OPPOSING JIM CROW

JUSTICE AND
SOCIAL INQUIRY

Series Editors

Jeremy I. Levitt

Matthew C. Whitaker

OPPOSING JIM CROW

African Americans and
the Soviet Indictment of
U.S. Racism, 1928–1937

MEREDITH L. ROMAN

University of Nebraska Press | Lincoln & London

A portion of chapter 1 was previously published
in "Robert Robinson: Celebrity Worker in the USSR,"
in *The Human Tradition in the Black Atlantic, 1500–2000*,
ed. Beatriz Mamigonian and Karen Racine, 133–45
(Lanham MD: Rowman and Littlefield, 2009). Reprinted
with permission.

Portions of chapters 1 and 2 were previously pub-
lished in "Racism in a 'Raceless' Society: The Soviet
Press and Representations of American Racial Vio-
lence at Stalingrad in 1930," *International Labor and
Working-Class History* 71, no. 1 (Spring 2007): 185–203.
Copyright © 2007 by The International Labor and
Working-Class History Society. Reprinted with the
permission of Cambridge University Press.

Library of Congress Cataloging-in-Publication Data
Roman, Meredith L. (Meredith Lynn)
Opposing Jim Crow: African Americans and the
Soviet indictment of U.S. racism, 1928–1937 /
Meredith L. Roman.
p. cm.—(Justice and social inquiry)
Includes bibliographical references and index.
ISBN 978-0-8032-1552-8 (cloth: alkaline paper)
ISBN 978-1-4962-1666-3 (paper: alkaline paper)
1. Anti-racism—Soviet Union. 2. Racism—Government
policy—Soviet Union. 3. Multiculturalism—Soviet
Union. 4. Racism—United States. 5. African
Americans—Civil rights—United States. 6. African
Americans—Soviet Union. I. Title. II. Series: Justice
and social inquiry.
DK268.4.R66 2012
305.800947—dc23   2011051678

Set in Swift EF by Bob Reitz.
Designed by A. Shahan.

In loving memory of Michael J. Roman (1972–92)

CONTENTS

ILLUSTRATIONS

Throughout the many years I have been working on this project, diverse people have asked me how I became interested in comparative Soviet and African American history. I always appreciated their curiosity but I could never adequately address the question because the answer is complex. At the most basic level, my response would have to begin with the small town in central New Jersey where I grew up. As a result of my hometown's all-white working-class population, which was the result of a history of "sundown" laws (de facto or otherwise), I quickly became aware of its notorious reputation as a place unfriendly to persons of color and to African Americans in particular. Placed in the context of this study, the town in which I grew up in the 1980s and early 1990s had the exact opposite image and reputation that Soviet authorities cultivated for the cities and towns of the USSR in the 1920s and 1930s.

Since I grew up in a household where racist attitudes were abhorred, I became increasingly embarrassed by my hometown's racist reputation and frustrated with my schooling experience. From elementary school through high school, the curriculum (in both history and literature) erased Asians, Latinos, First Nations Peoples, and African Americans, who were the main targets of my classmates' racist diatribes in spite of their physical absence from the school (and town). As I entered middle school, I did extra reading and chose topics for assignments that dealt with the history of racism and, more specifically, the history of African Americans. I was trying to make

sense of why the working-class whites in my small town would har-
bor such racial animus toward blacks, with whom they had virtually
no (meaningful) contact, and when African Americans were so obviously not the source of their economic oppression. At the same time,
I was also trying to signal my unequivocal rejection of the dominant
racial mores that many of my classmates espoused or tacitly accepted.
I recall all this not to claim that I was a remarkable youth, but quite
the contrary, to underscore how white privilege allowed me (and continues to allow me) to safely examine the history of racial injustice as
an intellectual problem rather than as a real life, everyday experience,
and to highlight the severe limitations that often accompany efforts
to pursue an antiracist agenda. To be sure, the dilemmas I wrestled
with as a teenager ultimately influenced—albeit indirectly—my decision to examine the first pursuit of state-sponsored antiracism in modern Europe and, by extension, African American and Soviet history.

My experiences in Freeport, Bahamas, though brief, expanded
my intellectual interest in the history of racial injustice beyond the
United States. I traveled with my family to this Caribbean island to
pursue alternate treatment for my nineteen-year-old brother, who
was soon to succumb to non-Hodgkins lymphoma, despite two years
of radiation and chemotherapy. Since we were not tourists confined
to the overwhelmingly white resort areas, I was exposed, as a sopho-
more in high school, to the extreme poverty that marked the lives of
most Bahamians of African descent. My history classes and my own
supplementary reading had left me ill-equipped to process the obscene
racialized economic disparities that Western imperialism and global-
ization had created beyond the borders of the United States.

I was not introduced to the history of the Soviet Union and the
direct challenges it posed to Western imperialism until I reached
college. At the College of New Jersey (then Trenton State College) I
first became acquainted with the promises of the Soviet experiment
through the lectures that Tom Allsen eloquently delivered. In supervis-
ing my senior honors thesis, Tom encouraged me to investigate Soviet
nationality policy, or what Terry Martin would term the policies of
the "affirmative action empire." My newfound interest in exploring

the Soviet experiment was now combined with a specific exploration of Soviet efforts to promote internationalism through the eradication of centuries of national inequality and injustice.

My investigation into Soviet internationalism evolved to include African Americans and became refined as an exploration of the Soviet Union's indictment of U.S. racism once I reached the Comparative Black History (CBH) Program at Michigan State University. The CBH Program is the final yet extremely critical component in adequately explaining how I arrived at a study of Soviet and African American history. Members of the then vibrant CBH Program (both professors and students alike) strongly encouraged the exploration of the history of the black diaspora and the black liberation struggle in its many incarnations. Combined with the indispensable support of Lewis Siegelbaum, my adviser in Soviet history, the atmosphere of dynamic intellectual inquiry and exchange of the CBH Program provided the necessary context for pursuing a subject that at the time had received minimal scholarly attention. Lewis's support was particularly valuable because some Western historians of the Soviet Union dismissed my project as having no significance to the history of the USSR. Excluded from this conservative group was, of course, Allison Blakely, whose monumental 1986 study *Russia and the Negro* was critical in inspiring my investigation into African Americans' role in Soviet antiracism.

In addition to some of the individuals mentioned above, there are many other people who made a comparative study like this possible. My thanks to the directors and staffs of the State Archive of the Russian Federation (GARF), the Russian State Archive of Social and Political History (RGASPI), the U.S. National Archives, the Schomburg Center for Research in Black Culture, the Houghton Library at the Harvard College Library, the Arthur and Elizabeth Schlesinger Library at the Radcliffe Institute for Advanced Study, and the Tamiment Library and Robert F. Wagner Labor Archives. I greatly appreciate the access to sources facilitated by the research librarians in the now defunct Baltic and Slavic Division of the New York Public Library and European Reading Room at the Library of Congress. J. Arch Getty and Elena Sergeevna Drozdova made the exasperating process of traveling to Russia to conduct research easier. The late Milton Muelder's generous donation to the Department of History at Michigan State University made possible the four-year fellowship from which I benefited in pursuing my PhD. The Union of University Professionals (UUP) of New York State also provided integral funding for this project through the Dr. Nuala McGann Drescher Affirmative Action/Diversity Committee Award. I thank my editors at the University of Nebraska Press, Heather Lundine and Bridget Barry, for their commitment to my project and for providing integral guidance at every stage of the publishing process.

I am grateful to Leslie Page Moch, Keely Stauter-Halsted, Laurent Dubois, Darlene Clark Hine, Curtis Stokes, Barbara Keys, Adrienne Edgar, Katya Vladimirov, James Heinzen, Scott W. Palmer, Matt Lenoe, Anastasia Kayiatos, Thomas Ewing, and Barbara Allen for their encouragement, insight, and suggestions for valuable sources. Barbara Keys was especially generous in sharing documents she obtained from the U.S. government concerning Robert Robinson. Katherine Clark, Wanda Wakefield, Steve Ireland, Jenny Lloyd, Anne Macpherson, and Alison Parker are among my colleagues in the Department of History at SUNY Brockport who have graciously given their time to reading and commenting on my work. Morag Martin deserves a special thank you for reading my book prospectus and insisting that I send it out.

A number of friends and colleagues associated with the once vibrant Comparative Black History Program at Michigan State University deserve mention. These include Kennetta Hammond Perry, Pero G. Dagbovie, John Wess Grant, Sowande' Mustakeem, Mona Jackson, Morey Lewis, Eric M. Washington, Dawne Y. Curry, Tracy K. Flemming, Marshanda Smith, Shannon Vance Harris, and Tamba M'bayo. I am extremely grateful to Matthew C. Whitaker for his interest in my work and for his empathetic responses to my inquiries about the publishing process. Eric D. Duke's friendship has been a tremendous gift to me, and I can never adequately express how much his sarcasm, encouragement, and thoughtfulness over the years has meant to me. I want to thank Jody Duke for her profound generosity, and Mya and Xavier Duke for always making me smile. Joseph M. Kassick and Monika Tomczuk helped me survive high school and the subsequent phases of our lives with their thoughtfulness, creativity, and laughter. Marcie Cowley has been an invaluable ally in Soviet history and I cannot imagine the historical profession or navigating Moscow without her.

I have been blessed with parents, Ronald and Cecilia Roman, who have selflessly supported—in countless ways—all my scholarly pursuits regardless of how much geographic distance it has placed between us, and made sure that I was well equipped to meet the many challenges I faced. They have visited me in every area of the United States in which I spent time. I can never repay them for their unconditional love and support. To members of the Quinn, Kuldoshes, Kaufmann, and Englehart families, thank you for always believing in me. Jenny (Kaufmann) Chalecki is owed a special thank you for her immense generosity.

My partner, best friend, and husband, Kenneth E. Marshall, is owed the greatest thanks. Over the years he has patiently endured endless discussions of diverse aspects and ideas in this book, read through and provided valuable feedback on several drafts of chapters, astutely recognized when coffee was needed, made me laugh when ideas and writing were not forthcoming, accompanied me to various conferences and listened to me practice numerous papers, and bravely made the trek to Moscow to remind me that my project was important. His love, intellect, and friendship have proven immeasurable. Last but certainly not least, I must acknowledge our newborn son, Julius Michael Marshall, who has brought such incredible joy to our lives, and whom we love so very much.

OPPOSING JIM CROW

Introduction

The Birth of a Nation

On December 1, 1958, amidst the Berlin Crisis, U.S. senator Hubert H. Humphrey had an unprecedented eight-hour-long meeting with Nikita Khrushchev in the Kremlin. Humphrey explained afterward that at one point during their conversation the Soviet leader "tore off on a whole long lecture like I wish I could remember [because it would have been] the best speech I could ever make in my life on antiracialism. Boy, he really gave me a talk on that."[1] Khrushchev's verbosity in "speaking antiracism" in 1958, which greatly impressed the U.S. senator, was not a new skill that the Soviet leader had cultivated in the 1950s as a result of Cold War politics.[2] Rather, it was from the 1920s through the mid-1930s that Khrushchev and other young party officials—with the help of African Americans—learned to "speak antiracism."[3] Decades before most American senators even expressed interest in giving speeches on "antiracialism," Soviet authorities used Jim Crow to claim the moral superiority of the USSR and contest America's image as the world's beacon of democracy and freedom.

Before the Nazis came to power in Germany, U.S. racism was identified in the Soviet Union as the most egregiously horrific aspect of capitalism, and the United States was represented as the most racist country in the world. This book investigates the Soviet indictment of American racial apartheid in the decades between the two world wars, and the role of African Americans in the first form of state-sponsored antiracism in modern Europe. Between 1928 and 1934, the pursuit of antiracism assumed the level of a priority or "hard-line" policy.[4] Photo-

1

graphs, children's stories, film, newspaper articles, political education campaigns, and court proceedings exposed the hypocrisy of America's racial democracy, represented the USSR as a superior society where racism was absent, and identified African Americans as valued allies in resisting an imperialist war against the first workers' state.

Notwithstanding the considerable propagandistic value that Soviet leaders stood to gain at home and abroad from drawing attention to U.S. racism, Soviet antiracism challenged the prevailing white supremacist notion—dominant throughout Europe and the globe—that blacks were biologically inferior and unworthy of equality with whites. At the same time it raised critical awareness of the routine violation of African Americans' human rights. To be sure, interwar America was a place of extreme racial apartheid; this was no exaggeration of Soviet propaganda. The 1920s and 1930s punctuate the time period that some African American historians identify as the "nadir" of black American life, beginning in the 1890s. In addition to the race riots, or mass violence perpetrated against black communities in the wake of the First World War, everyday life for the average African American consisted of routine racial degradation, lower wages, exclusion from most skilled labor and trade unions, inferior living conditions and public accommodations, and disproportionate rates of unemployment which the Great Depression exacerbated.[5] Moreover, despite their status as U.S. citizens, African Americans enjoyed little to no protection under the law. This was evidenced most clearly in the U.S. government's refusal to take any action to stop lynching or other extralegal acts of racial terrorism directed primarily against black men.[6] Confronted with America as a place of "unfreedom," U.S. blacks pursued a variety of strategies to protest and improve their less than equal status. It is within this context that African Americans of diverse political and socioeconomic backgrounds became instrumental contributors to the Soviet indictment of U.S. racism and architects of the USSR's image as a refuge from American "freedom."

Concerned with African Americans' involvement in Soviet antiracism, this book does not delve into the "hidden transcript" to capture black Americans' lived experiences in the first workers' state or

Soviet citizens' genuine feelings toward them.[7] A few recent studies address these important issues directly. These include Joy Gleason Carew's *Blacks, Reds, and Russians*, Kate Baldwin's *Beyond the Color Line*, Glenda Elizabeth Gilmore's *Defying Dixie*, the scholarship of Maxim Matusevich, and Allison Blakely's foundational 1986 study, *Russia and the Negro*.[8] Alternatively, an investigation of Soviet antiracism is the focal point of *Opposing Jim Crow*. To this end, my purpose is not simply to document Soviet antiracism but to present it as a discursive field in which its themes, images, and manifestations were glorified, redefined, and contested by various individuals and organizations—for an array of reasons—but with the same objective: representing the Soviet Union as a society where racism was absent. African Americans—not just those of prominence or with Communist Party membership cards—were indispensable creators of and participants in this discourse and, by implication, in shaping the USSR's identity as an emerging world power. They helped bring awareness of Jim Crow to the USSR, making African American oppression central to Soviet representations of U.S. democracy, and concurrently, central to representations of Soviet exceptionalism regarding race. In recognizing African Americans' substantive contributions to Soviet antiracism, this book furthers the scholarship of Kate Baldwin, Mark Naison, Robin D. G. Kelley, Mark Solomon, and William Maxwell, who demonstrate to varying degrees the integral role black Americans played in influencing Comintern policy and Soviet society.[9]

Throughout the 1920s and 1930s, contemporary Soviet and African American newspapers constructed, reformulated, and exhibited the Soviet Union as a society intolerant of racism. (Such efforts were particularly consistent in the Soviet press from 1930 through 1932 and from 1934 through 1937 in the African American [non-Communist] press.) Besides newspapers, this book employs the memoirs of several black Americans and the collections of Comintern, trade union, and propaganda organizations located in GARF, the State Archive of the Russian Federation (Gosudarstvennyi arkhiv Rossiiskoi Federatsii), and RGASPI, the Russian State Archive of Social and Political History (Rossiiskii gosudarstvennyi arkhiv sotsial'noi i politicheskoi istorii). The information found in these archival records, memoirs, and newspapers is read critically, with an appreciation for what they represent rather than as descriptors of Soviet reality.[10] Thus, the *Chicago Defender*, the records of the All-Union Central Council of Trade Unions (VTsSPS), and the pages of its organ, *Trud* (Labor), do not necessarily provide evidence that the USSR had eliminated racism. Instead, they demonstrate that in the 1930s trade union officials in the Soviet Union and editors of the non-Communist African American press in the United States were speaking their own brands of Soviet antiracism, that is, engaging in rhetoric that authenticated the USSR as a society where racism was absent. The discursive field of Soviet antiracism, in other words, traversed the Atlantic to include blacks who never set foot on Soviet soil.

Though this book focuses on the Soviet indictment of U.S. racism from 1928 through 1937, it does not suggest that hitherto, authorities in Moscow had ignored American racial oppression. Leaders of the Third International had demonstrated interest in the plight of black workers since the organization's First World Congress in 1919.[11] This interest received its first concrete expression in 1922, when the Fourth Comintern Congress organized a "Negro Bureau" and formulated a "Thesis on the Negro Question," which acknowledged the Comintern's support of all black liberation movements that helped undermine imperialism (conceptualized by V. I. Lenin as the highest stage of capitalism).[12] Otto Huiswood, a U.S. black Communist originally of Dutch Guiana, was appointed head of the bureau. Claude McKay, the Jamaican-born U.S. poet who traveled to Moscow independent of the Workers Party of America delegation (the predecessor of the U.S. Communist Party), was designated the face or "poster child" of the alliance that the Comintern officially forged with black workers at the congress.[13]

As several scholars and biographers of McKay have discussed, Comintern authorities' preference for McKay over Huiswood was based entirely on his darker skin color, which conformed to Russians' stereotypical notions of blackness. Huiswood's light complexion made him more tolerable to the white American Communists (who resented the Comintern's order that they include a black representative), yet less desirable to officials in Moscow. They were ignorant of the complexities of U.S. racism and wanted McKay's dark skin to authenticate Soviet enlightenment. As Joy Carew writes, "McKay's darker skin stood in greater contrast to the white faces of the Russians around him, and, therefore, his propaganda value as a symbol in photos and publications was also greater."[14] Huiswood, as Kate Baldwin likewise explains, "was too light-skinned to afford the crucial racial distinctions between black and white that could herald the Soviet Union as the true model for global internationalism."[15] "Color-struck" Comintern leaders invited McKay to sit on the platform and address the congress on the plight of U.S. blacks.[16] McKay's speech was subsequently published in *Pravda*, with strategic changes. Most notably, McKay's extended discussion of racism among American Communists was removed to confine racism to bourgeois society.[17] The Comintern's alliance with black workers, which the exhibition of McKay symbolized, extended beyond the halls of the Fourth Congress. Photographs of McKay posing with various Soviet officials and at key Russian historic sites appeared in central newspapers, and he spoke at factories and meetings of Soviet intellectuals. Huiswood was not excluded from these publicity engagements but became "black" by association with McKay; both men were consequently named to the Moscow City Soviet.[18]

In addition to publishing his Fourth Congress speech in *Pravda* in altered form, Comintern authorities commissioned McKay to write *Negroes in America* (1923), a one-hundred-page nonfictional work that presents U.S. black history and life from a Marxist perspective, and a collection of three short stories, titled *A Trial by Lynching: Stories about the Life of Negroes in North America* (1925).[19] *Negroes in America* was allegedly required reading for high-ranking Soviet officials, but a limited number of copies were printed; in 1932 Langston Hughes looked for a copy of this "African-American primer for Soviet beginners" that was already out of print.[20]

Despite this initial flurry of attention devoted to black workers, it did not extend in any substantive way beyond McKay's visit. Rather,

Soviet interest in exposing the contradictions in U.S. democracy's treatment of African Americans before 1928 is best conceived as a latent or soft-line policy.[21] Certainly, a few Soviet writers and officials who visited the United States in the early to mid-1920s commented on American racism in published accounts of their travels, but so had some of their prerevolutionary Russian predecessors.[22] The best-known example from the 1920s is the revolutionary poet Vladimir Maiakovskii, who indicted U.S. racial oppression (including white men's use of rape to terrorize black "girls") in verse and in a travel-ogue titled *My Discovery of America*.[23] Yet apart from the work of Claude McKay, Maiakovskii, and a few others among the Soviet elite, literary works by and about U.S. blacks were not printed consistently in the Soviet Union until the 1930s when, as chapter 2 outlines, the publication of these materials reached its peak.

Similar to literary works, information about U.S. race relations appeared sporadically in Soviet newspapers of the 1920s, therefore corresponding with what Jeffrey Brooks argues was the ambiguous but generally positive image of America found in the press during the first decade of Bolshevik rule.[24] Of equal significance, central authorities neither organized a political education campaign to condemn U.S. racism in the 1920s nor made a concerted effort to portray Soviet citizens as outraged by American racial injustice. Additionally, the number of black Americans who visited the USSR prior to 1928 paled in comparison to those who traveled to the country thereafter. W. E. B. Du Bois, the preeminent African American leader and intellectual, first toured the Soviet Union for two months during the late summer of 1926 (which included the celebration of International Youth Day in Moscow). But Du Bois generated absolutely no fanfare, something that would become unfeasible a few years later, not to mention in the decades after the Second World War (in spite of his light-skinned complexion).[25]

What helped elevate the Soviet indictment of U.S. racism to a hard-line or priority policy after 1928? What inspired propagandists to identify African Americans as allies of Soviet citizens (not just of the Comintern), and what encouraged a greater number of these African

American allies to traverse Soviet territory? Two major corresponding shifts in domestic and Comintern policy informed these developments. By 1929 central authorities abandoned the New Economic
Policy (1921–27), which sought to attain socialism through capitalist practices, and launched a campaign to build socialism through
rapid industrialization as outlined in the First (1928–32) and Second
(1933–37) Five-Year Plans. They simultaneously pursued various means
to represent the USSR as a superior, unmistakably "noncapitalist society."[26] The designation of U.S. industry as the model of development
and the recruitment of a substantial number of workers from the
United States (and other capitalist countries) to help eradicate the
Soviet Union's industrial inferiority made this objective particularly
imperative. The indictment of U.S. racism helped assuage anxieties
among officials in Moscow that they were simply reinstituting capitalism.[27] Having launched a campaign to build a new society and people,
the incentive emerged to represent Soviet citizens as committed to
racial equality and as appalled by the stark racial inequalities in the
United States.[28]

Moscow's heightened interest in condemning U.S. racism was also
motivated by the ascendancy of the Comintern's militant Third Period
(1928–35). In 1928 authorities of the Third International posited that
the "gradual and partial stabilization" of capitalism characteristic of
the "second period" (1924–28) was being replaced by an impending
crisis in capitalism that would bring with it a proliferation of revolutionary opportunities. To capitalize on these opportunities, Comintern
leaders ordered Communist parties around the world to abandon their
coalition policies with working-class parties while they assessed the
revolutionary potential of black Americans. As a result of this assessment, Comintern officials at the Sixth World Comintern Congress
in 1928 declared African Americans as an oppressed nation with the
right to national self-determination and anointed them the vanguard
among colonized nations.[29]

The "birth of the African American nation" at the Sixth Congress,
in conjunction with the project of building socialism, encouraged
the elevation of antiracism to a priority policy in the years that fol-

lowed. The decree effectively made American blacks "indispensable allies" to the USSR at a time when the country was building socialism in what Soviet leaders depicted as an extremely antagonistic capitalist world.[30] Paradoxically, America's status as the most advanced capitalist country not only rendered it the model of Soviet industrial development but also (by the logic of the militant Third Period) made the United States the USSR's most formidable enemy. Officially recognized as valued allies, a veritable fifth column that would resist the U.S. bourgeoisie's efforts to wage an imperialist war against the Soviet Union, African Americans henceforth received more sustained attention in the first workers' state. The increased persecution they suffered in the Depression-ridden United States was depicted as the first steps in the U.S. capitalists' plot to destroy the country of Soviets. Whereas Comintern officials spoke of U.S. racism as an impediment to the international revolutionary movement, in the Soviet Union it was represented as a threat, albeit indirect, to the country's national security.[31]

Due largely to the increased attention to African American oppression that these two monumental policy shifts precipitated, the number of U.S. blacks who visited the USSR in the interwar decades reached its height between 1928 and 1937. The Comintern's emphasis on militant agitation and elevation of black Americans' status in the revolutionary family meant that a larger number of black Americans were admitted to KUTV—the Communist University of the Toilers of the East (Kommunisticheskii universitet trudiashchikhsia Vostoka)—and the International Lenin School (Mezhdunarodnaia leninskaia shkola) and attended the organization's international congresses (and those of its affiliates). At the same time, the demands of the First and Second Five-Year Plans created opportunities in Soviet industry and agriculture, which the Great Depression in the United States made attractive to black workers who, as mentioned earlier, were hit hardest by unemployment. Additional black Americans traveled to the USSR during this era of capitalism in crisis to examine in person the country's image as a superior, raceless society.[32]

The movement of black Americans between the United States and

USSR, like Soviet interest in indicting American racism, dissipated by 1937. War seemed imminent on the continent, and suspicion of all foreigners intensified in the Soviet Union. Few if any newcomers joined the ranks of the small yet significant Soviet African American community after 1937 on either a temporary or long-term basis. By 1939 Paul Robeson had removed his son, Pauli, from the Moscow school where he was enrolled in 1936.[33] The majority of U.S. blacks who remained in the USSR by late 1937 stayed there at least through the duration of the Second World War. These African Americans, many of whom appear throughout this study, included Robert Robinson, Frank Goode (Robeson's brother-in-law), Homer Smith, Williana Burroughs and her sons Neal and Charles, Lloyd Patterson, Robert Ross, Oliver Golden, George Tynes, and Wayland Rudd. Like all inhabitants of the USSR, these African Americans were divested of their civil rights. Overwhelmingly, however, their blackness allowed them to escape persecution during the Stalinist "Great Terror" (1936–38) despite their foreign origins.[34]

The lone exception was Lovett Fort-Whiteman (James Jackson), a member of the Communist Party of the USA (CPUSA) and resident of Moscow since 1928. He was sentenced to internal exile in Kazakhstan in 1937 for "anti-Soviet agitation" and died in a Siberian labor camp in 1939.[35] Tragically, Fort-Whiteman's fate was the result of political infighting within the CPUSA, which stemmed from his persistent opposition to the Comintern's support of black self-determination and his eccentric personality. Fort-Whiteman's death could have been averted had U.S. Party leaders approved his request in October 1933 to return to the United States to work as an instructor in the New York Party School. Denied return, Fort-Whiteman's attacks on the Party escalated. By 1936 he had been expelled from the Party as a "Trotskyist," and William Patterson, a leading black American Communist, charged him with having a pernicious influence on Moscow's black American expatriate community. Despite running completely afoul of the Communist Party, Fort-Whiteman could have still escaped imprisonment and death had the U.S. consulate in Moscow approved his application for a passport in early 1936.[36]

While the threat of imperialist war against the USSR persisted in the second half of the 1930s, Soviet officials perceived its primary architects to be Nazi Germans instead of U.S. capitalists. As a consequence, African Americans ceased to be identified as valued allies of the first workers' state. It became advantageous for authorities in Moscow, intent on forging an antifascist alliance with the governments of the United States, France, and Britain, to "go soft" on U.S. racism, that is, pursue significantly less militant, Popular Front tactics, the effects of which informed Soviet propaganda prior to the Comintern's adoption of it as official policy in 1935.[37] The Nazis' rise to power in early 1933, along with the establishment of diplomatic relations with the United States that November, played a key role in subordinating the indictment of U.S. racism to antifascism. Though Germany had become the main enemy, Soviet leaders continued to reject as unenlightened and inferior a society defined by racism.

Soviet leaders' equation of modernity with the transcendence of racism seems all the more unique when placed within the context of a world that was witnessing the consolidation of racial theory and defining modern civilization in hierarchical racial terms.[38] Anxieties on the Left and the Right about racial decline, degeneration, and reinvigoration fueled the ascendancy of biological racism in Europe. The boundaries of national communities throughout the continent, including the new nation states of Poland, Hungary, and Romania, were redrawn to include members of one putatively homogenous ethno-racial biological group at the exclusion and discrimination of others.[39] Antiracist movements—many of which were affiliated with the Comintern—emerged in response to the burgeoning of scientific racism, especially in interwar England, as Susan Pennybacker has shown.[40]

Yet among European states, Soviet leaders alone promoted antiracism and posited that a superior, modern society did not use race to categorize or identify its populace. Francine Hirsch, Amir Weiner, and Terry Martin emphasize that Soviet authorities believed they were distinct from, and superior to, their Western capitalist contemporaries because they used the sociohistorical categories of nationality and class in managing the populace at the explicit rejection of the biological category of race. Eric Weitz contends that although officials in Moscow disdained use of the category of "race," Soviet population politics were essentially "racial politics without the concept of race."[41] Even if one agrees with Weitz's argument, Soviet authorities nonetheless insisted on the backwardness of racial hierarchies during an era in which government leaders in Europe, the Americas, Asia, and Africa celebrated the superiority of "white men's countries."[42] Only following the Second World War and the atrocities of the Nazi Holocaust did a "new international antiracist consensus" emerge among state leaders, making Soviet officials ahead of their contemporaries in playing the "race card."[43]

Juxtaposed with Soviet leaders' desire to represent the USSR as the champion of racial equality, the Nazi racial state took to the extreme the biological racism prominent in European social thought, and postulated as impossibility the equality of races.[44] As Mark Mazower argues, the Nazis modeled their racial politics after Western European colonial policies in Africa and Asia. This was epitomized in the 1935 Nuremberg Laws, which criminalized interracial sexual relations and codified Jews' exclusion from the racially defined national community of the *Volksgemeinschaft*. Viewed from this perspective, the Nazi quest for a racial empire, as Mazower avers, constituted the "culmination of the process of European imperial expansion that began in the 1870s" and merely turned inward onto the continent itself.[45]

Mazower's emphasis on the connections between Nazi and Western European imperial policy is consistent with the scholarship of Thomas Holt, Alice Conklin, and Sue Peabody, which demonstrates how discourses of liberal universalism contributed to British and French conceptualizations of superior and inferior races but prevented open promotion of racial hatred and legislation of racial exclusion on the level of the Nuremberg Laws.[46] The British and French governments increasingly introduced segregation and color bars in the colonies, made it extremely difficult for dark-skinned colonial subjects to receive full citizenship, and exhibited even greater concern in the early twentieth century with preventing miscegenation.[47] More specifically, the British condemned interracial marriage as a threat to the racial, class, and gender boundaries that sustained imperial rule, and deprecated the children that such unions produced as a disruption to England's purported homogeneity and harmony.[48] The French, moreover, quickly repatriated the North African and Indochinese laborers in France at the end of the Great War as a result of escalating violence and anxieties surrounding miscegenation. French officials replaced them with Polish and Italian immigrant workers to restore the semblance of European, that is, "white" order.[49] As reflected in British and French policies of the interwar era, the key to "racial survival" in the colonies and metropole was based on mutually reinforcing cultural and biological definitions of race, which required observing strict cultural and gender proscriptions and limiting interracial sexual contact.[50]

Despite non-European laborers' experiences with discrimination in France during the First World War, the Soviet Union was second to France as the most popular European "promised land" for many African Americans in the 1920s and 1930s. Certainly, less personal risk and sacrifice were involved in exploring the myth of French color-blindness. The USSR was logistically more difficult to reach, and travel there necessitated tolerance of atheism and Communist ideology and a willingness to deal with a foreign language that used the Cyrillic alphabet. More important, individuals who relocated to France risked neither ostracism from family nor additional stigmatization from a U.S. government that already treated blacks as second-class citizens. Stigmatization was especially severe prior to the establishment of diplomatic relations with the Soviet Union in November 1933.[51] As a consequence, regardless of individuals' specific intentions, travel to the USSR constituted a symbolic boycott of the U.S. racial regime.

Apart from the varied factors that made migration to the Soviet Union a precarious venture, the attractiveness of France was enhanced by the testimony of African American soldiers. Many U.S. blacks who had served in France during the First World War claimed that the French had treated them with more respect and warmth than any white people previously. Tyler Stovall attributes the favor accorded black Americans to Parisians' obsession with blackness, which was rooted in a crisis of European rationality and progress that the Great War inspired. Stovall therefore stresses that the French in no way purported that blacks were whites' equals, but considered their primitivism (i.e., "lush naive sensuality") and simplicity virtues rather than vices.[52]

Leaders of the Communist International, in contrast, recognized black equality at least in theory. They expressed a bias for African Americans, who they conceived as the least primitive and most poised for leading revolution within the African diaspora. According to Kate Baldwin, prior to 1928 Comintern authorities conceived of African Americans' "use value for the liberation of Africa, not their individual political existence as a nation."[53] The Sixth Comintern Congress (July 17–September 1) elevated their importance in the revolutionary family by declaring them an oppressed nation with the right to self-determination in the so-called black belt regions of the U.S. South. Numerous scholars have discussed at length the debates surrounding the 1928 decree, and African American Communist Harry Haywood, one of its main architects, documented them in his 1978 autobiography, *Black Bolshevik*. Suffice it to say that unlike Haywood, most African American Communists, including James Ford, Otto Hall, William Patterson, and Roy Mahoney, initially rejected the idea. They insisted that U.S. blacks constituted an oppressed racial minority, not an oppressed nation whose members sought inclusion in the larger American nation. Thus, they warned, black laborers would interpret advocacy of self-determination as segregation.[54]

Jay Lovestone, a white American Communist and leader of the soon-to-be-defeated Lovestone and John Pepper faction of the CPUSA, opposed the proposal for a different reason. Lovestone contended that because "a second industrial revolution" would eliminate the "slave remnants in southern agriculture," a black liberation movement could only be "reactionary." Comintern authorities denounced Lovestone's position as a "right opportunist" argument, and his opponent in the CPUSA, William Foster, wisely advocated African Americans' right to national self-determination. In the end, independent of the divisions within the CPUSA, the persistent support for the proposal of Comintern authorities Otto Kuusinen, Boris Mikhailov, Max Goldfarb, Charles Nasanov, and, most important, of J. V. Stalin effected the declaration in 1928 of African Americans as an oppressed nation with the right to self-determination.[55]

As Cedric J. Robinson and other scholars have argued, the policies of the African Blood Brotherhood (ABB) and Marcus Garvey's United Negro Improvement Association (UNIA) influenced the Comintern's recognition of African American nationhood.[56] But Soviet nationality policy and contemporary definitions of the terms "race" and "nation" also informed the Sixth Congress's decision. As Francine Hirsch details, Soviet anthropologists defined "race" as a phase of historical development that was replaced gradually by the "unification of peoples" into nascent "ethnohistorical units," or "nationalities" and "nations," which were founded upon a common language, culture, and consciousness.[57] According to this logic, if Soviet leaders classified African Americans as a "race" or even *narodnosti* (the lowest level of development within the process of nation formation), then they would have been characterizing them as behind in historical development. This would have made them no better than U.S. officials and Western imperialists who purposefully denied the historic national character of nonwhites, embedding them in the present to justify their subjugation.[58]

The 1928 Comintern decree was also consistent with Soviet nationality policy, which afforded the officially sponsored non-Russian nationalities of the USSR the nominal right to national self-determination. Besides encouraging their cultural development, Soviet leaders established an ethnicity-based affirmative action system that privileged non-Russians over ethnic Russians in terms of hiring, admissions, and promotions. Terry Martin and Yuri Slezkine argue that even after 1933, when authorities in Moscow began systematically promoting Russian language and culture, they neither abandoned affirmative action policies, especially with regard to the nationalities of the Soviet "east" (whom they deemed to have suffered the most from tsarist oppression) nor launched any concerted effort to eradicate their national identities.[59] Therefore, by demanding that white Americans place themselves in a disadvantaged position in relationship to African Americans, and recognize their right to national self-determination in the black belt regions of the U.S. South, Comintern officials were operating within the logic of the Soviet affirmative action empire. They were, in other words, holding white Americans as fellow members of an oppressing nation to the same standard as Russians.

However, in the two years following the Sixth Comintern Congress, the U.S. Communist Party failed to dedicate greater attention to work among African Americans. Its inaction was the result of continued apathy toward African Americans, as well as confusion over what the decree, also known as the black belt thesis, concretely meant with regard to everyday policy toward blacks, especially in the North. As a consequence, the Executive Committee of the Communist International (ECCI) issued a new resolution in October 1930 clarifying the Party's approach to African Americans in the U.S. North and South. Written largely by the Finnish Communist Otto Kuusinen, the resolution ordered U.S. leaders to actively recruit and fully incorporate black workers into the life of the trade unions, to educate and promote them to leadership positions, and to unite them with white laborers in common organizations in the North rather than segregating them in separate organizations.[60] The ECCI emphasized that in the North it was imperative for the U.S. Communist Party to promote black equality and integration while advancing the program of national self-determination in the South. Only through the promotion of the latter was it possible for southern black Americans, who "are living in slavery in the literal sense of the word," to have true social equality. This required seizing "the landed property of the white masters," redistributing it to black tenant farmers, who would control the governing bodies, and granting white residents minority rights if the black majority exercised the right to political separation. In addition to making these clarifications, the ECCI admonished white American Communists that in the "struggle for equal rights for Negroes," it was their Leninist duty, as members of the oppressing nation, "to march *at the head* of this struggle. They must everywhere make a breach in the walls of segregation and 'Jim Crowism' which has been set up by bour-geois slave market morality. . . . They, the white workers, must boldly jump at the throat of the 100 per cent bandits who strike a Negro in the face."[61] The October 1930 resolution, as chapter 5 demonstrates, became an important tool used by Communists on both sides of the Atlantic to condemn the conduct of members of the CPUSA, who con-tinued to underestimate and subordinate the struggle against racism.

Despite many African American Communists' initial opposition, the 1928 Comintern decree of nationhood was of immense signifi-cance to the black liberation movement. Mark Naison emphasizes that "by defining blacks as an oppressed nation, even in this bizarre fashion, the Comintern had, within the Leninist lexicon of values, endowed the black struggle with unprecedented dignity and impor-tance."[62] U.S. blacks were not the "reserves of capitalist reaction," the degraded status that some U.S. Communists had heretofore assigned them.[63] Instead, the struggle for black equality was itself integral to the revolutionary process and therefore not subordinate to the class question. Regardless of our personal opinions of the notion of "black self-determination," Robin D. G. Kelley argues, "the policy compelled the Communists to pay attention to black workers and farmers in the South. The point was not to promote separatism but to expose the basic denial of black citizenship in the South." Hence, "the Com-munists' 'black belt' policy," Kelley stresses, "resulted not in a sepa-ratist movement but in active support for black civil rights."[64] Alan Wald makes a similar point, writing that self-determination meant "the beginning of paying close attention to all issues—cultural as well as political—that affected African Americans."[65] As *Opposing Jim Crow* illuminates, the 1928 decree of African American nationhood also had immense implications for the importance afforded the struggle for black equality in the Soviet Union.

Chapter 1 argues that the first major event that signaled the emer-gence of Soviet antiracism as a priority policy was the August 1930 trial of two white Americans, Lemuel Lewis and William Brown, who assaulted Robert Robinson, an African American worker, at a major tractor factory in Stalingrad. Throughout the nationwide campaign against and trial of Lewis and Brown, trade union authorities and all-union editors depicted workers around the country as outraged at the racially motivated assault on "our brother" Robinson, and firmly committed to building a new socialist society where racists were absent. The Stalingrad court's decision to expel the white American assailants of a black worker sent a clear message that American technique and industrial knowledge were valued in the construction of Soviet modernity, but American racial norms were not. Robinson himself was depicted as an innocent, hard-working black laborer who represented all African American workers—the Soviet Union's allies—whom white Americans routinely victimized. His representation as the "poster child" for Soviet antiracism reached its culmination when he was elected, in December 1934, to the Moscow City Soviet. By drawing attention to the success Robinson had achieved as a skilled toolmaker and instructor to Soviet workers in the four years since the trial, officials could easily demonstrate how this black worker had tangibly reaped the benefits of antiracism since first arriving on Soviet soil.

Although Robert Robinson was made the poster child for Soviet antiracism, representations of U.S. blacks' inclusion in Soviet society and the indictment of U.S. racism were not limited to this black toolmaker and the Stalingrad trial of his white American assailants. Rather, as chapter 2 investigates, throughout the early 1930s, the black male body was used in the Soviet press and literature to simultaneously signify American racial apartheid and Soviet antiracism. African American males—adults and children, real and fictional—were portrayed in photographs, cartoons, articles, short stories, and poems as being excluded from American society by lynching, imprisonment, and discriminatory labor practices. Concurrently, Soviet workers were shown embracing black men as equals at political conferences, factories, and in classrooms. Acceptance in the Soviet body politic was shown restoring African Americans (represented in the black male body) to the full humanity that American racial oppression had denied them. Representations of African Americans as heroic, persecuted revolutionaries disappeared from the Soviet press and literature by the second half of the 1930s. The work of the popular Soviet humorists Il'ia Il'f and Evgenii Petrov best illustrates how a more ambiguous, depoliticized yet sympathetic portrayal of U.S. blacks assumed precedence by the second half of the 1930s, thereby signaling the shift to a more soft-line form of antiracism reflective of the policies of the Popular Front era (1935–39).

Chapter 3 examines the nationwide campaign to liberate nine African American male teenagers who were condemned to death in Scottsboro, Alabama, in April 1931 on false charges of raping two white women. By focusing sustained attention on the plight of nine young African American men, the Scottsboro protest personalized, or gave a "face" to, U.S. racism in the same way that the Stalingrad trial and election of Robert Robinson to the Moscow City Soviet personalized black males' inclusion in Soviet society. Soviet citizens from all corners of the USSR were represented as composing protest resolutions, letters, and poems and attending rallies en masse to voice their outrage at the persecution of their "revolutionary brothers" in Scottsboro. While it is impossible to determine whether Soviet antiracism cultivated a sincere conviction against racial prejudice among officials and citizens, the Scottsboro protest demonstrates that it succeeded in dominating the field of discourse in teaching citizens and authorities how to "speak antiracism."

African Americans of a wide array of socioeconomic and political backgrounds likewise spoke Soviet antiracism. George Padmore, the high-ranking Communist turned pan-African radical, and editors of African American newspapers like the *Pittsburgh Courier*, *Afro-American*, and *Chicago Defender* demonstrate how blacks who were bitter detractors of Communism and critics of Soviet opportunism nonetheless spoke of the USSR as a society where racism was absent. As chapter 4 shows, they forged the Soviet Union's antiracist image to bring the United States to account for the incessantly hostile treatment of its black citizens. The ill-fated Soviet film *Black and White* is especially instructive of African Americans' role as indispensable supporters and architects of Soviet antiracism. Due to its intended directness in attacking the U.S. racial regime, Comintern leaders abandoned production of *Black and White* in August 1932 out of fear of jeopardizing American diplomatic recognition, which then appeared imminent. This decision constituted the gravest threat to the USSR's antiracist image prior to the 1939 Nazi-Soviet Pact. Yet the majority of the black American cast members (most of whom were not Communist Party members) used the controversy to publicly reaffirm as sincere the Soviet commitment to antiracism, while privately articulating discontent to authorities in Moscow.

A pioneering group of African American Communists, who integrated Moscow's International Lenin School in 1931 and negotiated the power, promise, and limitations of Soviet antiracism, constitute the main protagonists of chapter 5. When reality failed to correspond with the image of Soviet racial equality, with regard to the conduct of white Americans and their treatment by school officials, these African American Communists criticized the disparities not only as "racist" but, more important, as "anti-Soviet." They demanded from Soviet leaders the freedom from racism that the country's antiracist image promised them. African American and African students at KUTV used similar strategies to voice their criticisms of aspects of Soviet society that they deemed problematic. Similar to the experiences of the African Americans who integrated the Lenin School, when an African student at KUTV violated Soviet antiracism by not merely criticizing its shortcomings but by challenging its validity with accusations that the USSR was just as racist as the United States, several African American Communists immediately responded by defending the Soviet Union's image as a society intolerant of racism. Like the majority of the *Black and White* cast members, they recognized that they had more to gain in actively supporting Soviet antiracism, or saying nothing publicly about it, than in joining their white American oppressors in dismantling it.

The epilogue uses Grigorii Aleksandrov's 1936 musical comedy, *Circus (Tsirk)*, to further demonstrate how the growing threat of fascism in Europe and the adoption of Popular Front policies made African American oppression a secondary or soft-line concern of Soviet propaganda. Although ostensibly about U.S. racism, the film elides the previously hallowed African American man, represents the white American woman as the primary victim of American racial injustice, and identifies the main villain as a German manager with Nazi-like features. In these and other important ways, *Circus* signals how antifascism or the Nazi racial state assumed precedence over U.S. racism in Soviet propaganda in the second half of the 1930s. While the United States resurfaced as a major enemy of the USSR after the signing of the Nazi-Soviet Pact in August 1939, African Americans could no longer be portrayed as revolutionary allies. It was not until the post–Second World War era that the Soviet indictment of U.S. racism regained the intensity of the early 1930s, and African Americans—returned to their status as valued friends of the first workers' state—again became valuable contributors to Soviet antiracism.

Before traveling to the USSR, most of the African Americans featured in this book had a history of prior migration. They had either moved from the Caribbean to the U.S. North (primarily to New York) as part of the flow of some 88,000 migrants to the United States from 1900 to 1932, or were part of the Great Migration of African Americans, an exodus from 1910 to 1940 of roughly 1,750,000 people largely although not exclusively from southern regions of the United States to northern cities.[66] For example, both Robert Robinson, the "heroic" worker in the Stalingrad trial, and George Padmore (whose original name was Malcolm Meredith Nurse), the future secretary of the International Trade Union Committee of Negro Workers (ITUCNW), belonged to the first group. According to Winston James, the overrepresentation of Caribbean migrants in U.S. radical movements like Communism was due to numerous factors, including their previous political and organizational experience, majority consciousness, educational and occupational accomplishments, previous travel experience, weaker attachment to Christian churches, and for those from the British Caribbean, a politically protected status in the United States.[67]

Robinson, who never joined the Communist Party, was born in Jamaica around 1907, grew up in Cuba, worked in Brazil, and later migrated to Harlem in 1923. He relocated to Detroit in 1927 before journeying to Stalingrad in 1930.[68] George Padmore, who joined the Party in 1927, was born in Trinidad in 1902 and migrated to the United States in late 1924 to study law at Fisk University in Nashville, Tennessee. He moved to New York City in 1926, from where he traveled back and forth to Howard University's School of Law in Washington DC before leaving the United States permanently by the decade's end.[69]

Although Padmore, Robinson, and others were born in the Caribbean, they were identified in the Soviet Union as black Americans and representatives of the African American nation. It would be easy to simply attribute this identification to Soviet leaders' ignorant, essentialist notions of blacks. However, the life of George Padmore illustrates that the situation was more complex than this. Padmore arrived in Moscow in 1929 as a representative of the U.S. Communist Party, an organization in which he became active, as noted above, in Harlem in 1927. Apart from representing a U.S. organization, Padmore had an incentive to identify as an African American since the Comintern had officially recognized U.S. blacks as the revolutionary vanguard. According to Mark Solomon, it was only in May 1931, when Padmore assumed editorship of the *Negro Worker* in Hamburg, Germany (see chapter 4 of this study), that he ceased acting as a representative of an American organization and identifying as an African American.[70] Moreover, the racism and class exploitation of the United States were the primary sources of and space for the radicalization of Padmore and other Caribbean migrants to the United States in the 1920s, not British imperialism in the Caribbean. While they may have had revolutionary leanings before reaching American soil, U.S. society effected their transformation into revolutionaries. As Cedric Robinson argues, it was in the United States that Malcolm Nurse became George Padmore.[71] For these reasons, Caribbean-born migrants to the United States who made the trek to the Soviet Union are referred to throughout this study as African Americans or U.S. blacks. The purpose is not to essentialize or erase the diversity among blacks in Moscow, but to underscore the importance of American racial apartheid in inspiring them to participate in Soviet antiracism.

James Ford and Harry Haywood represent the second major group of African Americans featured in this book. They participated in the massive internal migration of African Americans of the early twentieth century, which landed both men in Chicago before they ultimately traveled to Moscow. Ford, who was born in Pratt City, Alabama, in 1893, relocated to Chicago in 1919 where he became active in the postal workers' union and the American Negro Labor Congress (ANLC) and in 1926 joined the Communist Party. Ford served as a de facto spokesman and figurehead for African American Communists in Moscow in the late 1920s and early 1930s, was named as a member of the Profintern's executive committee in 1930, and ran as the U.S. Communist Party's candidate for vice president in the 1932 and 1936 presidential elections.[72]

Harry Haywood was the first African American student admitted to the Lenin School in 1927 and played a pivotal role, as mentioned earlier, in the Sixth Comintern Congress's declaration of African Americans as an oppressed nation. Haywood was born in Omaha, Nebraska, in 1898, but his family moved to Minneapolis and later Chicago where he became involved in the ABB, the Communist Youth League, and then, like his brother Otto Hall, the Communist Party.[73] While Ford and Haywood joined the Communist movement after migrating to Chicago, both men had also served as soldiers in the First World War.[74] The obscene racism that they confronted in the U.S. armed forces, America's insistence on maintaining the racial status quo after the war, and the racial tensions they encountered in the northern "promised land" of Chicago, which witnessed a major race riot in the "Red Summer" of 1919, undoubtedly proved critical in piquing their interest in Communism's promises of complete social equality.[75]

As reference to these four black men and the preceding chapter summaries indicate, Soviet antiracism was a masculine discourse. Even though it condemned all forms of U.S. racism, the specific sufferings of black men received the bulk of attention. The fact that African American men were the targets of the most sensationalized acts of racism helps to explain the gender imbalance of Soviet antiracism. Soviet leaders' own biases against and general ambivalence with regard to women also played a part. Rape, the primary form of racial violence that white men used to terrorize black women, was not consistently treated as a serious crime in Soviet society.[76]

Another reason for the masculine focus of Soviet antiracism is that, along with Soviet men, African American men were its main contributors. During the 1920s and 1930s, the opportunities for black American women (and women in general) to assume positions of authority in political movements like U.S. Communism were limited, and their male counterparts were more likely to travel abroad in search of industrial labor or for political purposes. Hence, though black women played indispensable roles in the American Communist movement, their importance was not reflected in the ranks of its leadership or the delegations sent to Moscow.[77] Yet even when black women were present in the Soviet capital, they often were excluded from participating on a level equal to their male counterparts. No black American woman (or white woman), for instance, actively participated in the debates to declare African Americans a nation at the Sixth Comintern Congress, despite the fact that Maude White was then a student at KUTV, as were some of her black American male colleagues who did participate.[78] Williana Burroughs (Mary Adams), another African American female delegate (see chapter 2), also seemingly played no active role in the debates regarding black nationhood.

Black women's exclusion from meaningful involvement in this monumental process replicated the representation of men (throughout history) as the active political and economic agents of a nation whose masculine accomplishments were responsible for its foundation and defense.[79] To be sure, Soviet men were depicted leading the struggle with African American men against Jim Crow, which assumed the form of a white American male capitalist.[80] Thus, the disproportionate attention given to African American men at the near omission of black women is not the intention of this book. Instead, it reflects the reality that Soviet leaders cast African Americans, like the non-Russian nationalities of the USSR, as "brothers" rather than "sisters" in class.[81]

It goes without saying that the Soviet Union was not the society free of racism that leaders in Moscow claimed in the 1920s and the 1930s. Yet it is equally problematic to go to the opposite extreme and portray it as riddled by virulent racism. Such a one-dimensional analysis makes the African Americans who contributed to Soviet antiracism appear as dupes of a Soviet Potemkin village. At the same time, it discounts what scholars have identified as a sincere commitment among many Soviet authorities and citizens to creating a new society where all forms of exploitation and injustice were absent. Additionally, any racism black Americans may have experienced in the USSR in the interwar era in the form of "sociological racism" (or racism "from below") was not reinforced *systematically* by "official racism" (or racism "from above"), as it was in the United States.[82] The racial climate in the present-day Russian Federation illustrates the significant difference that official racism, especially as represented in the authority of law enforcement officials, as opposed to official *anti*racism, can have on the growth of sociological racism.[83] As *Opposing Jim Crow* demonstrates, the Soviet Union in the decades between the two world wars was more complex and nuanced than any black and white depictions allow.

1

American Racism on Trial and the Poster Child for Soviet Antiracism

In an entry to his diary labeled "Stalingrad, August 1930," William Henry Chamberlin, then the Moscow correspondent for the *Christian Science Monitor*, recorded that he traveled with his wife to "the newly built Stalingrad tractor factory in order to attend the trial of two American mechanics." He wrote that the two defendants, "Mr. Lewis" and "Mr. Brown," were charged with "'racial chauvinism' for having become involved in a brawl with the sole Negro employed at the works."[1] The trial of two American racists to which Chamberlin alludes demonstrates that at a time when Soviet leaders admitted the country's industrial inferiority and recruited a substantial number of American (and other foreign) workers to help build socialism, they represented the USSR as superior to the United States in terms of its treatment of black or "dark-skinned" peoples. Placing U.S. racism on trial in Stalingrad constituted one important means by which officials in Moscow cultivated the Soviet Union's image as an enlightened, race-less society, that is, a society where race did not limit an individual's access to rights.[2]

To this end, Soviet trade union authorities did not want the trial to appear merely as the result of their own efforts. Rather, they depicted the campaign against "Mr. Lewis" and "Mr. Brown" as the product of the widespread indignation of foreign and Soviet laborers. These men and women had been brought together at Soviet industrial giants like the Stalingrad Traktorostroi, Magnitogorsk, Moscow Elektrozavod, and Nizhni-Novgorod Automobile Factory as a result of the demands of the First Five-Year Plan.[3] Throughout the month of August 1930, the central press systematically reported that the workers of these and other enterprises were enthusiastically attending factory meetings to protest the assault on "our brother," electing worker representatives to serve as public prosecutors at the trial and incessantly demanding that the assailants be expelled from the country. Among the central newspapers, *Trud* provided the most extensive coverage, printing on the front page an average of four articles and protest resolutions a day.[4] Thus, in spite of the persistence of national animosity and anti-Semitism in the USSR, the trial of two American racists combined with these frequently published reports made foreign and Soviet laborers appear to be members of a nascent international proletariat who were committed to inaugurating a new socialist society where racial and national discrimination were absent.[5]

All-union editors and central trade union officials simultaneously constructed Robert Robinson, the victim whom workers were shown as having risen to defend en masse, as the "ideal, heroic black worker." To fulfill this trope, information about Robinson in the press was limited to references concerning his blackness, innocence, and diligence as a laborer. Robinson the person necessarily remained a mystery. In this way, he was made to represent all black workers who were innocent victims of the routine racial discrimination engendered by capitalism. His image as the ideal, heroic black worker reached its culmination four years later, in December 1934, when he was elected to the Moscow City Soviet. On this occasion more information was revealed about Robinson than had previously been the case. The intention, arguably, was to personalize or give a "face" to Soviet antiracism. To be sure, Robinson was the perfect poster child for interwar Soviet antiracism; authorities could highlight how he had reaped its benefits since first arriving in the first workers' state in 1930.

On Thursday, July 24, 1930, around six o'clock in the evening at the Stalingrad Tractor Factory, Robert Robinson was walking away from the cafeteria when two white American men, Lemuel Lewis and William Brown, confronted him. All three Americans had been recruited from the Ford Motor Company in Detroit by Amtorg, the Soviet trading agency based in New York. They were in Stalingrad to help build and operate what Soviet leaders prized, along with Magnitogorsk, Elektrozavod, and Nizhni-Novgorod Automobile Factory, as one of the giants of the new socialist industry, the Stalingrad Traktorostroi, named for Feliks Dzerzhinskii.[6] Lewis and Brown had arrived together in May with the majority of the other American workers at the Traktorostroi, which numbered around 370 men. Robinson, in contrast, had arrived on July 20, just four days before the confrontation.[7]

If we consider the official trial record (the contents of which were not released in their entirety in the central press), along with the coverage in Soviet newspapers, the hearsay information afforded the U.S. legation in Riga, Latvia, and the account found in Robinson's 1988 autobiography, we can ascertain that the following scenario ensued. When the two white Americans—who were intoxicated—saw Robinson walking in their direction, Brown teased Lewis by remarking, "Look, here comes your brother!" Lewis responded by asking Robinson, "Where did you come from?" Because Robinson answered him with sarcasm, Lewis admonished his fellow worker not to forget that he was black and needed to answer him, a white man, with deference. Brown similarly reminded Robinson to "not forget your place" and threatened that if "you do not leave here in three days we will drown you in the Volga." Lewis then called Robinson a "black dog," as well as some other names that the local authorities described as unprintable. Robinson supposedly responded by calling Lewis a "bastard," emphasizing that if he was going to end up in the Volga, then a white man was going with him. Lewis and Brown then lunged at the black worker. In self-defense, as witnesses for both the defense and prosecution testified, Robinson picked up a stone from the ground, which initially forced Lewis to retreat.

But Lewis and Brown again pursued Robinson, who had started to walk away from them. Lewis, who caught up with Robinson first, punched the black worker twice in the face, knocking his glasses to the ground. When Robinson tried to grab Lewis, both men fell down. As Lewis pummeled him with his fists, Brown held back his arms to prevent him from retaliating. In an effort to free himself, Robinson clenched his teeth around Lewis's neck and refused to let go until a group of American workers, some of whom had been standing by laughing, pulled the three men apart.[8] Local police questioned and released both Lewis and Robinson that evening. Failing to recognize the political significance of the attack, neither they nor the factory's trade union officials conducted any further investigations in the weeks that followed. (This negligence would elicit severe public reprimands from central authorities and ultimately resulted in the reorganization of the Traktorostroi's factory committee.) Therefore, it was not until *Trud* exposed news of the assault on August 9, 1930, that officials in Moscow intervened and a campaign was organized to bring the American racists to justice.[9]

Central newspapers portrayed workers throughout the Soviet Union as quickly and simultaneously responding to the initial reports and near daily front-page coverage of the assault on Robinson. Yet for clearly strategic purposes, the foreign and Soviet laborers of the Moscow Elektrozavod were portrayed as the most active. As Sergei Zhuravlev argues, during and after the First Five-Year Plan Soviet leaders considered Elektrozavod to be such a high priority that it came to symbolize socialism.[10] It follows therefore that all-union editors presented workers from this particular giant of socialist industry as paragons of proletarian enlightenment, who were at the forefront in denouncing racist conduct as impermissible in a socialist society. According to the central press, Elektrozavod laborers organized a mass protest meeting at which they asked James Ford to speak. They also invited Robinson to work at their factory, and later issued a reassurance that "we are all on his side."[11] The press even credited the Elektrozavod community with suggesting that *Trud*'s editors, with the assistance of the Central Committee of the Metal Workers Union (CC VSRM), form an international workers' brigade. Comprised of nine to ten Soviet and foreign workers from the country's major industrial centers, members of the brigade would serve as community prosecutors at the trial. *Trud*'s editors promptly approved what was scripted as the workers' proposal and contacted representatives of the Metal Workers Union in Leningrad, Khar'kov, Rostov-on-Don, and Tula. They requested that each immediately hold a meeting to appoint a laborer to represent them and, by extension, the entire international proletariat in condemning the white American assailants of a black worker.[12]

The trial opened in one of the main halls of the Stalingrad Traktorostroi on Friday evening, August 22, 1930, roughly a month after the assault had occurred, but only two weeks after *Trud* had exposed news of it.[13] The seven male and two female members of the international workers' brigade had arrived in Stalingrad four days earlier. They were introduced in the press as Ozerov of *Trud*'s editorial board; Kirillov of the CC VSRM; Becker, whom trade union officials described as one of the "conscious" Americans in Stalingrad; Erast, a Latvian from the Khar'kov State Electric Factory; Gavrilov of the Central Committee of the International Organization for Assistance to Revolutionary Fighters (Mezhdunarodnaia organizatsiia pomoshchi bortsam revoliutsii, MOPR); Kondrat'ev of the Khar'kov Traktorostroi; Blaich of Sel'mashstroi in Rostov-on-Don; Rodzinskaia of Elektrozavod in Moscow; and Ferdinand Knut, a German concrete worker from Leningrad.[14]

Two large photographs of Knut and Rodzinskaia, in which both brigadiers are looking directly at the camera, were published on *Trud*'s front page three days prior to the start of the trial. Knut is shown with a pipe in his mouth and wearing a double-breasted suit and tie. Rodzinskaia looks younger than her male counterpart but is equally attractive in appearance; she has short, bobbed blond hair and is wearing a patterned jumper. She fits the model of the "youthful, vital, and attractive" woman that would become pervasive in the press by the end of the decade.[15] By displaying their images in such prominent fashion, *Trud* presented Knut and Rodzinskaia as representing the millions of "little heroes," the country's faceless rank-and-file workers—of Soviet and foreign origin—who were responsible through their everyday labor and comradely unity for building a new society where feelings of racial superiority were absent.[16] The use of Rodzinskaia, a young woman, and Knut, a mature-looking man, to represent the alliance between Soviet and foreign laborers reflects the high esteem that the latter were officially afforded during the First Five-Year Plan. As Sergei Zhuravlev explains, foreign workers were conceptualized as the more mature, proletarian "big brother" who was graciously sharing his technological knowledge and industrial skill with his younger, more inexperienced little brother.[17] When viewed in this context, the prominent photographs on *Trud*'s front page suggest that the maturity, skill, experience, and knowledge associated with the foreign worker assumed the male body. In contrast, the inexperience, youthfulness, humility, and subservient role of the Soviet worker were embodied in the female form.[18] Hence, somewhat paradoxically, Rodzinskaia symbolized the Soviet Union's moral superiority (specifically its alleged gender and racial equality) in relation to capitalist countries, while simultaneously signifying its status—albeit temporary—as industrially and technologically inferior.

The main objective of Knut, Rodzinskaia, and other members of the international workers' brigade was to prove that Lewis and Brown attacked Robinson only because he was black, or more precisely, because he was "by nationality a Negro." Clearly, from the white American assailants' perspective, "Negro" signified an inferior race; by assaulting Robinson they were transferring their American racial norms to Soviet society. Accordingly, in their statements in the central press, many workers, editors, and the defendants themselves attributed the assault on Robinson to racial hatred (*rasovaia nenavist'*) and racial enmity (*rasovaia vrazhda*). However, in the Soviet Union "Negro" signified a distinct nationality; thus, the crime for which members of the international workers' brigade needed to convict Lewis and Brown was "national chauvinism" rather than "racial chauvinism." Accordingly, in the Stalingrad courtroom the terms "national hatred" (*natsional'naia nenavist'*) or "national enmity" (*natsional'naia vrazhda*) were primarily used to describe Lewis and Brown's assault on Robinson. By condemning both "national and racial hatred," workers and all-union editors occasionally attempted to compensate for the difference between Lewis and Brown's motivations and the language of the Soviet law code.

Lewis himself employed this tactic. The day before the trial opened, he issued a statement in which he apologized to the Soviet proletariat for failing to comprehend the pernicious consequences of "national and racial dissension." He emphasized that he was a victim of the American capitalists who had imbued him with such prejudice.[19] Rather than reflecting a genuine change of heart, this apology was motivated by Lewis's desire to gain a more lenient sentence from the court. According to William Chamberlin, the leaders of the American colony at the Stalingrad Tractor Factory, known as the "American committee," helped him compose it. This was a group of men who shared Lewis's opinion of the Soviet commitment to racial equality. Chamberlin claimed that one of its "fascist-minded" leaders showed him a copy of the original apology when he was in Stalingrad attending the trial. When he asked this "middle-aged mechanic, faithful Republican, and proud member of the Methodist church" why a line was crossed out in it, the American committee leader explained that it "'was a direct apology to the nigger. *We crossed that out!*'"[20]

Lewis's efforts at feigning repentance for his racial offense were short-lived. During the trial, he retracted his apology, insisting that it had been a mere scuffle between two workers, that Robinson had been the aggressor (striking him on the head with a pail), and that his drunkenness had made him unaware of what he was doing.[21] The community prosecutors had a vested interest in refuting Lewis's claims. From a practical perspective, the charge of national chauvinism was a counterrevolutionary offense and carried a harsher penalty than mere physical assault.[22] Symbolically speaking, such a charge meant placing at the defendants' bench and condemning "the entire capitalist system and social-fascist trade unions," which had inculcated Lewis and Brown and all white workers with hatred of blacks.[23] *Rabochaia gazeta* (Worker newspaper) captured this objective in a front-page cartoon showing a nondescript white man under interrogation in a courtroom with the shadow of a capitalist lurking behind him. The headline identified the shadow as "the principal defendant who will soon appear before a proletarian court." The caption elucidated that "the American worker at the Stalingrad Tractor Factory assaulted the Negro-worker. The hand of the worker served American capitalism, which spreads racial enmity to further its own interests."[24]

In their opening statements to the court, members of the international workers' brigade made it clear that Lewis had been motivated by U.S. racism. Before a crowd of one thousand workers, and a larger audience listening to the trial broadcast in the dormitories and barracks, Rodzinskaia proclaimed that it was absurd to claim that Lewis "who today calls Russian workers red scum, and tomorrow Negroes black dogs," attacked Robinson independent of any prejudice.[25] Knut similarly stressed that chauvinism and racial hatred were clearly "the motives of this crime." Ozerov, who was equally adamant, put it another way: Lewis assaulted Robinson because in America "attacking a Negro is not considered a crime." In addressing the claim of intoxication, Rodzinskaia emphasized that the two white Americans committed the attack in a state of full consciousness. She then facetiously asked, "If Lewis and Brown were really in such a drunken state, why did they not beat each other?"[26]

The testimony of witnesses for both the defense and prosecution confirmed the "undoubted" racism of the two white American assailants while further revealing that U.S. racism was itself on trial before the workers' court. Peter Parch, for example, emphasized that "feelings of national enmity and hatred towards Negroes, which are especially strong in the southern states of the USA, played a principal role here since Lewis is a native of these southern states." Parch added that Lewis's frequent drinking exacerbated his hatred of black Americans. H. D. Chechell testified to the racial hostility that Lewis and Brown, and the larger American community at the Stalingrad Traktorostroi, exhibited toward Robinson. He, like international brigadier Ozerov, attributed their animosity to the U.S. government's failure to punish individuals who commit violence against black workers, which in turn encouraged their mockery, assault, and murder.[27]

In addition to the testimony of witnesses, Soviet newspapers claimed that the two defendants made the job of the prosecutors easier by often undermining their own argument that they had become involved in a scuffle with a worker who just happened to be black. *Rabochaia gazeta*, which had a particularly sensationalist style of reporting, was at the forefront of representing the two white Americans as unapologetic racists. For example, one article reported that when placed on the witness stand, Lewis claimed that he was unaware that participating in conversations with fellow members of the American colony "about the need to remove the Negro from the factory" was wrong and violated Soviet law. And with regard to the actual assault, the paper quoted him as explaining: "I did not think that I would be brought to trial. In America, incidents with Negroes—this is considered simply street fighting." Brown corroborated Lewis's statement, commenting that "in America, this would be treated as a joke." When asked to elucidate upon the source of white animosity toward black people in the United States, Lewis claimed that blacks were neither "clean" nor educated. Brown, who the prosecution repeatedly stressed was a member of the American Federation of Labor, allegedly responded by stating that "Negroes were slaves, and should remain slaves."[28] There can be little doubt that *Rabochaia gazeta*'s editors eagerly attributed these inflammatory comments to the two white American defendants. They epitomized the blatant racism and chauvinism of "civilized" America that the new socialist society, which the trial itself signified, had supposedly obliterated and rendered impermissible.

In 1941 George Padmore, who had been living in Moscow in 1930 when Lewis and Brown were placed on trial, recalled that "the Russian workers were so indignant at white men treating a fellow-worker in that fashion simply because of his race, that they demanded their immediate expulsion from the Soviet Union."[29] Padmore's reminiscence testifies to Soviet authorities' success in framing the Stalingrad campaign in a discourse of workers' indignation and incessant demands that the two American racists be expelled from the country. To be sure, indignation was the only proper "proletarian" way for Soviet and foreign laborers to respond publicly to this manifestation of American racism. "Proletarianness" and the code of conduct associated with the enlightened "New Soviet Person" thus entailed more than just punctuality, a readiness to exceed work assignments, maintenance of a clean home, and refraining from spitting on the floor.[30] It also required proficiency in "speaking antiracism," or expressing at least outward disdain for national chauvinism and racism. Articulating indignation at the racially motivated assault, then, whether individually or collectively, became a means for workers to prove their "proletarianness" and claim membership in the international proletariat.

When *Trud*'s editors broke the story, they claimed that the attack on a black worker at the Stalingrad Traktorostroi had provoked tremendous indignation (*vozmushchenie*) among the laborers there. In the days that followed, as reported in the all-union newspapers, the workers in Moscow factories such as Dinamo and Elektrozavod, as well as members of the city and oblast sections of MOPR, discussed the manifestation of racial prejudice and voiced their anger. In their protest statements, foreign workers in Kiev, Khar'kov, and Rostov-on-Don proclaimed that Lewis's "vile" (*gnusnoe*) behavior can only arouse "profound indignation."[31] Indignation was also shown to have affected the young proletariat. Participants at an International Pioneers Conference in Moscow and workers of the Siberian youth newspaper *Molodoi rabochii* (Young worker) articulated outrage at the assault. Editors frequently complemented these protest statements with general assertions that the Americans' conduct had "understandably" and justifiably elicited tremendous indignation throughout the country.[32] They only questioned the sincerity of a particular group's anger and their claims to proletarian status when the notorious American committee of the Stalingrad Traktorostroi issued a protest resolution prior to the start of the trial.[33]

In addition to protest resolutions in the central press, the trial of a Moscow worker modeled indignation as the proper proletarian response to racial injustice. The defendant in the August 17 trial was V. M. Tsiprus, a textile worker and former resident of the United States who had allegedly expressed approval of, rather than indignation at, the two Americans' conduct. When a *Rabochaia gazeta* reporter asked him, during a factory protest meeting, his opinion of the assault, Tsiprus supposedly remarked, "Negroes are snakes. They all need to be lynched or subjected to lynch law."[34] The central press depicted the country's laborers as outraged and united in their demand that trade union officials bring Tsiprus to account for his racist comments. According to Isaiah Hawkins, an African American Communist who attended the trial, Tsiprus's statements roused "all kinds of indignation among workers of the Soviet Union."[35] For failing to speak antiracism, a workers' court condemned Tsiprus to expulsion from the needle workers union for three months or until he was able to demonstrate, through community service, his commitment to proletarian internationalism.[36]

Robinson's assailants, with whom Tsiprus had reportedly voiced solidarity, faced a far more serious form of expulsion. As Padmore's above comment indicates, the widespread outpouring of indignation against Lewis and Brown was paired with what the press made to appear as the equally universal appeal that they be deported from the Soviet Union. This demand was attributed to two hundred foreign laborers in Leningrad, workers of Krasnyi Putilovets, Ruhr miners working in the lower Moscow basin, workers of the Moscow Automobile Society, laborers of Sel'mashstroi in Rostov-on-Don, the "conscious" American workers at the Stalingrad Traktorostroi, and American laborers of the Nizhni-Novgorod Automobile Factory.[37] During the trial, the press reported that Ferdinand Knut expressed this popular appeal by declaring, "In the name of the Leningrad proletariat and in particular the foreign workers working in Leningrad, I demand the severest punishment, their expulsion from the USSR." As Gavrilov likewise averred, "We together with the Russian proletariat request that the community court rule to punish the criminals severely, to banish them from the borders of the Soviet Union, because they contaminated the territory of the socialist republic."[38]

Why did trade union officials encourage workers to insist on expulsion rather than imprisonment as the most appropriate, harshest punishment for Lewis and Brown? On a practical level, deportation signaled a return to the vast unemployment and hunger of the Depression-ridden United States, which the two American laborers wanted to avoid. Symbolically, expulsion sent a message to the large number of (non-Communist) American workers who remained in the Soviet Union to help build socialism: racists belonged in a racist society. According to the all-union press, workers and authorities repeatedly reminded Lewis and Brown that they were in a country that was "building socialism," the tempo of which was made possible only by upholding "the equality of all people." As a front-page editorial in *Trud* declared, Soviet workers were "correct to consider the chauvinistic acts of the Americans Lewis and Brown as a strike directly against our great construction."[39] By attempting to practice racism—to "transfer to Soviet soil the fascist ways of America"—Lewis and Brown became "counterrevolutionaries" and "fascists" who had threatened to inhibit the construction of socialism. In the words of Rodzinskaia, the two white Americans were "puppets" of the "international counterrevolution," of "American fascism, who tried to sabotage" the socialist project.[40] How else, then, if the image of the Soviet Union as a society intolerant of racial and national chauvinism was to be maintained, could the Soviet working community be expected to respond to these racists but with indignation? And what other verdict short of expulsion could the proletariat of an antiracist society demand for them?

After six days of testimony from witnesses and various speeches of the defense and prosecution, the court issued its verdict on August 29, 1930, at ten o'clock in the evening. Lewis and Brown were found guilty and sentenced to two years' imprisonment under article 59 of the criminal code regarding national chauvinism. Almost immediately thereafter, their sentence was commuted to ten years' banishment from the Soviet Union. The *Pittsburgh Courier*, an African American newspaper, captured the court's verdict in a front-page headline that declared "Detroit and Toledo Race-Haters Must Return to America."[41] This decision was based on the premise that Lewis and Brown had been raised under the American capitalist system, which purposefully inculcated its workers with hatred of blacks.[42] The message here was clear. Any individual raised in the Soviet Union would be held to a higher standard and consequently given a harsher punishment if they ever dared to raise a hand to a black worker.[43]

Since the central press portrayed Soviet and foreign workers as calling for the expulsion of the two Americans en masse, the formal court proceedings appear merely as a theatrical fulfillment of their demand. In one sense, this was not unusual. The outcome of Soviet show trials of the 1920s and 1930s were often determined beforehand; their objective became proving the "legitimacy, correctness, or validity of the predetermined decisions."[44] Similarly, members of the international workers' brigade did not simply reiterate the appeal of "workers" that the men be deported. Instead, they concentrated on proving its "legitimacy, correctness, and validity" by demonstrating that Lewis and Brown attacked Robinson only because he was black.

Deporting Lewis and Brown was not the only measure that central leaders implemented to ensure Robinson's future safety; it was simply the most dramatic and most publicized. They also launched a campaign to institute international education among the foreign laborers at factories around the country, but especially among those at the Stalingrad Tractor Factory where Robinson remained employed until 1932.[45] International education, broadly defined as the antithesis of "capitalist education," meant instilling in workers the values of a socialist society. In early July 1930, during the Sixteenth Party Congress, Stalin had emphasized the need to improve international education to eliminate remnants of national and racial chauvinism throughout the USSR.[46] Since Lewis and Brown attacked Robinson only a few weeks later, trade union officials in Moscow condemned Traktorostroi authorities for making the racial violence "inevitable" by failing to conduct international education among the American workers there.[47] By November 1930, central authorities' efforts to correct the situation at the Stalingrad Tractor Factory resulted in the deportation of seventeen additional American workers who they deemed the most "fascist" and "reactionary." Impervious to international education, these white American men, like Lewis and Brown, had to be removed from Soviet soil. By refusing to even nominally respect the principles of speaking antiracism, they threatened to jeopardize Robinson's physical safety and the Soviet Union's image as a society that had discovered the cure for racism.[48]

Who was Robert Robinson, whom William Chamberlin had described only as "the sole Negro employed at the [Stalingrad tractor] works"?

Or, more significantly, how did Soviet authorities present him? Robinson was produced as the heroic black worker, and to some degree, the oppressed black victim during the nearly monthlong campaign to bring his white American attackers to justice. Personal information was necessarily omitted and replaced by constant assertions of Robinson's blackness and innocence. While on the one hand this emphasis nearly eliminated Robinson the individual, on the other it overturned the historical Western and, in this case, the particularly American dichotomy that paired blackness with guilt or immorality.[49]

When *Trud* and *Rabochaia gazeta* first identified Robert Robinson as the victim of the assault, they reported that Stalingrad Traktorostroi workers characterized him "as a highly skilled, conscientious worker" and "great comrade." Readers were also informed that Robinson had defied the order of a group of Americans to leave the cafeteria during dinner. As *Rabochaia gazeta* explained, Robinson specifically told his antagonists that he was in the Soviet Union and therefore did not have to listen to them. In an editorial, Mikhail Danilov emphasized that there was something very positive, if not exhilarating, in all this "kulak violence"—namely, that "THE NEGRO ROBINSON REFUSED TO SUBMIT TO THE SAVAGE DEMAND OF HIS WHITE COUNTRYMEN." Therefore, "the Negro Robinson already understands, what the American [L]ewis does not; that in the country of Soviets there is no racial inequality."[50]

On August 12, 1930, *Trud*'s editors printed a sketch of Robinson's profile on the front page, in which he was depicted wearing glasses and a shirt and tie. Robinson signed his name at the bottom of the sketch along with the message written in English, "Best wishes for your success," which must have been addressed to the laborers of Elektrozavod who had invited him to join their worker family. In a very short interview, Robinson thanked them but insisted that he must remain at the Stalingrad Traktorostroi because if he left, then he would only be giving the "American slaveowners" there what they wanted. Robinson explained that although some of the American workers and interpreters had begun to treat him with even greater contempt since the attack, the "Russian workers as usual have remained my friends." He also requested that the Elektrozavod workers stay in correspondence with him.[51]

Printed biographical information about Robinson was limited to the brief mention that he had worked in Cuba, the West Indies, Brazil, and Detroit.[52] Only two points about him were clear from published statements: Robinson was black and he was innocent. Variations of the phrases "only because he is black, not white" and "only because he is a Negro" became standard. From the outset of their coverage, *Trud*'s editors stressed that the "Negro-worker" was attacked "ONLY BECAUSE he is—a Negro."[53] *Rabochaia gazeta* similarly reported that the white American "beat up the Negro Robinson only for this, that he is BLACK." As deputy chairman of the Supreme Court of the Russian Soviet Federated Socialist Republic (RSFSR) F. Nakhimson put it, the two "reactionary" Americans thought they were in a type of "capitalist paradise where they could raise a hand to a Negro worker only because he is a Negro."[54] Foreign workers of the Moscow Elektrozavod followed the example of editors and authorities by declaring that it was humiliating for the entire proletariat that Robinson was assaulted "only because he is a Negro, not white." A group of over twenty American specialists at the First State Clock Factory in Moscow too denounced Lewis and Brown for attacking Robinson "only because he is black."[55]

Robinson emerged from all these articles, letters, and resolutions of protest as a hero who stood up to the American racists by asserting his rights as a black worker in the fatherland of all workers. He, unlike Lewis and Brown, did not treat as mere propaganda Soviet claims that the USSR was intolerant of racial animosity. After the assault, Robinson declared that he would remain at the Stalingrad Traktorostroi because he refused to acquiesce to the designs of the American racists. Workers wrote Robinson letters of support, and coworkers attested to his skill and diligence, while Robinson himself testified to the friendliness, and by implication, enlightened thinking of the Russian laborers with whom he worked. Very simply, the Robinson whom authorities constructed was easy to support if not like.

Interestingly, readers were never provided with the complete description of the altercation between Robinson and his two white antagonists, as narrated at the beginning of this chapter. In fact, with the exception of *Pravda*, Soviet papers continued to report that the incident took place in the dining hall.[56] Information that Robinson had fought back not only verbally but also physically was omitted from the central press. The community prosecutors repeatedly emphasized, and witnesses for the defense confirmed, that Robinson acted out of self-defense. Yet this information was obviously deemed inappropriate for the construction of the ideal, heroic black worker. Undoubtedly, evidence that Robinson physically retaliated against his attackers would have rendered more problematic the simultaneous effort to produce him as a victim, a victim of racial injustice (representing the racially oppressed of the world) who needed Soviet workers to defend him. As a member of the international workers' brigade emphasized in his closing remarks, the evidence presented during the trial confirmed that Robinson was "an honest, exemplary worker" whom "we must defend from racial prejudice."[57] In a sense, then, Soviet officials perpetuated the stereotype of black males as defenseless "Sambos" in need of white protection for their survival. The caretakers of Robinson's attack, in other words, reinforced the racist ideology they ostensibly sought to destroy, thereby further illuminating their own lack of understanding of racism.[58] As will be discussed below and elaborated on in subsequent chapters, such paternalistic images of African Americans pervaded most forms of Soviet antiracism.

An even more glaring omission in the creation of Robinson as heroic black worker was any mention of his occupational specialty. Although this could be guessed at when considering his place of employment, the Stalingrad Traktorostroi, it was still never clear exactly what type of work the "extremely well-qualified" worker did there (keeping in mind that the central newspapers never reported that his last employer was the Ford Motor Company).[59] This particular omission supports the argument that what was most important about Robinson was that he was black and innocent. In addition to his work specialization, any other personal information about Robinson, such as his age, marital status, family life, or educational level, could not be disclosed. This would have made it more difficult for him to stand in for and symbolize all black workers, whose rights the Soviet Union defended.

Such an erasure of Robinson the individual also furthered all-union editors' efforts to transform the confrontation between him and the two white Americans into an "event" that the working community could organize meetings around, discuss, and condemn. In several articles concerning the attack, Robinson's name was not even mentioned but was replaced by phrases like "the Stalingrad incident," "the incident in Stalingrad," and "the Stalingrad affair." Therefore, although authorities brought his white American assailants to justice, they rendered Robinson the person irrelevant to their story.

In renditions of the "incident" that were recounted in Soviet anti-racist lore after 1930, Robinson's name or identity was not the only casualty. It was common for basic information surrounding the case to be omitted. This included the year the trial occurred, the names of the defendants, and the specific tractor factory where it took place. Information was also frequently distorted to make the American defendants (or defendant, depending on the particular rendition) "skilled" laborers. A short story for children that appeared in *Murzilka* in 1933 exemplifies this pattern. Titled "Negro Pioneers," the narrative addressed the hard life of an African American Pioneer named "Jack" who was only fourteen years old but already had a full-time job. When Jack attended a meeting of white American Pioneers, he told them about an "interesting event" in the USSR. By Jack's account, some skilled American laborers at a Soviet tractor factory were tried before a workers' court and deported because they had attacked a "Negro worker" when he entered the American cafeteria.[60]

Even more egregious in its omission and distortion of information than the "Negro Pioneers" is the rendition of the "incident" that Dmitri Manuilskii, the head of the Comintern, recounted during a meeting with African and African American students in 1933. Manuilskii transformed Lewis—whom he identified (though not by name) as the sole white American involved—from a habitually inebriated rank-and-file worker to a leading American specialist who did not physically attack a black worker but simply objected to his presence in the cafeteria. Specifically, Manuilskii emphasized that by deporting Lewis for "refusing to sit in the cafeteria with a Negro," the country had "lost one of the best specialists." By reducing the severity of Lewis's racial offense and portraying him as an extremely valuable contributor to the construction of Soviet industry, Manuilskii made authorities' intolerance of racism appear even more uncompromising and genuine.[61] By November 1936, accounts of the Stalingrad trial had become even more convoluted. A Russian tour guide reportedly told a white American student from Oklahoma who was disbelieving of Soviet racial equality that three white Americans had been banished *recently* from the USSR at the behest of Russian workers because they had assaulted their black foreman.[62] Clearly, perpetuating the memory of the country's response to American racial violence assumed precedence over accuracy. That is to say, as long as the memory of the "incident" was preserved regardless of its imperfections, the Soviet Union's image as a society without racism persisted in spite of its imperfections.

Though erased from the memory of the "Stalingrad incident" and replaced by the generic "Negro worker," Robert Robinson's image as an ideal, heroic black worker never disappeared in the first half of the 1930s. Having decided to renew his labor contract in 1931, he subsequently became—though not as a result of his own designs—the poster child for Soviet antiracism. Representations of Robinson came to serve, apart from the memory of the Stalingrad trial, as additional, tangible evidence that Soviet antiracism was not mere propaganda. As George Padmore put it in April 1932, Robinson constituted "most convincing proof of the fact that any honest worker, whatever his nationality, race, etc., is welcome in the Soviet Union to participate in the great task of carrying out the Five-Year Plan."[63] As long as it could be shown that the black American worker was prospering in the Soviet Union, the country's antiracist image was secured.

English-language newspapers in the USSR and the African American Communist press were at the forefront of reporting Robinson's success. Editors' main objective was to convey the reality of Soviet antiracism to readers. This intention becomes especially clear when considering that Lewis and Brown's assault on Robinson served as the major impetus for the establishment, in October 1930, of newspapers for English-speaking workers in the Soviet Union. Central authorities emphasized that such publications were imperative to improving foreign laborers' international education and preventing similar incidents of American racial violence from occurring in the USSR.[64] Clearly, the representations of Robinson found in central papers like the *Moscow News* and *Workers News* (two papers that merged to become the *Moscow Daily News* in May 1932) were intended to remind readers that the boundaries of the Soviet community included and must continue to include black workers as equals. To put it differently, speaking antiracism was not an option but a requirement of residence in the first workers' state.

In August 1931, exactly a year after the trial, the *Workers News* reported that Robinson, an "honest worker," had been named co-leader of the Workers Correspondents Bureau. This was a committee that had been established to "make the work of the Americans in the Stalingrad plant one of the brightest spots in the success of the third, decisive year of the Five-Year Plan."[65] A month later, according to the *Liberator*, the organ of the League of Struggle for Negro Rights (LSNR), Robinson was vacationing in Paris where he had "the highest praise for the treatment of Negro workers by the Soviet workers and officials."[66] The following year Robinson resurfaced in the *Workers News*, first hailing the "wonderful achievements at Stalingrad" and then protesting the execution of nine young African American men in Scottsboro, Alabama, who were at the center of a Soviet and international liberation movement (see chapter 3).[67] The *Liberator* reported in late 1932 that in return for his humble dedication to building socialism, Robinson had been honored as a hero of labor. He had received this award for having contributed over twenty inventions at the First State Ball Bearing Plant in Moscow, where he had been transferred. The editors emphasized that his portrait was displayed in the Palace of Trade Unions with images of other heroes of labor—"those workers who have made outstanding contributions to the building of a new society of the Soviet Union, without classes and without race differences."[68] In 1933 the *Moscow Daily News* also discussed Robinson's "outstanding contributions" in a series of stories that praised him as one of the few

foreign laborers to effectively submit and push through to realization his inventions and suggestions to improve the inefficiency of the
gauge department at the ball bearing plant.[69] From all these reports,
Robinson reemerged as the ideal, heroic black worker: resolute in
his commitment to socialist construction, grateful for the benefits of
Soviet society, and concerned about the plight of his less fortunate
African American brothers who remained in the United States.

Despite this coverage of his success in the years immediately following the trial, it was not until his coworkers at the ball bearing plant
elected him deputy to the Moscow City Soviet in late December 1934
that Robinson returned most forcefully to the national spotlight. Prior
to Robinson, a few other U.S. blacks had been named to the Moscow
City Soviet. These included George Padmore in 1930 (see chapter 4) and
Claude McKay and Otto Huiswood in 1922. Yet Robinson was the only
one who was elected by coworkers—regardless of how contrived that
election was—rather than appointed as an honorary deputy by high-
ranking party officials. Sergei Zhuravlev contends that Robinson's election was similar to that of several German workers during the early
1930s, in that it constituted a way for Soviet leaders to demonstrate
that the USSR had become "'the homeland of workers of all lands.'"[70]
While it is important to view Robinson's election within the context
of other foreign laborers, it is equally imperative to recognize that it
held even greater significance. Simply put, Robinson was special. In
contrast to the sizable number of Germans and other European and
white American workers, Robinson was one of very few black men
employed in the Soviet Union. He represented (as he had four years
earlier in the Stalingrad trial) those U.S. citizens whom American
democracy systematically excluded from the political process because
of their skin color. His election, unlike that of other foreign workers,
indicted American racial apartheid. At the same time, it glorified as
enlightened the policies of the Soviet state, which had afforded him
the opportunity as a black man to excel in an age when biological racism and the ideology of white supremacy was ascendant throughout
Europe and the world.[71] Robinson's photograph, consequently, carried a powerful message regardless of the publication in which it was

printed. Whether shown in *Trud* sitting strategically next to a female delegate at the Third Congress of Soviets of the Moscow oblast, or in the African American newspaper *Chicago Defender* standing with the coworkers who elected him, Robinson appeared as a beneficiary of Soviet antiracism.[72] His image simultaneously signified the purported justice and progressive modernity of Soviet society and the ignorance and backwardness of the capitalist world.

As suggested by the representations of the black worker prior to December 1934, Robinson was presented as having become, after his election to the Moscow City Soviet, even more ideal and heroic as a result of living in the Soviet Union for four years. This enhanced heroism was attributed not necessarily to Robinson's own efforts—though it was clear that he was honest and hard-working—but to the enlightened policies of the Soviet state. In response to his new position as city soviet deputy, the *Moscow Daily News* quoted Robinson as saying that "the realization that I have been elected to such an esteemed and honored position as deputy to the Moscow city and provincial soviets fills me with gratitude and with love for the people of this country and of those who fought in the Revolution to create a better world for workers and toilers, and the oppressed nations and colonial peoples." Robinson's refusal to praise his own accomplishments while expressing indebtedness to the Soviet system was standard in the depiction of all Soviet heroes in the central press during the 1930s.[73] The implication was that the sacrifices of revolutionaries who had established the Soviet state, rather than Robinson's own hard work, skill, and knowledge, had enabled him, as a member of an oppressed nation, to receive such an honor. Robinson further downplayed his own agency by emphasizing the "immense possibilities" that awaited "all who want to work honestly and conscientiously" in the "land of socialism."[74]

While this "modest individual" refrained from praising his contributions to the socialist project, in a lengthy article about Robinson in *Vecherniaia Moskva* (Evening Moscow), the author Evgenii Mar made clear that "there was no more diligent and knowledgeable worker than Robinson" in the instrumental section at the First State Ball Bearing Plant. The "talented instrumentalist" had submitted nearly fifty valuable rationalization proposals, taught ten individuals his skill, and three of his students had already become qualified to teach others. A photograph of Robinson closely instructing a Russian worker reinforced his role as a respected teacher at the factory. Mar claimed that as a result of the admiration that a large circle of students and friends had for his intellect and skill, Robinson had "learned to speak Russian very well" and read Soviet newspapers and the works of Lenin and Stalin.[75] Robinson's language skills were likely more limited than Mar reported. The *Moscow Daily News* quoted Robinson as expressing regret that he was limited in his duties as city soviet deputy because he still possessed an insufficient command of the Russian language. Mar's desire to portray Soviet citizens as genuine in their acceptance of the black worker was not the only reason that he exaggerated Robinson's proficiency in Russian. He also sought to offset a potential flaw that he noted in the profile of the ideal, heroic black worker, namely, that Robinson was not a member of the Communist Party. By ascribing him a solid command of the Russian language, an interest in reading Soviet newspapers, and engagement with the writings of Lenin and Stalin, Mar reaffirmed Robinson's heroic identity—his loyalty to socialist construction appeared unequivocal in spite of his lack of party status.

Robinson's representation as a hero and poster child for Soviet antiracism reached its culmination in Boris Agapov's 1936 *Technical Tales* (*Tekhnicheskie rasskazy*), a collection of stories about the construction of several giants of socialist industry during the First and Second Five-Year Plans. The first section of the book's final chapter, titled "New Fatherland," features a sixteen-page biography of Robinson as one of the valued contributors to Soviet industry. The account is based on a meeting that the author allegedly had with Robinson at the ball bearing plant.[76] Yet instead of an objective, accurate record of his life, the biography reads like a short story, and Robinson—whom Agapov refers to from the outset as "Bob"—seems more like a character born of his creative license than a biographical subject. The significance of Agapov's narrative therefore rests not in determining where fact and fiction diverge but in examining how it authenticates Robinson's representation as the ultimate beneficiary of Soviet antiracism. Toward this end, Agapov did not merely provide evidence of Robinson's success in the USSR, which editors of the central press also documented. Rather, he dedicated the majority of the biography to detailing the black worker's former status as a victim of the capitalist world, a status to which he makes clear Robinson would quickly return should he leave Soviet soil. Due to the emphasis on his pre-Soviet existence, Robinson appears as being reborn in Soviet society, a fate consistent with that of all Soviet heroes of this era.[77]

The lengthy account of Robinson's "life" under capitalism begins with the poverty that young "Bob" and his family suffered in the Caribbean. His father, a dark-skinned sugarcane cutter who longed to own a plot of land and a horse, moved the family around Jamaica and Cuba in search of a decent wage. One could already see the glimmer of the ideal, heroic black worker in Bob as a young boy; accompanying his incessant hunger pangs was an irrepressible desire to study to become a skilled laborer. After becoming an apprentice to a craftsman for whom his mother worked as a laundress, Robinson excelled through constant hard work and studying to become a skilled worker and earn high wages. He was reminded, however, that education, hard work, and acquisition of skill do not negate blackness in the capitalist world. Bob was forced to leave a high-paying job and the region in Cuba where he was living because he struck a white man who had insulted his craft and intelligence. Having jeopardized his long-term safety on the island by transgressing capitalism's racial hierarchy, Bob began saving money to move to the United States where he naively—as a landlord later informed him—sought refuge from racism.

It was in the "land of freedom" that Agapov's representation of Bob as a tragic victim reached its apex. During the journey there by boat, he portrays the young migrant laborer as reading newspaper headlines which referenced lynching, skin lighteners, and employers seeking light-skinned blacks. Nonetheless, Bob still failed to realize that the United States "was not for blacks," not even for a skilled worker like himself.[78] Upon arriving in New York, he was shocked that he was forced to engage in menial, degrading work and was the target of routine racial insults. Despite learning the "art" of modesty and submissiveness in dealing with whites, Bob was unable to gain respectable work from New York to Washington DC. He eventually traveled to the Ford Motor Company in Detroit hoping to improve his fortunes, but Bob's experiences there only confirmed that America was not the land of opportunity he had envisioned. After four years working as a janitor and unloading trucks, a German foreman gave the skilled laborer a chance to operate a machine in the toolmaking shop. Regardless of the foreman's background, Agapov wanted to portray or emphasize (if true) that a German man was the only white person to give Robinson a break in the United States.[79] Bob performed so brilliantly in his new position that he was transferred to a more delicate section of the toolmaking shop, where for two years he worked without making a mistake. Yet success came at a high price. During those two years none of the workers spoke to him and they constantly tampered with his machine. Since Bob's only joy in America was taking classes in the evenings, he began saving money to return to Jamaica. It was during this low point as a black worker in the capitalist world that Bob was approached about working in the Soviet Union. Although a major decision for Robinson, Agapov portrays him as giving it no serious reflection.

Robinson's supposed naivety regarding American racial norms was paralleled by his alleged ignorance of Soviet attitudes toward persons of African descent. As a result, it was Soviet citizens' treatment of him, Agapov insisted, that startled Bob the most about the USSR. He first encountered this enlightened thinking during his journey to the first workers' state. Whereas Jim Crow laws had accompanied him during his voyage across the Atlantic, when Bob transferred to a Soviet ship, the Russian passengers conversed with him and invited him to eat at their table, the Soviet novelist Aleksei Tolstoi drank to his health, and all the Russian women expressed a desire to dance with him. As Agapov put it, their conduct infuriated the white American passengers who "preferred to starve rather than eat in the company of a Negro."[80] Whether Russian women wanted to dance with a (strange) black man is immaterial. What is most provocative is that Agapov used their alleged desire and Russian men's implicit approval to insist on the moral superiority of the Soviet people during an era when much of the Western world condemned interracial male-female contact as a threat to humanity (deemed white) and a justified provocation for violence against black men.[81]

Prefigured in the conduct of the Russian passengers, the Soviet Union was the "promised land" or refuge from racism for which Bob had been searching his entire life. Contrasting America's Jim Crow laws, Agapov stressed the intimacy with which tools were passed from Bob's "black hand" to the "white hands" of his Russian coworkers, the shared towels in the washroom at the ball bearing plant, and the Stalingrad trial of his American assailants in 1930. More than this, Agapov compared Bob to a virtuoso violin player whose brain and body were not those of an animal. He was completely unsuited for the mindless, unskilled labor to which his black skin condemned him—even as an ideal worker—in the United States. One white American teacher, Agapov claimed, had called Bob foolish for studying so hard when he would never have the opportunity to apply his knowledge to any appropriate occupation. This teacher, however, was the real fool. As Agapov triumphantly declared, "Robert Robinson had not studied for nothing, the virtuoso, soloist of delicate instruments had found, finally, his orchestra."[82] The enlightened policies of the Soviet state, in other words, had allowed Robinson to transcend his brutal victimization, reach his potential as a "virtuoso," and ascend to heroic heights. Even though he was not a member of the Communist Party, Agapov (like Mar) allayed any suspicions concerning the black worker's loyalty, stating that he was attending KUTV and evening lectures. His dedication and devotion to his "New Fatherland," the paternalistic state to which he owed his existence as a complete man, were unquestioned.

Agapov's portrayal of Robinson as a virtuoso of fine toolmaking who attended KUTV and taught Russian workers his craft is complicated by his simultaneous racialization of him as "Bob."[83] "Bob" is an extremely naive, noncontemplative laborer who is oblivious to matters that do not pertain directly to his work. He willfully clings to his ignorance of Americans' opinions of black people, despite reading newspaper headlines pertaining to U.S. racial apartheid, he gives no serious consideration before deciding to pursue employment in the USSR, and he is completely unaware of Soviet antiracism.[84] This last characteristic is especially curious since most African Americans who traveled to the Soviet Union during this era, as noted in the introduction, did so as "black 'pilgrims,'" explicitly seeking to investigate the validity of leaders' claims to have "discovered the cure for racism."[85] Moreover, by highlighting how Robinson's "black hand with white nails" held the pencil he used to solve trigonometry problems, Agapov presents Robinson (regardless of his specific intention) as a curiosity of sorts; the implication was that solving complex math problems and black skin were incongruent.[86] Overall, Agapov's biographical portrait of Robinson helps illuminate the contradictory images of blacks that Soviet antiracism often disseminated, an issue that will be elaborated more fully below with regard to this black American Soviet hero.[87]

Although more information was disseminated about Robinson after his election to the Moscow City Soviet, the heroic persona constructed of him remained hollow. The ostensibly personal material concerning Robinson's life was limited to his existence as a tragic victim of racism in the capitalist world, the details of his occupational specialty, and his indispensable contributions to Soviet industry. The honest, hard-working black laborer of 1930 had merely matured to become a black proletarian who was a highly respected instructor of fellow workers and an indefatigable, selfless builder of socialism. Any personal information that might have contradicted his representation as an ideal, heroic black worker was omitted. This not only included Robinson's supposed devotion to Christianity, but also any relationship he may have had with Russian women.[88] While Soviet editors and writers may have considered it too dangerous to represent the black laborer as having any romantic interest in Russian women, Robinson's image as a desexualized worker reflected the representation of all Soviet male celebrities in the 1930s. Only if these men were married were women mentioned, and this was merely to praise the latter for contributing to Soviet society through their housework.[89] The primary devotion of these male heroes, like that of Robinson, was to the paternalistic Soviet state (and increasingly to Stalin himself) which had given them life. By this logic, any indication of sexuality was simply anathema to hero or ideal worker status in the USSR.[90] Regardless of the specific motivations behind it, Robinson's representation as an ideal worker devoid of sexuality challenged the dominant Western image of the oversexed, virile black male who lusted after white women.[91]

The evolution of the well-crafted image of Robinson in the first half of the 1930s was similar to the memory of the Stalingrad trial in that it served as evidence of the Soviet Union's intolerance of racism. At the same time, however, it held even greater significance. It not only validated the actions of the workers who had rallied to Robinson's defense four years earlier. More important, it also validated the existence of Soviet antiracism, and specifically Soviet leaders' rejection of biological racism. Black workers, as Robinson's image demonstrated, were not inherently lazy, dishonest, unintelligent, inclined to insubordination, and incapable of skilled labor requiring innovation or creativity. Instead, they were victims of centuries of racial oppression—an oppression that the existence of capitalism necessitated—who had been systematically deprived of the opportunities to develop, reach their potential, and excel. If any Soviet, white American, or other foreign laborers had retained, consciously or subconsciously, any backward "capitalist" stereotypes regarding blacks, Soviet authorities offered up Robinson as an antidote.[92]

Yet while validating Soviet leaders' rejection of biological racism, Robinson's reincarnation as a more ideal, heroic black worker simultaneously perpetuated a form of racial paternalism. Robinson—who remained completely mild-mannered and nonthreatening in his representation—was not the agent of his own emancipation. In spite of his remarkable determination, hard work, and dedication to studying, Robinson would have remained a victim had he remained in the capitalist world. He needed the assistance or enlightened wisdom of whites across the Atlantic to realize his own liberation. The same was true for all black workers whom he represented, and was consistent with the conceptualization of the Soviet Union's non-Russian nationalities as "little brothers" who had needed the help of their Russian "big brother" to end tsarist oppression and attain a civilized existence.[93]

Certainly, in the 1930s Soviet citizens as a whole, and heroes in particular, were portrayed in the press, literature, and at major congresses as indebted to the paternalistic Soviet state, embodied in the father figure of Stalin, for their happy, cultured lives.[94] But the long history in Russia and the West of depicting nonwhite peoples as wild, "dark" savages in need of civilization makes it difficult to deny the racially paternalistic overtones of Robinson's image.[95] His representation as the poster child for Soviet antiracism thus reinforced some of the racist stereotypes that Soviet authorities may have intended for it to counter. This indicates the extent to which the ideology of black inferiority, whether rooted in sociohistorical circumstances or biology, was entrenched even in modern societies that attempted to define themselves in opposition to it.

Soviet racial paternalism becomes even more apparent when considering that Robinson's dark complexion made him well-suited to serve as the poster child for Soviet "emancipation." Officials in Moscow—obtuse to differences among persons of African descent—had established a precedent for equating dark skin with authentic blackness and racial oppression. As discussed briefly in the introduction, this was evidenced in Comintern leaders' decision to anoint Claude McKay as the representative "Negro American Communist" at the Fourth Comintern Congress in 1922 instead of the light-skinned Otto Huiswood. Authorities expressed similar distress ten years later in June 1932 when the African Americans who arrived in the capital to make *Black and White*, a film about American racism, had light complexions (see chapter 4).[96] Soviet officials' preference for dark-skinned African Americans reflects their use of non-Russians who appeared most ethnically "non-European" to exhibit—in the press and at national conferences—the progress of Soviet society.[97] As these examples suggest, Robinson's usefulness to Soviet authorities rested as much in his dark skin tone as his good work ethic. His distinctive "black" skin helped glorify the USSR as the world's beacon of enlightenment.

What is the significance of Stalingrad to this narrative? While Moscow was the primary stage from which leaders projected the Soviet Union's image as a brotherhood and later friendship of peoples, the fact that the assault on Robinson occurred at the Stalingrad Traktorostroi was fortuitous.[98] Placing American racism on trial at a giant of socialist industry reaffirmed that these massive industrial complexes were not merely producing the technological products that would facilitate the arrival of a new socialist society. They were also producing the enlightened new Soviet people who would populate it. Although American industrial technique and knowledge played a key role in their construction, these giants of socialist industry were represented as bulwarks against the racism that capitalist societies like the United States engendered. The central press provided further evidence of this by depicting the workers of another leading industrial enterprise, the Moscow Elektrozavod, at the forefront of the campaign to bring Lewis and Brown to account for their racist conduct. Apart from this, Stalingrad was significant for another reason. It could stand in for all provincial towns of the RSFSR to signify that racism and national inequality had been transcended throughout the entire country, not just in the capital of internationalism.

Trade union officials and all-union editors portrayed foreign laborers as particularly vocal in condemning the assault on Robinson. They were depicted formulating numerous protest resolutions and comprising the ranks of the international workers' brigade. Clearly, the authorities' objective was to distance other foreign workers in the country from any stigma that Lewis and Brown's racist actions may have conferred on them as a whole. Their role as the proletarian "big brother" to Soviet workers, with whom they were expected to share their technical knowledge, could therefore remain intact, if they were shown to be just as outraged as the Soviet laboring masses at white American men raising a hand to a black worker.

During an era when biological racism was paramount in European and American social thought, officials in Moscow claimed a monopoly on modern civilization and enlightenment in what was then a unique way: they cast themselves and their citizens as staunch opponents of racism. They defined socialism or the "anticapitalist" world that they were constructing not only in terms of the absence of capitalism's chaotic markets and "selfish individualism" but also its racial hatred.[99] The Stalingrad trial of two American racists visualized what Francine Hirsch and Amir Weiner have identified as Soviet leaders' resolute rejection of Western authorities' politics of racial exclusion.[100] It thereby established the foundation for the even more far-reaching protest that MOPR launched eight months later to liberate the young black American men condemned to death in Scottsboro, Alabama, on false rape charges (see chapter 3). The court proceedings in Stalingrad also provided the inspiration and model for the trials that the U.S. Communist Party organized to eradicate white chauvinism within its ranks. The first and most popular was the trial of August Yokinen held in Harlem on March 1, 1931, that is, five months after the Stalingrad proceedings.[101]

There can be little doubt that the slippage between the image of the Soviet Union as a society without racism and reality was considerable, and that the widespread participation of workers in the Stalingrad trial was orchestrated "from above." Still, this chapter does not discount the possibility that some Soviet and foreign workers may have been committed to inaugurating a new society where racist conduct like that which Lewis and Brown committed was absent. As several scholars have shown, many Soviet citizens were enthusiastic about and derived a tremendous sense of self-worth from participating in the construction of a new socialist world.[102] Moreover, Robinson's reminiscences about the trial in his 1988 autobiography demonstrate the need to exercise caution when examining Soviet antiracism. Robinson used his memoir, published by a company with connections to the CIA, to document that racism had not been eliminated in the USSR and to accuse Soviet authorities of holding him hostage in the country from the Second World War through the 1970s.[103] However, although these were his objectives, Robinson nevertheless claimed that Russian workers and officials had respected him at the Stalingrad Tractor Factory, and that the former had intervened during the assault in July 1930. Additionally, despite emphasizing that he only participated in the trial—which he described as a propaganda tool—to avoid deportation, Robinson explained that after the verdict was issued he was not on vigilant guard against any potential attackers for the first time in his life. He elucidated: "Everything looked the same, but I felt different. Breathing seemed easier, my heart felt lighter, and the tension that was always a part of me was gone. I was floating. 'This must be what freedom feels like,' I thought." Robinson added that the next morning, he continued to experience the same new tranquility: "As I was putting my clothes on, I even tried to think of things to worry about, so unnatural was this feeling of peacefulness."[104] As Robinson's powerful recollections reveal, Soviet antiracist propaganda created a complex, often contradictory reality that renders any black-white representation of Soviet attitudes toward racial prejudice problematic.

At a juncture in Soviet history when the privileged category of "worker" was reconfigured to include women, students, and peasant in-migrants, the Stalingrad trial extended those boundaries to embrace a black migrant laborer from Detroit and all black workers.[105] This reflected the contemporary shift in Comintern policy which, as noted in the introduction, elevated black Americans' importance in the revolutionary family, making them valued allies of the Soviet Union. Simultaneously, two white Americans were stripped of the identity of "workers" and expelled from the fatherland of all workers. They had assumed that their whiteness would automatically exonerate them for attacking a black laborer, while Robinson's blackness would automatically indict him. Soviet leaders used Lewis and Brown's underestimation of their commitment to the USSR's antiracist image to strengthen it.

2

"This Is Not Bourgeois America"

Representations of American Racial Apartheid and Soviet Racelessness

Robert Robinson constituted the "face" of Soviet antiracism, but representations of black Americans' inclusion in the USSR and the indictment of U.S. racism were not limited to the black toolmaker and the Stalingrad trial of his white American assailants. Rather, during the late 1920s and early 1930s, the Soviet press depicted real and fictional African Americans embraced as equals in the first workers' state and as lynched, imprisoned, and segregated in the United States. By juxtaposing blacks' inclusion in the Soviet body politic with their exclusion from U.S. society, central newspapers and magazines represented the USSR as the morally superior antithesis to "bourgeois America." The Soviet Union was imaged, in other words, both as a "raceless" society where race did not limit an individual's access to rights and as an antiracist society that condemned the racism of the capitalist world, but particularly of the United States, the most advanced capitalist country where racial hatred was shown to have reached its most depraved form. Since African American men were at the center of these representations, the black male body came to simultaneously signify American racial apartheid and Soviet racelessness.

The importance that Soviet leaders assigned the press in forging the new revolutionary order cannot be overstated. With regard to its "transformative role," Jonathan Becker argues that the press was intended "to do nothing less than foster the creation of a new people who would both forge and form a new society."[1] On a most basic level, the press taught young party and trade union activists the official language of the state. To better fulfill this goal, in the late 1920s and early 1930s Soviet newspapers adopted a more accessible, popular format and appearance that would appeal to the hundreds of thousands of individuals of working-class background, who were entering the ranks of the party and officialdom.[2] The coverage of U.S. racism assumed its most intense, sustained form during this era, teaching this large young cadre of party members—among other lessons—the language and grammar of antiracism. As suggested by the exchange between U.S. senator Hubert Humphrey and Soviet leader Nikita Khrushchev outlined in the introduction, this language served Khrushchev and other working-class "promotees" well into the late 1940s and 1950s.

The increased number of articles, short stories, photographs, and cartoons indicting U.S. racism in the Soviet press identified African Americans as valued allies and condemned the violence against them as a threat to the national security of the USSR.[3] Since the most sensationalized acts of racism were committed against black men, central newspapers and magazines elided black women and gendered African American militancy (and the Soviet Union's allies) male. The emasculation of black male workers was presented as the main impetus of the U.S. racial regime, and the revolutionary struggle as their remasculinization in homosocial alliance with Soviet men. Documenting the racial injustices committed against bourgeois America's black male citizens was meant to confirm for readers that their mission of building an anticapitalist society was a noble one.[4] It also served as an obvious distraction from the violence that the Soviet state committed against its citizens.[5]

The Soviet publication that dedicated the most attention to the persecution of African American male workers was *Internatsional'nyi maiak* (initially titled *Put' MOPR'a*). *Internatsional'nyi maiak* (International lighthouse) served as a major site of antiracist expression in the early 1930s. It was one of two journals (and the more popular of the two) that the Soviet branch of MOPR, or the International Organization for Assistance to Revolutionary Fighters, published to systematically expose the atrocities committed against "revolutionary fighters" in capitalist countries.[6] The consistent presence of black American men in this journal affirmed their identity as the revolutionary vanguard. Mainstream publications like *Komsomol'skaia pravda*, *Trud*, and *Ogonek* (Flame) were not published by Comintern-affiliated organizations like MOPR, they had a much broader readership, and they needed to be more economical with the space they devoted to U.S. race relations. Accordingly, their coverage is especially instructive of the major goals of Soviet antiracism.

Complementing the expanded coverage of U.S. racism in the central press, the increased number of African Americans who spent time in the USSR between 1928 and 1937 appeared frequently in Soviet newspapers and magazines. Though photographs of African visitors to Moscow were occasionally printed, U.S. blacks were *the* "Negroes" in the interwar Soviet press. African Americans' status as longtime residents and citizens of the United States, rather than imperial subjects who inhabited a distant, overseas colony, made them more attractive to display.[7] Each representation of African Americans' inclusion in the USSR—involving a real or fictional African American—highlighted the fallacy of American freedom while authenticating the racelessness or equal opportunity of the first workers' state.

Outside of newspapers, a major source of information about the United States for Soviet citizens was published in the 1930s, namely Il'ia Il'f and Evgenii Petrov's 1937 novel *One-Story America* (*Odnoetazhnaia Amerika*). During the fall and winter of 1935–36, Il'f and Petrov journeyed by car through twenty-five American states. They recorded their impressions of U.S. society in the aforementioned novel, excerpts of which were published in 1936 in the journal *Znamia* (Banner).[8] That same year, the popular magazine *Ogonek* printed a series of eleven photographic essays that Il'f and Petrov penned about their U.S. adventures. The writings on America of these two satirists demonstrate that Soviet antiracism assumed a "softer" form in the second half of the 1930s, rendering African Americans apolitical victims instead of revolutionary allies who were actively fighting the common capitalist enemy.

The heightened indictment of U.S. racism in the Soviet press during the late 1920s and early 1930s established U.S. blacks as the most exploited segment of the populace, and the group most prime for revolution in capitalist America. The African American nation was conflated with class and gender, making its agents proletarian and male.[9] Newspapers and magazines informed readers that the exploitative labor practices of U.S. capitalism had reduced African Americans to virtual slaves. Articles discussed how they were assigned the most difficult, dangerous, dirtiest work; were confined to unskilled positions; earned less money than their white counterparts even when they performed the same tasks; lost their jobs first during any economic crisis; and remained unorganized because the "reformist" trade union leaders believed, like the bourgeoisie, that blacks were not human.[10] As *Prozhektor* (Searchlight) summarized in a 1928 exposé, African Americans "suffer from merciless exploitation no less harsh than slavery which existed until the Civil War."[11] *Pravda* elucidated just how easy it was for white landowners, who were desperate for free labor as a result of the Great Depression, to reenslave African Americans. The paper reported in 1932 that in Dallas, Texas, local police colluded with cotton plantation owners to raid black neighborhoods, arresting the unemployed. Plantation owners then paid five dollars' "bail" for each African American "prisoner," and put him to work on their fields in what amounted to "slave labor."[12]

To keep the "slaves" of U.S. capitalism in their proper place, Soviet newspapers explained, black male workers faced the constant threat of lynching. Lynching, no doubt, made it easy for Soviet officials to portray the United States as the world's most racist country. Editors most often adopted the terms "*linchevat'*" (to lynch) and "*sud Lincha*" (lynch law) to describe the extralegal executions of African American men instead of the Russian term "*samosud*" (mob law or literally "judging by oneself").[13] Soviet readers were therefore introduced to the vocabulary of U.S. racism and encouraged to understand that "lynching" was a particularly heinous act of violence peculiar to the advanced capitalist society of the United States. Even ignorant, "counterrevolutionary" white Americans like Lemuel Lewis and William Brown were depicted as instinctively recognizing the inconceivability of lynching in the USSR. As Elena Stasova, the head of MOPR's Soviet branch, remarked with regard to their attack on Robert Robinson, "Naturally, the white Americans here did not dare to attempt to lynch the Negro."[14]

If the enlightened racial consciousness of Soviet citizens rendered mob violence against black workers beyond the realm of possibility in the first workers' state, "a lynched Negro," as *Prozhektor* claimed, was "the monument of American civilization."[15] A cartoon that *Rabochaia gazeta* published on the front page in 1931—without any articles regarding U.S. racism—made this point explicit. The image showed the grim reaper disguised as the Statue of Liberty, which was a common feature of Soviet cartoons. Graphic artists used the famous monument as "an iconic metaphor to underline their vision of the disparity between the American promise of social and political equality and the reality of racial and economic injustice."[16] In this instance, hanging from Lady Liberty's skeletal arms were ten nooses with black corpses dangling at the end of five of them. The headline explained that this was "American 'Democracy,' as It Really Is," and the caption elucidated that "For Negro-workers in 'free' America there are many free nooses."[17] The cartoon's reference to "many free nooses" and depiction of five victims visually reinforced the Soviet press's emphasis that the distinctively American monument of "civilization"—the lynched black worker—was becoming an even more common feature of the U.S. landscape. In addition to cartoons like this one, lynching photographs in newspapers, magazines, and on postcards confirmed as "factually correct" reports that the number of extralegal executions of African Americans had escalated in response to their growing militancy.[18]

Like the "American 'Democracy'" cartoon, lynching photographs were published in the Soviet press with brief captions amidst unrelated articles. They were just as likely to accompany reports concerning the latest achievements in the First Five-Year Plan and the recent production figures of a particular Soviet factory than news items that addressed U.S. race relations. Oftentimes, readers were expected to know intuitively that the photographs had been taken somewhere in the United States. The details were inconsequential—it was just another example of the horrific racial violence in capitalist America. A superimposed American flag sometimes served as the primary visual

1. "American 'democracy,' as it really is." *Rabochaia gazeta*, August 17, 1931, 1.

cue. The dissemination of lynching photographs in this manner points to the sensationalist function they served in the USSR. At the same time, by not disclosing the location of the execution, the date when it occurred, or the name of the victim, these photographs conveyed a message similar to those printed on postcards and sold at Moscow kiosks: these extralegal murders occurred with such frequency in America that they could happen to any black male worker at any time and under the pretext of any "crime."[19] "For Negro-workers in 'free' America," in other words, "there are many free nooses."

The photograph that appeared most often in the Soviet press and on the front pages of *Trud* and *Komsomol'skaia pravda* depicted the August 1930 double murder of Abraham Smith and Thomas Shipp in Marion, Indiana.[20] Despite the photograph's relatively wide exposure, minimal information concerning the execution was disclosed. The standard caption stated: "The trial by lynching [*sudom Lincha*] of two Negroes." The crowd of well-dressed white men and women posing proudly beneath the two black men's corpses, smiling shamelessly at the camera, made it especially appealing to print. The white Americans' conduct spotlighted the moral depravity of U.S. modernity and provided the ideal contrast to the progressive, antiracist "Soviet" consciousness that all inhabitants of the first workers' state supposedly possessed.[21]

A lynching photograph printed in *Rabochaia gazeta* in August 1930 served a similar function. A caption read: "The charred corpse of a Negro who was burned alive in America, in Sherman, the state of Texas." The victim's name, the alleged offense that he had committed, and the fact that he had been murdered three months earlier on May 9, 1930, were omitted.[22] The surrounding articles discussed the latest efforts to bring Lewis and Brown to justice for assaulting Robert Robinson. By publishing the photograph in this context, *Rabochaia gazeta* juxtaposed the justice afforded black men in the Soviet Union with the license that whites possessed over black male bodies in the United States where, as lynching images like this one made clear, the "law was white."[23] Unsurprisingly, this was not the only lynching photograph printed in the Soviet press during the campaign against

Lewis and Brown. Rather, it was during this roughly monthlong period in August 1930 that lynching photographs appeared with the greatest frequency.

The implication behind the dissemination of lynching photographs in the USSR was that the victims had been punished for the "crime" of class consciousness. At times, newspaper editors made this explicit by distorting or fabricating information.[24] For example, the caption to a lynching photograph on *Komsomol'skaia pravda*'s front page described the man as "a Negro-worker, victim of mob law at the hands of a band of landowners in Marion (America)," who was "hanged simply because he (together with other Negroes) actively participated in preparations for a strike. Police appeared only after the murderers finished their 'work.'" The editors added that these "same police" arrive in a few minutes when they are called on to break up a "demonstration of unemployed workers."[25] *Komsomol'skaia pravda* erred in reporting that this man had been executed by mob law in Marion. The aforementioned Shipp and Smith constituted Marion's only recorded lynch victims, and neither had been involved in labor activity. Yet this inaccuracy was immaterial. By identifying the lynch victim as a labor activist whose murder law enforcement officials sanctioned through their inaction, the paper represented U.S. blacks as members of the revolutionary vanguard whose efforts at mobilizing were met with barbaric violence by the same white landowners who ultimately sought to destroy the first workers' state.

A lynching cartoon in *Komsomol'skaia pravda* reinforced this message. A bare-chested black man was shown with his mouth contorted in agony and noose around his neck. The caption called on "Workers! To Struggle against the lynching of your Negro-proletarian brothers!" and the headline promised that through this unity, "We will chop off the clutches of the hangman." The "hangman" assumed the familiar form of an extremely fat white male capitalist wearing a top hat, long coat, and gun holster. He was depicted posting a sign above the victim's head that warned black workers, "Do not dare to struggle for your rights." By using the standard image of the capitalist, the cartoon visualized how African Americans and Soviet citizens were fighting

2. "We will chop off the clutches of the hangman." The capitalist's sign reads, "Do not dare to struggle for your rights." The line underneath the headline indicates that the drawing had been published in the *Daily Worker*. *Komsomol'skaia pravda*, August 26, 1930, 4.

the same enemy, and that black men constituted the frontline casualties in a war that would eventually be directed at the USSR.[26] Soviet representations of lynching therefore were meant to convince readers of the superiority of Soviet society and to remind them of the need to work more diligently for its construction in the face of a growing threat of imperialist war.

In addition to the extralegal wrath of the lynch mob, central newspapers exposed how African American men faced the equally lethal "legal" violence of law enforcement officials. The instance of police brutality that received the most attention in the Soviet press was the July 1930 murder of Alfred Levy in New York City. As *Rabochaia gazeta*, *Trud*, and *Komsomol'skaia pravda* reported, Levy was an African American Communist and delegate to a convention of unemployed workers whom New York police brutally beat to death at an antilynching meeting. Several weeks after his murder, *Pravda* printed a photograph of the honor guard standing in front of Levy's coffin. The headline provided the only information about the police murder victim. As was standard with photographs in the Soviet press documenting African American oppression (like the lynching photographs just discussed), this was a "floating image"; none of the surrounding articles mentioned the United States let alone police violence against workers (white or black).[27]

Besides murder, the Soviet press depicted the capitalist enemy as using imprisonment to suppress African Americans' burgeoning militancy. John Spivak's 1932 *Georgia Nigger* provided the most damning evidence of the systematic human rights violations committed against black male prisoners. Published in the Soviet Union in 1933, in Russian and English, the book combined investigative journalism and fiction to expose African American chain gang life and peonage.[28] *Komsomol'skaia pravda* and *Internatsional'nyi maiak* printed documentary photographs from the book's appendix that showed black prisoners subjected to torture. *Internatsional'nyi maiak* published these images with serialized excerpts from the text, while *Komsomol'skaia pravda*'s editors printed them on the front page without any reference to Spivak's study and politicized the subjects as persecuted revolutionaries.[29]

Soviet newspapers pursued even more basic methods to associate proletarian militancy and intensified repression with a black male face. For instance, *Trud* published a stock photograph of African American Communist Herbert Newton, with a headline identifying him as one of five "prisoners of American capital" threatened with execution via the electric chair. A caption described Newton as the leader of an organization of black workers in Atlanta, whose crime was conducting labor activity among blacks.[30] Although most of those arrested were white, by showing Newton's image alone, *Trud* reinforced African Americans' status as the allies of Soviet citizens whom the common capitalist enemy targeted for persecution. To be sure, due to this alliance, *Pravda* reported in August 1932 that U.S. leaders were reducing the number of African Americans in the military because in the future imperialist war (against the USSR) they could not trust them to defend "white bourgeois society."[31]

As if to confirm as well-founded the U.S. bourgeoisie's growing "distrust of Negroes with weapons," the politicization of African Americans was represented as even including boys. To illustrate, *Trud* published a photograph of two African American boys packing cotton bales. A caption explained that despite the high unemployment rates among African Americans, employers used the labor of black children. It added that a broad Pioneer movement had developed among them, and identified the two boys as the secretary and head of a Pioneer organization. Like the majority of photographs discussed above, this was a "floating image"; that is to say, adjacent articles discussed neither the United States nor child labor. Rather they addressed Spanish labor organizations, French workers' opposition to imperialist intervention in the USSR, and a German Social Democratic leader's exposure of social fascists. By placing the mobilization of African American boys in the context of the struggle of the historically advanced European proletariat, *Trud* conferred prestige and importance on the African American struggle.[32]

Children's publications too portrayed African American men and boys as mobilizing to make Soviet society the American reality.[33] Two short stories in *Murzilka* from the early 1930s are representative. The first, titled "Jim Crow," details how an African American boy named "Tom" finds refuge from his apartheid existence in a school operated by his father's trade union.[34] Whereas cartoons show white American policemen assaulting the young boy for entering a white neighborhood and glaring at his father with their fists cocked, Tom learns from John (his new white friend at the school) about the Soviet Union where Jim Crow is absent and all people are treated equally. The final cartoon shows Tom and his father smiling and looking lovingly at each other; their smiles signify the hope that accompanied the discovery of the interracial revolutionary movement and the USSR.[35]

In another *Murzilka* story titled "Negro Pioneers," the young black male Pioneer named "Jack" is already on the interracial revolutionary path and enlightens a meeting of white American Pioneers about the Soviet Union. Jack informs them that while he works full-time picking cotton because his father is unemployed, in the USSR all children attend school (regardless of their skin color) because racism is not tolerated there. To corroborate his claim, Jack (as mentioned in chapter 1) recounts a brief rendition of the Stalingrad trial. The youngest white Pioneer in the group responds to Jack's story by exclaiming that he does not want to be an American but a "Negro." He then quickly corrects himself to declare that it was best to be a Soviet boy. In the final scene, a bewildered Jack asks the Pioneer leader whether this boy was really unaware that America would also become a Soviet republic.[36]

As "Jim Crow" and "Negro Pioneers" demonstrate, U.S. racism's impact on African American boys was intended to remind Soviet youth that the USSR was "the *best* place in the world for children." Stories like these also instructed the future generations of the first workers' state that their "happy childhood" came with the responsibility of "instinctively" recognizing African Americans as "friends."[37] The absence of a black mother figure from these narratives reflects the de-emphasis on motherhood in the Soviet Union of the early 1930s, and the elision of black women from the Soviet indictment of U.S. racism.[38]

As the examples discussed in this section reveal, the Soviet press portrayed African American men as posing a greater threat to America's racial democracy because of their increased politicization and alliance with the USSR, and as a consequence eliciting greater violence and repression from the capitalist enemy.[39] Quite paradoxically, then, representations of the injured black male body came to signify not only the enormity of U.S. racism and alleged moral superiority of Soviet society but also African Americans' growing militancy. Certainly, by portraying African American men as militant revolutionaries, Soviet antiracism challenged the dominant, historically Western image of blacks as criminals, savages, fools, or clowns. Yet since their politicization was met with more intense violence, Soviet citizens were primarily exposed to representations of their valued allies—except when shown on Soviet soil—as persecuted and, in some cases, defeated, tragic victims.[40] With the exception of the children's stories in each instance, the angry white lynch mob, law enforcement officials, or racist employers struck them down on the path to freedom.

The lack of representations of African American men in the United States as defiant revolutionaries who escaped *any* injury (with the exception of children) served several functions. First, it articulated international solidarity and empathy, while satisfying an interest among Soviet citizens (young and old alike) for what Evgenii Steiner terms "sadistic discourse," that is, stories about torture and violence.[41] Second, it underscored the severity of the capitalist threat to the USSR and made the struggle to build socialism seem more imperative.[42] Third, and perhaps most important, it rendered the intervention of the Soviet Union—in some form though never clearly defined—indispensable to securing the ultimate freedom of African Americans. In this way, the plight of the African American nation mirrored that of the non-Russian nationalities, the "little brothers" of the USSR, who were conceptualized as having realized liberation from tsarist oppression with the guidance of their Russian "elder brother."[43] It was furthermore consistent with Soviet leaders' views that the success of any revolution in the colonies of Western Europe was contingent on the "direction and aid" of Moscow.[44]

The simultaneous image of black men in the United States as heroic revolutionaries and tragic victims was thus driven by the desire to cast the USSR and Soviet citizens in a paternalistic, pseudomessianic role. As Maxim Matusevich puts it, this was "a vocation cherished by the country's Communist elites and apparently internalized by large segments of the general population."[45] Soviet officials may have not intended to relegate African Americans to a perpetually inferior, subordinate position, but representing the USSR as revolutionary savior necessitated this negative depiction. At the same time, though the Soviet Union's role was indispensable, revolution in the United States was portrayed as unfeasible without the contributions of African Americans. By the mid-1930s, as the last section of this chapter demonstrates, this politicized image of African Americans ceased to exist, making them appear simply poor and oppressed.

Among the increased number of African American visitors to the USSR in the late 1920s and early 1930s, delegates to political congresses were at the forefront of representations of Soviet racial equality. Soviet officials established this precedent in 1922, when they designated Claude McKay as the face, or "poster child," of the Comintern's alliance with black workers. Yet it was not until the end of the decade, with Soviet antiracism elevated to a hard-line policy, that Soviet authorities were again interested in using African American delegates (of whom there were a larger number from which to choose) to "prove" the Soviet commitment to antiracism. No other proceeding was as important in furthering this objective as the Fifth Congress of the Profintern, or Red International of Trade Unions (RILU, Krasnyi internatsional prof-soiuzov), which convened August 15–30, 1930. This was the first major international congress organized in Moscow after Comintern leaders had conferred nation status on African Americans, and by design it boasted a large number of U.S. black delegates.[46]

A sizable African American presence at the Fifth Congress was intended to reflect the Profintern's commitment to eradicating the organization's previous apathy toward recruiting black laborers into the revolutionary trade union movement. As part of this new commitment, the Profintern had sponsored an international conference of black workers in Hamburg, Germany, in July 1930 and established the International Trade Union Committee of Negro Workers (ITUCNW).

Indicative of their status as the revolutionary vanguard, several African Americans, including James Ford, Helen McClain, Isaiah Hawkins, and George Padmore, were appointed to the ITUCNW's executive bureau.[47] The scheduling of the ITUCNW conference in July 1930 was strategic; it allowed the African American delegates to simply travel east to Moscow once the proceedings concluded to await the start of the Fifth Profintern Congress on August 15.

With a large number of African Americans in attendance, the Soviet press, and *Rabochaia gazeta* in particular, capitalized on the fact that the Profintern proceedings coincided with the trial of Lewis and Brown. Editors printed photographs of African American delegates adjacent to headlines that announced: "This is not Bourgeois America," "In the USSR there is no Place for Racial Enmity," "In the USSR There is Neither White nor Black," "The USSR is the Fatherland for the Black, Yellow and White Races," and "The Country of Soviets is the Society of All Workers."[48] As a specific, particularly representative example, on August 9 *Trud* published on the front page (centerpiece) a photograph of African American delegate Helen McClain (Jenny Reid) next to the article that exposed Lewis and Brown's assault on Robinson. The smiling image of this black female textile worker from Philadelphia complemented the story's corresponding headline, which declared, "We Do Not Permit in the USSR the Ways of Capitalist America." Clearly, McClain's photograph was published for symbolic purposes: the Profintern Congress did not begin until six days later and there were no articles concerning either it or the global conference of female workers, which a caption mentioned she also attended.[49] As this example indicates, it was common for photographs of African Americans who were visiting the USSR—like lynching photographs discussed in the previous section—to appear as "floating images," that is, without any related articles.

Given McClain's identity as an African American woman and the Profintern Congress's official black female delegate, her image had particular appeal for Soviet editors. McClain's visage appeared again in *Trud*, as well as in *Pravda*, *Komsomol'skaia pravda*, and *Mezhdunarodnoe rabochee dvizhenie* (the Profintern's publication). Although on these occasions her likeness accompanied articles regarding the congress, none mentioned McClain, black women, or the United States. Interestingly, two years later, in 1932, McClain's photograph—the same one that had appeared on *Trud*'s front page—was published in *Internatsional'nyi maiak* without any articles that referenced her, the United States, the 1930 conference of female workers, or the Profintern proceedings of the same year. Instead, the surrounding articles broadly addressed the mobilization of female workers.[50] McClain's image—recycled in various Soviet publications—signified the racial, national, and gender equality that allegedly existed in the Soviet Union and international revolutionary movement.

Helen McClain was not the first African American female conference delegate to grace the front page of a Soviet paper. Two years earlier, during the Sixth Comintern Congress in 1928, *Trud* printed a photograph of an African American woman and her two sons on the front page (centerpiece). A caption stated that the woman—who unlike McClain was not identified by name—was attending the congress with her children, who were Pioneers. The unnamed black female delegate was Williana Burroughs, a member of the U.S. Communist Party and a New York City schoolteacher.[51] Burroughs's image appeared without any articles that specifically mentioned her, the children, or blacks in general. The adjacent article discussed Soviet workers' warm reception of participants of the "world revolution."[52]

Burroughs, in contrast to Helen McClain, did not reappear in the Soviet press, but her sons Charles Jr. and Neal (still not identified by name) resurfaced on *Trud*'s front page five days later. Having exchanged their Pioneer scarves for ties, the two boys were shown smiling and posing with a white man who was identified as "one of the participants of the Comintern congress with Negro pioneers." The five-year-old Neal was seated next to the white delegate with a hand resting on his shoulder, and his nine-year-old brother Charles Jr. was standing behind them. None of the surrounding articles referenced this interracial, intergenerational male trio.[53] Similar to the image of the young African American cotton pickers previously discussed,

3. This photograph of Williana Burroughs and her sons, Charles Jr. and Neal, appeared on *Trud*'s front page on August 11, 1928. Langston Hughes Papers, 1862–1980, Beinecke Rare Book and Manuscript Library.

this photograph portrayed African American boys—already Pioneers mobilizing for world revolution—as the future generation of the revolutionary African American nation that Comintern leaders officially recognized at the Congress.

Interestingly, Charles Jr. reemerged four years later as "Pioneer Jim" in a 1932 issue of *Internatsional'nyi maiak*. After the Sixth Comintern Congress in 1928, Williana Burroughs had enrolled her sons in an elite Moscow school for the children of Soviet and foreign Communists. In a brief article, "Pioneer Jim" explained that his mother wanted him and his younger brother, Neal (identified by his real name), to experience living in a "free country." His unfamiliarity with the Russian language initially made school difficult, but, he claimed, unlike in the United States where blacks are not considered human, all the children treated him as their brother. After emphasizing the tremendous pride he and his brother derived from being young Leninists, Pioneer Jim appealed to Soviet children to help the oppressed in capitalist countries by joining MOPR's youth organization.[54] Regardless of whether young Charles Burroughs Jr. took part in the composition of this article, it and the accompanying photograph furthered the image of Soviet racial equality and politicization of African American boys as revolutionary allies.

Although numerous African American men attended the 1928 Comintern Congress, Burroughs and the two boys constituted the only African American presence in the central newspapers. The prominent mother-and-son image was arguably intended to symbolize the birth of the African American nation that the Sixth Congress decreed. Two years later, McClain's photograph notwithstanding, black male delegates to the 1930 Profintern Congress came to embody the new African American nation in the Soviet press. Images of these black men—by themselves, with white workers and/or delegates, or in large groups with African, Asian, and white delegates—were especially important to print since African American men were those shown excluded from the American nation.[55] A delegate whose image received considerable exposure was Isaiah Hawkins (Jack Bell), a black miner and leader of the National Miners Union in Pittsburgh, Pennsylvania. Sketches of Hawkins appeared in *Pravda*, *Izvestiia*, and *Mezhdunarodnoe rabochee dvizhenie*. He was also depicted in a photograph on the front pages of *Komsomol'skaia pravda* and *Trud*, and in *Mezhdunarodnoe rabochee dvizhenie* shaking hands with a Russian male delegate in what all three editors labeled a "brotherly meeting."[56] This blatant dramatization of African Americans' inclusion in Soviet society as "brothers" was therefore reenacted in three separate publications targeting different audiences. In each instance, the photograph appeared as a floating image: an adjacent article referenced neither man. The interracial brotherhood exhibited in the aforementioned photograph of the Burrough boys and the white male delegate had in two years matured: African Americans had become men.

Another photograph on *Trud*'s front page celebrated the brotherhood and equality that the Soviet Union supposedly afforded African American men. The image featured James Ford, a member of the Profintern's executive bureau who, among U.S. black delegates, appeared most often in the central press.[57] Ford was standing with his arms around several workers at the Moscow Elektrozavod, in what the caption described as "brotherly unity." Unlike the photographs previously discussed, an adjacent article bore direct relevance to the image; it contained excerpts from a speech that Ford had delivered at a factory meeting organized to protest the assault on Robert Robinson. The published excerpts bolstered the photograph's message of Soviet national and racial equality. In "the fatherland of all nationalities," Ford was quoted as declaring, "there is no place for racial dissension. Hand in hand all people (*narod*) are together building socialism." A protest resolution attributed to Dinamo factory workers, which appeared beneath the photograph, echoed Ford's sentiment. No one, these Moscow laborers admonished, "is permitted to violate the brotherly unity of the workers of all nationalities, a number of whom are Negro workers."[58]

Pravda, Izvestiia, Rabochaia gazeta, and *Trud* also printed the speeches that black American male delegates like Ford and Hawkins delivered at the Fifth Congress regarding the revolutionary movement among black laborers.[59] By printing the photographs and speeches of African American male delegates (there is no record that McClain formally addressed the assembly), the Soviet press represented the USSR as a place where black men were allowed to be men, or more precisely, thinkers, speakers, and leaders without any threat to their physical safety. Concurrently, it fostered the impression that Soviet citizens were concerned about the plight of their black brothers in the capitalist world. Representations of African American men in positions of respect, if not leadership, in Moscow provided a sharp contrast to the photographs of black men lynched in the United States.

African American delegates to international conferences were the most important but not the only black American faces that Soviet newspapers displayed to prove the racelessness of Soviet society. For instance, in January 1932 the *Workers News* printed a photograph of Lovett Fort-Whiteman surrounded by ten white children whom, as a caption explained, he taught at an English-language school in Moscow. According to Glenda Gilmore, Fort-Whiteman's position as a science teacher at the American School was his most visible job since he made the Soviet Union his permanent home in 1928. The two adjacent articles referenced neither Fort-Whiteman nor the school. The first, which was written by George Padmore, addressed imperialists' efforts to suppress the revolutionary movement among black laborers. The other article, authored by an African American Lenin School student, discussed black workers' efforts to carve out a meager existence in the United States.[60] By situating Fort-Whiteman's photograph with these articles, the Workers News juxtaposed the persecution and struggles of blacks in the capitalist world with the position entrusted to Whiteman in the Soviet Union of teaching white youth.

Since only a one-line caption accompanied Whiteman's photograph, there was no explanation regarding who he was, why he had originally traveled to the Soviet Union, or how long he had been there. This was not uncommon with "floating images" of African Americans who were in the USSR as neither conference delegates nor entertainers on tour. To further illustrate, on September 2, 1930, Trud published a large photograph of a black woman with a caption that read: "Comrade Bruce at the machine." The adjacent articles provided no clues as to why her photograph was printed, where she worked, or why she was in the Soviet Union. Instead, they addressed fascism in Austria and self-criticism within the party.[61] The message behind the publication of the photograph of "Comrade Bruce" and others like it was that the equality and friendship afforded African Americans in the USSR were reason enough—why would they not live in the Soviet Union? The United States, as the Soviet press made clear, was a place of "unfreedom" for African Americans in spite of their nominal citizenship. In contrast, these photographs represented African Americans' acceptance in the Soviet community as automatic regardless of their personal profile or the specific place where they worked. Moreover, by omitting reference to how long they had been in the country or the date they had arrived, it was as if these African American men and women had been in the Soviet Union since its inception.

Photographs of African Americans in the USSR appeared less frequently in the Soviet press by the mid-1930s, as the growing threat of fascism in Europe eclipsed Soviet interest in indicting U.S. racism.

When they did appear it was most often as musicians or singers who performed in the USSR. On those rare occasions when the photograph of an African American nonentertainer was published, it was in the same ostensibly random yet purposeful manner characteristic of the floating image of the first half of the decade. For example, in July 1936 *Izvestiia* published on the front page a photograph of African American Robert Ross marching across Red Square in a Physical Culture parade with two other people, a white man, who was in the center carrying a flag, and a white woman. The caption identified Ross, who was dressed in a tank top and shorts, as a trainer at the Central State Institute of Physical Culture named for Stalin; the white male, who was similarly clad, was named as a teacher at the institute; and the white female as a student.[62] No article referenced the parade, Ross, or the institute. Hence, the reader was left with no information regarding why Ross chose to work in the USSR or when he had arrived but simply with the impression that he was completely integrated in Soviet society.[63]

Short stories and poems likewise represented as seamless Soviet society's acceptance of African Americans. Interestingly, the main protagonist of these fictional accounts was consistently gendered male and often named "Tom" (as in the aforementioned short story "Jim Crow"). The pervasiveness of this name suggests the influence of Harriet Beecher Stowe's *Uncle Tom's Cabin*, which had been published in Russia in book and serial form since the nineteenth century, and the "massively" popular film *Little Red Devils* (1923), which generated several sequels and had as one of its three main characters a young black performer named "Tom" (see the epilogue).[64] Another common feature of these fictional accounts was their portrayal of the black male protagonist as unaware of the freedom that the USSR afforded blacks until he encountered Soviet citizens. As noted in chapter 1, Boris Agapov's biography of Robert Robinson portrayed "Bob" as having no prior knowledge of Soviet attitudes toward race. This trope of surprise is particularly curious when considering that the majority of African Americans who traveled to the USSR were motivated—to some degree—by the desire to examine, in person, Soviet claims of racial equality. Writers arguably used the element of surprise to heighten and magnify the emotions that these characters experienced upon discovering the total freedom—"the promised land"—that life under U.S. capitalism had made seemingly unattainable.

A representative example is a short story published in *Murzilka* in 1932 about a young African American boy named "Tom Jones," who moves to the Soviet Union with his father.[65] Unaware of Soviet citizens' enlightened attitudes toward blacks, Tom Jones fears that the vast multitude of white people in Moscow will beat him and his father to death since "whites can do anything." When Tom expresses apprehension about attending school with all whites, his father simply reminds him that they are no longer in America. At school, Tom is escorted to the classroom by a blond-haired girl named Mary, who is ecstatic to have a new classmate who is black. Tom remains petrified that the students will attack him as they had done in New Jersey (which the author locates in the U.S. South). The purely amicable behavior of the other students—several of whom had German names like Otto Zimmel and Bruno Wolf—bewilders Tom. He is further shocked to discover that the teacher is a black man named "Comrade Walker" (perhaps inspired by Lovett Fort-Whiteman), who reassures Tom that he has nothing to fear because "Friend! You are in the USSR, in a free country. You are not in America."[66]

As "Tom Jones" illustrates, fictional accounts regarding African Americans' encounter with Soviet society further established the United States as the antithesis of the only truly "free country"—the USSR. Though the Soviet Union afforded Tom complete equality and freedom, he could not initially appreciate it; the ultraviolence of the U.S. racial regime had scarred him to such an extent that he found it inconceivable that white people (even children) would not physically attack him and his father. Since the white students at the English-language school embraced Tom, the implication was that Soviet soil eradicated the "capitalist education" or racial prejudice to which children from capitalist countries had previously been exposed. While an ostensible objective of "Tom Jones" was to represent black Americans as friends whom Soviet children should accept as equals, the caricatures of Tom that graced *Murzilka*'s cover and accompanied the narrative reintroduced notions of black inequality. Specifically, Tom Jones was drawn with a very large forehead, oversized eyes with strikingly large white irises that made him seem possessed, an exaggerated, broad nose, and excessively bright red lips. A blond-haired girl wearing a red shirt, red Pioneer scarf, and a light blue skirt is depicted leading Tom by the hand; she most likely represents the character of Mary. She is standing tall with a smile on her face, striding confidently into the future and pulling Tom with such force that he appears literally off balance. Her impeccable posture and self-confidence stand in stark contrast to the confusion, uncertainty, and near haplessness exhibited by her black companion, who is looking to the side rather than straight ahead into the future. Without Mary's guidance, Tom would be lost.[67]

Tom Jones's physical appearance mirrored the stereotypical images of blacks that appeared in Soviet advertisements, plays, and children's books, about which Lovett Fort-Whiteman and other African American Communists first raised concerns to Soviet officials in 1924.[68] Evgenii Steiner contends that such racist imagery was the result of illustrators who thought persons of African descent were inferior, and others who sought to advance proletarian internationalism yet still produced stereotypical images of blacks.[69] Yet, since many stories including the previously discussed "Negro Pioneers" and "Jim Crow" depicted their protagonists without racialized features, the potential clearly existed in Soviet society—independent of African Americans' criticisms—for illustrators to refrain from producing dehumanizing caricatures of blacks. Soviet failure and/or refusal to see the contradiction between the indictment of U.S. racism and racist images like those of "Tom Jones" further illuminates the limitations of their understanding of racism and commitment to African Americans' struggle for freedom. As demonstrated throughout this study, paternalistic language and racist imagery oftentimes contradicted the cause of African Americans' equality which Soviet leaders advanced.

This unfortunate paradox is also evidenced in "John and the Unfamiliar Word," a feuilleton that *Krokodil* published in 1931. Similar to "Tom Jones," the main protagonist, an African American worker named John, was drawn with excessively large lips and jet black skin, making him appear grotesque in comparison to the drawings of the white characters. Yet, as with "Tom Jones," the narrative did not articulate the antiblack sentiment implicit in these drawings. The narrative described John as an extremely hard-working lift operator in an upscale New York City hotel, who was grossly underpaid and virtually invisible to the affluent whites to whom he showed utter subservience. One day Ellen, a black chambermaid at the hotel, suggested that they flee to the USSR, where she emphasized all races and nationalities lived in harmony and equality. Upon arriving in Moscow, Ellen and John immediately acquired work in a textile factory in the Central District. In their new lives, as the story insisted, they "felt not like Negroes but members of a giant family of workers." Ellen's role (though brief) was significant. Apart from lending a rare female presence to Soviet narratives about African Americans, she was the reason why she and John were in the USSR feeling "not like Negroes" but full human beings.

With the USSR firmly established as the "promised land" for African Americans, the remainder of the feuilleton—which constituted the bulk of the text—focused on John's efforts (Ellen subsequently disappears) to find someone who could explain adequately the meaning of the term "bureaucratism." John's incomprehension was indicative of neither inferior mental faculties nor his status as a foreigner, since the most high-ranking Soviet official had trouble explaining the "unfamiliar word."[70] The use of an African American male protagonist as the backdrop to a story that satirized the state's campaign against "bureaucratism" is noteworthy. It suggests that the trope of African Americans' inclusion in Soviet society was just as pervasive during the early 1930s as the stereotypical images of blacks that effected their exclusion—whether intentionally or unintentionally—as racialized others. Viewed alternately, although Soviet citizens may have perceived African Americans in the manner shown in the caricatures, that is, as "black curiosities" or racialized "others," stories like this one instructed that they were nevertheless supposed to accept them into their world as automatically and unquestioningly as the narratives' Soviet characters. To be sure, these fictional accounts assured Soviet readers that African Americans—despite their appearance—were not "others" but, to a large degree, their equivalents: selfless, hardworking, and morally irreprehensible.

"Tom," the main protagonist of a poem in *Internatsional'nyi maiak* bearing his name, exemplifies this black quasi-saint common in Soviet narratives about African Americans, and is reminiscent of the representations of Robert Robinson discussed in the preceding chapter. The poem's narrator is an anonymous Soviet male worker who lives in a new, large workers' home next to Tom and his family. Due to the enlightened attitudes of workers like the narrator, the acceptance of Tom's family into Soviet society is understood to have been seamless. The narrator (like all Soviet citizens) does not see Tom as a curiosity or racial other; rather he views the unfamiliar capitalist world that he left behind as the curiosity. From frequent visits with his favorite neighbor he has learned that in America Tom's existence was a struggle to survive. Tom worked his entire life in New York as an unskilled laborer, yet still did not earn enough money to feed his family. Tom's situation became even worse when the Great Depression left him and his wife unemployed. As his anger at their impoverished condition grew, Tom found out about the "great country in which Lenin was born." By the spring (arguably because of its association with rebirth) the black worker moved his family to the USSR. In a letter to his friend Claude in the United States, Tom explained that he had found his true homeland and his people in the Soviet Union. Driven by immense gratitude and a strong desire to strengthen the society that had restored him to full humanity, Tom became a shock worker.[71]

The Soviet press was not the only printed source of information about real and fictional African Americans in the interwar decades. The indictment of U.S. racism also carried over into the realm of literature. In the 1920s Soviet publishers printed the work of a few African American writers like Claude McKay, but it was the 1930s when the publication of African American literature, and those writing about the lives of American blacks, reached its peak in the Soviet Union. As

Glenora and Denning Brown argue in their study of American literature in the USSR, "Soviet publishers in the thirties were alert for the appearance of new works by and about Negroes, and particularly those with a strong ingredient of social protest." The Browns attribute this to a general interest in literature that criticized American society from a leftist ("though not necessarily Marxist") perspective. But the surge in the publication of African American writings was also inseparable from the elevation of Soviet antiracism to priority status in the first half of the 1930s.[72]

Among the more prominent African American writers to have their novels, short stories, poetry, and plays translated into Russian, Langston Hughes enjoyed the distinction of being the most popular. His work appeared frequently in the Soviet press in the 1930s.[73] The literary works about U.S. racism of a few white American authors such as John Spivak's aforementioned *Georgia Nigger* and Myra Page's *The Gathering Storm: A Story of the Black Belt* were also published in the USSR in the early 1930s.[74] Coexisting with this literature concerning black American social protest was African American folklore that included the stories of Joel Chandler Harris about Brer Rabbit and Uncle Remus. The traditional stereotypes of blacks that these stories reproduced competed with and undermined the politicized representation of African Americans as militating against their oppression in ways that transcended the traditional realms of folklore, humor, and music.

While the publication of African American literature was an important expression of the Soviet antiracist impulse, most Soviet citizens' literary encounter with African Americans came through the work of Il'ia Il'f and Evgenii Petrov. According to Hans Rogger, Il'f and Petrov's *One-Story America* was the "most widely read Soviet book about the United States."[75] Reading the work of African American authors necessitated a curiosity about the lives of U.S. blacks. *One-Story America* attracted a much broader audience, who as fans of Il'f and Petrov were interested in learning about the United States—a country that fascinated most Soviet citizens—from the Russian writers' experiences there.[76] Indicative of the widespread interest in America and the two humorists' popularity, in 1936 *Ogonek* printed eleven photographic essays that Il'f and Petrov composed about their American road trip.[77] The Soviet satirists dedicated one article in *Ogonek* and a book chapter to "Negroes" and referenced African Americans in a few others.

Il'f and Petrov's commentary on U.S. blacks provides insight into what central authorities considered most appropriate for Soviet citizens to learn about American racism during the Popular Front era. Unlike the hard-line antiracism characteristic of the late 1920s and early 1930s, African Americans were no longer identified as valued allies of the first workers' state. Hence, the racial violence committed against them no longer posed an indirect threat to the USSR's national security. Accordingly, physical violence against African Americans was a minor theme in *One-Story America* and the *Ogonek* essays. Il'f and Petrov ridiculed the "logic" or "reasoning" that white Americans used to justify the existence of the U.S. racial regime, rather than detail the specific injustices that American blacks suffered as its primary targets. In the process they underscored the degree to which white American workers were themselves tragic victims of this racial illogic.

Their encounter with a sixteen-year-old white male hitchhiker from South Carolina—which appeared in the *Ogonek* essay on "Negroes" and was reproduced in the book chapter of the same title—is emblematic of this approach. Il'f and Petrov emphasized that they had not embellished the account, thereby suggesting that they may have been amazed and/or disturbed by what it had revealed. The young hitchhiker, they explained, lacked the funding to attend college, his father's farm was doing poorly, and he was currently working at an unemployment camp established by the federal government. Yet in spite of all this, he was "completely free from any shadow of worry." This was because he "knows that he's young, he's healthy, he's got white skin, and he plays baseball. This means that everything is okay—*all right*—and he'll get by somehow."[78] By introducing the young man in this manner, Il'f and Petrov alluded to the effectiveness of white "privilege" in deluding white American laborers into supporting the status quo, rather than mobilizing with blacks to gain genuine power.

They further exposed the power of white privilege by questioning the teen about the reasons for the severe impoverishment of black communities in the Carolinas. The young white man conceded that African Americans were generally good people who were neither dirty nor lazy. Moreover, when they asked if it was possible for him to fall in love with a black woman, he said that he found some black women attractive. Despite these frank admissions, the white male hitchhiker demonstrated no interest in learning why African Americans were so poor, why his family and other white families would never eat with blacks, why he would never marry a black woman if he fell in love with her, and why a black man would be hanged if he married a white woman. In fact, when the Soviet writers refused to accept "that's just the way it is" as a satisfactory response to their queries, the incurious hitchhiker dismissed them as hailing from New York, which they noted southern whites mistook as a bastion of progressive, radical thought.[79] The white American teen emerged from this conversation as a tragic figure who was willfully unconcerned with how he was complicit in his own oppression. Though he was not the virulent racist of the Ku Klux Klan, Il'f and Petrov insinuated, he was more dangerous.

As their use of a hypothetical African American woman to broach the issue of miscegenation indicates, black women were not excluded from Il'f and Petrov's commentary on U.S. racism. The Soviet writers even used their encounter with an "old hunched over black woman" walking along a southern highway to expose how the "logic" of American racial apartheid structured all forms of contact between whites and blacks.[80] Il'f and Petrov, however, did not always represent African American women in an unproblematic manner. The writers' representations of black women are emblematic of their stereotypical portrait of African Americans as a whole. As an example, in recounting their brief interaction with the black woman who worked in the home of "Mr. Adams," their American tour guide, Il'f and Petrov neither commented on her status as a domestic laborer nor conjectured how U.S. racism shaped her life.[81] Instead, they remarked how her "African teeth" lit up the vestibule when she opened the apartment door and smiled. Though they made this comment in passing, and arguably without malicious intent, it nonetheless racialized the woman and invoked the stereotypical image of the grinning, "good-natured" black servant or "smiling darkey"—much like the one they would acknowledge was common in U.S. films—who was depicted with extremely large and very white teeth.[82]

Il'f and Petrov presented a young black male janitor in a similar fashion. In *One-Story America*, they described how a lanky young man, "whose legs seemed to start at his armpits," danced for visitors of the Grand Canyon with "great pleasure" and then retreated to a corner, grabbed a broom, and flashed a large smile.[83] In *Ogonek*, Il'f and Petrov placed this same janitor in Alabama and insisted that he would prosper as a dancer in Moscow, where Muscovites were no amateurs in assessing talent. By raising the issue of wasted talent in *Ogonek*, they (or perhaps the magazine's editors) replicated a practice common in the first half of the 1930s, namely, they counterposed U.S. society's denigration of black men against the alleged equal opportunity or racelessness of the first workers' state. And yet the passing reference to the janitor as a victim of U.S. racism was complicated by a photograph that showed him dressed in overalls and grinning widely.[84] This photograph demonstrates the degree to which the goals of Soviet antiracism had changed with the advent of the Popular Front era. A photograph that featured a young black male worker in the United States smiling broadly would not have appeared in the Soviet press during the first half of the decade. The image would have undermined the representations of America as the most racist country in the world and its black (male) citizens as militant proletarians poised to stage revolution and defend the USSR in an imperialist war.

Il'f and Petrov deviated further from the representation of African Americans as revolutionaries by introducing readers to the "fanatical followers" of the "crafty old man" named Father Divine, a discussion that appeared only in *Ogonek*. They relayed how in a parade of Father Divine's followers in Harlem, black men played instruments and black women carried signs declaring the "clever prophet" God. (Several photographs confirmed this scenario.) Depictions of African Americans, especially in an urban environment like New York, embracing a man who advertised himself as "God" on his "nice Rolls Royce" would have been unthinkable, if not counterrevolutionary in the early 1930s.[85] Il'f and Petrov mentioned an antiwar/antifascism demonstration that also occurred in Harlem, but the two accompanying photographs depicted nothing that would indicate that Il'f (who was the photographer) had taken them at a political event. The first showed a black and white woman standing on a sidewalk; the other featured a black mother standing with her two children on a corner. These women could have just as easily been waiting for a bus as consciously attending a political rally.[86] Moreover, unlike the African American women who were actively praising "their God" in the Father Divine photographs, these black women—even if they were attending an antifascism demonstration—were mere bystanders rather than active participants. Though African American militancy had been gendered exclusively male in the late 1920s and early 1930s, the elision of black women was arguably less pernicious than their depiction as "fanatical followers" of a "crafty old man"; this image was not balanced by their representation as agents of revolutionary change.

As Il'f and Petrov's commentary on African Americans reveals, the image of blacks as the most exploited segment of the U.S. populace remained constant in the second half of the 1930s. The satirists may have even enhanced this image by discussing how African Americans faced far greater degrees of exploitation, discrimination, and impoverishment than working-class whites and Native Americans—a group that was virtually absent from representations of U.S. race relations under hard-line antiracism. Yet the African Americans whom readers encountered in Il'f and Petrov's writings were not responding to this extreme oppression by becoming increasingly militant, and thus were not experiencing greater violence and persecution as a consequence. In fact, Il'f and Petrov claimed that blacks refrained from exercising their legal right to enter white establishments (outside their servile roles) to avoid the violence such political "experiments" would evoke.[87] Indeed, African Americans were shown enduring their impoverished conditions, following crooked religious leaders, dancing and performing with great ease and natural ability, and exhibiting characteristics that helped make them the "soul" of the United States. Dance, religion, curiosity, an appreciation for nature, and dogged endurance sustained African Americans rather than strikes, protests, labor organizations, and the promise of revolution epitomized in the Soviet Union.[88]

Although they depicted African Americans as tragic, "hopelessly" impoverished victims, Il'f and Petrov nevertheless indicted U.S. racial mores at a time when biological racism was at its apex throughout the world. It would have been impossible for the satirists, who were on assignment for *Pravda*, to have visited the United States and not condemned U.S. racism. The fact that they were "unusually (for Soviet writers) candid in their appreciation" of various aspects of U.S. society, as Maxim Matusevich remarks, seemingly made a discussion of African American oppression imperative.[89] Letters to the publisher regarding *One-Story America* underline the necessity for the Soviet humorists to have commented on African Americans. A few letter writers praised Il'f and Petrov for providing a clear picture of the lives of U.S. blacks, but another reader who identified himself as a member of the Communist Party criticized them for allotting insufficient attention to the degradation of African Americans and workers. Whether these readers' assessments were positive or negative is not the issue here. These letters—even if Soviet publishers contrived them—further reveal that speaking antiracism remained a form of "speaking Soviet" throughout the 1930s.[90]

Yet to acknowledge that antiracism remained part of the field of discourse is not to say that Il'f and Petrov were apathetic about the plight of African Americans and addressed it out of ideological necessity alone. Their personal letters suggest that coming into contact with African Americans, who to some degree they viewed as "curiosities," left a strong impression on them. For example, in a letter to his wife in early January 1936, Petrov explained that their tedious travels had suddenly become interesting because "everywhere are Negroes, Negroes, Negroes." Special bathrooms, churches, movie theaters, and sections of streetcars were designated for blacks who lived, Petrov stressed, in deplorable conditions. He then noted, however, that this was already well known, there was nothing he could add, and he was eager to return home. Apart from growing homesick, Petrov's remarks indicate that the information about African Americans that he recounted was already general knowledge at least among educated segments of the Soviet populace. Still, Il'f likewise felt compelled to comment to his wife about the racial segregation, poverty, and suffering among blacks that he and Petrov observed.[91] Thus, while antiracism persisted as part of the field of discourse, Il'f and Petrov's letters indicate that they may have been taken aback, if not slightly shocked, at seeing firsthand the oppression of African Americans that they had only heard or read about in the Soviet Union. To attribute their commentary about U.S. racism to politics alone, therefore, would be misguided.[92]

As the indictment of U.S. racism in the central press confirms, Soviet antiracism was not meant to advance in any comprehensive manner the Comintern's line on African Americans as an oppressed nation. Certainly, the increased coverage of U.S. racism and the equation of black skin with revolutionary feeling (and persecution) in the Soviet press demonstrate how the policy of the Executive Committee of the Communist International (ECCI) regarding African Americans penetrated Soviet society.[93] But the Comintern's advocacy of African Americans' self-determination in the black belt regions of the U.S. South was rarely mentioned in the central press.[94] Additionally, the ECCI's official line on the United States instructed that white American laborers were increasingly recognizing that they shared a common plight with African Americans and that they were organizing an inter-racial struggle to bring down capitalism.[95] Yet the dominant image of white American workers that emerged from the indictment of U.S. racism was ambiguous at best. Black was *the* color of American class consciousness in the Soviet press. This ambiguous depiction of white American toilers contradicted the Comintern line on revolution in the United States, but it was most effective for illuminating the enlighten-ment of the Soviet people. It also insinuated that only with the latter's help could revolution in the United States be realized and racism be eradicated. Highlighting Soviet exceptionalism thus held the greatest precedence in the central press.[96]

This objective did not change in the second half of the 1930s.

Germany, however, replaced the United States as *the* quintessential "country of racial bigotry" against which Soviet enlightenment was juxtaposed.[97] By 1936 the press ceased conflating racism with fascism, and distinguished the racism of fascist countries from that of bourgeois democracies. The racist practices of nonfascist states like the United States remained deplorable manifestations of capitalism and warranted continued approbation (i.e., antiracism), but journalists acknowledged that readers were already familiar with U.S. racism (and especially lynching, as one writer noted) and emphasized that the Nazi Party's policies constituted the graver threat to citizens of the first workers' state.[98]

The frequent presence of African Americans in the Soviet press in the late 1920s and early 1930s bespeaks the special status they enjoyed as valued allies of the USSR. To be sure, African Americans appeared in central newspapers in the decades after the Second World War as both victims of U.S. racism and visitors to the first workers' state; the fanfare surrounding Paul Robeson and W. E. B. Du Bois's visits to Moscow makes this most obvious. Yet due to the changes in the international climate and political exigencies of the Soviet state, they had lost their exclusive interwar status as *the* revolutionary vanguard among oppressed nations and *the* black faces in the Soviet press.[99] The unprecedented number of African dignitaries and students who traveled to the USSR in the wake of decolonization gave Soviet officials a much broader array of persons of African descent to use to "prove" Soviet enlightenment. Yet compared to the interwar era, they also had greater incentive to display their images. By the mid-1950s Soviet leaders expressed interest in winning the esteem of Asians, and especially Africans, for which they were competing with the United States for influence.[100] While African Americans had played a critical role in forging the identity of this emerging world power in its bid to establish an alternate, more progressive, and humane model of modernity, Soviet leaders expanded upon their commitment to and "friendship" with the African continent to consolidate and secure it.[101]

3

The Scottsboro Campaign
Personalizing American Racism and Speaking Antiracism

While a black migrant laborer from Detroit became the de facto poster child for Soviet antiracism, in the early 1930s nine black male teenagers from Tennessee became the faces of U.S. racial apartheid. They were, of course, not the only African American males presented as victims of the U.S. racial regime (as chapter 2 demonstrates), but they were certainly the most visible.[1] From May 1931 through the fall of 1932, these young men constituted the subject of pamphlets, banners, news articles, poems, protest resolutions, rallies, cartoons, and photographs. On March 25, 1931, police had hauled the nine black teenagers off a freight train in Paint Rock, Alabama. They initially charged them with assaulting a group of white male hitchers until they persuaded two white prostitutes, whom they had also pulled off the train, to accuse the nine unsuspecting black youth of rape. The trials, for which the alleged gang of rapists were refused impartial legal counsel, began on April 6, 1931, in Scottsboro, Alabama, with a lynch mob surrounding the courthouse. Although evidence in the case was extremely weak, by April 9 an all-white jury had condemned eight of the defendants to death and sentenced the youngest (who was only thirteen) to life imprisonment. Their execution was scheduled for July 10, 1931.

A campaign to liberate the Scottsboro prisoners was organized in the USSR by the Soviet branch of MOPR, or the International Organization for Assistance to Revolutionary Fighters, known more popularly abroad as International Red Aid (IRA). As a subsidiary organization of the Communist International, MOPR was best suited to oversee the protest; its main organizational objectives were systematically exposing the atrocities (acts they termed "white terror") committed against revolutionaries in capitalist countries and fostering support among the Soviet toiling masses for their imprisoned brethren.[2] MOPR leaders instructed branches of the organization in the United States, as well as throughout Latin America and Europe, to lead similar protests. As a result of these campaigns and the efforts of the International Labor Defense (ILD), which was MOPR's American affiliate, the Scottsboro prisoners were not executed in July. After the ILD successfully appealed other execution dates, the U.S. Supreme Court in November 1932 ordered a new trial for the young black men on the grounds that the rights guaranteed them under the Fourteenth Amendment had been violated.[3]

As James Miller, Susan D. Pennybacker, and Eve Rosenhaft argue in their important 2001 article in the *American Historical Review*, the Scottsboro campaigns in England, Germany, the Soviet Union, and the United States fostered a global racial dialogue in the 1930s.[4] This chapter adds nuance to their conclusion by situating the Scottsboro protest within the broader Soviet indictment of U.S. racism. It demonstrates that MOPR authorities conceived of it as the duty of the Soviet people, as citizens of the first country to be building a socialist society, to lead this antiracist dialogue and raise the most massive, far-reaching Scottsboro campaign. More precisely, as the "shock brigade of the international proletariat," they were supposed to lead the struggle to liberate the nine African American prisoners and to inspire toilers around the world to follow their example.[5]

MOPR's use of the liberation movement to glorify the Soviet state as enlightened rendered it distinct—in both content and form—from the Scottsboro campaigns in the United States and Europe.[6] As will be elaborated below, expressing solidarity with the Scottsboro defendants became an alternate means of expressing support for the project of building socialism. The Scottsboro protest made abundantly clear, in other words, that "speaking antiracism" was another form of "speaking Bolshevik." Accordingly, segments of society that had been perceived as suspect in their loyalty to the Soviet state were portrayed rallying to the Scottsboro prisoners' defense with particular enthusiasm. This included members of the Soviet intellectual and cultural community who, in the spring of 1931, were just emerging from the most militant phase of the Cultural Revolution (1928–31). Their prominent role in a campaign to denounce the hypocrisy of freedom in "bourgeois" America served as evidence that "bourgeois" elements had been eradicated from the intellectual spheres of Soviet society. Similarly, workers and collective farmers who inhabited border regions of the USSR, agricultural areas subjected to forced collectivization, and/or republics that had a history of ethnic conflict or recent anti-Soviet unrest, appeared among the most active in condemning American racial injustice.[7] Simply stated, the Scottsboro campaign represented Soviet citizens as unified in defense of nine black teenagers in Alabama with whom their fate was intertwined.[8] In forging this representation, the protest sheds further light on the complex and often contradictory role that African Americans directly and indirectly played in the creation of Soviet identity.

In late May 1931 MOPR's Executive Committee sent a directive marked "urgent" to authorities at the national republic, *krai* (region), and *oblast'* (province) levels regarding the need to immediately launch a mass campaign on behalf of "8 Negro proletarians" who had been condemned to death in Scottsboro, Alabama. This included, among other measures, organizing mass meetings at industrial enterprises, schools, and state and collective farms to inform citizens of the status of the revolutionary movement, the plight of U.S. blacks, and the impending execution of the eight African American "proletarians." Their execution reflected the intensification of the class struggle, the directive instructed.[9] In addition to sending this directive to MOPR officials around the country, the Executive Committee appealed to members of the intellectual and cultural community—recently "proletarianized" in the wake of the Cultural Revolution—to assume a leading role in popularizing the protest.

Less than a month later, a Defense Committee comprised of seventeen "distinguished representatives of science, literature, and society" was formed with the illustrious Russian writer Maksim Gor'kii as its leader. Gor'kii had been criticized the previous year for allegedly producing "unproletarian" work, but had more recently been hailed upon his return to the Soviet Union in mid-May 1931 as the "great writer of the proletariat."[10] Other "distinguished members" of this body included Elena Stasova, the head of MOPR USSR and long-standing member of the Executive Committee of the Communist International; Lovett Fort-Whiteman and George Padmore; representatives from the All-Union Council of Trade Unions and the Academy of Sciences; editors of *Rabochaia gazeta* and *Komsomol'skaia pravda*; and Anatolii Lunacharskii, who had lost his position as Commissar of Enlightenment during the Cultural Revolution.[11] Merely a few months after its formation, MOPR leaders would credit the Defense Committee for enabling them to mobilize nearly all Soviet society to the protest in such a short period of time.[12]

In their first official action, the Defense Committee, also known as "the Committee for Saving the 9 Negroes," issued an appeal on June 21, 1931, to all male and female workers in the Soviet Union and around the world with the demand that they "raise a protest against the verdict and execution of 9 Negro workers."[13] They called on their "brothers in class" to recognize that "saving the lives of the prisoners in Scottsboro rests entirely in the hands of the working masses" and that it was necessary to "gain the freedom of the Scottsboro prisoners at any cost." In collectively expressing their outrage at the death sentence, its members denounced as an old form of "racist 'trickery'" the accusation that the young men, who represented "the doubly oppressed and persecuted Negro proletariat," raped two white women. They insisted that the real "crime" for which the "bourgeois-fascist American court" made the young black men "candidates for the electric chair" was their involvement in "rally(ing) black and white workers for the struggle against the unbridled terrorism of the maddened bourgeoisie."[14]

The Defense Committee's June 1931 appeal, which was published in *Izvestiia*, *Trud*, *Rabochaia gazeta*, *Komsomol'skaia pravda*, and the *Workers*

News, is significant: it unofficially launched the Scottsboro campaign in the Soviet Union and modeled how to speak antiracism for the country's citizens.[15] In accordance with the aforementioned MOPR directive, the Defense Committee portrayed the Scottsboro prisoners not as unemployed teenagers who had hopped on a freight train in search of work and medical treatment. Rather, they had become champions of interracial proletarian unity, persecuted for their class consciousness and revolutionary activity. Although this depiction was fabricated, it quickly became replicated as fact at rallies and in the essays and protest resolutions of workers, collective farmers, students, and other intellectuals. For example, less than a week after the committee issued its appeal, a protest resolution with the signatures of 140 writers and cultural figures appeared on *Literaturnaia gazeta*'s front page. It declared that the Scottsboro prisoners were going to be "burned to death on the electric chair" because they refused to remain "slaves" and had "advanced the slogan of international solidarity of the working class."[16]

The transformation of the Scottsboro defendants from "boys"— which was their dominant identity in the European and U.S. campaigns—to "revolutionaries" was strategic: it effectively made the nine African American teenagers the allies of Soviet citizens.[17] By implication, their impending execution—and the escalating violence against all African American workers that it was portrayed as representing—signified the first steps in the U.S. capitalists' plot to wage an imperialist war against the Soviet Union.[18] As the Central Committee MOPR USSR made particularly explicit in one appeal, the true crime for which the Scottsboro "revolutionaries" were sentenced to death was their efforts to expose the military preparations of the American imperialist bourgeoisie to invade the first workers' state.[19] Demands for the liberation of the nine black defendants thus became equivalent to expressing a readiness to defend the USSR.

Since revolutionary activity was the real offense of which "our Negro brothers in Scottsboro" were guilty, the myth of the black rapist, the "traditional lie" as *Prozhektor* called it, had become a counter-revolutionary weapon. The American bourgeoisie no longer just used it to incite animosity among workers and to "lynch thousands of black workers," as they had done, MOPR leaders emphasized, for the past several decades. Even more perniciously they now also used it to "legally" send Soviet allies to the electric chair.[20] Due to its politicization, the myth of the black rapist—a subject that had been limited largely to references in literature and travel narratives—became a focus of the Soviet indictment of American racism.[21]

Throughout the two-year campaign but especially in the weeks preceding the defendants' initial execution date of July 10, 1931, Soviet writers, academicians, and artists—whether motivated by sincerity, obligation, or a combination of both—used the parameters established in the Defense Committee's June appeal to speak antiracism. They wrote poems, essays, and speeches, attended and led protest rallies, and created cartoons—all of which demonstrated that as the intelligentsia of the world's first workers' state, they had risen to lead the toiling masses of the Soviet Union and the globe in gaining the freedom of "our Negro brothers." Protest rallies were a particularly effective stage for showing that Soviet intellectual toilers had become the conscience of the international revolutionary movement.[22] For instance, at a mass meeting held in Leningrad on July 4, 1931, 1,500 writers, artists, lawyers, and scientists reportedly gathered to condemn the preparations for the "brutal murder" and to "demand," as Soviet novelist Aleksei Tolstoi declared, "the liberation of our black comrades."[23] Led by George Padmore and Wilhelm Pieck, a German Comintern official and fellow Defense Committee member, the rally juxtaposed the U.S. holiday's celebration of liberty and justice with the Scottsboro prisoners' scheduled execution five days later. Though uncertain whether 1,500 representatives of Leningrad's intellectual and cultural community actually attended this rally, what is most important is that MOPR wanted to portray them as doing so. That is to say, this was certainly how the intellectual toilers of the USSR—as the fatherland of all workers—were supposed to conduct themselves.

Protest rallies held in theaters were intended to highlight the extent to which the campaign had penetrated the cultural community.[24] One such Scottsboro rally occurred in Moscow's Kamernyi Theater on July 5, 1931, after the first act of Eugene O'Neill's play *All God's Chillun Got Wings* (billed as *Negro*). The play, which Alexander Tairov (the theater's founder) produced, premiered in 1929 and remained part of the repertoire during the first half of the 1930s. It serves as an important reminder that the Scottsboro protest was just one expression, albeit a very significant one, of the larger indictment of U.S. racism in the USSR in the late 1920s and early 1930s. To this end, this rally, like others, did not simply focus on the specific circumstances surrounding the Scottsboro case; its leaders also addressed African American oppression as a whole. M. Musso, a Defense Committee member and Comintern official from Indonesia, opened the protest gathering (which was reportedly broadcast on the radio) by discussing the Jim Crow segregation and "savage hatred" to which African Americans were subjected in the United States. Specifically, Musso emphasized that in America, "for Negroes there are special restaurants, special schools—forbidding them from associating with whites."[25] One of *Chillun*'s "black" male characters—who performed in blackface—assumed the identity of an African American man and recited a seventy-line-long poem by Mikhail Svetlov concerning American blacks' centuries-long struggle for equality and freedom.[26] *Literaturnaia gazeta* published the text of this poem on the front page the following day. The actor lamented: "From childhood because of my black skin they called me swine. Because of the color of my skin, they made a laughingstock of me, trying to put me in chains to lynch me." He implored members of the audience "from the front row to the last" to recognize the urgency of "rais(ing) your voice of protest" to liberate the Scottsboro prisoners.[27]

Soviet graphic artists likewise alluded to the connection between the lynching of African Americans and the impending execution of the Scottsboro defendants via the electric chair. A provocative cartoon published in both *Komsomol'skaia pravda* and *Internatsional'nyi maiak* showed a wire that could easily be mistaken for a rope spelling the acronym USA. Yet in the places where there should be knots to form each letter, the artist V. Federovskii drew the heads of the Scottsboro prisoners with the rope-wire looped around each of their necks. The

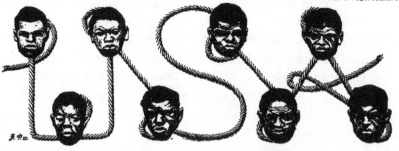

ОБОРВИТЕ ПРОВОДА ЭЛЕКТРИЧЕСКОИ ГИЛЬОТИНЫ!

Рис. В. ФЕДОРОВСКОГО

4. "Snap the Wire of the Electric Guillotine." *Komsomol'skaia pravda*, January 27, 1932,
4. Drawing by V. Federovskii.

headline appealed to onlookers to "Snap the Wire of the Electric Guillotine." As this image suggests, the wire of the electric chair—modern bourgeois "civilization's" improvement on the guillotine—was equivalent to the rope used to extralegally lynch them; both were "barbaric" tools used to suppress black revolutionaries and uphold "lynch justice" in the "USA."[28]

The essays and poems of Soviet intellectuals were equally forthright in condemning the hypocrisy of American lynch justice and the racial mores that sanctioned it. In a lengthy essay in *Komsomol'skaia pravda*, Anatolii Lunacharskii summarized with a discernible tone of disbelief that eight black teenagers will be murdered, and the ninth (the youngest) "will spend his entire life in prison," though there was absolutely no proof that they physically violated "two white professional prostitutes." Lunacharskii attributed this travesty to white Americans' attitudes toward race, which he claimed were backward in comparison with those of Soviet citizens. Even the more "open-minded" white Americans, he explained, who opposed the death sentence on the grounds that the black defendants had been denied a fair trial, nevertheless believed that if it could be proven that they had even just "made advances" at the two white women, then they deserved to be deprived of their lives. This was because, Lunacharskii argued, by white Americans' logic, "'the black dogs'" needed to "understand that it was entirely impermissible for them to raise their eyes to white women, whom their white brothers in Christ can acquire for a few dollars." He insisted that the four actual "crimes" for which the "bourgeois-fascist American court" had sentenced the Scottsboro defendants to death were their blackness, working-class status, unemployment, and revolutionary activity.[29]

In a poem in *Literaturnaia gazeta* titled "A Song about Alabama," Nikolai Aseev, a leading poet of the Russian avant-garde of the 1920s, also disparaged white Americans' perverse notions of what constituted a "crime" punishable by death for black men. Aseev explained that in Alabama, if a black man, above whose head constantly hangs a "long, sturdy noose," even smiled at a white woman, then he would be "burned alive" whether by the extralegal "laws of lynch" or the legal means of electricity. He emphasized that this systematic terrorism against African Americans, whom whites in Alabama still considered "slaves," was inseparable from the ultimate threat of imperialist war against the USSR. The inhabitants of this barbaric southern state, Aseev warned, sought to "replace the power of the Soviets with the cross of the fascists."[30]

While the Scottsboro campaign exposed the complicity of the white American masses in perpetrating violence against the USSR's African American allies, it identified as the main villain the bourgeoisie who had blinded them with the ideology of white supremacy. Graphic artists were especially pointed in conveying this message. A Dmitri Moor cartoon that *Komsomol'skaia pravda* published on the front page in March 1932 is particularly representative of this imagery. Moor, the "unofficial 'commissar of propagandistic revolutionary art,'" depicted an obese white male capitalist disguised as the Statue of Liberty.[31] With his mouth open and bearing razor-sharp teeth, the capitalist appears resting his plump left hand on a guillotine while raising an electric chair in his right. On the right shirt cuff he wears a small swastika cufflink. At the base of Lady Liberty's pedestal, miniature figures of the eight Scottsboro prisoners (drawn in proportion to the guillotine and electric chair) are shackled to one another by their wrists. Two white men are standing on either side of the defendants:

5. "The executioners are switching on the electric current." *Komsomol'skaia pravda*, March 3, 1932, 1. Drawing by D. Moor.

a sheriff in a ten-gallon hat armed with an extremely long rifle, and a Christian bishop dressed in a long robe and miter with a cross. To emphasize their status as the capitalist's henchmen, Moor drew the pair slightly taller than the black captives but still dwarflike compared to the "Statue of Liberty."

Moor's depiction of the villain as an obese white male capitalist was of course consistent with the iconography found in Soviet political posters since the October Revolution.[32] Similar to the lynching cartoon in chapter 2, this bourgeois capitalist "everyman" was shown to be not only their own formidable enemy as residents of the first workers' state, but also the bloodthirsty adversary of their African American allies, who the Scottsboro prisoners represented.[33] *Komsomol'skaia pravda*'s editors situated Moor's capitalist amid demands of workers, collective farmers, and students for the liberation of "our Scottsboro brothers." In this way, the youth newspaper represented Soviet citizens as astutely aware that the "executioners" of the Scottsboro prisoners, who the cartoon's headline warned "are switching on the electric current" were also the "conspirators against the Soviet Union."[34]

Moor's juxtaposition of the electric chair with the Statue of Liberty reflects the Soviet campaign's insistence that "the electric chair" is the "true symbol of American democracy"—a message that was also conveyed in a cartoon on *Pravda*'s front page featuring a Ku Klux Klan member as Lady Liberty raising an electric chair instead of a torch.[35] By having the bourgeois capitalist rest his left hand on the "medieval" guillotine while raising the nominally "modern" technological invention of the electric chair in his right, Moor was claiming that the counterrevolution had found a putatively more "sophisticated" and "civilized" method for dealing with its enemies; this was also the message Federovskii's "USA" cartoon conveyed. The swastika, which in this case could easily be overlooked because of its small size, became, according to Victoria Bonnell, a feature of the capitalist in Soviet iconography in the early 1930s. At the same time, it was also consistent with the protest's rhetoric, which routinely referred to the Alabama court and the executioners as "bourgeois American fascists."[36] The term "fascist" was intended to place the "civilized executioners" of the Scottsboro prisoners in league with capitalists throughout the Western world. At this juncture it and the swastika signified a general anti-Soviet stance rather than specific forms of fascism (such as that in Italy or Nazism in Germany).[37] Hence, as mentioned in chapter 1, the white American assailants of Robert Robinson were denounced as "fascists." Finally, by identifying one of the Scottsboro "guards" as a Christian authority, Moor indicted the church for sanctioning the execution of eight innocent black men and the U.S. bourgeoisie's designs to destroy the USSR.[38]

In an agitational pamphlet, Maksim Gor'kii warned Soviet citizens that the common enemy—Moor's "Statue of Liberty"—had intensified his attack on their allies. Three million copies of the pamphlet, titled "Capitalists' Terror against Negro Workers in America," were allegedly released simultaneously in twenty-four areas of the USSR in the summer of 1931.[39] Gor'kii elucidated that the American bourgeoisie, feeling increasingly threatened, sentenced the Scottsboro defendants to death in an attempt "to scare Negroes" back into their "proper" place. "This murder," he continued, is a "'preventative measure.'"[40] He cited the then recent atrocities at Camp Hill, Alabama, of mid-July 1931, to underscore that American capitalists had escalated their violence against black workers. As Gor'kii explained, "400 policemen and armed fascists" stormed a Scottsboro protest of black sharecroppers, murdered their union leader (Ralph Grey), lynched four other black men, and set fire to the homes of several black families. Gor'kii was not the first to mention the violence at Camp Hill. *Rabochaia gazeta, Trud, Komsomol'skaia pravda, Leningradskaia pravda, Internatsional'nyi maiak*, and the *Workers News* had published articles about the atrocities, which MOPR leaders instructed officials to present at Scottsboro meetings. Camp Hill reinforced the campaign's emphasis that it was imperative for the world proletariat—led by inhabitants of the first workers' state—to fight in defense of the Scottsboro prisoners, all African American workers, and by implication, the Soviet fatherland.[41]

In an essay in *Izvestiia* and the *Workers News*, Aleksei Tolstoi similarly admonished that the American bourgeoisie had become even more desperate and violent as a result of the growing class consciousness of black workers like the Scottsboro prisoners. At the same time, he also condemned the white American masses who blindly supported their efforts. Tolstoi's essay affirms that Soviet antiracism constituted one way for intellectuals to demonstrate their allegiance to the socialist project.[42] The novelist prefaced his lengthy criticism of the U.S. racial regime by declaring that he was speaking on behalf of all "Soviet writers" who were "taking part as far as our strength will allow in the building of the foundation of socialism." He then proceeded to discuss how white Americans would have accused the defendants of whatever "crime" necessary to justify their execution—regardless of its absurdity. To illustrate his point, Tolstoi quipped, "Ten thousand white farmers rushed into the small town of Scottsboro, to condemn to death eight Negro workers. If for this purpose it was necessary to prove that the Negroes had stolen the moon from the sky ten thousand whites would have shouted: Yes!" As a result of the preparations of "10,000 horsemen, mounted farmers, sons of frightened bourgeoisie," and "members of the Young Men's Christian Association" to murder eight innocent black workers in Scottsboro, Tolstoi lamented, "really one is ashamed to call himself a white man."[43]

Despite the essay's obvious class overtones, Tolstoi's use of the racial identifier "white" (in reference to himself and the American lynch mob) is instructive. It suggests that an underlying objective of the Scottsboro protest, or at least that of some of its participants, was to disassociate the "whiteness" of Soviet citizens from the "whiteness" of (white) Americans. To be sure, MOPR leaders identified eradicating black workers' distrust of whites as one of the organization's main goals.[44] Yet Russians' history of contested whiteness, and contemporary representations of the Soviet Union and the Bolsheviks as nonwhite because of their perceived "efforts to overthrow white supremacy in the West," make Tolstoi's comment and those of other intellectuals especially provocative.[45]

Members of the Academy of Sciences, who had been a major target of the Cultural Revolution's antibourgeois offensive, also ridiculed white Americans for their racial mores. *Rabochaia gazeta*, for instance, quoted A. N. Samoilovich as remarking that "Soviet citizens cannot find sufficient words for articulating their anger and surprise that in our day a manifestation of such barbarity would be permitted in a country which purports to belong to a higher civilization." Fellow academician N. S. Derzhavin also reportedly posited that because U.S. intellectuals help keep workers racially divided, "in the area of culture, we have long surpassed America. Our new ethical outlook, our national policy, our Soviet civilization, stands immeasurably higher."[46] As the protest writings of intellectuals illuminate, a major goal of the Scottsboro campaign—like all forms of Soviet antiracism—was encouraging Soviet citizens to take pride in the new society and civilization they were building. The superior system of socialism was based on the recognition of national and racial equality, rather than the oppression of dark-skinned peoples as epitomized in the U.S. racial regime.[47] At least implicitly, therefore, the Scottsboro campaign did not simply challenge Russians' historical exclusion from the ranks of the "civilized" or "white." It also insisted that they were in fact the most "civilized" or "white" among European-descended groups, to whom white Americans were an embarrassment.

Intellectuals' claims of Russian exceptionalism had long historical precedent save the distinct ideological (Marxist-Leninist) component, and the notion that Soviet citizens possessed a different, more civilized form of whiteness was not without basis. Many African Americans perceived the "whiteness" of Russians as more benign and enlightened than the "whiteness" of their fellow Americans, an issue that chapter 5 will address at greater length. Yet with good reason, they also did not conceive of it as entirely unproblematic.[48] To be sure, Soviet antiracism challenged the definition of "civilization" but did not challenge its association or equation with whiteness. Consequently, the superiority of whiteness was reaffirmed, and it assumed the form of a racial paternalism that, as addressed in previous chapters and elaborated below, subordinated African Americans and other groups to Russians as the "first among equals."

The toiling masses of the USSR were represented as mobilizing to defend their African American comrades on a scale that paralleled their counterparts in the intellectual and cultural community. Their forms of speaking antiracism confirmed that the Scottsboro death sentence constituted an attack, albeit indirect, on the new civilization they were building. On June 27, 1931, roughly a week after the Defense Committee issued its initial appeal, *Rabochaia gazeta* reported in hyperbolic fashion that thousands of protests against the execution of the Scottsboro defendants had risen "from all ends of the Soviet Union: from Arkhangel'sk to Viatka, Novosibirsk to Vladivostok, the Donbass mines to the Baku oil fields, the cotton fields of Central Asia to the textile factories of Ivanovo-Voznesensk."[49] The following year, the Executive Committee of MOPR similarly asserted as fact, in equally picturesque language, that the protest had pervaded the vast territory of the country: "Throughout the whole of the Soviet Union, from Leningrad to Vladivostok, from Minsk to Tiflis, the mighty voices of millions thunder: 'Freedom for the Scottsboro Prisoners!'"[50]

To complement broad, dramatic statements like these the central press published numerous protest resolutions that they attributed to Russian and non-Russian workers, collective farmers, and students from around the country. Among the central newspapers, *Komsomol'skaia pravda*—whose editor was a member of the Defense Committee—printed the most, often displaying between three and seven resolutions at one time on the front page.[51] Similar to MOPR's Central Committee, which claimed to have received thousands of protest statements, a disclaimer often prefaced the resolutions in *Komsomol'skaia pravda*, *Leningradskaia pravda*, and other papers claiming that the editorial office had been flooded with protest resolutions from various factories, institutions, and Red Army units, rendering it impossible to print all of them.[52] Editors of *Internatsional'nyi maiak* were especially efficient in maximizing the space devoted to statements of opposition. They typically printed the complete text of three or four, and then listed several other factories, construction sites, and collective or state farms that they claimed had likewise sent protest statements, but which "unfortunately" there "was insufficient space" to publish.[53]

Although the publication of these resolutions was intended to serve as evidence of the spontaneous and widespread nature of Soviet citizens' outrage, it helped to reveal the degree to which they were contrived. As evidenced from those in the central press and included in MOPR records, Scottsboro resolutions assumed two standard forms, among which there was generally minimal variation regardless of who was identified as the author(s). Workers, collective farmers, Red Army soldiers, and students were thus shown speaking antiracism in two main ways. The first consisted of a short statement articulating indignation and demanding justice for the Scottsboro defendants. MOPR authorities had sanctioned indignation as the "proletarian" or "Soviet" response—just as trade union officials had done during the campaign against Lewis and Brown in 1930. In one particular statement, they insisted that "the indignation of workers and peasants in the country of soviets who have risen in opposition to the Alabama courts and American racism is natural and comprehensible."[54] As a typical example of this form of antiracist expression, on July 7, 1931, *Trud* reported on the front page that sixteen thousand workers at a factory in Nikolaev (southern Ukraine), "with great indignation[,] are protesting the American bourgeoisie's barbaric execution of eight Negro workers." In their resolution, they "'demand(ed) the immediate repeal of the bloody sentence and the liberation of our brothers in class! Down with the bloody terror of fascism! Long live international proletarian solidarity!'"[55]

In the second form of resolution, workers, collective farmers, and students followed the standard "angry" denunciation of the "vile" death sentence with a pledge to engage in activities on behalf of the joint goal of building socialism and liberating the Scottsboro prisoners. This included forming shock brigades, engaging in socialist competition, eliminating illiteracy, sowing additional plots of land, establishing new MOPR cells, collecting donations, and/or subscribing to the bond "The Five-Year Plan in Four Years."[56] Reflective of this era in Soviet history, forming shock brigades was the most popular pledge; *Internatsional'nyi maiak* even published a photograph of one such brigade named for the "7 Negroes."[57] *Sputnik moprovtsa*, the organ published for MOPR functionaries, printed lists of activities that different groups supposedly had promised to engage in to protest U.S. lynch law.[58] Central newspapers, on the other hand, published the full text of a few groups' resolutions. For instance, on *Komsomol'skaia pravda*'s front page on July 4, 1931, amid several other statements of opposition, laborers in Ufa were quoted as declaring: "Having listened to a report about the preparations for the execution of eight Negro comrades, we are creating a new shock brigade named for the eight Negro comrades to struggle by all means possible for the fulfillment of the Five-Year Plan in four years, and for strengthening the power of the USSR—the fatherland of the world proletariat."[59] Similarly, in an attempt to illustrate the far-reaching nature of the Scottsboro protest (and by implication Soviet power), MOPR reported that to express their outrage, "non-Russian women at their meetings in Makhachkala (Dagestan) set themselves a number of tasks, i.e. the formation of shock-brigades, collection of funds, and the recruitment of members into MOPR, and called on a number of towns to take their example."[60]

It is unsurprising that citizens from around the country were represented as demonstrating their outrage at the impending execution by pledging to engage in tasks to strengthen socialist construction. Indeed, at the outset, MOPR's Executive Committee had instructed officials that along with an expression of indignation, this was the proper way for the Soviet masses to express solidarity with the Scottsboro defendants.[61] To this end, by early August 1931 they reprimanded authorities in twenty-five regions of the country for failing to send protest resolutions containing these pledges, followed by the advisement that they relay this information to Moscow immediately.[62] The objective in having citizens appear to be participating in the liberation movement in this manner was twofold. First, it affirmed the connection between the Scottsboro prisoners' execution and the threat of an imperialist war against the USSR that members of the Defense Committee and other Soviet intellectuals articulated at rallies and in poems, cartoons, and essays. MOPR's elevation of American race relations from the realm of U.S. domestic affairs to an issue of international concern was further legitimated. Second, it reinforced the representation of the USSR as the "fatherland of the world proletariat," as the Ufa laborers put it, *the* defender and protector of the world's oppressed masses. Hence, only by making the USSR stronger could the lives of the Scottsboro prisoners be saved and the liberation of all African Americans be realized.

Whether workers, students, and collective farmers actually fulfilled any of the promises to strengthen socialism that they were portrayed as making in Scottsboro protest resolutions is secondary. Daniel Peris discusses similar pledges found in the reports of the League of the Militant Godless (another Soviet propaganda organization) during the early 1930s. Peris argues that "these were rituals of declaration much more loudly declaimed than actually observed. . . . Revolutionary discourse was running far ahead of revolutionary reality and was increasingly divorced from it."[63] These "rituals of declaration" were thus not meant to reflect the types of activities the Soviet toiling masses were actually engaging in to protest the Scottsboro death sentence. Rather, these were the activities in which the revolutionary citizens of a new socialist, that is, antiracist society *should be* engaging.

As noted earlier, MOPR leaders consistently emphasized that workers of the world looked to Soviet citizens to lead the fight on behalf of their oppressed brethren around the globe. Consistent with this mission, the press published articles about and photographs of Scottsboro meetings reportedly held in various regions of the Soviet Union (alongside those in the United States, Latin America, China, and Europe).[64] MOPR leaders likewise sent directives to local officials outlining the campaign's success in different regions of the Soviet Union, as well as in Germany, France, and the United States.[65] Disseminating information about the campaign abroad was intended to serve as evidence that members of the nascent international proletariat community were not only acting in unity with, but also in theory following the example of, inhabitants of the "fatherland."[66] Apart from this, it also functioned to remind MOPR authorities throughout the USSR that they could not afford to be upstaged by the campaigns in the capitalist world.

MOPR's Central Committee did, however, compile specific "data" to represent workers, collective farmers, Red Army soldiers, and students in diverse regions of the country—including several of the previously derelict regions—as fulfilling these pledges and attending Scottsboro meetings en masse.[67] While they likely had fabricated these numbers or taken considerable creative license with them, important insight can still be gained into which social groups and regions of the country MOPR leaders thought should appear as the most active in condemning U.S. racial injustice. In one survey of six regions that included Azerbaijan and Armenia, the two Transcaucasian republics were shown as having organized the most Scottsboro mass meetings and group discussions. Azerbaijan was identified as holding over 300 more mass meetings than Armenia (405 to 72, not including the 6,960 small group discussions that Azerbaijani officials also allegedly held), but Armenian officials supposedly managed to involve about 30,000 more participants (125,000 to 82,350).[68] Though the numbers at first glance seem disparate (perhaps to foster the impression that they were not contrived), both republics appeared to have achieved nearly the same level of success; Armenia was just portrayed as holding fewer meetings of a more massive character. Therefore, in spite of past territorial disputes over Nakhichevan and Nagorno-Karabakh, and the insurrection in northwest Azerbaijan in 1930 to establish an Islamic state, this "data" demonstrated that the Scottsboro campaign was educating Armenians and Azerbaijanis in "the spirit of proletarian internationalism."[69] Mention of the third Transcaucasian republic of Georgia, which had not been involved in these particular hostilities, was omitted.

In another more detailed survey that charted attendance at Scottsboro meetings, collective farmers in the Central Black Earth Oblast' were listed as the most active participants (over five times more than industrial workers).[70] Certainly, peasants who willingly joined the collective farm may have been most committed to the project of building socialism and to articulating outrage at racial injustice in bourgeois America. Yet the Central Black Earth Oblast' was also a region with one of the country's highest rates of forced collectivization and dekulakization.[71] Significantly, the same survey included the Urals and listed industrial workers as the segment of the populace most involved in the protest gatherings there.[72] MOPR officials arguably sought to convey the message that with their assistance the agricultural revolution had begun to raise the level of consciousness in the countryside to where it paralleled that of the proletariat in the Soviet Union's major industrial centers.[73]

The data concerning Ukraine give this argument further credence. MOPR records depict inhabitants of this republic as far surpassing other regions of the country—including the Urals—in terms of forming shock brigades on behalf of the Scottsboro prisoners, sowing extra hectares of land in the name of the Scottsboro defendants, and donating resources for the construction of socialism and liberation of their African American allies.[74] This portrayal of Ukraine as fully mobilized to the Scottsboro campaign was highly strategic: the republic was a site of substantial turmoil due to collectivization; it suffered a severe grain requisitions crisis in the fall of 1932, devastating famine in 1933, and repression of tens of thousands so-called Ukrainian nationalists who were accused of plotting with the new Nazi regime and Polish government to have the republic secede from the USSR.[75] How could its inhabitants be starving and discontented, and how could their loyalty be considered suspect, when they supposedly donated more funds, labor, and resources than their fellow citizens to the project of building socialism and to improving the welfare of the Scottsboro prisoners and their relatives? Who would have suspected that, at least from 1931 through 1932, the heart of Soviet antiracism and bulwark of support for the socialist project outside Moscow (according to MOPR's central records) was located in the Ukrainian Soviet Socialist Republic?

Since their records were not for public consumption, MOPR leaders compiled and fabricated this data to demonstrate for internal (party) purposes that they had achieved considerable success in inciting the populace to the protest and, by implication, gaining their allegiance to the socialist cause. This would have been a priority in 1931 and 1932. As chapter 1 discussed, party and trade union authorities in Moscow had interpreted the 1930 assault on Robert Robinson as revealing an absence of international education throughout the Soviet Union. International education was supposed to eradicate the racial and national animosities that "capitalist education" had inculcated in the masses, and raise their awareness of and empathy for the plight of their laboring brothers in capitalist and colonial countries. Although the responsibility fell in part on trade union officials, MOPR—for whom international education was a primary organizational objective—was also implicated.[76] Accordingly, throughout the Scottsboro protest, MOPR's Central Committee emphasized the urgency of strengthening international education, particularly among new working-class cadres, not simply because of the two Americans' assault on Robinson, but also in light of manifestations of anti-Semitism, "Great Power" chauvinism, and local nationalism around the country. Only by improving international education, MOPR authorities admonished, would the organization fulfill its vital role in "educating and creating" the "new person for the new society."[77] MOPR leaders compiled this data to prove that even in those regions that had experienced some type of turmoil, they were using the Scottsboro protest to facilitate the emergence of this New Soviet Person.[78]

A twelve-page, single-spaced informational guide that was intended for individuals to consult when delivering lectures and leading discussions at Scottsboro gatherings around the country provides some insight into MOPR's curriculum in international education. Titled "The Lynching and Persecution of Negro Workers in the USA" ("Linchevanie i presledovanie negritianskikh trudiashchikhsia v SASSh"), it is uncertain how often this guide was consulted and the information found within it disseminated at protest rallies. Yet its contents—which contain no references to the Scottsboro case—demonstrate that MOPR authorities wanted to depict Soviet citizens as receiving a general lesson in U.S. racism when they were attending protest meetings en masse, as the press and their organizational records claimed.

The guide opens with statistical data that established blacks as the most oppressed segment of the U.S. populace. Thereafter, each section addressed a form of African American oppression that included Jim Crow and the struggles of hard-working black farmers. The majority of the guide, however, dealt with lynching and other forms of white mob violence. One section explained that after the "emancipation" of the slaves, lynching came to be employed almost exclusively against African American men on false allegations of raping white women. Lecturers were encouraged to admonish attendees against believing such accusations, and to particularly emphasize (the passage was underlined in the original) that "in the course of two centuries incidents of violence committed by black men against white women are not only rare, but are completely unknown." To corroborate this claim, the guide's fifth section referenced criminologists' studies that showed that men belonging to nationalities other than "Negro" (including Russians, Italians, and Hungarians) were more often arrested on rape charges. Two additional sections of the guide provided lecturers with extensive statistical data documenting how incidents of lynching had increased in number since the Great Depression, and gave four graphic accounts of the torture and murder of African American men (and one woman) that personalized these figures.[79]

As the content of the "Lynching and Persecution of Negro Workers in the USA" suggests, MOPR leaders identified instruction about African American oppression (especially in its most physically violent forms) as a vehicle—at least in theory—for cultivating an enlightened racial consciousness, while also no doubt satisfying an interest among Soviet citizens for what Evgenii Steiner (as mentioned in the previous chapter) calls sadistic discourse. The lecture guide also points to the critical role that African Americans played in fostering the emergence of this New Soviet Person, since African Americans were behind the production of this and other Soviet knowledge about U.S. racism. Substantial portions of "The Lynching and Persecution of Negro Workers in the USA" had appeared in articles that George Padmore authored for a few Soviet publications, making it highly likely that Padmore was the guide's author, or at the very least contributed substantially to its compilation. In 1931 Otto Huiswood likewise authored materials regarding the details behind the Scottsboro case which MOPR's Executive Committee forwarded to all sections for use in leading protest meetings.[80] In addition to Padmore and Lovett Fort-Whiteman, who served on the Defense Committee, MOPR records and publications claim that other African Americans like Oliver Golden and Robert Ross (who became an official propagandist) addressed meetings around the country.[81]

African Americans certainly exercised a position of power in the Soviet protest by helping to forge the "new people" for the "new society." This position of power, however, was predicated on MOPR's desire to use African Americans' "blackness" to authenticate the alleged enlightened wisdom of the Soviet state. More precisely, Soviet authorities enlisted the help of their African American allies (directly and indirectly) in cultivating an antiracist consciousness among Soviet citizens, but that consciousness—at least among the country's leaders—was also understood to preexist their intervention. The Scottsboro protest thereby affirmed African Americans' identity as allies and integral players in the international revolutionary struggle, at the same time it established their subservient role within that struggle. The simultaneous elevation and subordination of the African American nation, in alliance with the first workers' state, becomes especially clear when closely examining representations of the "men" at the center of the campaign itself: the Scottsboro prisoners.

The iconography of the Scottsboro protest made the "9 Negroes" the "face" or "faces" of African American oppression in the USSR. The Scottsboro defendants, in other words, were used to personalize the plight of the country's African American allies. Photographs of the Scottsboro prisoners and cartoons with figures bearing their likeness (including the aforementioned cartoons of Dmitri Moor and V. Federovskii) appeared frequently in the central press and on posters that adorned the public spaces of Moscow and other major urban centers from 1931 through 1932.[82] Sam Langford, Morris Wikman, and Abraham Lewis—three black American laborers who visited the country in 1931—claimed to have seen photographs of the Scottsboro prisoners "everyplace—on street corners, in factories, in hotels and clubs."[83] These dark-skinned young men, who were dressed in overalls, came to typify the stereotypical image of African Americans among Soviet citizens. Several African Americans who visited and/or lived in the USSR testified to the confusion they confronted among Russians who believed

6. "Stop the Executioners!" *Pravda*, April 11, 1932, 4. Drawing by V. Federovskii.

that all African Americans were poor, had dark skin, and wore tattered clothes.[84] Hence, while the Scottsboro campaign affirmed African Americans' status in the revolutionary family as valued militants, it simultaneously fostered essentialist views of black people as in need of the empathy and assistance of the Soviet state and its people.

To be sure, the alleged revolutionary activities of the Scottsboro defendants (like those of the more nameless and faceless African Americans in chapter 2) had gotten them nowhere but sentenced to death, a fate that photographs and cartoons were most pointed in illustrating. Prison bars and an electric chair were sometimes superimposed over photographs of the black defendants. Cartoons, too, showed them with electrocution caps on their heads, nooses around their necks, and standing with hands bound on a chess board opposite three fierce-looking white men: an obese male capitalist, Ku Klux Klan member, and fat sheriff.[85] In a *Pravda* cartoon by V. Federovskii in which these instruments of bourgeois justice are absent, a Soviet male worker stands with his right arm extended and hand open, ready to "stop the executioners" from harming the Scottsboro defendants, who are shown standing (smaller in size) behind him.[86]

The protest rhetoric complemented this imagery by presenting the liberation of the Scottsboro prisoners as contingent on the intervention of the world's proletariat led by "toilers of the USSR."[87] Variations of the phrases "We Must Save the 9 Negroes" pervaded cartoons, essays, placards, protest resolutions, and rallies. The Defense Committee was known alternatively as the "Committee for Saving the 9 Negroes" (as mentioned earlier) and newspaper headlines announced that "the Scottsboro victims are waiting our help."[88] Posters reminded passersby that the Scottsboro executioners were the "conspirators against the Soviet Union" while also assuring that "We Will Break Free the 8 Scottsboro Negro Youth from the Clutches of the Executioners."[89] Moreover, MOPR leaders often referred to the movement as the "Campaign to Save the 9 Negroes" and advocated use of the slogan "Save the victims of Scottsboro" to make the protest the most massive international campaign in the organization's history.[90]

In short, the Scottsboro protest reflects the fundamental problem of Soviet antiracism: since its objective first and foremost was the glorification of the Soviet state rather than black equality, in the process of raising critical international attention to African American oppression, it perpetuated a variant of the ideology of white superiority that the campaign ostensibly was supposed to counter, namely, paternalism. Somewhat paradoxically, therefore, in the Soviet Union the Scottsboro "boys" were politicized or transformed into militant revolutionaries at the same time that they became the poster boys or poster children for black men in interwar America; they needed the paternalistic beneficence of the Soviet state to realize their complete emancipation.[91] The simultaneous portrayal of the Scottsboro defendants as revolutionaries and dependents was necessary to creating a "super state" and people—a promised land—that was powerful enough to defeat Dmitri Moor's larger-than-life white male capitalist and to afford African Americans both immediate and ultimate salvation.

To showcase the salvation that the Soviet state promised for the Scottsboro prisoners and all African Americans, the Soviet liberation movement represented African Americans in the USSR, real and fictional, as restored to the full humanity that America's racial democracy had systematically denied them (much like the representations addressed in chapter 2). A poem titled "The Other Shore," which juxtaposed the fate of a fictional African American man named "Gary" with that of the Scottsboro defendants, makes this particularly obvious. Gary flees the lynching, imprisonment, and daily injustice that are the lot of blacks in the United States, seeking refuge on the "Other Shore," that is, in the USSR. Even though as a refrain reminds readers, the earth is relatively small, the ocean that separates the Soviet Union from the United States is vast. Its vastness reflects just how disparate are the attitudes toward blacks in these two societies. As the poem elucidates, whereas the electric chair is the fate of African Americans like the Scottsboro prisoners in the United States, in the Soviet Union the color of Gary's skin is immaterial and he is able to work, "grow," and "develop" in complete equality. Despite having arrived on the "Other Shore," Gary is acutely aware that he and Soviet citizens share the responsibility of saving from the electric chair, which the Statue of Liberty elevates in her right hand (imagery reminiscent of Moor's cartoon), the brothers he left behind in the "land of Lady Liberty."[92]

Scottsboro rallies likewise celebrated the Soviet Union as the "promised land" that was responsible for African Americans' liberation. A two-day protest rally and carnival in the Park of Culture and Rest in the summer of 1932, which reportedly attracted thirty thousand people, illustrates this point.[93] The more notable in attendance included Sen Katayama, a Japanese scholar and Comintern official; Fort-Whiteman and Padmore; twenty-one African American male and female cast members of the Mezhrabpom film *Black and White*; and Emma Harris, a sixty-two-year-old African American woman and longtime resident of Moscow.[94] According to Langston Hughes, who was a member of the *Black and White* cast, though Harris disagreed with many of the Soviet state's policies, she supported its energetic condemnation of U.S. racism and spoke at all the Moscow rallies. Hughes claimed that Soviet officials always introduced Harris as "our own beloved Negro comrade, Emma, who before she came to the Soviet motherland, knew the stinging lash of race hatred in her native America."[95]

The presentation of Harris in this manner is instructive. Referring to an adult black woman by her first name was probably intended to convey friendship and familiarity, as suggested by the use of the terms "beloved" and "comrade." But it could also be seen as a reflection of the racial paternalism and superficial understanding of American racism that influenced most forms of Soviet antiracism. Additionally, introducing her as having known the "stinging lash" of U.S. racism before reaching the "Soviet motherland" deliberately fosters the impression that she had arrived just a few years previously, with the explicit purpose of seeking refuge in the USSR from American racial persecution. Harris had in fact not only been living in Moscow since 1901 but had enjoyed what some contemporaries claimed was a rather lucrative and content existence as a singer and brothel owner for sixteen years. Soviet antiracism, however, rendered Harris's personal history impossible. Only in the Soviet Union, and not in its tsarist predecessor, could Emma Harris find salvation as a "Negro comrade" in her "motherland." Thus, although she nominally occupied a position of power in this rally as one of its speakers, this was undercut by the implication that Harris was indebted to the Soviet state for it. That is to say, she and the other African American participants were no longer victims in need of being "saved"; travel to the USSR had brought them the complete equality and freedom for which they were now struggling with Soviet citizens to bring the Scottsboro prisoners.

Scottsboro rallies not only displayed the "emancipated" status of African American residents and visitors. MOPR authorities also intended these events to exhibit the antiracist consciousness and international education of Soviet citizens that made African Americans' emancipation possible. More precisely, a large, enthusiastic turnout of Soviet citizens at such events was arguably intended to provide tangible evidence to African American visitors that whiteness in a socialist society signified enlightenment rather than ignorance with regard to race. This, MOPR leaders may have reasoned, could then potentially encourage them to return to the United States and deliberately or inadvertently propagate the Soviet Union's identity as an antiracist society simply by speaking of their experiences there. A remark attributed to Dorothy West, a member of the *Black and White* cast, suggests that this was a consideration. The *Moscow Daily News* reported that West was impressed by the level of knowledge Russian workers possessed about the Scottsboro prisoners. As a result, the paper stressed, she and other cast members learned about developments in the case from them when they attended rallies in Moscow.[96]

The mention of Emma Harris and Dorothy West raises another important issue related to the Scottsboro campaign and the revolutionary alliance between African Americans and Soviet citizens that demands attention, namely, its masculinized nature. Harris and West lent a rare black female presence to the discourse and organization of the liberation movement in the USSR. The circumstances of the Scottsboro case, combined with the fact that African American and Soviet men were predominantly the contributors to the campaign's discourse, reinforced the elision of African American women from Soviet antiracism. To be sure, the caretakers of the Soviet protest did not maximize the opportunities that the Scottsboro case afforded them to portray black women at least as secondary or auxiliary victims of American racial injustice. Several of the defendants' mothers, but especially Ada Wright, who toured Europe in 1932, played prominent, highly visible roles in the Scottsboro campaigns in the United States and throughout Europe. In contrast, her name and image appeared sporadically in Soviet publications, and by the time her tour reached Moscow, Wright was too ill to address MOPR's International Congress.[97] Yet the low profile that Wright and the other mothers were allotted in the Soviet protest may also reflect its unique representation of the Scottsboro defendants as revolutionary allies, and its designation of the Soviet Union as assuming a semimessianic role in their liberation. Specifically, the Soviet campaign's depiction of the Scottsboro prisoners as militant, revolutionary workers instead of mere "boys" rendered prominent mother figures dispensable and established the paternalistic Soviet state, the fatherland of all workers, as their main "guardian."

Just as the African American revolutionary militants (and consequent targets of American racial injustice) were gendered male, the Soviet liberation movement cast white male capitalists and their white male henchmen as the primary agents of American racism. But the nature of the Scottsboro case, and the Soviet protest's emphasis on dispelling the myth of the black rapist (of white women), ensured that white American women's role in the oppression of African Americans would not be ignored completely. On occasion they were mentioned as providing white men with "justification" to lynch black men—through legal or extralegal means—by falsely accusing them of rape. This role was epitomized by Ruby Bates and Victoria Price, the two white women whom authorities persuaded to accuse the nine teenagers of rape. Notwithstanding the acknowledgment of this white female involvement, the Soviet campaign conceptualized the struggle against U.S. racism—like the larger international revolutionary movement it was supposed to reflect—as a masculine affair. Women—African American, white American, and Soviet—occupied secondary, auxiliary roles in a conflict that pitted white American men against African American men who, in turn, needed Soviet men to help them turn the tide in their more than three-hundred-year struggle. Otherwise, the implication was that racism would remain the hallmark of American "democracy."

This discussion is complicated, however, by the fact that a woman, Elena Stasova, served as the head of the Soviet branch of MOPR during the Scottsboro protest. Yet despite her leadership position, the organization rather than Stasova was publicly associated with and credited for leading the Soviet campaign. Maksim Gor'kii, his male-dominated Defense Committee (of which she was a member), and other male intellectual and cultural figures assumed more visible, personal roles in popularizing the protest than did Stasova. Consistent with official representations of women revolutionaries who were ascribed the ideal female revolutionary trait of modesty, Stasova's activities were largely invisible. At the same time, since a major function of the Scottsboro campaign, and of MOPR itself, was educating the masses and providing assistance to the nine imprisoned revolutionaries, it could be argued that Stasova was in charge of an organization that was concerned with traditionally "feminine" responsibilities, namely, the spiritual and moral (if not "mothering") aspects of the international revolutionary movement.[98] Under her leadership, MOPR was helping to "nurture" Soviet men by providing them with the knowledge that would inspire them to take up the fight to liberate their African American brothers (and the entire African American nation) and to defend the fatherland.

The Scottsboro protest furthered two major objectives of Soviet antiracism. First, it glorified the Soviet state by representing the USSR as the most enlightened country in the world. Representations of the Soviet populace as unified around a higher cause of the defense of justice and human rights arguably had tremendous moral capital in the USSR and abroad, while countering rumors of unrest and disunity in the face of an impending imperialist war, which the Scottsboro death sentence supposedly signaled. Second, the Scottsboro protest succeeded in dominating the field of discourse. That is to say, it helped to imbibe Soviet authorities and citizens with an awareness of American racial apartheid and with knowledge of what constituted the "Soviet" or enlightened response to it.

Indeed, white American businessmen who visited the Soviet Union in the early 1930s often expressed frustration to U.S. State Department officials with Soviet citizens' knowledge of U.S. race relations and their agility at speaking antiracism. One such white American was Raymond Price from Washington DC, who worked in the Soviet Union in 1931. Price informed U.S. consulate officials in Riga, Latvia, that the Russians with whom he spoke during his residence there believed that African Americans were not allowed to attend schools or universities with whites; and that they refused to believe otherwise when he tried to tell them differently. Isador Besbek, who visited the Soviet Union in 1932, informed the U.S. consulate of a similar encounter that he had had with the daughter of a Moscow University professor. Besbek recounted how the young woman asked him, "Don't you people in the 'free' United States of America lynch Negroes?" Besbek tried to persuade the young woman that she had been misinformed, emphasizing that lynch victims, regardless of their skin color, deserved it.[99] African Americans like Paul Robeson and the aforementioned Dorothy West also expressed amazement at the extent of Soviet citizens' knowledge about the plight of African Americans.[100]

Yet to acknowledge that antiracism was part of the field of discourse or another form of "speaking Soviet" during the 1930s is not to deny that some Soviet citizens may have been genuinely outraged at American racial injustice and sincere in their expressions of solidarity with the victims. Certainly, as this chapter demonstrates, the Soviet Scottsboro campaign was the product of official state action rather than the result of Soviet citizens' initiative and popular outrage, as authorities claimed. At the same time, it would be irresponsible to claim that Soviet citizens responded to the campaign with indifference and apathy alone.[101] As noted throughout this study, scholars of the Soviet Union have demonstrated how many individuals during the 1920s and 1930s possessed a strong desire to act as "the agents of historical progress" and help inaugurate a new, superior society where racial and national hatred was absent—a desire that the Soviet state no doubt harnessed.[102] As Maxim Matusevich argues, it was not until after the Second World War that Soviet citizens' enthusiasm for antiracist rhetoric had worn thin, as many increasingly saw the state's indictment of American racism as just another dimension of the Cold War struggle with the United States.[103]

Moreover, as noted elsewhere, Russian intellectuals had a long history of insisting on the superiority of Russian civilization over the morally bankrupt societies of the West. Although they had largely focused on the countries of Europe rather than the fledgling United States, some nineteenth-century writers had articulated disdain for American racism and emphasized the negative impact that racial slavery and the extermination of Native Americans had on U.S. civilization.[104] Thus, while Soviet antiracism reflected the state's identification of the United States as the most advanced capitalist society and, hence, a bitter adversary of the Soviet Union, it must also be viewed within the context of a longer Russian tradition of insistence on the inferiority of Western values and culture.[105]

Since representing the USSR as a superior society and teaching inhabitants how to speak antiracism were its primary objectives, the Scottsboro protest did not continue in the Soviet Union until all the defendants were released from prison.[106] To the contrary, after the U.S. Supreme Court issued its aforementioned monumental legal decision in November 1932 and ordered a new trial for the Scottsboro defendants, the protest resolutions, rallies, poems, essays, and cartoons expressing solidarity with the African American prisoners disappeared from the central press and MOPR literature and records.[107]

The Japanese occupation of Manchuria and the Nazis' assumption of power in January 1933 played a major role in the dissipation of the Scottsboro campaign in the USSR after 1932. "Suddenly threatened on two sides," as Norman Saul puts it, Soviet leaders were anxious to establish diplomatic relations with the United States, which the election of Franklin D. Roosevelt to the U.S. presidency in November 1932 made a distinct possibility.[108] Soviet authorities assumed correctly that propaganda would be one of the new president's primary points of contention, and in November 1933, rapprochement was achieved.[109] By no means a coincidence, throughout 1932 the most intense condemnation of the Scottsboro death sentence in the Soviet press had coexisted with articles alleging collusion between American and Japanese imperialists against the USSR.[110]

Cultivating the image that Soviet citizens had united en masse to condemn the persecution of African Americans, and by implication, U.S. preparations for an imperialist war against the USSR, was beneficial to the Soviet state as long as diplomatic relations with the United States seemed distant.[111] Once they seemed imminent, however, it became a potential detriment. Paradoxically, then, it was the perceived threat of war that encouraged MOPR to represent Soviet citizens as unified in demanding justice for their African American allies, and which prompted them to withdraw it roughly two years later.[112]

African American Architects of
Soviet Antiracism and the
Challenge of *Black and White*

African Americans, as the preceding chapters have alluded to, were
indispensable to Soviet officials' and citizens' efforts to speak antiracism. This chapter closely examines the various ways and venues in
which American blacks themselves spoke Soviet antiracism. In the
process it further decenters the production of Soviet antiracism, illuminating how African Americans of a wide array of political backgrounds were integral to creating and disseminating the USSR's image
as a society where racism was absent. As will be shown, espousing the
master narrative of Soviet antiracism did not preclude African Americans from articulating an anti-Communist perspective, from publicly
criticizing Soviet leaders for opportunism, or from privately expressing discontent. While it served as a means for authorities in Moscow to
celebrate the Soviet Union's alleged moral superiority, African Americans across the political spectrum contributed to Soviet antiracism to
advance the cause of black freedom—however they defined it.

The *Liberator* and the *Negro Worker* were publications (founded in
1930 and 1931) in which African American Communists routinely
spoke Soviet antiracism. The *Liberator* was headquartered in Harlem
and constituted the organ of the League of Struggle for Negro Rights
(LSNR), which in 1930 replaced the nearly defunct American Negro
Labor Congress (ANLC). Despite attempts in late 1931 to extend its
circulation beyond the United States, African Americans were its primary subjects and readers.[1] The *Negro Worker* was the organ of the
ITUCNW, a subsidiary of the Profintern mentioned in chapter 2, and

was originally based in Hamburg, Germany.[2] Its subject matter and intended audience was designed to include blacks in the United States, Africa, and other parts of the diaspora (especially the West Indies). As products of the militant Third Period's heightened interest in black workers, the *Liberator* and *Negro Worker* were the most vibrant and were printed consistently in the early 1930s; by the second half of the decade they ceased publication. While it is unsurprising that these two Communist periodicals represented the USSR as a raceless society, this chapter uses the person of George Padmore, the preeminent pan-African leader who was the ITUCNW's secretary and the *Negro Worker*'s second editor (from 1931 to 1933), to argue that many blacks with experience living in America's racialized society—independent of political affiliation—shared this objective.

The ill-fated 1932 Mezhrabpom film *Black and White* provides particular insight into how and why African Americans spoke Soviet antiracism. On June 26, 1932, twenty-one African Americans, most of whom were nonactors and none of whom were members of the U.S. Communist Party, arrived in Moscow to begin production on *Black and White*. *Black and White* was supposed to expose the systematic racial discrimination against African American workers and place it in a historical context of racial bondage. As the *New York Times* reported in June 1932, the film also promised to represent black life truthfully, without the "sentimentality and buffoonery" that marked most cinematic representations of African Americans.[3] *Black and White* would have constituted the third main component in the triumvirate of hard-line Soviet antiracism that included the Stalingrad trial and the Scottsboro protest (which was then in its second year). But due precisely to the film's intended directness in attacking the U.S. racial regime, Soviet leaders abandoned the project in August 1932. Instead of substantially bolstering representations of Soviet intolerance of racism, *Black and White*'s cancellation threatened to dismantle them. Disaster was averted, however, when the majority of the African American cast members publicly affirmed as sincere the Soviet commitment to antiracism while privately articulating their grievances to authorities in Moscow.

An unorthodox, yet critical site for the production of the Soviet Union's antiracist image in the 1930s was the African American "bourgeois" (non-Communist) press. Similar to the *Negro Worker* and *Liberator*, publications like the *Chicago Defender*, *Afro-American*, and *The Crisis* printed articles, photographs, and testimonials of African Americans that buttressed Soviet claims to have "solved racial and national problems." Though Communist or Communist-affiliated organizations did not commission these periodicals, and in fact, officials in Moscow generally disdained them, the visual and discursive images that they disseminated of blacks' inclusion in the USSR constitute important artifacts of the public transcript of Soviet antiracism.[4] Since they had a substantially wider circulation than the more obscure Communist organs like the *Negro Worker* and *Liberator*, black "bourgeois" publications no doubt were the primary arena in which most African Americans became acquainted with the promise of Soviet racial equality.

Photographs were the most obvious way that the *Negro Worker* and the *Liberator* represented the USSR as a society without racism. Standard were white and black children smiling together gleefully, and Soviet national minorities, dressed in distinctly "ethnic" garb, holding political office. Captions and headlines typically read: "In the only country where all races are equal," "Youth in Russia. Where Blacks and Whites are Equals," and "To Hell with American Race Prejudice!"[5] Both periodicals affirmed African Americans' status as the revolutionary vanguard by reporting on their role in Soviet society as teachers, workers, agricultural experts, and political figures. Among them were the eleven African American scientists who were organized by Oliver Golden, an African American Communist and former KUTV student, with the help of George Washington Carver. The group arrived in the USSR in 1931 to assist in the development of the cotton industry.[6]

The *Liberator* encouraged its African American readers to pursue the employment opportunities available in the Soviet Union, and organized competitions that awarded the worker who gained the most newspaper subscriptions with a trip there. Editors attempted to entice potential migrants and contestants by stressing that the "workers' government of the Soviet Union is the only government in the world that will not tolerate Jim Crowism, discrimination or lynching."[7] As evidence that a black man has the possibility "for development unrestrained by the pressure of national prejudices and discrimination from which he suffers in America," the paper cited the expulsion of Robinson's white American assailants.[8] The memory of the Stalingrad trial, as the *Liberator*'s competition and recruitment notices suggest, was frequently invoked in black Communist publications. Even Edward Wilson, in his classic 1974 study, *Russia and Black Africa*, mentioned the numerous references to "the Stalingrad incident" in the *Negro Worker*.[9]

Among the various artifacts of the Stalingrad campaign that the periodicals reproduced was the "brotherly unity" photograph which, as discussed in chapter 2, showed James Ford with his arms around a group of Elektrozavod workers. Originally published on *Trud*'s front page in August 1930, the *Negro Worker* reprinted it six months later in February 1931, while the *Liberator* reproduced the photograph more than two years later, in November 1932. In the *Negro Worker*, the image accompanied the resolution that black delegates to the Fifth Profintern Congress had issued condemning the racially motivated assault. Opposite the photograph, a cartoon promised that interracial unity among male workers—like that shown in the photograph—would overthrow capitalism (imaged as the standard fat white man) and eliminate chauvinism. Readers were encouraged to "DO IT NOW."[10] In the *Liberator*, the "brotherly unity" image complemented an article titled "How Soviet Russia Freed the National Minorities." A caption inaccurately identified the white men with Ford as automobile factory workers.[11] Similar to the U.S. lynching photographs in the Soviet press, accuracy and the lapse of time between when the photograph was taken and when it appeared in these periodicals was immaterial. What was most significant is that each time it was printed, the photograph reenacted African American men's inclusion as "brothers" in the Soviet body politic. It also reinforced one of the major messages of the *Liberator* and *Negro Worker*: class-conscious whites, epitomized by inhabitants of the Soviet Union, could be color blind and thereby trusted.

To be sure, African American visitors to the USSR testified that the bonds of trust and friendship that they forged with Soviet citizens were so strong that they considered the Soviet Union their true homeland. To illustrate, in a 1935 article in the *Negro Worker* Margaret Glascow, an African American hair stylist, declared that in the USSR, "I am Among My Own People in My Own Country." Glascow, who moved to Moscow in 1934 and worked in an automobile factory, claimed that "from force of habit I thought that I would meet with a hostile attitude among the white people here. . . . 'Comrade,' that was the first word I heard. . . . I have quite forgotten that I am black. I feel that I am a person like everybody else."[12] As evidenced in the Glascow article, blacks' articulation of mistrust of whites, albeit within certain parameters, was deemed acceptable and justified. Persons of African descent were not expected, in other words, to automatically trust white people of any country given their experiences with centuries of enslavement and oppression in the United States and throughout the African diaspora. Rather, white people needed to emulate Soviet citizens and prove themselves worthy of blacks' trust.

The *Liberator* consolidated Soviet citizens' image as exemplary whites by publishing letters in which Soviet workers and children expressed interest in the plight of African Americans and especially the Scottsboro prisoners.[13] Though the *Negro Worker* also reported on the Soviet Scottsboro campaign, its coverage never equaled that of the *Liberator*. Arguably, since the latter's audience was overwhelmingly African Americans who lived in a white majority society (unlike blacks in the colonies of Western Europe), where many white Americans sanctioned the Scottsboro defendants' execution, representing Soviet citizens as outraged assumed a greater priority.

As the above examples confirm, an obvious objective of the *Liberator* and *Negro Worker* was to sell Communism as the solution for blacks' problems by representing the Soviet Union as a society that had discovered the cure for racism.[14] While acknowledging the propagandistic function of the two Communist publications, it is important not to devalue their significance in the first half of the 1930s. On the most basic level, the notions of black equality implicit in the circulation of these periodicals, and made explicit in their content, threatened to upset the white supremacist principles upon which Western societies rested. British and French officials' concerted efforts to disrupt the *Negro Worker*'s dissemination underscore this point.[15] As Edward Wilson argues, their actions serve as a reminder that the "revolutionary ideas in the *Negro Worker* held the real promise of radicalizing indigenous political attitudes in Africa."[16] Hence, despite their clear propagandistic purpose, Western government leaders did not disregard as harmless the *Liberator* and *Negro Worker*. To put it differently, as distant as the image of Soviet racial equality found in these journals may have been from reality, it nevertheless threatened to disrupt the status quo that naturalized white over black.

Of equal significance, the *Liberator* and *Negro Worker* were not simply "creatures of Soviet intentions" which expressed only the agenda of officials in Moscow.[17] Rather, as several scholars have shown, their editors exercised a relative degree of autonomy and published material that was seemingly antithetical to their Communist affiliation. Robin D. G. Kelley, for instance, explores the black nationalist discourse printed in the *Liberator* (especially under the editorial direction of Cyril Briggs from 1930 through early 1933) in spite of the emphasis on interracial internationalism and injunctions against bourgeois nationalism.[18] Brent Hayes Edwards likewise stresses the *Negro Worker*'s role as a vehicle for politically educating workers throughout Africa and the diaspora. Edwards argues that when George Padmore edited the journal in the early 1930s, he dedicated substantial attention to contemporary African politics and quotidian problems that workers of African descent confronted around the world.[19] Yet black nationalist and Pan-African themes were not the only authentic expressions of the editors' personal interests. As the career of George Padmore reveals, advancing the Soviet Union's image as a raceless society was an objective that officials in Moscow and national Communists likely had in common.

Padmore's rapid rise in the ranks of international Communism between 1929 and 1933, in which he became the Comintern's leading "expert on race and imperialism," mirrored the ascendancy of the militant Third Period with its heightened interest in black workers, and elevation of Soviet antiracism to a hard-line policy.[20] Indeed, Pad-more was a simultaneous product and producer of hard-line antira-cism. As alluded to in the preceding chapters, during the years that Padmore lived in Moscow (between 1929 and 1931), he contributed substantially to the Soviet indictment of American racism, writing numerous articles on African American oppression for various Soviet publications. As the head of the Negro Bureau of the Profintern, he had an office in the Kremlin, was afforded a prominent place atop Lenin's mausoleum, and was "elected" deputy to the Moscow City Soviet. Years later Padmore supposedly told C. L. R. James, his close friend and associate, that he was never given any responsibilities as a deputy. Rather, the purpose of his "fictive election," he claimed, was to shame George Bernard Shaw, who visited Moscow shortly thereafter, into addressing why the British Parliament had no black representa-tives given England's vast colonial holdings.[21] Apart from this sym-bolic position, as secretary of the ITUCNW Padmore helped organize the first and only international trade union congress of black workers in Hamburg, Germany, in July 1930, and, as previously noted, served as the second editor of the *Negro Worker*.

According to James, Padmore was astutely aware of his own pro-pagandistic value and usefulness to Soviet leaders. He insisted that Padmore allowed officials to use him as a trophy of Soviet racial enlightenment (even though he never believed in Stalin's brand of socialism) because the USSR provided him (at that time) the most space to advance his anticolonial agenda.[22] Yet Padmore's actions as the *Negro Worker*'s editor and then as a leading advocate of Pan-Afri-canism and anti-Communism, suggest that he may have also lent his assistance to forging the Soviet Union's antiracist image because he believed that that image was valuable to the black liberation struggle. Two letters that Padmore sent to Robert Robinson at the Stalingrad Tractor Factory in 1932, as the *Negro Worker*'s editor, bear out this point. Padmore requested that Robinson write an article for the jour-nal about his experiences in the USSR, which would include photo-graphs. He emphasized how important Robinson's image was to black workers around the world, whose only source of information about the Soviet Union was the bourgeois press. Black laborers, especially in Africa and the West Indies, wanted to hear from him, since Robinson, Padmore stressed, constituted "most convincing proof of the fact that any honest worker, whatever his nationality, race, etc. is welcome in the Soviet Union to participate in the great task of carrying out the Five-Year Plan." He argued that it would be a travesty if the (largely white) readers of the *Workers News* and *Moscow News*—to which Robinson had contributed stories—were alone exposed to his story.[23] Padmore's letters indicate that he considered it important for blacks throughout the diaspora to be exposed to the images of black achievement and equality in Soviet society (even if it was motivated by opportunism) that Robinson's experiences encapsulated.

Padmore's interest in popularizing the Soviet Union's antiracist image—irrespective of Moscow's wishes—becomes more evident after his acrimonious split with the Comintern in 1934. The Nazis' assumption of power in January 1933 forced the relocation of the *Negro Worker*'s headquarters from Hamburg to Copenhagen (and eventually to Brussels, Harlem, and Paris), and Padmore was arrested, prompting him to flee to London.[24] In the late summer of 1933 (roughly a year after sending the above letters to Robinson), Padmore resigned from his positions as the *Negro Worker*'s editor and ITUCNW's secretary. Having heard rumblings about Moscow's plans to dissolve the organization and suspend the journal's publication, Padmore accused Comintern authorities of abandoning the cause of black workers in an attempt to appease Western imperialists with whom they sought to forge an antifascist alliance. Even if, as some scholars argue, such an alliance was in the (long-term) best interest of anticolonial movements, Padmore refused to tolerate any vacillation in Moscow's commitment to revolution in the colonies.[25] His irreparable spilt with Communism became official in February 1934; Comintern leaders expelled Padmore from the organization, denouncing him as a bourgeois nationalist who had blasphemously emphasized race to the detriment of class. They also accused him of betraying black workers on a more personal level by disclosing to French police the identities of black sailors involved in revolutionary activity.[26]

In light of this rancorous split, one would assume that Soviet leaders had lost one of the most critical architects of, and contributors to, Soviet antiracism. However, throughout his subsequent career as one of the most prominent leaders of Pan-Africanism and outspoken critics of Communism and Soviet opportunism, Padmore continued to speak Soviet antiracism. For example, in September 1941, Padmore published an article in *Left* identifying Soviet racial equality as one of the major reasons that British workers and inhabitants of the colonies should defend the USSR from the Nazi invasion. Padmore acknowledged the country's limitations in terms of democracy but emphasized its multiethnic federated structure and the representatives of "dozens of races" who comprised the government. He claimed that "in the Soviet Union, colour-bar (rampant in Britain) and racial segregation, widespread throughout the Empire have no place. I have visited most European countries and America, and I have never come across people more sympathetic to coloured races than the Soviet people." Consistent with the master narrative of Soviet antiracism, Padmore cited the Stalingrad trial as evidence of the USSR's intolerance of racism. Contrary to what he allegedly told C. L. R. James, Padmore explained that because he was a deputy of the Moscow City Soviet at the time of the attack on Robinson, Soviet authorities had asked him to investigate it. As a result of Russian workers' indignation, Robinson's assailants were immediately expelled from the Soviet Union—a situation that Padmore averred was unheard of in "'democratic'" Britain. It was this country, whose white inhabitants were most sympathetic to the "coloured races," Padmore admonished, that Hitler sought to subordinate to his "'master'" race.[27]

Over a decade later, with the threat of fascist annihilation of the Soviet Union no longer an issue, the Pan-African leader nonetheless continued to testify to the racial enlightenment of the USSR's inhabitants and leaders, notwithstanding its myriad problems. Specifically, in his 1955 book *Pan-Africanism or Communism*, Padmore insisted that "Communist power politics apart, the Russian people are undoubtedly the least colour-conscious white folk in the world." He posited that inhabitants of Soviet Central Asia "enjoy absolute racial equality with those of Slav descent" and only experienced persecution for political errors but never as a consequence of their "race." Padmore continued: "No doubt, it is this absence of racial intolerance that influenced Mr. Paul Robeson, the internationally-known singer and actor, to have his only son educated in the Soviet Union; for the great artist has himself been the victim of racial snobbery in his own country and Britain. In this respect, I can myself endorse Mr. Robeson's admiration for the Soviet regime."

To further justify his position, Padmore again invoked the memory—with its own inaccuracies—of the Stalingrad trial. He recalled that "in 1930, while I served as a deputy on the Moscow Soviet, the authorities ordered the deportation of two white American engineers employed on the Five Year Plan who objected to eating in the same factory restaurant with an American Negro engineer named Robinson. The Soviet leaders, whatever may be said against them, treat any manifestation of racial chauvinism with great severity." Padmore highlighted Soviet citizens' adoration of Aleksandr Pushkin, the Russian poet of African ancestry, as additional proof of the absence of racial prejudice in the USSR. He likewise contended that "Soviet film and plays, unlike in the West, never treat the Negro race with ridicule and contempt. This sympathy for the blacks is reflected in all levels of Russian society." Padmore condemned the racism of white American and British Communists for extinguishing "much of the Negro's instinctive sympathy for Russia, which, with all its imperfections, has suppressed all forms of racial distinctions and colour bars within its borders."[28]

Padmore's loyalty to Soviet antiracism, which included a frequent invocation of the Stalingrad trial, is compelling. At the very least, it indicates that the consistent presence of the Stalingrad incident in the *Negro Worker* in the early 1930s, which Wilson termed "a curious device," was as much the result of Padmore's editorial influence as it was of the dictates of Moscow. Clearly, the Pan-African leader did not see his articulation of Soviet antiracism as incongruent with his rejection of Marxism-Leninism as the "'solution to all the complex racial, tribal, and socio-economic problems facing Africa.'"[29] To the contrary, he may have seen it as an effective means of retaining a modicum of autonomy in his alliance with the same U.S. and British leaders who he had condemned Soviet authorities for trying to align with in 1933.

Manning Marable argues that Padmore directed his harsh anti-Communist rhetoric at British and especially U.S. officials (rather than African workers) because he wanted them to lend economic assistance to Africa on the level of the Marshall Plan.[30] Padmore may have also intended his espousal of Soviet antiracism for British and American officials. While he openly condemned white American and British Communists for their opportunism, Padmore's allegiance to the Soviet Union's antiracist image allowed him to indict and challenge the British and American *anti*-Communists with whom he was working. That is to say, by speaking Soviet antiracism, Padmore pursued the financial benefits for Africa that accompanied colluding with leaders of the Free World, while simultaneously criticizing and challenging these leaders—albeit indirectly—to correct their hypocritical racist politics. His comments in *Pan-Africanism and Communism* about the supposed absence of racialized, degrading images of blacks in Soviet culture seem particularly directed at his bourgeois democratic partners. He must have been aware of the protests that African American Communists had raised to Soviet leaders as early as 1924 regarding the offensive depictions of persons of African descent in Soviet plays, books, and advertisements.[31] These remarks therefore undoubtedly reflect Padmore's desire to effect positive changes in the dominant depiction of blacks in Western capitalist societies.

In the end, Padmore's struggle for black freedom remained inseparable from the image of Soviet racial equality, which since 1929 he had been instrumental in constructing. His experiences as a Pan-African leader and avowed anti-Communist who chose to speak Soviet antiracism sheds light on the stance that African Americans who firmly opposed Communism assumed throughout the 1930s. To this point, the ugly split between Padmore and the Communist International was not the first instance in the early 1930s that Soviet leaders' support of black workers was attacked as opportunism. And yet, as will be elaborated in the following two sections, due to the actions of Afri-

7. The *Black and White* cast, June 17, 1932. Langston Hughes Papers, 1862–1980, Beinecke Rare Book and Manuscript Library. Reprinted by permission of Harold Ober Associates Incorporated.

can Americans who were not taking orders from Moscow, the Soviet Union's image as a society without racism weathered these challenges and persisted in its indictment of America's racialized society.

The *Black and White* film project attracted the interest of a diverse group of twenty-two predominantly nonactors from across the United States who were willing and able to pay for their travel expenses to New York and then to the USSR. They had been recruited in the spring 1932 by Louise Thompson, a young Harlem activist, who at the urging of James Ford organized the Cooperating Committee for the Production of a Soviet Film on Negro Life, an interracial, multipolitical group that sponsored the *Black and White* cast's journey to the Soviet Union.[32] Involvement in *Black and White* provided participants the opportunity to explore the land that claimed to have eliminated racial and national inequality and to participate in what promised to be a landmark film in terms of its condemnation of U.S. racism and dignified depiction of African Americans. Also, the four-month contracts that this group of college students, social and postal workers, and writers and journalists signed in Moscow afforded them salaries unavailable to most African Americans in interwar America. The group's only white member, Alan McKenzie, a salesman, appears to be the only member of the U.S. Communist Party in 1932. Langston Hughes, the highly acclaimed writer and the group's highest-profile figure, was supposed to serve as a consultant on the film's screenplay and write its English-language dialogue.[33]

Yet roughly five weeks after the *Black and White* cast arrived in the USSR in June 1932, the film was cancelled. The Soviet archives have confirmed that Col. Hugh L. Cooper, an American engineer and businessman who was instrumental in the construction of the Dnieprostroi dam, played a leading role in making sure the film was never made. In late July 1932 Lazar Kaganovich and Viacheslav Molotov informed Stalin that Cooper had visited them and spent an hour emphasizing that the travel of over twenty African Americans to the Soviet Union to make a film about U.S. racism posed a serious obstacle to establishing diplomatic relations with the United States.[34] Cooper had threatened that if the film was made, then he would immediately withdraw his assistance from the construction of the dam and cease acting as an advocate of rapprochement.[35] Shortly after relaying Cooper's message, Kaganovich sent a note to Stalin in which he advised that the film was "unnecessary" and that the Central Committee had not even approved its production. A few weeks later, on August 22, the Politburo voted to cancel the film based on the present circumstances, advising against the release of any formal announcement.[36]

Newspapers in the United States and Europe, however, had already reported almost two weeks earlier, on August 9, that the film had been cancelled. The reports accurately attributed the decision to Soviet leaders' desire to avoid jeopardizing rapprochement with the United States, and specifically, to their interest in strengthening the USSR's position in the Far East against Japan.[37] Editors of the mainstream American press celebrated the abandonment of *Black and White* as evidence that the Soviet indictment of U.S. racism could be compromised to Great Power politics. Comintern officials denied these reports and insisted that the film had merely been postponed for technical reasons and would be made the following summer.[38]

While political maneuvering sealed its fate, to state that production of *Black and White* had been cancelled is misleading. In the five weeks that the cast had been in Moscow, production on the film had not begun. Dissension among Mezhrabpom officials rather than the political exigencies of the Soviet state was the reason for the inactivity. Mezhrabpom (Mezhdunarodnaia organizatsiia rabochei pomoshchi, or International Workers' Aid) was the only major semiprivate film studio in the USSR during the first half of the 1930s.[39] Its leaders demanded that the *Black and White* cast arrive in Moscow by July 1, even though they had yet to secure additional actors or construct the sets. Especially egregious, they had failed to reach a consensus on the script and the ability of the German director, Carl Junghans, to make the film.[40]

The disputes concerning Junghans and the film's script, of which there were at least two versions, were interrelated. The first script was written by Georgii Grebner, a professional Russian scenarist, and Lovett Fort-Whiteman.[41] By the time Fort-Whiteman completed translating the Grebner script into English, the *Black and White* cast had already been in Moscow two weeks. After reading it, Hughes declared the script implausible and unsalvageable, a verdict that offended Fort-Whiteman. Emblematic of its implausibility, one scene featured the son of a wealthy industrialist inviting a black female servant to dance during a dinner party at the home of an Alabama factory owner, a scenario that apparently was consistent with Fort-Whiteman's fantastical short stories.[42]

According to Glenda Gilmore, a second script, whose primary author was Junghans, more accurately depicted black life in the U.S. South due largely to the input of Hughes and perhaps others. Yet it was too short and "stilted."[43] Of equal importance, the Junghans script did not have the support of the company's Russian officials, even though a few Soviet directors, whose advice they had sought, also favored it. In fact, these Russian authorities had no use for Junghans altogether. Langston Hughes claimed that only Otto Katz, Mezhrab-pom's production manager (originally director of the company's German division), and the Italian Francesco Misiano, head of the Moscow studio, believed Junghans was capable of making the film.[44]

Junghans, who reportedly spoke very poor English and Russian, had never visited the United States and had neither firsthand experience with nor knowledge of life among African Americans. He had been selected as *Black and White*'s director simply because he had worked with Africans when directing another film (*Strange Birds of Africa*).[45] Embittered by *Black and White*'s cancellation, Junghans told cast members that Mezhrabpom officials did not "understand Negroes" (which he did), that they believed in blacks' racial inferiority, and were divided by a left contingent that wanted the film to include a "little propaganda" and a right that emphasized artistic expression.[46] Significantly, this was not the first time that dissension among Mezhrabpom authorities impeded the efforts of a German director to make a film in the Soviet Union. The previous summer, a similar division that pitted Katz and Misiano against the company's Russian officials had prevented the production of Hans Richter's *Metal*.[47] Thus, irrespective of the political climate, given Mezhrabpom's internal politics and its then recent history, it seems unlikely that *Black and White* would have been made.

Notwithstanding the various factors that conspired against the film's production, political machinations ultimately determined its fate, making *Black and White* the gravest threat to the USSR's antiracist image prior to the 1939 Nazi-Soviet Pact. But of the twenty-one African American cast members of *Black and White*, only four confirmed the reports of the non-Communist Western press accusing Soviet leaders of opportunism. Henry Lee Moon, Theodore Poston, Thurston McNairy Lewis, and Laurence Alberga constituted the four public detractors.[48] In an official statement dated August 22, 1932, they rejected as "unsound, insufficient, and insulting to our intelligence the reasons offered by Meschrabpom Film Corporation for the cancellation of the 'Black and White' film project." Alluding to Cooper's role, they insisted that the film's cancellation constituted a concession to the "racial prejudice of American Capitalism and World Imperialism." They accused Mezhrabpom and its supporters of "base betrayal of the Negro workers of America and the International Proletariat" and of sabotaging the "Revolution."[49] In another statement that Moon and Poston sent from Berlin weeks later, they reiterated that "'once again the forces of American race prejudice have triumphed, and this time in a land where it would be least expected—the Union of Soviet Socialist Republics.'"[50]

What is particularly striking about the statements of the four public dissenters is that they used the language of Soviet antiracism to voice their protest.[51] That is to say, while they may have intended to mock the rhetoric of Soviet leaders, the four cast members validated the existence of Soviet antiracism. By accusing officials in Moscow of allowing "the forces of American race prejudice" to triumph "in a land where it would be least expected," they invoked the Soviet Union's antiracist image and characterized authorities' conduct as racist and anti-Soviet. Hence, even as they sought to separate themselves from the Soviet worldview, they affirmed that it was the one by which world leaders ought to be judged.[52]

On the other hand, the majority of the *Black and White* cast members insisted that Soviet leaders had not compromised their antiracist principles, and they reiterated the Comintern line that the film had been postponed. In a collective public statement, the fourteen cast members also denied erroneous reports—most likely the result of Colonel Cooper's misinformation—that they were stranded in Moscow without food, money, or way home. Such slanderous reports, they emphasized, "are readily utilized by the press" to arouse the distrust of white and black workers. They concluded by positing, "'We deeply regret these malicious and unfounded attacks upon people whose guests we have been and who are doing everything possible for our comfort and entertainment during our stay in the USSR.'"[53]

A few of the fourteen cast members also issued individual statements declaring as sincere the Soviet commitment to antiracism. For instance, Loren Miller, a future Los Angeles attorney, posited, "We have seen with our own eyes how this is the one country where all races and peoples are free, and where they have achieved real equality and self-government. This is a cardinal principle of Soviet life. The Soviet Union is the best friend of the Negro and of all oppressed peoples." Louise Thompson, who expressed similar sentiments, asserted that "we have been afforded opportunities here that, as Negroes and working people, would never have been open to us in any other country."[54] James Ford, who was then the Communist candidate for vice president of the United States, corroborated their testimony, citing both his personal experiences living in the Soviet Union and, of course, the Stalingrad trial of Robert Robinson's assailants.[55]

It is impossible to determine the reasons that four male cast members refused to speak Soviet antiracism while fourteen others, conversely, publicly defended as uncompromising Moscow's intolerance of racial prejudice. In addition to these eighteen, the three other black cast members, Leonard Hill, Katherine Jenkins, and her fiancé, George Sample, remained silent during the controversy, signing their name to neither group's statements. It would be easy to portray the majority of the cast members as the puppets of Soviet leaders, who were blinded by the equalities afforded them in the USSR and who loyally fulfilled Moscow's will. Viewed in this way, the public dissenters acted heroically, "unblindly" holding Soviet leaders accountable to the antiracist code of conduct that they espoused, and condemning their acquiescence to U.S. "race hate." The reality of the situation was, however, more complex.

Personal gain on some level arguably motivated the four public discontents. Moon, Poston, Lewis, and Alberga likely concluded that whatever personal advantage they could garner from the controversy outweighed any intangible political value that came with validating the image of Soviet intransigence to racism. The path that they chose promised to eradicate some of the stigma (among U.S. officials) that accompanied travel to the USSR and involvement in a film project to indict U.S. racism. It also entailed a more immediate tangible financial and professional incentive. Joy Carew discusses how upon returning to the United States Poston, Moon, and Lewis "sold their version of the story to the white and black press." She adds that the controversy allowed the two journalists, Poston and Moon—the most outspoken critics—to finally fulfill their dreams of appearing in the *New York Times*.[56]

W. A. Domingo, who chaired the Cooperating Committee for the Production of a Soviet Film on Negro Life, remarked in correspondence with Louise Thompson that he was "truthfully" unsurprised by Poston's decision to openly criticize Soviet leaders. Domingo elucidated that "what I saw of him at the meetings left me with the impression that he was not a very serious person and that he was given to frivolity and wise-cracking."[57] Thompson agreed with Domingo's assessment of Poston as lacking political savvy. She attributed the conduct of Poston and the others to the pernicious influence of Lovett Fort-Whiteman, whom she despised (much like her future husband, William Patterson, did). Thompson claimed that they had foolishly become embroiled "in the internal intrigues of a struggle over authorship" of the *Black and White* script at which Fort-Whiteman was at the center.[58]

The motivations behind the decision of fourteen cast members to reiterate the Comintern line on the film are equally complex. Mark Naison contends that they were somewhat relieved by the film's cancellation since most had traveled to the Soviet Union not for "the opportunity of artistic expression" but for the escape it provided from U.S. racism.[59] Several members of the group wanted to extend their stays in the USSR, and publicly criticizing Soviet leaders was obviously incongruent with these plans. Glenda Gilmore argues that their kindly treatment blinded them to the Soviet Union's faults and "discouraged them from questioning their hosts' motives for abandoning the film."[60] Yet the detailed grievances that the fourteen cast members presented to Comintern leaders regarding the film's cancellation and their treatment by Mezhrabpom officials suggest that they were more politically astute than these interpretations allow. Owing in part to their warm reception in Soviet society, it appears that they had concluded that making their discontent public was futile. Remaining publicly loyal to the master narrative of Soviet antiracism, in fact, allowed them to voice at length their complaints to Comintern leaders.

Anticipating his career as a prominent attorney, Loren Miller served as the group's spokesperson in meetings and correspondence with Comintern officials. Indicative of their incredulity that the film was postponed, Miller exclusively used the terms "abandonment" and "cancel" to articulate their grievances; he reserved use of the term "postpone" for public statements.[61] Among the documents he presented to Comintern leaders, a two-and-a-half page statement detailed the negative political repercussions that would result from *Black and White*'s nonproduction. Implicit in this tactic was the understanding that political reasons motivated the decision to "postpone" the film, and that alternate political reasons could alone persuade officials to follow through on its production. This interpretation is given further credence when considering that Miller, speaking on behalf of the majority of the cast, went to extensive lengths (in a separate two-page document titled "Reasons for Abandonment") to expose just how "insufficient" and "almost trivial" were "Meschrabpom's reasons for the abandonment of the film"; the implication here is that political pressure had necessarily played a role.[62] Miller also emphasized that cast members had, weeks earlier, raised their concerns to Comintern officials regarding Cooper's threats that *Black and White* would be cancelled because it jeopardized U.S. recognition. Miller reminded Comintern authorities that they had responded by reassuring the group that the "film would never be abandoned on that ground" and that "such a situation was impossible."[63]

Though the abandonment of *Black and White* served as the greatest source of the group's discontent, they also accused Mezhrabpom of mistreating them. The blatant disregard for the sacrifices that the cast members had made to arrive in the Soviet Union by Mezhrabpom's deadline of July 1, when the studio was not ready for them, was at the forefront of their disgruntlement. They also criticized Mezhrabpom officials for never providing them with a competent translator; promising numerous excursions, few of which materialized; sending them away from Moscow (to Odessa) "at the time of the greatest uncertainty about the film"; failing to inform the group's journalists about the film's cancellation first, so that they could issue a statement ahead of the bourgeois press; and dispatching a representative with whom they had no prior contact (Boris Babitskii, director of Mezhrabpom) to relay the news.[64]

An additional grievance that Miller presented to Comintern authorities on behalf of his thirteen fellow cast members warrants mention. They were insulted by Mezhrabpom's claim that their light skin tone and professional class status made them "inauthentic blacks," rendering it necessary to "postpone" the film's production. Several scholars have referenced Soviet authorities' dismay at the light complexions of the *Black and White* cast, comparing it to Comintern leaders' decision at the Fourth Congress in 1922 to anoint Claude McKay rather than the light-skinned Otto Huiswood as the figurehead of the organization's alliance with black workers. Yet the Mezhrabpom officials who lamented the absence of "real Negroes" among the group were not only Russians but also Germans, including Otto Katz and Carl Junghans. The United Press had even reported Junghans's dissatisfaction with the physical appearance of the African American cast who "turned out to be too light colored and intellectual for his purposes."[65] Such racial obtuseness may have been one of the few qualities that united the Russian, German, and Italian representatives of Mezhrabpom. Their response underscores the ignorance among Europeans of this era about persons of African descent, including those who ostensibly sought to dismantle racist images of blacks in film. With palpable exasperation, Langston Hughes remarked to Comintern authorities that Mezhrabpom should have been more specific regarding the "type" of African Americans they wanted when they sent their initial invitation.[66] But given Mezhrabpom officials' lack of knowledge about the history of African Americans, such a consideration was beyond the realm of possibility.

As the above discussion reveals, the decision to speak Soviet anti-racism did not mean that the fourteen *Black and White* cast members found life as "perfect" in the USSR as they publicly claimed. Although opportunism motivated the Soviet indictment of U.S. racism, leaders in Moscow no doubt hated the fact that international developments had placed them in a position whereby they felt compelled to capitulate to the demands of American businessmen.[67] The exposure of the Soviet Union's vulnerability arguably inspired most *Black and White* cast members to refrain from publicly condemning as opportunistic its leaders' opposition to white supremacy.

To be sure, this opportunism notwithstanding, Soviet antiracism translated into a level of freedom and equality for African Americans unavailable to them in the United States. Even Laurence Alberga, one of the four public dissenters, testified to this reality in a letter to W. A. Domingo. Alberga outlined his grievances regarding the film's cancellation but also emphasized that they had been "well received" in the Soviet Union and traveled throughout the country as "honored guests."[68] Dorothy West, a cast member who remained in Moscow for nearly a year after the film's cancellation, candidly discussed in letters to her mother the impact that this warm reception had on her disposition. In a letter dated November 1932, for example, West commented, "Hope you are as half as happy as I am. Nothing has happened. It's simply that life is very good right through here, and I haven't any worries." Several months later, in March 1933, West wrote, "I would never be so carefree again as I have ever been since I've been here."[69]

The "carefree" existence that many African Americans enjoyed in the USSR relative to their experiences in the United States was not lost on Colonel Cooper and the outraged U.S. businessmen for whom he spoke. When Cooper met with Molotov and Kaganovich "in a spirit of great indignation," he had also threatened the withdrawal of his assistance "'if those niggers are not sent out of Russia by the 10th of August.'"[70] As his threat indicates, the mere presence of the twenty-one African Americans in Moscow, who were lodged at the prestigious Grand Hotel—which, incidentally, Dorothy West described to her mother as "really a grand hotel"—had roused considerable discontent among white Americans in the Soviet capital.[71] In debriefings with U.S. consulate officials, one of these white American men remarked with disdain that upon his leaving Moscow in September 1932, these African Americans, who he overestimated as "about forty Negroes from the Harlem district," were still "having a good time playing around Moscow" despite Cooper's demands.[72] When considering that the white American enemies of racial equality deemed Soviet antiracism dangerous in spite of the "shameless" opportunism that motivated it, it becomes even clearer why most *Black and White* cast members—including the three who remained silent throughout the controversy—refrained from helping them attack it.

Due to the implicit threat that Soviet antiracism posed to the United States' racialized society, editors of the mainstream American press published Poston, Moon, Lewis, and Alberga's attacks on Soviet leaders and elided the voices of the fourteen black cast members who defended them. In light of these circumstances, it is unsurprising that African American editors adopted a more nuanced position on the *Black and White* controversy. Though most published editorials echoing Poston and Moon's cries of Soviet opportunism, at the same time they printed statements of the fourteen others.[73] To illustrate, *The Crisis*, the organ of the National Association for the Advancement of Colored People (NAACP), an organization that had an antagonistic relationship with the U.S. Communist Party, indicted Soviet authorities for failing to adequately explain *Black and White*'s nonproduction. The magazine also, however, printed an article by Louise Thompson in which she insisted that the film would be made in the summer of 1933, she differentiated Soviet leaders from Mezhrabpom officials, and she emphasized the "eager" efforts of the mainstream press "to discredit in the eyes of American Negroes the one country in the whole world which gives them complete equality."[74]

Of course, contrary to Thompson's public assertions, the summer of 1933 passed without the production of *Black and White*. Despite this confirmation that Soviet leaders had bowed to "American race hate," the African American press continued to publish, in the years that followed, articles and photographs that represented the Soviet Union as "the one country in the whole world which gives" as Thompson put it, "complete equality" to American blacks. While the Communist press served a similar function, as W. A. Domingo remarked in a letter to Thompson, "no one reads the *Daily Worker*," black or white.[75] The complete discrediting of the Soviet Union's antiracist image which could have resulted from the cancellation of *Black and White* was thus averted thanks largely to the black bourgeois press. Similar to George Padmore, many African American editors did not see their rejection of Communism and disdain for Soviet opportunism as incongruent with propagating the image of Soviet racial equality. As larger numbers of African Americans traveled to the USSR in the 1930s, the black press provided them with a venue to speak Soviet antiracism.[76]

Among the personal testimonials of Soviet racelessness that appeared in the African American press of the mid-1930s, Langston Hughes wrote the most poignant piece, titled "Going South in Russia." Published in *The Crisis* in June 1934, the essay reveals how Hughes and other African Americans viewed Soviet society through the lens of U.S. racism.[77] Hughes, who toured Soviet Central Asia for several months, described how his travels aboard the Moscow-Tashkent Express allowed him to think as he had when he was a child, before U.S. racial proscriptions conditioned him to act like an inferior member of society.[78] Since he was accustomed to having the U.S. conductor order him to the last car when the train reached Washington DC, Hughes expected to receive a similar command as the Soviet train moved south farther away from Moscow. Since Jim Crow was not universal, he never received such an order. Instead, Hughes ate hot meals in the dining car and reclined leisurely in the sleeping compartment—two areas forbidden to blacks on American trains. As he wrote, "I am riding South from Moscow and am not Jim-Crowed, and none of the darker people on the train with me are Jim Crowed." Hughes conveyed his surprise that a nonwhite man in the front car was the mayor of Bukhara—even though he was "almost brown as I." Anticipating the retort that this "brown" passenger owed his position to racial tokenism, Hughes stressed that it would be impossible for a man of his color to become mayor of any Mississippi town even if it was just symbolic. Acknowledging the train's shortcomings in terms of Western standards of comfort, Hughes asserted that "racial freedom was sweeter than the lack of it" and "dirt without Jim Crow was bad—but dirt with Jim Crow for me, would have been infinitely worse."[79]

In addition to powerful testimonials like Hughes's, the most consistent site of Soviet antiracist expression in the African American press of the 1930s was the columns of Homer Smith. Smith had traveled to Moscow in June 1932 as a member of the *Black and White* cast and was one of the three men who pursued full-time employment there. He, like most other cast members, was not an actor. Smith had graduated from the University of Minnesota's school of journalism but worked as a U.S. postal clerk because of the lack of opportunities available to black journalists. Due to his experiences in the U.S. Postal Service, Smith gained a high-ranking position as a consultant and inspector for the Commissariat of Posts and Telegraphs in Moscow.[80] After spending three years helping to reorganize the Soviet postal service, Smith became a full-time news correspondent for the African American press, often writing under the pen name of "Chatwood Hall" in periodicals that included the *Chicago Defender*, *The Crisis*, and the *Afro-American*, the black newspaper most sympathetic to Communism.[81]

The "Column from Moscow" that Smith published weekly in the *Chicago Defender* in December 1934 demonstrates how the African American press expanded the bounds of acceptable Soviet antiracist discourse. For example, Smith did not attribute Soviet citizens' racial enlightenment to their "class consciousness." Rather, they treated blacks as equals because, unlike the white inhabitants of "Christian" America, they practiced the Ten Commandments on a daily basis. For this reason, Smith claimed, "non-Christian" Communist Russia was the most "Christian country" in the world. He reported that Soviet citizens used the materials from the destruction of churches to help those in need and assigned greater significance to the date in the Scottsboro case ("set by a 'Christian' judge, in a 'Christian' state, in a 'Christian' country for the execution of two innocent boys, Patterson and Norris") than the Christmas holiday.[82]

Smith also encouraged African American readers to identify with Soviet citizens by reminding them that most white Americans and Europeans defined Russians as falling outside the bounds of whiteness. He condemned a white American visitor to the USSR who in his "Nordic conceit" disparaged Russians as inferior or "Asiatic." Smith emphasized that the cornerstones of modern civilization emerged from the supposedly inferior "East," including science, religion, and the very same printing process that allowed the racist white American to express his ignorant views in the *San Francisco Chronicle*. Smith insisted that the putative enlightened West had a lot to learn from the East, which had also produced the first society (i.e., the USSR) to eradicate social, economic, and political inequality.[83] At a time when leaders in Moscow were representing Soviet culture as progressive and unmistakably European, Smith connected the culture's progressiveness to its Eastern or Asian roots.[84]

Certainly, editors of the African American press were not seeking to sell Communism as the solution to blacks' problems by publishing articles like Smith's praising the superior racial consciousness of Soviet citizens. This was not even an objective of the *Afro-American*. Although its editors, Carl Murphy and William N. Jones, often treated Communism favorably, they never offered an uncritical endorsement.[85] What then were editors seeking to accomplish? On the most basic level, representations of the Soviet Union as a raceless society demonstrated that racial prejudice was not universal and that systems of racial inequality could be eradicated rapidly in a few decades rather than gradually over the course of a century.[86] Stories testifying to the inclusion of African Americans in Soviet society therefore served as an inspiration for readers to continue the struggle for equality.[87]

Articles about African Americans' experiences in Soviet Russia were also intended to foster a sense of racial pride. The *Chicago Defender* and *Afro-American* highlighted Robert Robinson's election to the Moscow City Soviet in December 1934 ("U.S. Youth Is Soviet Leader") and discussed the numerous inventions he contributed to Soviet industry. The *Chicago Defender* hailed Homer Smith as "Another American Youth Making Good in Moscow," reporting in a feature article that Smith "is reputed to hold the highest government post of any foreigner in the Soviet Union."[88] The *New York Amsterdam News* introduced readers to "Mr. and Mrs. Joseph Roane," college graduates who moved to the Soviet Union in 1931 and, as the article's headline announced, "rave about Soviet jobs."[89] Though African American accomplishment in the USSR was largely framed in a masculinist discourse (in both the

Communist and non-Communist press), *The Crisis* extolled the success of "A Black Woman in Red Russia," Coretta Arle-Titz, who completed her musical education at the Moscow and Leningrad Conservatories, performed at the Bolshoi Theater for over ten years, and was honored on Soviet radio for her achievements.[90] *Opportunity*, the organ of the Urban League, likewise spotlighted the "highly valued" contributions of sixty-three-year-old Emma Harris (see chapter 3) to the construction of socialism in the USSR where she had become unaccustomed to "racial prejudice."[91]

As evidenced in the above examples, Soviet authorities were not the only ones who celebrated the achievements of Harris, Robinson, and other African Americans in the USSR. Beyond serving as a source of pride, their accomplishments disproved the pervasive theories of blacks' biological inferiority and underscored the need for serious structural changes in American society that would allow African Americans to excel. That is to say, editors of African American newspapers and magazines propagated the image of Soviet racial equality because of its potential to effect positive change for blacks in the United States.[92]

Yet the change desired was not a workers' revolution. Although they were ostensibly reporting on the first workers' state, class was infrequently mentioned while race assumed absolute precedence. Thus, the emphasis was on Soviet elections that were not a "white man's primary" rather than not a "bourgeois man's primary."[93] Concurrently, economic issues related to affordable housing, food, health care, and higher education were generally eschewed, with the exception of a few articles in the *Afro-American*.[94] Hence, somewhat paradoxically, the depictions of Soviet racelessness in the African American press affirmed its editors' commitment to the American capitalist ideals of property, profits, and rugged individualism.[95]

Indeed, they used the Soviet Union to envision capitalist America as a racially integrated society where the promise of U.S. democracy—of equal opportunity "without regard to color or race"—was realized.[96] Jim Crow did not inhibit the movement, thought, or aspirations of African Americans. Literary writers with African roots and "Negroid features" (like Aleksandr Pushkin) were lauded as national heroes.[97] African American men and women could freely pursue occupational goals, "rear children without prejudice," and fall in love and marry without the harassment of antimiscegenation laws or the lethal violence of lynch mobs.[98] Indeed, white people did not have license to physically attack, let alone lynch, African Americans, a reality that was confirmed in the trial of Robert Robinson's white assailants, to which even the conservative *Pittsburgh Courier* dedicated front-page coverage.[99] Overall, editors of the African American press perpetuated the Soviet Union's antiracist image as a means of seeking integration and full citizenship in U.S. society for African Americans.

Despite the different objectives that motivated contributors, expressions of Soviet antiracism often assumed a similar appearance. As demonstrated by the publication of two photographs, the front page of the *Chicago Defender* on January 26, 1935, could have been taken from any Soviet or Communist newspaper. The first photograph showed Robert Robinson surrounded by the Russian male workers who had elected him to the Moscow City Soviet, while the other depicted Paul Robeson with Sergei Eisenstein standing on his right side and the "famous cameraman" A. P. Tisse on his left. These displays of interracial brotherhood bore a striking resemblance to the photograph of James Ford and the Elektrozavod workers that first appeared on *Trud's* front page in 1930 and was later reprinted in the *Negro Worker* and *Liberator*. The *Chicago Defender's* message was clear: the USSR was a space where white men embraced African American males as men not only in the realm of culture and art but also in the spheres of technological innovation and politics. The degree to which this image of the first workers' state accurately represented Soviet reality was immaterial for the paper's editors; what was certain is that this was the American reality to which they aspired.

For this reason, as noted briefly above, the black bourgeois press, like its Communist counterpart, dedicated substantive attention to the deportation from the USSR of Robert Robinson's assailants in 1930. The constant threat of lynching that black men faced in the southern

United States, and the U.S. government's refusal to pass antilynching legislation, makes this coverage unsurprising. Editors were seeking, at the very least, to encourage U.S. leaders to engage in similar "shameless" opportunism, if it translated into a similar guarantee of bodily safety from the physical violence of white men.

In the mid-1930s, African Americans who were not members of the Communist Party, and African American publications that bore no affiliation with international Communism, served as the greatest conduits of and sites for Soviet antiracist expression. Homer Smith was most instrumental in effecting this paradox. While cancellation of the film *Black and White*, which originally brought Smith to the USSR, posed a serious challenge to the Soviet Union's image as a society where racism was absent, Soviet antiracism gained an indispensable ally in Smith, who played a critical role in redeeming it.

Smith's status as a foreign correspondent who provided black America with images of Soviet racial equality shielded him from much of the antiforeigner bias and suspicion that marked Soviet society during the second half of the 1930s. It also allowed him to avoid the pressure that other Americans in the USSR experienced to relinquish their U.S. citizenship. During the Second World War, Smith earned the distinction of becoming the first African American war correspondent. But in 1946 Smith accepted a position in the Ethiopian Press Service and left the USSR permanently; the wartime hopes that Soviet Russia would pursue a more democratic path had been quickly dispelled. The following year officials in the Ethiopian embassy managed to obtain an exit visa for Smith's Russian wife.[100] More than fifteen years later, when Smith wrote about his experiences in *Black Man in Red Russia* (borrowing from his *Crisis* article on Coretta Arle-Titz), he emphasized the absence of basic civil rights and the brutally repressive conditions under which Soviet citizens lived, particularly during the mass repression of the second half of the 1930s. However, his 1964 autobiography, like his columns of the mid-1930s, provided pages of testimony of the full human equality that African Americans—most of whom were men—experienced in the USSR. Smith, like other blacks who were instrumental contributors to Soviet antiracism in the 1930s, continued to espouse the practical humanizing benefits that it had on the lives and psychological well-being of black men.[101]

The cancellation of the *Black and White* film project in August 1932, along with George Padmore's expulsion from the Comintern in February 1934, signaled the ascendancy of antifascism as the primary concern of Soviet propaganda and Moscow's adoption of a much "softer" line on U.S. race hatred. The ITUCNW was not dissolved in 1933 and the *Negro Worker* continued publication under the editorship of Otto Huiswood until 1937, but neither, as scholars have argued, regained their vibrancy or significance of the early 1930s.[102] Moreover, a major film condemning U.S. racism, titled *Circus*, was ultimately made in 1936. However, as the epilogue demonstrates, it achieved this objective in a much more indirect, bizarre manner than had been intended with *Black and White*, and it represented Nazism as the main villain. To be sure, by the time of *Circus*'s production, Mezhrabpom had ceased to exist. After the *Black and White* fiasco, antifascist films became Mezhrabpom's overriding focus, and in 1935 Comintern leaders dissolved the company in favor of Popular Front organizations.[103]

While Nazi Germany became the overwhelming focus of Soviet propaganda by the mid-1930s, Soviet leaders refused to completely surrender the American race card. If the U.S. businessmen who comprised Moscow's American colony had had their way in 1932, then authorities in the Kremlin would have "entirely reversed" the "kindly treatment" afforded African Americans in the USSR.[104] Speaking Soviet antiracism—an enterprise in which a diverse number of African Americans engaged throughout the 1930s—served as a constant reminder that although the power that white American businessmen exercised was tremendous, it had its limits—that is, even they could not mold the world in their vision.

5   The Promises of Soviet Antiracism and the Integration of Moscow's International Lenin School

The year before twenty-one African Americans traveled to Moscow to make a film that would indict U.S. racism, the Soviet capital had been the site of a different sort of antiracist experiment. In September 1931 twelve African Americans enrolled in the International Lenin School (ILS), embarking on a unique experiment in American racial integration on Soviet soil. This pioneering group of black American integrationists was very different from the *Black and White* cast; they came from modest working-class backgrounds and had minimal primary education. They were all members of the U.S. Communist Party and all but one of them were men. As the grandsons of slaves and sons of sharecroppers, most had participated in the Great Migration of African Americans from the U.S. South to northern cities. Their humble origins notwithstanding, they were astutely aware of and ready to challenge Soviet leaders to "keep real" the promises of Soviet antiracism. As their experiences demonstrate, African American Communists in Moscow had a vested interest in speaking Soviet antiracism, which they did not perceive as simply a paternalistic, abstract discourse.

Certainly, the CPUSA was supposed to serve as a "working model of ethnic and racial integration" in interwar America, and it often organized interracial social events in places like segregated Chicago.[1] The white and black Americans enrolled in the Lenin School in the fall of 1931 faced a far greater challenge; they were required to coexist as equals in classrooms, dormitories, and cafeterias for an entire year. As Orlando Patterson argues, twentieth-century efforts at integration often led to greater conflict and misunderstanding, rather than reso-lution and unity, due to white and black Americans' previous lack of experience dealing intimately with each other.[2] The Lenin School, as will be shown, was no exception despite the institution's namesake.

While African Americans had entered its corridors before 1931, no more than two or three U.S. blacks had attended the Lenin School at one time. The absence of a meaningful African American presence may have continued had a group of African American students at KUTV, or Communist University of Toilers of the East, not decried the hypoc-risy of this "integration" in January 1930, accusing the Comintern of operating "white" and "nonwhite" universities. Since the mid-1920s, African Americans had primarily studied at KUTV together with stu-dents from Soviet Asia, colonial countries, and the Middle East, while white Americans and Europeans exclusively attended the more presti-gious Lenin School.[3] William Weinstone (William Randolph), the CPUSA representative to the Comintern, emphasized in a letter to the U.S. Secretariat that the justification for this de facto segregation, namely, the Lenin School's higher requirements defined in terms of Party and industrial experience was no longer viable.[4] The recent groups of white Americans that the CPUSA had sent to the Lenin School had not even met its political prerequisites, thereby justifying the African American students' charge of discrimination.[5]

The African Americans who the U.S. Communist Party subsequently sent to the Lenin School to quell accusations of institutional racism lend important insight into the ways in which black Americans in Moscow negotiated the power, promise, and limitations of Soviet anti-racism.[6] As will be shown, when their white American colleagues com-mitted racist offenses, they consistently invoked Soviet antiracism, demanding the freedom from racism it promised them. In the process they defined what antiracism and freedom from racism looked like. Hence, even when Lenin School authorities failed to meet their expec-tations of proper "Soviet" or antiracist conduct, they appealed to the Executive Committee of the Communist International (ECCI) and dis-trict committee of the All-Union Communist Party (CPSU), criticizing their actions as not only racist but also as "anti-Soviet."

African Americans who attended the Lenin School were not alone in viewing Soviet antiracism as more than a paternalistic, abstract discourse.[7] To elaborate on this point, this chapter concludes by switching venues to KUTV, where in 1933 a group of African American and African students met with Dmitri Manuilskii, the head of the ECCI. During this meeting, the students drew upon and challenged the master narrative of Soviet antiracism to criticize certain aspects of Soviet society and culture as racist.[8] When a few African students, however, challenged Soviet antiracism by calling into question its validity, three black American students criticized them, adamantly defending the USSR's image as a society intolerant of racism. Indeed, African Americans at KUTV and the Lenin School saw greater value in constructively criticizing and contributing to Soviet antiracism than in supporting the reactionary and divisive political forces of racial inequality in attacking it.

Only within the past two decades have the African Americans who attended the Comintern's universities become visible in the historical record. The black men and few black women who attended KUTV have received the bulk of scholars' attention, while the history of African Americans (the overwhelming majority of whom were also men) enrolled in the Lenin School remains virtually unexplored.[9] The lack of attention to their experiences reflects the broader silence with regard to the Lenin School in scholarship on the Comintern, European and American Left, and Chinese Communist Party. Scholars who have begun to research its place in the history of British and Chinese Communism attribute this silence to the particularly high level of secrecy in which the Lenin School was "shrouded."[10] Since the school was responsible for creating an international revolutionary elite out of the leading cadres of foreign Communist parties (many of which were illegal), neither family members and friends nor rank-and-file party members were supposed to know who national leaders sent to the Lenin School.[11] Despite occasional violations of this conspiracy, reconstructing the identities let alone the experiences of many of these individuals—who assumed a second alias in Moscow—remains a challenge.[12]

Since anonymity was essential to their program, the African Americans who attended the Lenin School and KUTV were not displayed in the Soviet press as trophies of Soviet racial enlightenment, as were those African Americans (discussed in previous chapters) who traveled to the USSR as conference delegates, entertainers, workers, and tourists. Nonetheless, these African American male students were very visible to the white American (male) architects, engineers, and businessman who spent time in Moscow in the early 1930s. In their debriefings with U.S. consulate officials in Riga, Latvia, many of these white American men commented on their encounters with these African American students, while rarely remarking on the presence of their white American colleagues. This was largely because they were unaccustomed to seeing African Americans with equal access to education, money, public facilities, and with regard to black men, openly associating with white women. As their comments reveal, the manner in which the African American students simply moved about the city and carried themselves in the company of whites was striking—and hence troubling to them. Harry Haywood, the first African American student enrolled in the Lenin School in 1927, emphasized the pride and confidence that he and his fellow African Americans gained from sojourns in Moscow. When he returned to the United States to work in Birmingham, Alabama, African American Communists Hosea Hudson and Joseph Howard admonished him to stop walking quickly with his head held high. They reminded Haywood that he needed to start slumping his shoulders and shuffling his feet to avoid trouble.[13] The nearly four years that he had spent in Moscow, in other words, had caused Haywood to "unlearn" the mannerisms of self-preservation that governed black male movement, especially in the southern states.[14]

The white American engineers and architects who spoke with U.S. authorities found this black confidence and pride extremely problematic. As several of them warned with palpable disdain, "the reception and kindly treatment which American Negroes have had in Russia," where they are "well looked after," had caused them to adopt an "extremely offensive" attitude toward all white Americans in Moscow.[15] Some directly attributed this "pompous" demeanor to their fraternization with Russian (white) women, alleging that "the Negroes say: 'we are just like white men; we marry white women.'" One white American singled out Isaiah Hawkins, an African American Communist discussed in chapter 2, as filling their minds with such "nonsensical" ideas.[16] The larger underlying fear of these white male visitors was obvious: young black men would return to the United States with these nonsensical ideas and demand to be treated "like white men."

In spite of their nominal espousal of black equality, the white Americans who enrolled in the International Lenin School in September 1931, found it just as difficult as the white American businessmen and technicians treating African Americans "like white men" on a daily basis. Such difficulties were of course not unique to this particular group of white American Communists but reflected the lack of racial consciousness for which members of the U.S. Communist Party had become notorious, and which the policies of the militant Third Period were supposed to address.[17] Yet, prior to the fall of 1931, the white American Communists who attended the Lenin School only had to interact with two or three African Americans at one time. The lack of a sizable African American presence meant that it was easier for racial incidents to be dismissed, and less likely that white Americans' conduct toward blacks would be scrutinized.[18] For example, in 1929 Harry Haywood had been the subject of malicious rumors concerning his fraternization with Russian women in Yalta. As only one of two African American students in the Lenin School at the time, the racism behind such rumors was never addressed, and Haywood was encouraged to consider reevaluating his conduct.[19]

In contrast to Haywood's experiences, the presence of more than ten African Americans in the Lenin School in the fall of 1931 meant that the criticism of the white American students' behavior began immediately. Three of these African American students were holdovers from the previous school year who had completed the roughly nine-month Short Course and enrolled in the two- to three-year Basic Course in September 1931. This included H. R. Hutchins (Robert Mann/Harry Reed) of Seattle, George Hewitt (James/Timothy Holmes) of Brooklyn, and

Romania Ferguson (Romy/Harriet Dayton) of Dayton, Ohio, who was the Lenin School's only African American female student that fall.[20]

These three African American Communists were joined at the Lenin School by nine young African American men who enrolled in the Short Course; they constituted the largest incoming African American student body in the school's history. Among them were Leonard Patterson (Cotton Terry) of Goldsboro, North Carolina, who had worked (among other jobs) in a shoe factory in New York City; William O. Nowell (Cooper) of Georgia, who was employed as an auto worker in Detroit; John Youngblood (Skoven), a steelworker from Pittsburgh (by way of South Carolina); Charles White (Earl Shumaker), a bootblack originally from Georgetown, Georgia; John W. Brown (Carl Jacoby) of Detroit; Edward Williams (George Washington), who joined the Party in Cleveland; Mack Coad (Jim Wright/Bill Carpenter), a barely literate sharecropper from Alabama; George Walker (James Edwards), a truck driver from Elizabeth, New Jersey; and Henry Shelton (Shepard), who appears to have left the school before the end of the year.[21] Otto Huiswood, who was already in Moscow in 1931 conducting work for the Profintern, was also supposed to enroll in the Lenin School that fall.[22] Since all English-speaking students were organized in the Anglo-American Sector or "Sector D" of the Lenin School prior to 1934, these twelve African Americans became acquainted with a few African Communists, most notably Albert Nzula (Tom Jackson), the South African Party's first black secretary who also enrolled in 1931.[23]

The relationship between Hutchins and Hewitt and the white American students was strained when the nine young African American men arrived at the Lenin School. However, the tensions that ultimately divided the American student body along racial lines, and prevented the Lenin School from becoming the site of a successful experiment in racial integration, originated in the new group's journey to Moscow. Much of the animosity stemmed from their experiences aboard the *Majestic*, the vessel that conveyed the interracial group across the Atlantic in late August 1931. A resolution dated August 13, 1931, had underscored the need "to send the Negro Comrades to the ILS, uniting them into one group with the Americans" rather than sending them separately to Moscow.[24] The yearlong experiment with integration was supposed to begin immediately. Yet it was their integrated journey that was the source of their problems. In his 1981 memoir *American Radical*, Steve Nelson (enrolled as "Louis Evans"), a white American Communist and the only student from this group to write an autobiography, recalled fifty years later that racial animosity divided them the entire year they were in Moscow because of events that transpired during their travels together.[25]

U.S. Party leaders had placed a four-person (student) commission in charge on the *Majestic*, assigning one African American, John Youngblood, to the commission with three white Americans. The other African American Communists were suspicious of U.S. Communist leaders' motives in designating Youngblood. Unlike some of his colleagues who had previously traveled to the Soviet Union and/or had several years of Party experience, the Pittsburgh steelworker had joined the Party that March. The subsequent decisions of the commission compounded their suspicions that Youngblood was chosen as a token who would be less inclined to oppose the proposals of its more experienced white members. To prevent the disclosure of the group's identity, the Central Committee had instructed the commission that they should conform to segregation, particularly with regard to the contact between white female and black male Communists, but only if it was the policy on the *Majestic*. In spite of this directive, the commission decided that the group would practice segregation even though it was not observed among the vessel's general populace.[26]

As a result of the Jim Crow policies that the white American Communists rather than the *Majestic*'s authorities imposed, tensions quickly developed. In meetings held later that fall with school officials to discuss these tensions, the African American Communists emphasized that when their white colleagues communicated with them on the *Majestic*, it was most often to relay orders. The few who interacted with them outside of giving orders adopted, as William Nowell charged, a condescending "paternalistic" attitude toward "us," making it clear "that 'we' fight for Negroes." At times they did not even convey their orders directly but instead sent Youngblood to relay them.

This was how the order barring the African American students from the dance floor in the *Majestic*'s dining room was conveyed. Specifically, one evening when Charles White, John Brown, and some white students were dancing, Rose Riley sent Youngblood to tell White and Brown to leave the dance floor. Riley, several black students alleged, had feared that the two young black men would start dancing with her if she approached them.[27]

By the time the group reached Moscow, what little trust the African American Communists may have had in their white colleagues was gone. Before arriving in London, Mary Dalton (Molly Piatek/Mary Dorn) had exacerbated tensions by advocating that a white Communist be assigned to chaperone each African American Communist.[28] Then, during their first week in the Soviet capital, several white American students had chided Leonard Patterson and John Brown "to do the jig" and sing spirituals when a group of Russian workers surrounded them on the street out of curiosity. Patterson and Brown emphasized that this request was extremely offensive, explaining that white slaveholders had forced their slaves to dance and sing under the threat of being struck with a whip, a practice that they stressed some southern white landowners had not abandoned. As Patterson elucidated, by telling them to start dancing the jig in the street, they felt like their white colleagues viewed them as having just emerged from the jungle and should act like the mad, uncivilized people they perceived them to be. After listening to these charges, Lenin School authorities expressed confusion, noting that when Russian workers had asked Harry Haywood to perform "the dance of slaves" several years ago, he did not consider their request racist. Patterson stressed that unlike Russians, white Americans had a long history of enslaving black people and propagating the myth that "dancing the jig" was the extent of their talent. Since it had historically constituted an important tool of white domination in the United States, white Americans were obliged to never make this request of African Americans.[29]

Consistent with these references to U.S. slavery, the African American students attributed the white American Communists' conduct to their "slaveowner psychology" and specific anxieties about black men and white women interacting. Such anxieties, they insisted, had led them to ostracize the interracial married couple of Pearl Demery (Gladys Payne/Molly Beckman) and William Nowell. As Brown described it, the discrimination against Demery and Nowell was "one of the rankest, bitterest forms of white chauvinism toward the Negroes in the Lenin School," which negatively affected all the African American Communists. Dalton, Anna Bush (Maria Rock), Jenny Bowers (Fanny Cooper), Rose Riley, and Emma Bentley had refused to assign Demery any practical work at a Soviet factory or collective farm despite her status as a long-standing Party member. They also denigrated her for sitting with and supporting the African American male Communists at meetings, remarking that if she was separated from Nowell for a minute, then she would die.[30]

Patterson explained that women like Demery were perceived inside and outside the Party as whores, degenerates, and traitors of their race, while Nowell and other black men were treated as sexual predators who were only interested in Communism because it gave them (sexual) access to white women. To this point, George Walker stressed that he refused to accept Gus Hall's claim that he had merely been joking when on several occasions he told a young German woman not to associate with him. Patterson likewise complained, even relaying a few examples as corroboration, that the women with whom he spent time in Moscow were the constant subject of malicious rumors among the white American students.[31] He and Nowell criticized U.S. leaders for reinforcing these perceptions of African American Communists as intellectual inferiors and sexual predators by largely confining them to "Negro work," thereby ensuring that white American Communists would rarely have to contend with blacks in leadership positions.[32]

Overall, the white American Communists responded to their African American colleagues' criticism of their conduct and charges of racism by denouncing them as a "gang of nationalists" who were hopelessly sentimental, inherently opposed to school authority, and instigators of an atmosphere of "negritudeness" or chaos in the Lenin School.[33] They likewise supposedly disparaged as opponents of the CC CPUSA and proponents of "social democratic tendencies" those white Americans—like Demery—who had crossed the racial divide by socializing and siding with the African American students.[34]

Authorities of the International Lenin School confronted a situation in the fall of 1931 that they undoubtedly had not anticipated when they agreed that 25 percent of the Americans admitted to the Short Course that year should be black.[35] Based on the CPUSA's persistent problems with racism in its ranks, few in Moscow or New York should have been surprised that the American students ended up racially divided. Grossly underestimating the deep-seated, insidious nature of U.S. racism, officials on both sides of the Atlantic thought that the key to integration was simply "to send the Negro Comrades to the ILS, uniting them into one group with the Americans," and to appoint an African American to serve on the four-person commission on the *Majestic*. In their estimation there was even no need to designate an African American Communist who had experience comparable to that of the three white members. Given the fact that John Youngblood had only been in the Party a few months, they most likely chose him as the token "Negro." Since these were the only measures that they pursued to make integration work, American and Comintern officials overestimated the white Communists' ability to transcend racial prejudices and African American Communists' willingness to endure the racial obtuseness of their white colleagues. That is to say, they arguably thought that the African Americans would be, or more accurately, should be content with just attending the same prestigious institution as their white brethren, and would therefore not create "trouble."

If this was indeed their mindset, then they had chosen the wrong group of African American men. While Lenin School authorities were no more prepared than U.S. officials to address their grievances, Soviet antiracism held them to a higher code of conduct that the African American students determined they failed to meet. As a consequence, in December 1931 they sent a nine-page letter to the ECCI and the district committee of the CPSU documenting the unbridled growth of racism in the Lenin School and the role they claimed school authorities had played in it. Though the few African students in the Anglo-American Sector seemingly supported their efforts and signed the letter, its contents dealt exclusively with the experiences of the African American Communists, and incidentally, William Nowell's aforementioned white wife, Pearl Demery.

Before addressing their specific criticisms, it is important to note that Lenin School authorities were at that time easy targets. The African American Communists' decision to compose this letter in December rather than a month earlier, after school officials had issued a formal resolution on the situation, suggests that they were keenly aware of this. The Lenin School leadership was then reeling from the general fallout that was occurring in Soviet academic institutions as a result of an October 1931 letter Stalin had written in *Proletarskaia revoliutsiia* criticizing certain historians for their Trotskyist errors. Among those implicated was Emel'ian Iaroslavskii, the preeminent Marxist historian who had published a four-volume history of the Soviet Communist Party in 1929. Institutions were required to organize discussions of Stalin's letter to reflect on its significance and engage in self-criticism. In December, the CPSU district committee criticized several Lenin School officials—many of whom the African American students criticized in their letter—for mistakes they made during these discussions.[36] The school's director, Klavdiia Ivanovna Kirsanova, who was also Iaroslavskii's wife, was held politically responsible for these errors and temporarily removed from her position.[37] Under even greater scrutiny at the time was Isaak Mints, whom the African American Communists criticized most often in the letter. In addition to the high-ranking positions he enjoyed at the Institute of Red Professors, Mints taught a course at the Lenin School on the history of Leninism and had served as head of the Anglo-American Sector. As a protégé of Iaroslavskii and contributing editor to the disputed fourth volume of the Party history, Mints's tenuous position became even more precarious after Lazar Kaganovich, the secretary of the Central Committee and head of the Moscow party, criticized him for "Trotskyist interpretations" of history.[38]

The Party's efforts to eradicate "Trotskyite tendencies" in the Lenin School necessarily affected the way the African American Communists composed their letter. This is not to say that they fabricated the charges and found school officials guilty of no wrongdoing. Rather, they shrewdly recognized the importance of maximizing the current political climate to ensure that the ECCI and district committee would be especially receptive to their criticisms, demands, and decision to exercise Soviet antiracism. The content of the letter, which they described as a "statement of facts," had two overriding, interrelated objectives. The first was to establish that over the previous and current academic year Lenin School authorities had pursued "wrong theories and methods" with regard to the "Negro Comrades." These wrong methods and theories included routinely minimizing their charges of racism; reiterating the white Americans' slanders of them as "sentimental" and "supersensitive" (feminizing terms); making the fight against black nationalism the sole priority in the Lenin School; and supporting the white Americans' cliques, the most prominent one of which they claimed centered around Isaak Mints. The formation of any "groupings" or factions in the Party was of course considered a serious offense and to connect it to Mints was strategic. The letter alleged that "the Mintz clique" had used "unprincipled" methods to turn the African American Communists against each other, and specifically had bribed Romania Ferguson into slandering her black male colleagues and Pearl Demery. This accusation was no doubt meant to explain why Ferguson had no hand in crafting the letter and failed to raise any accusations against the white American students or Lenin School authorities (an issue that will be addressed at length below).[39]

The African American Communists' second major objective in writing this letter was to dispel any notion that they were a band of incorrigible, hypersensitive black nationalists. To this end, they conceded to having made several mistakes; pledged their commitment to fighting black nationalist tendencies; and emphasized their willingness to "cooperate" with anyone interested in seeking a "real solution" to the problem. They warned that they would accept "nothing less," implying that this had not been the goal of Lenin School authorities. Curiously the students invoked the name of Robert Robinson, "the ideal black worker" and poster child for Soviet antiracism. They identified Robinson as an associate of William Nowell, who some white Americans had tried to expel from the Lenin School as a Trotskyite. To further redeem their names, the African American Lenin students made a passing, calculated reference to Russian workers. They explained that when George Hewitt (James) had filed a grievance against a white student for calling him a "nigger," Lenin School officials had responded by describing Hewitt as "rather suppersensitive [sic]." Confronted with this injustice, "the only thing," the letter declared, "that supported Comrade James was the splendid manner in which he was treated [by] . . . the Russian Workers."[40] Of course, whether Hewitt believed that Russian workers treated him "splendidly" and found solace in this is not the issue. The African American Communists affirmed that although they were criticizing Lenin School authorities, they recognized the fact of Soviet enlightenment. In making this statement they invoked the official image of workers in the early 1930s as the embodiment of proletarian virtue and morality, whose spirit intellectuals like Mints and other Lenin School officials needed to reclaim and emulate.[41]

When considered closely, the underlying problem that the African American Communists outlined in their nine-page appeal to the ECCI and CPSU district committee was that Lenin School authorities had denied them the power to "see" or determine what constituted racism. Specifically, Lenin School officials did not consistently agree that the conduct that the African American men were identifying as racism was "actually" racism, and therefore implicitly sanctioned rather than corrected it. As the first section of this chapter suggests, Leonard Patterson, William Nowell, and John Brown served as de facto spokespersons for the group in meetings with the school's investigative commission. This was not simply the result of their seemingly outspoken personalities but was primarily because they were at the center of what authorities termed "concrete" examples of racism. By more often scrutinizing, minimizing, and questioning their charges of racism rather than empathizing with and vindicating them, school officials had effectively disqualified as "biased" the ability of the African Americans to define what qualified as white chauvinism because they were not "white."[42] It was for this offense that the African American Communists appealed to higher authorities.

Comintern leaders' response was undoubtedly more consistent with the African Americans Communists' visions of how Soviet antiracism was supposed to work. They responded immediately and validated their criticisms of the white American Communists and Lenin School officials. The ECCI stated that the latter had gravely erred: "Instead of immediately, without delay, correcting and condemning the mistakes of the individual white comrades which were manifestations of remnants of white chauvinism, they tried to create a certain balance between the mistakes of this kind made by some white comrades, and the mistakes of another kind committed by some Negro comrades." Since they erroneously applied a "mechanical implementation" of the Bolshevik struggle on two fronts, they had exacerbated hostilities and lost the African American students' confidence.[43]

Shortly after the African American Communists sent their letter to the ECCI and district committee of the CPSU, Earl Browder, the U.S. Communist Party's general secretary, and Clarence Hathaway, who had replaced Weinstone as the CPUSA representative to the Comintern, arrived at the Lenin School to lead an emergency three-day meeting (December 22–24, 1931), which representatives of the CPSU and Comintern supervised.[44] Embarrassed by the situation, Browder and Hathaway criticized the African American Communists for not having first appealed to them before taking their complaints to the ECCI and CPSU district committee. Again Comintern leaders vindicated the African Americans' actions. They emphasized that as current members of the CPSU they unequivocally had the "political right" to appeal to them and demand that they take immediate action to eliminate the rampant racism within the Lenin School. At the same time, the ECCI admonished that it had been the "political *duty*" of the white Communists to bring the problem of white chauvinism to their attention; this was an injunction directed at both the white Communists and the American leadership. The racial tensions in the Lenin School served as further evidence that the CC CPUSA had still not taken seriously the Comintern's directives to conduct a fierce struggle against racism within the Party's ranks. And even though it was their political right, the African American Communists' decision to appeal to Soviet rather than American leaders demonstrated that they had far greater confidence in the former to treat their grievances seriously.[45]

At this late December meeting, the white American students were called on to criticize their failure to lead the struggle against racism in the Lenin School. This possibly could have relieved some of the tension dividing the American student body, but their self-criticism fell painfully short of Comintern leaders' expectations, a situation a few white students even acknowledged. Several white Americans conceded that some of their actions could be seen as racist and that they had not fought against racism—admissions they had refused to make in meetings with the school's authorities a month earlier. They simultaneously negated these begrudging admissions of accountability by subsequently emphasizing the mistakes that a particular African American Communist had made or by complaining that the African American Communists had "vulgarized" the charge of racism so that they feared saying anything to them. As Samuel Vint (Samuel Bly) observed, because many of his fellow white Americans had posed the question "How can I be a white chauvinist?" when they were supposed to be engaging in self-criticism, they revealed that they "do not know what is the sign of a white chauvinist mistake." In addition to this majority, there were others who, as Pearl Demery stated, refused to even criticize themselves for racism simply for the sake of appearances.[46] After witnessing the white Americans' inability if not unwillingness to even speak antiracism, Comintern authorities declared that members and leaders of the American Communist Party still failed to comprehend the "far-reaching political significance" of the struggle against racism.[47]

A resolution that an ECCI investigative commission issued in February 1932 elaborated on this conclusion. It connected the expressions of racism in the Lenin School to its recent manifestations within the CPUSA and attributed both to the deepening U.S. economic crisis and intensification of the class struggle. As a result of these developments, ECCI investigators reiterated that it was "THE MOST IMPORTANT

TASK of the American Party and above all the first duty of the white comrades" to lead the struggle for black equality and "to conduct a relentless war against every manifestation or even slightest echo within its own ranks of the ideology of white chauvinism, which is the main danger to the successful carrying through of the task of unifying white and Negro workers for common struggle." They reprimanded U.S. leaders for the white Communists' failure to apply theory, namely, Lenin's nationality policy, to everyday interactions with their black colleagues.[48] Rather than "lead the struggle for black equality," they had committed numerous acts of racism while insisting on their innocence. Furthermore, on those occasions when African American Communists made mistakes, the white American Communists did not make "certain concessions in order to overcome more quickly this mistrust and these prejudices" as Lenin had instructed, but had denounced them as "'bourgeois nationalists.'"[49]

Overall, the ECCI resolution served as an even more formal validation of the African American Communists' perspective; it identified racism as the main "evil" and placed the onus on the white Communists to reevaluate and alter their conduct to make integration work. Yet the follow-up investigation that Comintern authorities and Lenin School officials conducted in April 1932 revealed that the white American students had made relatively no effort to change the way they interacted with their African American colleagues. Instead, most had celebrated the ECCI resolution as a "petty" personal victory simply because it acknowledged that the African American Communists had made errors. As a result of their distortion of the resolution's meaning, most white American Communists had continued to attribute the hostilities in the Lenin School to the "distrust of Negro comrades toward white comrades." As one investigator remarked, with palpable frustration, if "obliged to judge the situation of the American Party on the basis of the situation of the American Lander group here, I would receive a very bad impression of the American Party."[50] Though authorities identified as encouraging the organization of a Scottsboro campaign in the school, a few white students had offended some African American students with "tactless" efforts to involve them.[51]

At a meeting held to discuss investigators' findings on April 22, 1932, some white American Communists conceded that they had given little attention to implementing the ECCI resolution and therefore to struggling against racism. But once again, an admission of guilt did not necessarily indicate that they would improve their conduct. The actions of Samuel Nessin (Gary Kelly) bear out this point.[52] Four months earlier, during the December meeting, Nessin had given an impressive performance in speaking antiracism. He had criticized himself and his fellow white students at length for treating black nationalism as the main danger and for leaving the fight against racism entirely "in the hands of the African American students." However, in early April 1932, Lenin School authorities reprimanded Nessin for attributing the hostilities in the school to African American students' "sustained mistrust" of their white colleagues. At the April meeting, Nessin explained his inconsistent behavior by articulating what had by then become a standard refrain among the white Communists in discussions about racism. Specifically, Nessin expressed disbelief that he could be guilty of racism, when for the past seventeen years he had led the struggle against his town's Ku Klux Klan and been at the forefront of mobilizing African American laborers.[53]

As Nessin's statements indicate, most white American Communists in the Lenin School were much more comfortable organizing against the Ku Klux Klan, that is, in occupying a superior, caretaking role in relation to blacks as victims. They were completely unprepared to deal with self-determined African Americans who possessed the agency to point out their complicity in perpetuating white supremacy and who demanded the serious structural changes that would make the end of racism possible. Put another way, the black American Communists refused to see the white Communists in the way the latter wanted to be seen, that is, "as the friends of blacks." If these grandsons of slaves had only complied, the white American Communists must have reasoned, then integration would have worked. The notion that African Americans were observers of white behavior and that whites did not exercise total control over how blacks perceived them was a reality that most white Americans during this era did not have to contemplate. Rather than deal with this reality, the white American Communists dismissed these "seeing" blacks as hypersensitive, incorrigible, angry nationalists, thereby invalidating their perspective. By denying African American Communists the ability or authority to see them and criticize their conduct, they refused to concede the privileged position of power that white supremacy invested in them. Such a refusal subverted (and continues to subvert) efforts at eliminating racial inequalities and effecting interracial unity.[54]

At the end of the April 1932 meeting, Comintern leaders had emphasized that this investigation would be their last. This of course did not mean that racism ceased to be a problem in the remaining months of the academic year. Yet the two major incidents that occurred did not involve white Americans directly. The first case concerned a British student named Jim Ancrum (James Mills), who spread the rumor that John Youngblood had raped a woman in Yalta when the group was there in July and August 1932. School authorities were again slow to respond to the incident, which they attributed to the students' failure to immediately bring the case to their attention. They denounced the rumor as "one of the lying bourgeois slanders raised against Negro workers in order to incite race hatred and white chauvinism" and used to justify "the wholesale lynching of Negro workers." Since Ancrum had already returned to England, they instructed leaders of the British Communist Party to address the offense.[55] With regard to the second major incident, which also involved Youngblood, the ECCI was forced to intervene. A Canadian Communist ("Ek") identified as a member of a clique of Canadian and American students called Youngblood a "black son-of-a-bitch" and spat in his face. Comintern leaders expelled the student from the party and school, and condemned the incident as a manifestation of the liberal attitude toward racism that continued to exist in the institution.[56]

The African Americans who integrated the Lenin School in 1931 exercised the power that Soviet antiracism had given them to demand an environment free from racism, while also experiencing its limits. As evidenced above, the ECCI ordered the white American Communists to lead the struggle for black equality and to treat their African

American colleagues accordingly, eradicating through word and deed the latter's justified mistrust of them. Yet, as Steve Nelson recalled in his aforementioned autobiography, in spite of Comintern leaders' intervention the racial tensions that divided the group remained unresolved. An environment free from racism was not realized.[57]

Conceivably, Comintern officials could have expelled from the Lenin School all white Americans who refused to comply with their directives and committed expressions of racism. As discussed in chapter 1, Soviet authorities had expelled from the USSR roughly twenty white Americans working at the Stalingrad Tractor Factory in 1930. But these men were not Communists and had openly espoused racist attitudes. Unapologetic white American racists were undoubtedly far easier to deal with and reconcile within the Marxist paradigm than the putative enlightened, class-conscious white Americans who did not want to be called "racists." Expelling them from the Lenin School would have been tantamount to conceding defeat, or acknowledging that the problem of racism was not simply a problem of class, and would not automatically be resolved with the workers' revolution. Unlike the fictional accounts discussed in chapter 2, Soviet soil did not magically eradicate the deep-seated racial prejudices among white Americans (or British and Canadians), notwithstanding their working-class origins, Communist Party membership, and in some cases extensive experiences championing the rights of black workers in the United States.[58]

While Comintern leaders consistently criticized CPUSA leaders for failing to appreciate the far-reaching political significance of the struggle against racism, they were equally reluctant to admit just how extensive was the power of white supremacy. To acknowledge such a harsh reality would have required blurring still further (and more substantially) the lines between the class-first and race-first policies that had allowed for antiracism to be elevated to a priority policy. Hence, they simply disbelieved that these students were as Earl Browder described them, "the best we have in America," and strongly advised the CC CPUSA to pay closer attention to the students they sent to the Lenin School in the upcoming year.[59] The Anglo-American Secretariat of the Comintern no doubt hoped that the next group would include white American Communists with a bit more racial consciousness and African American Communists who were more inclined to disregard the chauvinistic errors of their white colleagues.

Among the charges of racism that this group of African Americans raised while attending the Lenin School, the ECCI refused to validate the accusations that some of their African American colleagues were guilty of "Uncle Tomism." They rejected, in other words, the notion that a black student could encourage white chauvinism by overemphasizing the danger of black nationalism, and condemned such name-calling as an impediment to interracial proletarian unity.[60] Comintern leaders' response is curious given the history of Bolsheviks of non-Russian descent who underemphasized the fight against Russian nationalism.[61] From their perspective, Uncle Toms could only exist in a racialized, capitalist society where "whites" occupied a privileged position (based on their racial identity) in relation to "blacks," and where there was an incentive for the latter to act in such a fashion. African American bourgeois leaders who colluded with the white bourgeoisie to keep the black American underclass oppressed were, within this logic, the true "Uncle Toms." Since there was no basis for Uncle Toms to exist in the USSR, the ECCI attributed the African American Communists' accusations to an atmosphere of unbridled racism in the Lenin School and their exacerbated mistrust—although justified—of anyone who worked closely with the white American students and the CC CPUSA.[62]

Regardless of Soviet leaders' specific reasons for condemning the name calling, the charges did not stop. The African American Communists simply replaced the term "Uncle Tom" with "Judas."[63] Their persistence in leveling these accusations points to the different strategies they had adopted for navigating the integrated but still overwhelmingly white world of the Lenin School (a reality that Comintern leaders likely failed to understand). To put it differently, the African American Communists had different standards of conduct to which they held white Americans and Soviet authorities accountable. If someone in the group appeared to hold whites to too low a standard of conduct, then they became the target of "Judas" or "Uncle Tom" charges, that is, of accusations of betraying the cause of black freedom. This is evidenced most clearly in the relationship between Romania Ferguson and her African American male counterparts.

Ferguson was the only student consistently at the center of these accusations. As mentioned earlier, Ferguson never publicly expressed any grievances against the white American Communists or school authorities in the two years that she spent at the Lenin School. She is, however, on record criticizing her African American male colleagues. In the meetings held in December 1931 and April 1932, Ferguson charged several African American male students with black nationalist offenses and for "harmful" distrust of whites. She identified black nationalism as the main danger and denied the existence of racial tensions in the school prior to the fall of 1931. In their nine-page letter to the ECCI and CPSU district committee, the African American male Communists also listed several slanderous remarks that Ferguson supposedly had made about them, Otto Huiswood, and Nowell's white wife, Pearl Demery. Though they claimed that the "Mintz clique" had bribed her into acting in this fashion, they resented Ferguson for the stance she had assumed.[64]

Admittedly, there may have been instances in which a few African American male Communists manipulated the charge of racism to avoid or abet criticism of their actions.[65] At the same time, it is highly unlikely, in the two years Ferguson spent at the Lenin School interacting daily with white American Communists and the school's authorities, that she never confronted any racial hostility. Judging from her criticisms of the African American male Communists, which signified an effort to censure their conduct, it is more probable that Ferguson had a different understanding of what they as African Americans were entitled to expect from white people under Soviet antiracism, and what it in turn permitted them as African Americans to do and say. She seemingly deemed problematic their unwillingness to ignore certain paternalistic comments or actions, which she perceived as creating unnecessary "trouble." More precisely, Ferguson may have considered it foolish or unreasonable for her African American male colleagues to define such behavior as racist and to expect white Americans to have developed such a sophisticated sense of racial consciousness. Yet by not criticizing the conduct of her white American colleagues in any way, Ferguson validated their refusal to accept any accountability for the racial tensions in the school, which amounted to a broader denial that they played any role in maintaining the structures of white supremacy.

Ferguson's status as the school's lone African American female student testifies to the discrimination within the CPUSA and larger U.S. society against black women.[66] Conversely, her alternate strategies to navigating life in the Lenin School appear to reflect the historic racialization of black men as posing a far graver threat and menace to American society. Hence, the whites there most likely perceived and treated her differently, racializing her—like black women throughout history—as more loyal and amenable than African American men, the embodiment of the "old Mammy" stereotype.[67]

Perhaps for these reasons, Ferguson apparently also disapproved of her African American male colleagues' associations with white women. Some of the remarks the African American male students charged her with making suggest this. The experiences of Harry Haywood as a student in Moscow in the late 1920s also lend insight. Haywood recounts in his autobiography how Marie Houston, a black American KUTV student, criticized him for socializing with white women, accusing him privately of "scandalizing our name."[68] Thus, though many African American female Communists were challenging "normative modes of respectability" through their work in the Party, Ferguson, like Houston, may have still retained and respected some of its constitutive elements.[69] That is to say, she may have nonetheless wanted her African American male counterparts to conform to more conventional notions of respectability, particularly with regard to sexuality, to avoid reinforcing whites' stereotypes of blacks. Indeed, implicit in the myth of the black rapist was the myth of black women's perpetual promiscuity. Overall, Ferguson seemingly rejected her African American male colleagues' pursuit of a "new" oppositional form of black manhood that privileged sexuality and physicality over self-restraint and denial, and sanctioned a level of outspokenness, willfulness, and self-expression in interactions with whites that resisted the more constrained notions of respectability, character, and reason that constituted more traditional understandings of black masculinity.[70]

Though the power of Soviet antiracism to create an environment free from racism was limited, most African American Communists in the Lenin School in 1931–32 valued its existence. A specific charge of racism that they raised against a white American Communist named John Marr (Cass) best illustrates this. They accused Marr of racism for claiming that Soviet workers, like white American workers, hated black people. According to John Brown, when the group was in Khar'kov, he had made the following remark to Marr: "These workers seem to like the Negro workers here, as it is not like America here, we get a good smile from the workers." Marr, Brown explained, responded to his observation with skepticism, stating, "'Don't be so sure about that,' as he had seen some workers spit on the ground as we passed . . . as if trying to tell me there was hatred among Russian workers toward Negro workers."[71]

When Lenin School officials questioned Marr about the comment, he did not deny making it. Instead, he recounted how he had formed a different impression than Brown of Russian workers' attitudes toward blacks. This was because, when walking with other students in the group, he always stayed at the back to observe with "great interest" the way children gathered around African Americans. On one occasion, Marr elucidated, he saw a small girl stare intently at Brown and Mack Coad, "vehemently" spit on the ground, and mutter something as they walked by her. Marr admitted that he had interpreted the child's actions as a "white chauvinistic expression," even though he was unaware of what she mumbled. He insisted that by relaying the incident to Brown, he was not implying that all Russian workers were "infected" with racism but simply that racism still existed in the USSR.[72]

Unlike their handling of the other accusations of racism that fall, the ECCI and African American Communists approved of the manner in which the school's officials responded to this particular charge. Lenin School authorities criticized Marr for failing to appreciate the high level of consciousness among Soviet workers which made the construction of socialism possible. Marr, they emphasized, had denied the "Leninist conception" that white chauvinism was the class weapon of the bourgeoisie and instead had made "it the ideology of all whites including even the workers of the Soviet Union." One school official added that "undoubtedly, among the backward elements of the Soviet workers occur incidents of chauvinism, against which the party decisively struggles." He stressed that these were only remnants, and in most cases of an anti-Semitic rather than antiblack nature.[73] At the end of a meeting organized to address Marr's offense, the American student body collectively affirmed Soviet antiracism, "unanimously condemn[ing] the behavior of Comrade Cass [Marr] in regards to accusing the workers of the USSR with having the presence of white chauvinism."[74]

Whereas the conduct of his white colleagues had exposed the CPUSA's shortcomings with regard to eradicating racism, Marr's offense exposed its failings in teaching white members the importance of speaking Soviet antiracism. When Marr engaged in self-criticism during the emergency December meeting, he followed the precedent many of his fellow white Communists had set: he emphasized the work he had done to struggle against racism in Detroit, which had, in his opinion, made it unfeasible for him to be guilty of it. Although he refused to identify it as a form of racism, Marr criticized himself for violating Soviet antiracism, an offense that he lamented had prompted several white students to chide him as a "counterrevolutionary." By propagating a theory about the continued existence of racism in the USSR based on one small girl's actions, Marr repented, he had risked damaging the country's antiracist image among African Americans. This, he continued, would have made it even more difficult for the CPUSA to mobilize them to the Soviet Union's defense. Marr stressed how fortunate he was that Brown did not receive the "wrong impression," question whether racism was pervasive among Russian workers, and become "antagonistic" toward them.[75]

Marr was correct to note that Brown did not receive the "wrong impression" from his "theory" about the existence of racism in the USSR. More important than not receiving the "wrong impression," Brown had chosen to raise the accusation of racism against Marr. His first impulse had been to ignore Marr's theory; he only brought it to the attention of school authorities after his African American colleagues had persuaded him to do so. Lenin School officials reprimanded Brown for not following their counsel sooner, and Brown criticized himself for concealing an act of white chauvinism by failing to immediately report it.[76] As this episode reveals, the African American Communists had discussed Marr's comment, weighed its importance, and consciously chose not to disregard it as Brown had intended. Their collective, deliberate decision indicates that they had a vested interest in actively defending the Soviet Union's image as a society without racism. Whether they believed the image reflected reality is immaterial.[77] As they saw it, Marr did not breach an idealistic, abstract antiracist discourse. Rather, he directly affronted the real, practical albeit limited power that Soviet antiracism afforded them to forge a new set of conventions to structure black-white interactions to uphold the basic principles of black equality and dignity. No wonder they came to its defense.

African American Communists at KUTV adopted a similar stance during a meeting that Dmitri Manuilskii convened at the school on January 19, 1933. The purpose of this meeting was to allow African American and African students to voice their concerns regarding three main issues. The first pertained to conditions at the school and their professors' inadequate command of the English language. These grievances had previously been a problem at KUTV and would remain a source of contention among foreign students in Moscow universities into the late Soviet era.[78] The two other issues, which constitute the focus of this discussion, pertained to the manner in which Soviet citizens treated them and the offensive representations of persons of African descent in Soviet books, advertisements, and plays.

The racist caricature of blacks in Soviet books, advertisements, and plays was not a new complaint on the part of African American Communists. As mentioned in chapter 2, Lovett Fort-Whiteman had first raised this issue with Anatolii Lunacharskii, the Commissar of Enlightenment, in 1924. Nearly ten years later little had seemingly changed except that these racist representations paradoxically coexisted with a more intense indictment of U.S. racism and African American oppression. For example, Scottsboro protest rallies were held during the intermission of Eugene O'Neill's *All God's Chillun Got Wings* at Moscow's Kamernyi Theater, one of three plays the KUTV students mentioned during the meeting for its problematic depiction of blacks. While they did not identify their specific concern with *All God's Chillun* (the play, as mentioned in chapter 3, reinforced stereotypes of black men and used actors in blackface), the students were pointed in their criticism of *Geisha*, a musical by the English composer Sidney Jones that was critically acclaimed in Europe, then showing at a Moscow theater.[79]

The future Kenyan leader Jomo Kenyatta (James Jochen) opened the meeting by emphasizing their surprise at the egregious manner in which blacks were depicted in *Geisha*.[80] Wallace Daniels, an African American student, too insisted that the production provided Soviet citizens with an inaccurate portrayal of blacks who had been enslaved. Daniels argued that he was descended from slaves and never saw a black person who looked the way blacks were portrayed in *Geisha*. Blacks of numerous backgrounds were in the room, he added, and none of them looked like those shown in *Geisha*. Significantly, Daniels stressed their awareness that the intentions of this play's director and others were not malicious, and that they were trying "to show Russian workers how the class of capitalists exploited Negroes." But since most Russians' impressions of blacks came from books and plays from capitalist countries alone, it was imperative that they be exposed to accurate portrayals of black people. Daniels further noted that because blacks in *Geisha* were called "dogs," people had left the theater referring to them in this manner.[81]

Monroe Vallade (Bradford Bennett), an African American Communist from Harlem who spoke next, criticized the popular children's play *The Negro Child and the Monkey* (*Negritenok i obez'iana*) for fostering the association of blacks with monkeys.[82] He also protested the existence of a 1931 Russian dictionary that defined the word "negro" as "nigger" and "negro child" as "pickaninny." Vallade reasoned that since the Soviet Union was building socialism and working to eradicate all national and racial prejudices, a dictionary that used such contemptuous terms in describing peoples of African descent should be removed. Otherwise, he warned, African American reformist leaders would use these remnants of chauvinism against "us." Apropos of this concern, Vallade asked Manuilskii to address the status of *Black and White*, the "postponement" of which had placed them in a precarious position with these leaders.[83] As Vallade's line of argument and use of the first person plural illuminates, the KUTV students, and particularly the African American students, made clear that their purpose in highlighting the inconsistencies in Soviet antiracism was to strengthen and protect it against criticism from the common enemy. Roddy Lister, an automobile mechanic from Cleveland, followed up Vallade's remarks by reiterating the need to eradicate all depictions of blacks with bright red lips and large white eyes and teeth, and to remove the word "nigger" from the Russian dictionary, an issue he claimed Lenin School students had brought to the Comintern's attention the previous year.[84]

While Kenyatta, Daniels, Lister, and Vallade directed their criticisms at Soviet society and culture, three African students who subsequently spoke, Edwin Mofutsanyana (Greenwood), the future secretary of the South African Communist Party, Samuel Padmore (Hamilton) from the Gold Coast, and especially Pierre Kalmek (Robert) from the French colonies, shifted the tone and direction of the conversation by criticizing as racist the conduct of Soviet citizens.[85] Kalmek raised the issue and was the most bold in his pronouncements; he claimed to have confronted an inordinate amount of racism in the first workers' state. As a sailor he had traveled throughout Europe, "but nowhere did I see such chauvinism as in the Soviet Union. Why did I come here," he queried, "because I heard a lot and read in newspapers, that the USSR was the homeland of oppressed peoples, a country without chauvinism." Disappointingly, "I have encountered more chauvinism than in the capitalist countries. I was in Italy, India, and other countries. No one there ever spat at me as they spat here in Moscow at me around three–four times." Kalmek recounted how this had occurred to him recently at a Moscow factory, and that on one occasion a woman came up to him and said, "Who is this? Is this a monkey?" Even at KUTV, he explained, a woman pointed at him, laughed, and told her children, "This is a Negro."[86]

Edwin Mofutsanyana claimed that his experiences were similar. He could excuse the conduct of Russian children who said, "Come look at the Negro," when he was walking down the street, because children were instinctively curious. With regard to their parents he was less tolerant. Samuel Padmore likewise related how when he was return- ing from festivities commemorating the October Revolution some adults had remarked, "Look at the Negro. Why is he so black? Prob- ably because he does not bathe." Padmore stressed his disappointment that Soviet citizens were unable to distinguish themselves from the inhabitants of capitalist countries in terms of their attitudes toward persons of African descent.[87] Two other African students, Samuel Free- man (Charlie Lafayette) of Monrovia and Nathan Varne Gray (Smith) of the Gold Coast, testified to having confronted similar prejudice.[88]

In contrast to these four African Communists, four other students— three of whom were African Americans—contested rather than cor- roborated Kalmek's testimony and took particular offense at his claim that the Soviet Union was the most racist country in the world. Walter Lewis (Robert Wells), a semiliterate steelworker from Birmingham, Alabama, emphasized that he had lived in the USSR for more than two years and had traveled around the country, but had never con- fronted racism. Besides the fact that no one ever spat at him, he found that Russian workers were very sympathetic toward blacks. The Soviet citizens whom Kalmek confronted, Lewis conjectured, had possibly picked up some prejudices toward blacks through books and plays from capitalist countries, like *Geisha*, which, he reiterated, needed to be removed from the theater's repertoire for this reason.[89]

John Hyde Rhoden (Dewing), who also hailed from Birmingham, was equally adamant in disputing Kalmek's comments, while still articulating disdain for the offensive depictions of blacks in Soviet plays and the Russian dictionary that used racist terms. Rhoden, like Vallade, warned that if blacks in capitalist countries knew that a book like this existed in the first workers' state, then it would "be very difficult to lead any type of work among them on behalf of the USSR." After registering his criticisms, Rhoden asserted that Kalmek had no right to claim that the Soviet Union was the most racist country. Similar to his fellow Alabama native, Rhoden testified that he had lived over two years in the Soviet Union and never encountered white chauvinism. When Russian workers surrounded them and asked why they were black, Rhoden argued that it was simply because they had never before seen persons of African descent and wanted to become acquainted with them. He pointed to the way in which Russian workers protested the Scottsboro death sentence to underscore that Kalmek was out of line for describing the USSR as a citadel of racial hostility.[90]

Nikin Sobia (Jack Hilton) of South Africa echoed the sentiments of Lewis and Rhoden, scoffing at Kalmek's claim that the Soviet Union was the "most chauvinistic country in the world." Assuming a different stance than his fellow South African Mofutsanyana, Sobia emphasized that he came from a country where blacks suffered tremendous oppression. With regard to the woman calling him a "Negro," Sobia wondered whether Kalmek would have considered it chauvinism had she not spoken to him at all. He reminded Kalmek that the USSR had always defended black people and, like Rhoden, cited the Scottsboro protest as the most recent and obvious example.[91] Roddy Lister, who spoke earlier in the meeting, interjected to likewise insist that Kalmek was wrong to posit that racial chauvinism existed in the Soviet Union. Having been in Moscow since September 1930, Lister questioned how Kalmek was defining racism since, in his view, it consisted of blacks being forbidden from using public transportation with whites, which was the case in the United States, not in the USSR.[92]

When Dmitri Manuilskii addressed the students' grievances, he did not take issue with their criticisms of the offensive representations of blacks in Soviet plays and books. He did not even try to rationalize their existence. The ECCI secretary was apparently already somewhat familiar with these charges, and in leveling them the students had stayed within the proper boundaries of the master narrative of Soviet antiracism. It may seem that just by lodging these complaints, students were questioning as a farce the Soviet Union's racially enlightened image. Yet the act of criticism in itself constituted an "affirmative gesture" of that image and the antiracist discourse that produced it.[93] Kalmek, however, had crossed the line between challenging Soviet antiracism to correct its inconsistencies and questioning its validity. Hence, unsurprisingly, Manuilskii focused his remarks on attacking Kalmek's "blasphemous" charge that the Soviet Union was the most racist country in the world.

Manuilskii first denounced Kalmek's position as dialectically impossible: there was simply no economic basis for racism—"a class weapon of the imperialist bourgeoisie"—to exist in the Soviet Union. Then, as Lister had briefly done, he compared the pervasiveness of institutional racism in the capitalist world with its absence in the USSR. He challenged Kalmek to provide an example of rights afforded white people in the Soviet Union that blacks were denied. He stressed that in Central Africa English workers earned twice as much as African laborers, and in the United States "whites have the privilege to lynch Negroes, but Negroes do not have the right to lynch whites." This, he argued, was white chauvinism. Manuilskii belabored the point by asking, "Do we have a difference here between the salaries of Negro and white workers? Do we have the right to lynch Negro citizens?"[94]

Kalmek interjected to clarify that his contention was that white chauvinism was a problem among the populace, not the state. Manuilskii countered by insisting that much of the behavior that Kalmek and a few others identified as "chauvinism" was not chauvinism at all. In some cases they were confusing racism with what historically Europeans had disparaged as Russian or "Asiatic" barbarity. Russians, he elucidated, have traditionally failed to adhere to the putative notion of "European politeness," whereby "civilized" people believed it was discourteous to speak in a direct manner toward each other. Until recently, he emphasized, Russia had been quite a "backward" country: "We never saw colored races." Instead of acting refined, as if they had previously seen a person of African descent, Russians often said whatever was on their minds. With regard to Russian children, Manuilskii posited that their behavior was universal, so that children in Africa would stare and shout at him because of his different physical appearance.[95]

Though he attributed many of Kalmek's experiences to Russians' unrefined character, Manuilskii conceded the existence of "remnants" of white chauvinism among Soviet toilers. However, he stressed that Soviet authorities, unlike their capitalist counterparts, were mobilizing resources toward eradicating them. He urged them not to lose sight of the obstacles they faced in attempting to fulfill this goal, particularly the legacy of centuries of tsarist rule, which included bloody pogroms against Jews, widespread anti-Semitic propaganda, and ethnic conflict between Armenians and Turks. As evidence that Moscow was committed to realizing this objective at "all costs," Manuilskii cited the Stalingrad trial and distorted Lemuel Lewis's position as an "ordinary mechanic" who was notorious for drinking and starting fights, portraying him as one of the Traktorostroi's "leading specialists." The distortion of Lewis's profile made more impressive the Soviet state's insistence on expelling him for his racist conduct. While he reaffirmed the Soviet commitment to antiracism, Manuilskii cautioned that recent international developments had rendered it imperative that the Soviet Union's national security assume precedence over all other issues (including the production of a film like *Black and White*), since the country's destruction would signal certain defeat for the liberation of the world's oppressed masses. He nevertheless asked the students to draw up a letter documenting the grievances they had presented at the meeting so that the Comintern could better address them.[96]

Were the experiences of the African American Communists at KUTV really that different from their African colleagues, or were they merely not as "honest" about them? Jochen Hellbeck argues that it is dangerous to automatically dismiss any voice that speaks positively about the USSR as a "performance" or an exercise in propaganda, while treating those that speak negatively as the only "authentic" expressions.[97] Lewis's and Rhoden's progress reports dated May 25, 1933, suggest that the two men were forthright about their experiences; κυτν officials noted that neither man showed interest in returning to the United States.[98] The white American businessmen and engineers mentioned at the start of this chapter would have corroborated their testimony. The outrage they expressed to U.S. legation officials serves as particularly provocative evidence of the unprecedented level of freedom that African Americans experienced in Soviet society in the interwar years. Although historically they had little contact with peoples of African descent, it is not unreasonable to assume that Soviet citizens may have perceived and treated African Americans differently from Africans simply because of the former's association with the wealth, power, and Western "civilization" of America (which, as discussed in chapter 2, many Russians were fascinated with) as opposed to the European subjugation of the putative "Dark Continent." Moreover, as noted in chapter 1, Robert Robinson recalled in his 1988 memoir *Black on Red* that Russian workers at the Stalingrad Tractor Factory respected him when he worked there in the early 1930s. Since his objective in writing the autobiography was to challenge Soviet claims to have eradicated racism, Robinson would have had a clear interest in mentioning and playing up incidents of Russians (at the Stalingrad Traktorostroi) spitting at him or calling him a monkey, had they occurred.

Overall, African Americans may have also had different experiences because Soviet antiracism privileged them by making the indictment of U.S. racism its primary focus. African Americans and not Africans had been christened as the revolutionary vanguard. The Stalingrad trial and the Scottsboro protest concerned defending African Americans, not Africans, from racism. Even the ill-fated film *Black and White* was set in the United States and condemned the oppression of African American workers. While the racial atrocities of European imperialism were condemned, Soviet antiracism had not yet developed the strong anticolonial focus that it assumed in the decades after the Second World War, when Soviet leaders sought to spread socialism to former colonial countries, opened the doors of Moscow State University to Africans, and established Patrice Lumumba Friendship University.[99] Accordingly, Jomo Kenyatta even complained during the meeting that the "Comintern really neglects Negroes from colonial countries."[100] All this is not to say that African Americans had somehow escaped racism in the USSR in the 1930s, but to suggest that their African colleagues may have experienced it at a higher incidence (as they would into the post-Communist era). Thus, African American students' defense of Soviet antiracism can be attributed in part to their status as its primary beneficiaries.[101]

At the same time, it is impossible to say with certainty whether African Americans encountered less racism in Soviet society than their colleagues from the continent of Africa. What is clear is that they had adopted a different strategy for dealing with it. This may have been because African Americans came from a country with a white majority. Their experiences with white Americans may have made them, in other words, more willing to forgive certain conduct on the part of Russians, or less willing to openly define such conduct as racist.[102] It seems reasonable to assume that due to their experiences with American "whiteness" (including the attitudes of the aforementioned white American men incensed by African Americans' "kindly treatment" in the USSR), many African Americans saw Russians' whiteness differently than did most of the African students. Just as discussions in the Lenin School had revealed differences in the ways that white and black Americans defined racism, so this meeting with Manuilskii suggests that overall, many of the African and African American students at KUTV had different notions of what constituted racism on the part of Russians. Whether they encountered less racism and/or defined it differently, African Americans responded to Kalmek's comments by either remaining silent or defending the Soviet Union's antiracist image. Their response indicates that they saw this image as having some intangible value in the struggle for black freedom in the United States.

Wallace Daniels, who did not respond to Kalmek's remarks at the meeting, penned an article in the *Moscow Daily News* a few weeks later titled "The Negro Feels at Home in the USSR." It expressed the perspective that Lewis, Rhoden, Sobia, Lister, and Manuilskii had articulated, emphasizing Russians' lack of experience with and friendly curiosity about blacks and the absence of institutional racism in the Soviet Union.[103] Of course, any reference to the offensive representations of blacks was omitted. In the letter that Daniels and the other KUTV students sent to Comintern leaders about these representations, they obviously did not claim that they felt *completely* "at home in the USSR," as the *Moscow Daily News* article alleged. But prior to registering their complaints, they dedicated the first two pages of the letter to affirming that this was Soviet authorities' goal. They emphasized how they disbelieved as propaganda bourgeois leaders' contention that the Comintern had forsaken black workers, and were convinced of the Soviet state's intolerance of racism as proven in the Stalingrad trial, Scottsboro protest, and the prominent place afforded blacks in the commemoration of the fifteenth anniversary of the October Revolution. After insisting on the sincerity of Soviet antiracism, they reiterated their criticisms of the offensive representations of blacks in the USSR and the negative impact these images had on Soviet citizens' interactions with them. They even attached a set of formal "Resolutions in Connection with the Derogatory Portrayal of Negroes in the Cultural Institutes of the Soviet Union."[104] By organizing the letter in this fashion, they strategically condemned the degrading images of blacks in the USSR as racist and antithetical to Sovietness. The letter, when juxtaposed with the *Moscow Daily News* article, demonstrates how black Communists (similar to the *Black and White* cast members) practiced two forms of speaking antiracism: one for public consumption and the other for communications with Soviet authorities, but always with the same goal of advancing black equality.

Despite expressing their grievances to Comintern leaders in verbal and written form, the dominant images of blacks in Soviet society as a whole remained the same. This outcome is unsurprising given the absence of tangible results that African American Communists like Fort-Whiteman had earlier seen after lodging similar complaints.[105] Soviet officials simply lacked the motivation, desire, resources, and necessary consciousness (understanding) to eradicate racist caricatures of blacks. Conceivably, the African and African American Communists at KUTV could have openly denounced as hypocrisy this dissonance between the Soviet espousal of racial equality and the offensive depictions of persons of African descent in the USSR. They probably reasoned, however, that in an age of biological racism there was little if nothing to gain in doing so. At this time, most whites in the United States and Europe subscribed to some notion of black intellectual inferiority, which they either lauded as virtue (as in whites' obsession with "the primitive") or condemned as vice. Hence, in a world in which Josephine Baker achieved stardom by exploiting and reifying whites' racist associations of blacks with the jungle (and lush sensuality), they most likely concluded that the images of blacks found in the *Negro Child and the Monkey* and other Soviet cultural media were not worth surrendering their audience with officials in Moscow.[106]

If their criticisms of racist caricatures of blacks were unlikely to effect immediate change, and since they rejected as counterproductive exposing Soviet authorities' failure to act on them, why did the African and African American Communists still bother to raise them? Certainly, such images assaulted the dignity and very humanity of persons of African descent and subverted efforts to end racial inequality. The act of registering these criticisms therefore functioned as an act of humanization, an affirmation of black humanity, and a means of forging and/or preserving a positive sense of self in spite of not reaping any immediate tangible rewards.[107]

Concurrently, as several scholars of the Soviet Union argue, the act of criticism (staying within negotiated limits) was a means of expressing identification with and contributing to the project of building socialism. Our knowledge of the innumerable mass atrocities perpetrated by the Soviet regime makes it easy to understate, if not devalue, the tremendous sense of hope, self-worth, and belonging that many Soviet citizens derived in the 1930s from the knowledge that they were contributing to the construction of a new, superior world where exploitation was absent.[108] A similar sense of hope, self-worth, and belonging arguably motivated African and African American Communists to not give up trying to teach Comintern leaders that offensive images of blacks perpetuated the white supremacist ideology that they ostensibly condemned, and undermined the more progressive form of modernity they were seeking to construct. In drawing attention to the sheer power of white supremacy, they affirmed that it could be challenged, transformed, and dismantled. Viewed in this context, not voicing their criticisms would have been tantamount to surrendering hope that the black liberation struggle would ultimately be victorious.[109]

Paradoxically, American racism became a major problem in a school that was supposed to constitute a bastion of internationalism, at a time when the CPUSA was gaining greater respect among African Americans for its leading role in the Scottsboro liberation movement.[110] Yet as the discussions about racism in the Lenin School illuminate, white American Communists had little problem condemning flagrant acts of racial injustice. Their real difficulties rested in recognizing the ways in which the same system of American racial apartheid, which produced blatant racial atrocities like the Scottsboro legal lynching, structured their own attitudes and interactions with blacks in subtle and not so subtle ways. The white American students' lack of racial consciousness was evidenced most clearly in their attitudes regarding the interaction between white women and black men. Interestingly, white American female students played a role equal to white men in censuring these interracial relationships. Perhaps out of fear that black males had a rapacious appetite for white women or concern with preserving their own reputations (that is, of not being called a whore for associating too closely with black men), most white American women in the Lenin School helped uphold a U.S. societal myth in Moscow that contributed to their own oppression as white women.[111]

It goes without saying that Soviet antiracism and representations of the USSR as a society without racism did not eliminate racism. But African American Communists nonetheless derived a position of authority and a sense of dignity from Soviet antiracism. Hence, when a white American student in the Lenin School and African students at KUTV violated it by claiming that Soviet workers were racist, African Americans in both institutions defended the Soviet Union's image as a raceless society. Some scholars might argue that the white American and African men were speaking honestly, that each was expressing his "authentic self" by publicly articulating dissent, whereas the others were merely acting, making remarks similar to the former in private. While this may have been true in some if not most cases, it would be irresponsible to claim that it holds true for all. We cannot discount all African American voices that extolled the racial equality that they experienced in the Soviet Union as performances.[112] Some of these African Americans who were overwhelmingly men may have faced no racism in the Soviet Union, or whatever they did experience paled significantly in comparison to the systematic degradation that they confronted in the United States.

As the episodes involving John Marr and Pierre Kalmek reveal, Comintern and Party authorities admitted that "remnants" of racism existed among Soviet citizens. What they objected to was that both men used these remnants to posit that Soviet citizens were racists. Thus, Soviet leaders were not making the unrealistic claim—at least privately—that the image of the Soviet Union as a country without racism was perfect in the early 1930s. They did seek recognition that they were working toward making reality correspond with that image. Clearly, African Americans were not alone in speaking two forms of Soviet antiracism.

The African Americans who helped integrate the Lenin School in 1931 and 1932 did not become the high-profile leaders that their training was supposed to make them. Due to America's legacy of racism and anti-Communism, it is difficult to determine what even happened to most of these individuals upon their return to the United States. The few exceptions are those persons who eventually became professional anti-Communists or government-paid witnesses for the House Un-American Activities Committee (HUAC) in one of its various incarnations. This included George Hewitt and two of the most outspoken Lenin students, Leonard Patterson and William Nowell. Of the three men, William Nowell's decision to testify in roughly "forty trials and hearings between 1948 and 1954" is least surprising. Nowell had been the most educated member of the group and had conducted himself with an air of superiority. Party leaders had sent Nowell to the Lenin

School to have his viewpoints "corrected" with regard to the Comintern's position on African Americans as an oppressed nation, which he continued to reject, and they expelled him five years later, in 1936.[113] According to Manning Marable, after his expulsion Nowell "promptly worked as an agent in Henry Ford's 'goon squad,' threatening and beating other autoworkers."[114] Mack Coad, the barely literate sharecropper from Alabama, is the only African American alumnus from the 1931–32 academic year who was not a government-paid witness but about whom we have information regarding his future beyond the Lenin School. Around roughly the same time that Nowell embarked on the ignoble path of betraying the revolutionary work of fellow African Americans, Coad again crossed the Atlantic, this time to serve the cause of antiracism and freedom by joining the Abraham Lincoln Brigade in the Spanish Civil War.[115]

Epilogue

Circus *and Going Soft on American Racism*

On nearly every occasion in which the topic of this book was mentioned, scholars of Russian history responded by uttering the title of a 1936 Soviet film: *Circus*. As the response of these historians suggests, Grigorii V. Aleksandrov's film about a white American woman who finds refuge in the USSR with her two-year-old black son is the remnant of interwar Soviet antiracism that has endured in popular memory.[1] Considered independently of the press coverage, political education campaigns, and court proceedings that constitute this book's focus, *Circus* appears as a fleeting aberration of Soviet interest in condemning U.S. racism before the late 1940s and 1950s when U.S. race relations became central to Cold War politics. Although *Circus* constitutes the most enduring emblem of interwar Soviet antiracism, the popular musical comedy is very different from the hard-line expressions that preceded it in the first half of the 1930s. The film most effectively illuminates the shift in the mid-1930s to a more "soft-line" indictment of the U.S. racial regime reflective of Popular Front policies and the ascendancy of Nazi Germany as the overriding priority of Soviet propaganda.

Circus was the most successful but not the only cinematographic expression of interwar Soviet antiracism. The first noteworthy Soviet film to include a black male protagonist and an antiracist subtheme was the immensely popular *Little Red Devils* (1923) which generated several sequels.[2] *Little Red Devils* centers on the Civil War adventures of fifteen-year-old Misha, his sister Duniasha, and their friend Tom Jackson, a black street performer whom the brother and sister duo rescues from a crowd of "urchins" and two dishonest musicians.[3] The three friends seek revenge against the counterrevolutionary forces of Nestor Makhno for the murder of Misha and Duniasha's father and elder brother. Racial paternalism, discussed throughout this study, marks their friendship; the instance of rescue on which it was founded is repeated throughout *Little Red Devils*, with Tom consistently appearing as the weakest link. The three youths join forces with the famous Red Army commander, S. M. Budennyi, who uses them as scouts. The Red Army soldiers, like Misha and Duniasha before them, accept Tom without hesitation. But upon first meeting him, they attempt to remove what they naively mistake as paint from his face, a common trope in Soviet fictional accounts involving a black protagonist, including Aleksandrov's *Circus*. Tom's acceptance as an equal does not allow him to forget the horrors he endured as "a slave in the colonies of 'civilized' nations," about which, in one scene, he has a nightmare. As this scenario indicates, though historians and film archivists sometimes refer to Tom Jackson as an African American, he was scripted as a Senegalese sailor who "jumped ship in Sevastopol" during the Civil War, deserting "the French intervention forces."[4] American racism and African Americans (with the exception of Claude McKay) had yet to garner the special status they would command in the USSR by the early 1930s.

Accordingly, eight years later, in 1931, the Ukrainian national cinema released a film directed by Pavel Kolomoitsev titled *Black Skin* in which the indictment of U.S. racism is the central theme. Kador Ben-Salim, who played Tom Jackson in all the *Little Red Devils* films, assumes the role of an African American worker named Tom—further evidence of the influence of Harriet Beecher Stowe's *Uncle Tom's Cabin* on Soviet fictional portrayals of black men. After Tom and two white workers, Sam and Mary, are fired from the Ford factory, they pursue employment in the Soviet Union. During their journey, Sam treats Tom with contempt and refuses to share a room with the "racial inferior" when they arrive in the USSR. Indignant, Soviet workers ostracize Sam, who ultimately recognizes the ignorance of his capitalist ways and embraces Tom as his brother. The power of Soviet society to eradicate the racial prejudices of white American workers is thus affirmed.[5]

The following year Kolomoitsev and the Ukrainian national cinema released another film exposing U.S. race relations titled *The Negro from Sheridan*. Set in the United States in the late 1920s, the film explores the efforts of the class enemy, whose name is Dan, to dissolve an interracial strike committee. Dan spreads the rumor that Murray, a black woodcutter and one of the committee's members, is in love with the sister of the Smith brothers who are also on the committee. Faced with the threat of lynching, Murray seeks the help of a wealthy African American whom he discovers is not his "blood brother" when the latter has him arrested. Imprisoned as a "Bolshevik agitator," Murray meets the "Communist Hartwell," who was falsely charged with violating the "dry" law. Despite lacking leadership, the workers continue the strike. In the film's final scene, Murray tells Hartwell that he "finally found his 'blood brothers' in the proletariat regardless of skin color."[6]

A better-known 1932 film in which the indictment of U.S. racism constitutes a subtheme is *The Return of Nathan Becker*. Released by the Belorussian national cinema in both Russian and Yiddish, the film follows the adventures of Nathan Becker, a Jewish bricklayer who returns to his Belorussian village after living for twenty-eight years in the United States. Becker brings with him his African American friend named Jim (played by Ben-Salim), whom he informs that "'You, too are going home.'"[7] Reminiscent of the Red Army soldiers in *Little Red Devils*, the village's inhabitants are fascinated and perplexed by Jim's skin color. Eventually, Jim, Nathan, and the latter's father, Tsele (played by S. Mikhoels) move to Magnitigorsk to assist in building the new giant of socialist industry. To underscore the multiracial harmony which the socialist future guarantees, at the film's end, Tsele is shown teaching Jim a Jewish song.

As these films demonstrate, in contrast to Mezhrabpom's *Black and White*, which was cancelled in 1932, productions that implicated U.S. racism but did not involve an African American cast and had more modest budgets made it to the silver screen.[8] Hence, when *Circus* was released in May 1936, Soviet audiences would have been acquainted with films with antiracist themes.[9] But unlike these other films, *Circus* was a production of Mosfilm, the most prominent and powerful of Soviet studios, and commanded the widest viewing audience.[10] Some viewers may have been familiar with *Circus*'s underlying premise, since it was based on a play by Il'ia Il'f and Evgenii Petrov titled *Under the Big Top* (*Pod kupolom tsirka*), which premiered at the Moscow Music Hall on December 23, 1934.[11] After viewing the production in 1935, Aleksandrov recruited Il'f, Petrov, and Valentin Kataev, who was Petrov's brother, to write the film's screenplay. The partnership did not last, however. The three writers removed their names from the film after Aleksandrov—without their approval—made changes that politicized the script.[12]

Circus, unlike *Under the Big Top*, opens in America in a small Kansas town. The local paper, the *Sunnyville News*, announces on the front page that the renowned circus performer, Marion Dixon, was at the center of a "scandal."[13] An angry white mob chases the young white woman, who is carrying a baby that, it is later revealed, was fathered by a black man. Dixon barely eludes the grasp of her stone-throwing white male pursuers by leaping onto a departing train on the "Southern Railway, USA." She falls fainting into a compartment near Franz von Kneishits, a German man, who becomes her manager and the film's villain.[14] The addition of this brief "American" scene replete with an angry lynch mob constitutes one of the main ways that Aleksandrov politicized Il'f and Petrov's story.[15]

The film's next scene shifts to the Soviet Union, where Dixon is making special appearances in the Moscow Circus for the exorbitant salary of five hundred dollars a month. Despite her success, the young American woman fears the exposure of her "shameful" secret. The abusive von Kneishits uses her two-year-old black son, Jimmy, to blackmail her into staying with him. Neither the American nor the German realize that the Soviet people have a superior, enlightened attitude toward race. Dixon, consequently, pretends that Jimmy is the son of a black female domestic servant who lives with her in the new Hotel Moscow overlooking Red Square.

By the time her contract expires with the Moscow Circus, Dixon does not want to return to the capitalist world. She has fallen in love with the joyfulness of Soviet society, apropos of Stalin's declaration that "Life has become more joyous, comrades," and with Ivan Martynov, a handsome Russian circus performer. Martynov is a strong, principled Soviet man (with a very Aryanlike appearance) who represents the superior system of socialism.[16] His extremely powerful physique, handsomeness, and light-colored (typically white) clothing are juxtaposed with the weak, puny frame and dark clothing of the immoral von Kneishits. As the embodiment of Nazism, von Kneishits wears inflatable padding to increase the size of his shoulders and chest. Body type and clothing therefore leave no doubt with regard to who represents "good" and "evil" in *Circus*.[17]

Since Martynov has guided her to consciousness, Dixon is willing to work in the circus for a fraction of her previous salary if not for free, but she needs to escape the ruthlessly exploitative grasp of von Kneishits.[18] Dixon tricks the latter into thinking she is leaving the Soviet Union with him and absconds to the circus to perform a new act with Martynov. When the villain discovers her duplicity, he returns to the circus, displays Jimmy to the audience, and declares that Dixon's "racial crime" renders her unfit for "white civilized society." Dixon hides out of fear that the spectators will assault her as the white American mob had attempted. However, the audience, comprised of representatives of various Soviet nationalities including Georgians, Jews, Ukrainians, and Central Asians, dismisses von Kneishits's intolerant ranting, rescues Jimmy from von Kneishits, and sings him a lullaby in their native languages, and sings the chorus in unison in Russian (a scene that is absent from *Under the Big Top*). The final two spectators who sing to Jimmy are a young, blond-haired white woman and Robert Ross, an African American man who, as noted in chapter 2, appeared on *Izvestiia*'s front page in 1936 as a trainer in a Physical Culture parade.[19] As Beth Holmgren writes, "This crowd, in pointed contrast to the American mob of the prologue, laughs away his [von Kneishits's] ugly rhetoric and literally embraces Jimmy, removing him bodily from von Kneishits as soldier-patrons move forward to block the German from pursuit."[20] A bewildered Dixon is further stunned when Martynov says that her black son does not diminish his love for her. The film's final scene (which Aleksandrov also added to the script) features the happy couple participating in the May Day parade on Red Square. Dixon's face is radiant with the love she has for the new joyous life that the USSR has bestowed upon her. She and the other participants enthusiastically sing the popular "Song of the Motherland" by Isaak Dunaevskii.[21]

In an interview with the *Moscow Daily News* in May 1935, a year before filming and releasing *Circus*, Aleksandrov explained that by addressing "'the relations between a white woman and a black man,'" the film would highlight Soviet "'equality of all peoples regardless of nationality or the color of their skins.'"[22] With this as its underlying objective, *Circus* is consistent with the manifestations of Soviet antiracism discussed in the preceding five chapters. *Circus*, however, pursued its realization in a very different manner. Soviet antiracism of the late 1920s and early 1930s, as this book has shown, favored the African American man, specifically depicting black male workers as the primary targets of U.S. racial apartheid and the main beneficiaries of Soviet racelessness. *Circus*, in contrast, completely elides the African American man, focusing instead on how the "relations between a white woman and a black man" affect the white American woman, Marion Dixon, who finds refuge from American racial prejudice at the side of a Russian man in the USSR.

The image of the white American woman as a victim of racism had not only been absent from Soviet antiracism of the first half of the 1930s, but the emphasis on dispelling the myth of the black rapist had underscored white women's integral role in perpetuating the U.S racial regime (a role that several white American female Lenin School students gave credence). Moira Ratchford argues that the designation of a white American woman as the target of American race hatred made the film effective in encouraging antiracist sentiment among Soviet citizens. According to Ratchford, "by vicariously experiencing Marion's terrifying encounter with a mob of racists, the Soviet viewer undoubtedly felt a far deeper and more lasting sense of distress and disgust at American racists than by simply reading a newspaper article about the Ku Klux Klan."[23]

While perhaps effective in inspiring sympathy in the viewer, did the focus on the plight of a white American mother of a black child require the erasure of the African American father? Was he a husband, friend, fellow circus performer, or casual lover?[24] Had he been lynched, imprisoned, or had he managed to escape from the mob that would have definitely hunted him if it had chased Dixon? These are important questions that would have likely been expounded upon had the film been made a few years earlier. Instead, the sole evidence that this African American man exists, since Dixon is never portrayed thinking about him, is his light-skinned son, Jimmy. The casting of a light-skinned child to play Jimmy was certainly a radical departure from contemporary Hollywood productions, which often used white actors in blackface to play African American characters. And the intimate mother-child scene between Dixon and Jimmy in *Circus* would have been unthinkable in an American film of this era.[25] Yet at the same time, Aleksandrov had considered using an actor in blackface, a frequent practice in Soviet plays and films with black characters. Moreover, the inclusion of a black actor does not mean the inclusion of a black voice. Due to Jimmy's young age, he has no speaking lines; he can neither articulate his feelings nor testify to the existence of his African American father.[26] The common trope in Soviet cultural productions of depriving the racial other of the capacity for speech is thus exhibited in Aleksandrov's *Circus*.[27]

The presence of Ross and his white female companion at the Moscow Circus would seem to imply that the new Soviet constitution's guarantee of national and racial equality would have rendered Jimmy's African American father an equal in the USSR.[28] But again the black spectator has no voice, and this interracial couple is featured only in the circus. They are conspicuously absent from the triumphant march across Red Square, in which the grandfatherly circus director (rather than Dixon or Martynov) carries Jimmy. Fairs, carnivals, and circuses have historically constituted realms of liminality, where it has been acceptable to transgress or blur the gender, class, and racial boundaries that serve as the foundation of the putative social order.[29] In the end, it is not entirely clear whether the equality of Jimmy's African American father would have been upheld beyond the Big Top's world of illusions.

The portrayal of a white American mother who is an affluent, non-industrial worker as one of the film's two heroines—second to the Soviet motherland that had afforded Dixon a joyous life—reflects developments in Soviet society of the mid-1930s. This was an era in which women's identity as mothers (regardless of class) and the female identity of the Soviet Union as the motherland were celebrated.[30] The official reemphasis on family, motherhood, and children is manifest in the film in various other ways including the male-female couples in the circus's audience who assume a parental role by singing a lullaby to Jimmy; the elderly Russian circus director who declares that Dixon could have as many children as she wants regardless of their skin color "because in our country we love all children"; and the "Song of the Motherland" that Martynov teaches Dixon and that the new Soviet couple sings with the parade's other participants while marching across Red Square.[31] Karen Petrone argues that the song was intended to capture the intimate connection that every male citizen was supposed to have with the motherland, which they were to love "'as we would a bride.'" This bond, symbolized in Martynov's relationship to his "bride" Dixon, promised Soviet men "mastery of the motherland in exchange for her defense."[32]

Partly for this reason, Dixon's black child was scripted male. Like Martynov, upon maturation into manhood, Jimmy would defend and love the "motherland" because it had provided him the opportunity to grow up without the threat of physical "harm," an opportunity that the multiethnic spectators emphasize in the lullaby. But Dixon's child was also male because African American girls were nonexistent in interwar Soviet antiracism (as evidenced in the short stories discussed in chapter 2). In the early 1930s, prior to the state's reemphasis on motherhood, the parent-child relationship was entirely masculine or between an African American father and son.

The film's elision of the African American father could be explained independent of race by the official emphasis on women as mothers, if *Circus* had also devoted attention to African American women and/or mothers.[33] African American mothers were in fact not unknown in Soviet society of the 1930s. The most notable was Williana Burroughs, who as mentioned in chapter 2 placed her two sons in an elite Soviet school so that they could grow up without U.S. racial discrimination. Also, Margaret Glascow, the African American grandmother of the actor who played Dixon's son, Jimmy, in the film, moved to Moscow in 1934 (see chapter 4). Despite these examples, *Circus* ignores the African American woman. The film does not sanction an interracial union between an African American woman and a white American or Russian man, even though such relationships likewise existed in the Soviet Union (such as in the persons of Coretta Arle-Titz and Mildred Jones) during this era. Even more problematic, the film features one unnamed black woman (played by Vivian Jones), but she has no lines and no voice.[34] Equally egregious, Dixon's employment of this woman—who appears in full maid's regalia—as her domestic servant is presented as unproblematic; that is, as a way of life instead of signifying the racially discriminated status of African American women.[35] In this way, *Circus* perpetuates the desexualization of black women as the "Mammy" whose sole purpose in life was caring for the children and domiciles of white women even if they lived in Moscow.[36] Thus, while the film was in some ways far ahead of Hollywood's treatment of race, it also replicated some of its major shortcomings and stereotypes.

Aleksandrov's decision to focus on Soviet tolerance of interracial relationships to glorify the state's policies as enlightened is not surprising when considering the "hysteria over miscegenation" in the United States and Germany, and the international campaign of the early 1920s to remove French colonial troops from the Rhineland under false allegations that they were sexually assaulting German women.[37] Since the early 1930s, many African American men experienced what they publicly portrayed as a freedom previously unknown to them, as a result of their ability to date and marry white women (i.e., Russian, European, or American) in the USSR. Yet precisely because examples did exist in Soviet society of African

American men who married and fathered children by white women, it is curious that the film highlights Soviet society's tolerance and enlightenment by depicting a love story between a white American woman and a Russian man. The most obvious example was the interracial marital union of the parents of James Patterson, who played Jimmy. James's father was Lloyd Patterson, an African American cast member of *Black and White*. Shortly after arriving in Moscow in June 1932, Patterson married a Russian artist with whom he had three children; James, the oldest, was born in 1933.[38] The interracial grandparents of Yelena Khanga, the journalist and future Russian television celebrity, could have also served as a model. Khanga's grandfather was Oliver Golden, an African American Communist who, as mentioned in chapter 4, led a team of scientists from Tuskegee Institute, Wilberforce University, Harvard University, and Virginia Normal College to Uzbekistan in 1931 to assist in the development of the Soviet cotton industry. In 1935 Golden and his wife, Bertha Bialek, a Polish-born Jewish American woman, decided to remain permanently in the USSR due to the birth of their daughter, Lily (Khanga's mother).[39] Additionally, when *Circus* was released in late May 1936, Jane Emery, a white American woman and her husband, African American Communist Herbert Newton, reportedly moved to the Soviet Union with their children, explicitly seeking refuge from the incessant racial persecution they faced in the United States. The *Afro-American* quoted Emery, who was forced to undergo psychiatric evaluation when her marriage to Newton was exposed, as declaring that "'I am going to stay in Russia, where my marriage will be approved.'"[40]

In contrast to the varied examples of African American men and white women marrying and having children in the USSR in the first half of the 1930s, the case of a white American woman moving to Moscow with her young black son, blackmailed by a conniving German circus promoter and unaware of Soviet promises of racial equality, was utter fantasy. In his 1976 memoir, *Epokha i kino*, Aleksandrov remarked that "singing the praises of Soviet laws and the internationalism of Soviet society was all the more convincing when contrasted with the barbaric, hateful, racist laws of fascism. I encountered fascists, and offensive incidences of racism more than once in the USA. I gathered the materials for the prologue [of *Circus*] from eyewitness accounts.'"[41] In this statement, Aleksandrov elides the distinction that his film and Soviet officials drew in the mid-1930s between the racist policies of fascist countries and those of bourgeois democracies like the United States.[42] Even more important, he claims that he used eyewitness testimony to create the film's prologue. Lynch mobs, however, rarely pursued white American women who had black children, and such incidents are unknown for the mid-1930s. Aleksandrov's experiences in the United States in the early 1930s, and any superficial amount of research, would have made this evident. A lynch mob pursuing an African American mother would have been consistent with reality.[43]

Why, therefore, did Aleksandrov deal with interracial relationships and showcase Soviet racial and national equality in this circuitous manner? The lessons learned from *Black and White*, and Soviet authorities' desire to avoid incurring the ire of U.S. leaders, undoubtedly played a role. But it appears that Aleksandrov and Soviet officials were also unwilling or unable to bear a love story between an African American man and a white woman (or a black woman and a white man). It could be alluded to in the form of the interracial couple shown briefly in the final circus scene, but to allot it primary focus where character development was necessary was beyond the realm of possibility. This is most likely why the viewer is told nothing of Jimmy's father. Although the use of a black child and the images of Dixon soothing Jimmy were unfathomable in Hollywood films of this era, *Circus* exposes Soviet limitations in challenging the dominant racial taboos of the era.[44]

Beyond mirroring the changes in Soviet gender relations and the limits of Soviet antiracist expression, *Circus* reflects how the focus of Soviet propaganda had shifted by 1936 from antiracism and an attack on U.S. race relations to antifascism and Nazi Germany. This development, as noted above, was most clearly evidenced in the film's villain, von Kneishits. In *Under the Big Top*, von Kneishits, despite his name, is consistently identified as an American artist. In *Circus*, the character is not associated with the United States; he speaks Russian with a German accent and the "von" prefix added to his name fixes him as a

German aristocrat. Moreover, von Kneishits is depicted unmistakably Nazilike in physical appearance and demeanor: stern, tall, and lanky with a wiry mustache, dark hair, and dark eyes. As Richard Taylor posits, since von Kneishits's hair is parted on the right side, his character invokes viscerally the person of Hitler.[45] To be sure, *Circus* dramatizes socialism's defeat of Nazism in two main ways. First, the multinational circus spectators laugh at von Kneishits's racist diatribe and liberate Jimmy from the clutches of the stereotypical Nazi. Second, the physically strong, attractive, and racially enlightened Martynov defeats the puny, evil von Kneishits in the battle for Dixon's love.

Thus, notwithstanding the film's condemnation of U.S. racism, *Circus* affirms in the person of Dixon that there is hope for America. Dixon rejects the notion that interracial relations are a "racial crime"; she comes to recognize socialism as the superior system and disavows her old infatuation with material items. Soviet socialism rather than German Nazism wins the heart and mind of the representative American. While *Circus* therefore alludes to the similarities between the racial mores of the United States and Nazi Germany, it is the latter embodied in von Kneishits that constitutes the graver threat to Soviet civilization and against which the USSR and America (Martynov and Dixon) align to defeat. To put it differently, there was promise for America not in terms of an imminent workers' revolution that would make it a moral equal but as a potential ally in a future war against Nazi Germany, which had replaced the United States—in Soviet propaganda of the second half of the 1930s—as the most racist country in the world.

Although antifascism eclipsed antiracism as the overwhelming focus of Soviet propaganda by the second half of the 1930s, its rich imagery and discourse were not forgotten. The legacy of interwar antiracism enabled Nikita Khrushchev, as cited in the first pages of this book, to impress U.S. senator Hubert Humphrey with his effortless espousal of polished antiracist rhetoric in December 1958. And yet, while antiracism of the 1920s and 1930s informed the Soviet indictment of racism in the decades after the Second World War, salient differences also made them distinct. The most obvious distinction was that leaders of the Western world epitomized by Senator Humphrey now recognized the value of speaking antiracism. Indeed, Soviet depictions of American race relations reflected this change. Even prior to the emergence of the bus boycotts, marches, and sit-ins of the modern U.S. civil rights movement, the Soviet press reported that various "progressive" and "democratic" organizations in the United States opposed the violence against African Americans and were demanding that federal and state officials act decisively to end it.[46] Since an increasing number of white American citizens and officials had begun to conceive of violence against African Americans as an injustice and source of national embarrassment, widespread outrage about American racial apartheid could no longer be scripted as uniquely "Soviet" or as evidence of the exceptional antiracist consciousness of the New Soviet Person.

The Soviet indictment of U.S. racism after the Second World War was also distinct from its predecessor because propagandists did not need to rely primarily on violence against African Americans to represent America as an imperial, belligerent aggressor. In contrast to the era of American isolationism of the 1920s and 1930s, they could (and did) spotlight U.S. actions around the globe to challenge its leaders' claims to be defenders of the putative "Free World." Moreover, Soviet authorities used the "Rise in Anti-Negro Terror" in the late 1940s and 1950s to expose the hypocrisy of U.S. democracy, but *not* to signal an imminent imperialist war against the first workers' state. In other words, unlike the interwar era, U.S. racial violence was not depicted as a threat to the USSR's national security and thus did not carry the same sense of urgency or meaning for Soviet citizens. Their fate was no longer represented as inseparable from that of U.S. blacks. Certainly, African Americans continued to be identified as friends of the Soviet Union, as exhibited in the fanfare surrounding the visits of Paul Robeson and W. E. B. Du Bois to Moscow. To be sure, by the 1950s Robeson had become, and in many ways remains, the enduring "face" of Soviet antiracism. Yet African Americans lost their exclusive interwar status as *the* Soviet Union's valued allies; this designation was shared with Asians, and especially Africans, for whom Soviet leaders were competing with the United States for influence by the mid-1950s. As the competition between these two countries-turned-superpowers went global after the Second World War, the Soviet indictment of racism assumed a much more international (rather than primarily American) focus.

Introduction

1. Quoted in Taubman, *Khrushchev*, 406–7.
2. On the primacy of race to Cold War politics, see especially Dudziak, *Cold War Civil Rights*; Borstelmann, *Cold War and the Color Line*; and Anderson, *Eyes Off the Prize*.
3. Khrushchev was in Moscow during this period, first studying engineering at the Industrial Academy and then serving as its party secretary before becoming the general secretary of the Ukrainian Communist Party in 1938. The phraseology "speaking antiracism" is a variation of Stephen Kotkin's "speaking Bolshevik." See *Magnetic Mountain*, 198–237.
4. For the use of the term "hard-line policy," see Martin, *Affirmative Action Empire*, 83, 122–23.
5. The term "nadir" was coined by Logan in *Betrayal of the Negro*. See also Blackmon, *Slavery by Another Name*; Tuttle, *Race Riot*; and Brophy, *Reconstructing the Dreamland*. The apartheid existence of U.S. blacks is well documented in scholarship on the first Great Migration to northern U.S. cities during and after the First World War. See note 66 below.
6. The scholarship on lynching is vast. For excellent recent works, see Dray, *At the Hands of Persons Unknown*; Goldsby, *Spectacular Secret*; Waldrep, *African Americans Confront Lynching*; and Wood, *Lynching and Spectacle*.
7. On the concept of the "hidden transcript," see James Scott, *Domination and the Arts of Resistance*.
8. Blakely, *Russia and the Negro*; Carew, *Blacks, Reds, and Russians*; Gilmore, *Defying Dixie*; Matusevich, "Exotic Subversive" and "Journeys of Hope."
9. Baldwin, *Beyond the Color Line*; Kelley, *Hammer and Hoe*; Maxwell, *New*

Negro, Old Left; Naison, *Communists in Harlem*; Solomon, *Cry Was Unity*. These scholars have challenged the paradigm that depicted blacks who embraced Communism as subordinating their autonomy to Moscow.

10. For a discussion of this methodology and approach, see Trouillot, *Silencing the Past*.

11. American Communist John Reed spoke of the growing militancy among black workers in the United States. See especially C. Robinson, *Black Marxism*, 218–28; n.30.

12. C. Robinson, *Black Marxism*, esp. 220–22. Sen Katayama, a Japanese Communist who spent time in the United States, arranged for McKay's inclusion in the Congress. On the remarkable career of Katayama as a valued friend to blacks in Moscow, see especially Mukherji, "Erasure of American Anticolonialism."

13. For an overview of Huiswood's life and career, see Carew, *Blacks, Reds, and Russians*, 20–25.

14. Carew, *Blacks, Reds, and Russians*, 23.

15. Baldwin, *Beyond the Color Line*, 50.

16. McKay, *Long Way from Home*, 172–74.

17. Baldwin, *Beyond the Color Line*, esp. 40–46. Baldwin also explains that the *Pravda* version depicted blacks as possessing an innate "warrior" quality.

18. McKay, *Long Way from Home*, 171, 192; Baldwin, *Beyond the Color Line*, 49–51; Carew, *Blacks, Reds, and Russians*, 19–25. See also W. Cooper, *Claude McKay*; and Tillery, *Claude McKay*.

19. McKay, *Negroes in America* and *Trial by Lynching*. For an in-depth analysis of these works, see Baldwin, *Beyond the Color Line*, 59–80; and Maxwell, *New Negro, Old Left*, 71–93.

20. Hughes, "Negroes in Moscow." David Levering Lewis claims that it was required reading for high-ranking Soviet officials. See *W. E. B. Du Bois*, 194 (quotation).

21. For the term, see Fitzpatrick, "'Soft' Line on Culture," and *Cultural Front*, 91–114.

22. See, for example, Rogger, "America in the Russian Mind."

23. Maiakovskii, *Maiakovskii ob Amerike*, 120–21.

24. Brooks, "The Press and Its Message."

25. David Levering Lewis emphasizes the solitariness of Du Bois's trip, which he planned on short notice. Du Bois traveled to the USSR a second time in the fall of 1936, which included traveling to Manchuria

on the Trans-Siberian Railroad. See Lewis, *W. E. B. Du Bois*, 199–205, 389–418. On Du Bois's engagement with the USSR following the Second World War, see Baldwin, *Beyond the Color Line*, 149–201; and Horne, *Black and Red*.

26. Kotkin, *Magnetic Mountain*, esp. 2, 152–53. Russian leaders and intellectuals have a long history of defining the country's image in relation to the West. Under the Bolsheviks, this impulse assumed a distinct, Marxist-Leninist ideological mission that coexisted uneasily with Great Power imperatives. See Smart, *Imagery of Soviet Foreign Policy*, esp. 48–53; and chapter 2 of this study.

27. On these anxieties, see Rogger, "*Amerikanizm* and the Economic Development."

28. On the attributes of the New Soviet Person, see especially Hoffmann, *Stalinist Values*, 3–4, 45–54; and Peris, *Storming the Heavens*, 71–75.

29. On the militant "Third Period," see Eley, *Forging Democracy*, 251–52; and Chase, *Enemy within the Gates*, 1–9.

30. Solomon, *Cry Was Unity*, esp. 85–89.

31. Soviet leaders similarly connected the fate of the Loyalists in the Spanish Civil War with the security of the USSR. See Kowalsky, *Stalin and the Spanish Civil War*. On the "siege mentality" characteristic of this period of Soviet history, see Rittersporn, "Omnipresent Conspiracy"; and Peris, *Storming the Heavens*, 102–17.

32. For comprehensive accounts of these sojourners, see note 8 above.

33. Duberman, *Paul Robeson*, 206–8, 221–22. See also Robeson, *Undiscovered Paul Robeson*.

34. Carew makes this argument with regard to Robinson. See *Blacks, Reds, and Russians*, 168–69. Scholarship on the Great Terror is extensive. See, for example, Khlevniuk, *1937-i*; and Getty, Naumov, and Sher, *Road to Terror*.

35. Klehr, Haynes, and Anderson, *Soviet World*, 218–26; Carew, *Blacks, Reds, and Russians*, 180–83. For an extended discussion of Fort-Whiteman's activities in Moscow, see Gilmore, *Defying Dixie*, 31–66.

36. "Lichnoe delo-Fort Uaitman Lovet," Rossiiskii gosudarstvennyi arkhiv sotsial'noi i politicheskoi istorii (RGASPI), fond 495, opis' 261, delo 1476, listy 6, 7–8, 14–140b, 15, 21, 29.

37. This was evidenced most obviously in the Soviet Union's entry into the League of Nations in 1934. See Eley, *Forging Democracy*, 266.

38. For a similar argument with regard to Cuba in the late nineteenth century, see Ferrer, *Insurgent Cuba*.

39. Hobsbawm, *Age of Extremes*, 117–19, 131–32; Mazower, *Dark Continent*, 51–64; Livezeanu, *Cultural Politics*, 297–312; Hanebrink, *In Defense of Christian Hungary*; Plach, *Clash of Moral Nations*.

40. Pennybacker, *From Scottsboro to Munich*.

41. See the discussion about "racial politics" that involved Eric Weitz, Francine Hirsch, and Amir Weiner in the spring 2002 edition of the *Slavic Review*, 1–53. See also Martin, *Affirmative Action Empire*, esp. 126–26, 450–60; Holquist "'Conduct Merciless Mass Terror'"; Weiner, *Making Sense of War*; and Hirsch, *Empire of Nations*, esp. 295–96.

42. Weitz, "Racial Politics." For "white men's countries," see Lake and Reynolds, *Drawing the Global Colour Line*.

43. Mazower, *Dark Continent*, 102–3. See also note 2 above.

44. See Lusane, *Hitler's Black Victims*; Kershaw, *Nazi Dictatorship*; and Burleigh and Wippermann, *Racial State*.

45. See especially Mazower, *Hitler's Empire*. See also Mazower, *Dark Continent*, 70–73, 99–103. Mills makes a similar argument in *Racial Contract*. On racial defilement, see Szobar, "Telling Sexual Stories."

46. Holt, *Problem of Freedom*; Conklin, "Colonialism and Human Rights"; Peabody, *"There Are No Slaves in France."*

47. Mazower, *Dark Continent*, 56–61. On the coexistence of the principles of universality and exclusionary citizenship laws, see Brubaker, *Citizenship and Nationhood*; F. Cooper and A. Stoler, "Between Metropole and Colony"; and Moch, "Foreign Workers in Western Europe," 103–16.

48. Jenkinson, *Black 1919*; Bland, "White Women and Men of Colour"; Tabili, "Women 'of a Very Low Type.'"

49. Stovall, "Color Line behind the Lines" and "Colour-blind France?" On preserving the racially homogenous identity of France, see also Fletcher, "City, Nation, and Empire."

50. Anderson, *Imagined Communities*; Mazower, *Dark Continent*, 74–75; Peabody and Stovall, *Color of Liberty*; Stoler, *Race and the Education of Desire*.

51. See Saul, *Friends or Foes*, 269–301; and Phillips, "Rapprochement and Estrangement."

52. Stovall, *Paris Noir*, 32, 53, 81, 154–63, 323–24.

53. Baldwin, *Beyond the Color Line*, 36–37.

54. These debates are documented in three large files in the document collections of the Negro Bureau of the Eastern Secretariat of the Executive Committee of the Communist International. See RGASPI, f. 495, op. 155, dd. 56–58. Many of the articles written by the debates' participants and

the Comintern's resolution are reprinted in Foner and Allen, *American Communism and Black Americans*, 163–200. For Haywood's account, see *Black Bolshevik*, esp. 218–81.

55. For a meticulous account of these meetings, see Solomon, *Cry Was Unity*, esp. 68–91. See also note 56 below. Theodore Draper overemphasizes Stalin's role in these deliberations. See *American Communism and Soviet Russia*, 334.

56. See C. Robinson, *Black Marxism*, 224–28. Haywood acknowledges the influence of the ABB. See *Black Bolshevik*, 124–25, 230. William Maxwell contends that McKay's *Negroes in America* also influenced the Comintern's 1928 decree, an argument which Claude McKay would have supported. See *New Negro, Old Left*, 72, 80 89; and McKay, *Long Way from Home*, 179–89.

57. See Hirsch, "Race without the Practice of Racial Politics." On Soviet distinctions within ethnoterritorial units, see Hirsch, "The Soviet Union as a Work-in-Progress," 268, 272–75.

58. See, for example, Duara, *Rescuing History*; Gilroy, *"There Ain't No Black"*; and Pratt, *Imperial Eyes*.

59. Martin, *Affirmative Action Empire*, 125–26, 450–60; Slezkine, "USSR as a Communal Apartment." See also Hirsch, "Toward an Empire of Nations"; and Suny and Martin, *State of Nations*. For the foundational study of the repressive paradigm, see Pipes, *Formation of the Soviet Union*.

60. See "For the Political Secretariat," RGASPI, f. 495, op. 155, d. 91, ll. 6–9.

61. "Tezis po negritianskomu voprosu v SASSh," RGASPI, f. 495, op. 155, d. 94, ll. 21–42; Kuusinen, "Directives for the Thesis on the Negro Question in the United States," RGASPI, f. 495, op. 155, d. 94, ll. 205–8, 212–16. See also Kelley, *Hammer and Hoe*, 13.

62. Naison, *Communists in Harlem*, 18.

63. Solomon, *Cry Was Unity*, 85–89.

64. Kelley, *Scottsboro, Alabama*, xiii.

65. Wald, "Black Nationalist Identity," 12. On the labor defense movement, which established this precedent in the southern states, see Hill, *Men, Mobs, and Law*, 221–22.

66. Winston James argues that economic distress, natural disaster, and colonial policy helped precipitate migration to the United States. See *Holding Aloft the Banner*, 7–8, 12–20, 32–35, 38–41. Scholarship on the first Great Migration is immense. See, for example, Gottlieb, *Making*

Their Own Way; Grossman, *Land of Hope*; Thomas, *Life for Us*; and Trotter, *Great Migration*.

67. James, *Holding Aloft the Banner*, 1–6, 50–51, 69–89.

68. R. Robinson, *Black on Red*, 19–26. The migration of Robinson's family from Jamaica to Cuba was typical of the era. See James, *Holding Aloft the Banner*, 26–30.

69. Hooker, *Black Revolutionary*, 2–16.

70. Solomon, *Cry Was Unity*, 178.

71. C. Robinson, *Black Marxism*, 255.

72. According to James Ford's official biography, Ford's grandfather had been lynched in Georgia, and their last name was Forsch until a white foreman in Alabama changed it to Ford. See "Lichnoe delo Ford Dzheims," RGASPI, f. 495, op. 261, d. 6747, ll. 9–12; and "Negro Worker Nominated for Vice President," *Negro Worker* 2 (June 1932): 25–26.

73. Haywood's parents were originally from Tennessee and Missouri. See *Black Bolshevik*, 5–14.

74. In 1930–31 only 1,000 African Americans were members of the U.S. Communist Party, and roughly half lived in Chicago. By 1936 black American members numbered 3,895 or 9.5 percent of the Party. See Klehr, *Heyday of American Communism*, 331–33, 338–39, 347–48.

75. For the premier study on the first Great Migration to Chicago, see Grossman, *Land of Hope*. For the 1919 race riot, see William Tuttle, *Race Riot*. On African Americans in the First World War, see Williams, *Torch-bearers of Democracy*. On the role racism played in radicalizing the British West Indies Regiment, see James, *Holding Aloft the Banner*, 52–72; and Howe, *Race, War, and Nationalism*.

76. On the rape of black women, see especially Hine, "Rape and the Inner Lives of Black Women," 292–97. For an overview of Soviet leaders' ambivalence with regard to women and disregard of sexual crimes, see, for example, Lapidus, "Women in Soviet Society," 213–36; and Naiman, *Sex in Public*, 250–88.

77. See McDuffie, *Sojourning for Freedom*; and Harris, "Running with the Reds," 21–43.

78. White was a schoolteacher who stayed at KUTV for three years. See "Lichnoe delo-Uait Mod," RGASPI, f. 495, op. 261, d. 3234; and Haywood, *Black Bolshevik*, 217.

79. See, for example, Gilroy, "One Nation under a Groove"; McClintock, *Imperial Leather*, 352–88; and Verdery, *What Was Socialism*, 61–82.

80. On the similar masculinist articulation of the interracial proletarian movement in the United States, see Kelley, *Race Rebels*, 112–14.
81. On the "little brother, big brother" paradigm, see Martin, *Affirmative Action Empire*, 432–37, 452–60.
82. Balibar, "Racism and Nationalism."
83. See, for example, J. Allina-Pisano and E. Allina-Pisano, "'Friendship of Peoples' after the Fall"; and Roman, "Making Caucasians Black." On law enforcement officials as conduits of official racism, see Rowe, *Policing, Race, and Racism*; and Leo Lucassen, "'Harmful Tramps.'"

1. American Racism on Trial

1. Chamberlin, *Russia's Iron Age*, 362–64 (quotation 362). Chamberlin (1897–1969) served as the correspondent for the *Christian Science Monitor* from 1922 to 1932. He composed a two-volume history of the Russian Revolution. See Chamberlin, *Russian Revolution*.
2. Barbara Keys has explored the American response to the Stalingrad trial. See "An African-American Worker in Stalin's Soviet Union." Only a few other scholars mention the trial. These include Blakely, *Russia and the Negro*, 101; McClellan, "Africans and Black Americans in the Comintern Schools," 376; and Zhuravlev, *"Malen'kie liudi" i "bol'shaia istoriia,"* 260. Tim Tzouliadis, a journalist, discusses the trial to portray Soviet leaders as ruthlessly using Americans for propagandistic purposes and then discarding them. He bases his account on a literal reading of Robert Robinson's 1988 autobiography, which, as Barbara Keys notes, was printed by Acropolis, a company associated with the CIA. See Tzouliadis, *The Forsaken*.
3. During the most intensive phase of industrialization, nearly thirty-five thousand foreign workers, specialists, and their families were living in the Soviet Union, most of whom were Germans followed by Americans. See Zhuravlev, *"Malen'kie liudi,"* 29–31. Besides John Scott, who wrote about his experiences in Magnitogorsk in *Behind the Urals*, the most notable American to work in a socialist giant was Walter Reuther. Prior to his long tenure as president of the United Auto Workers in 1936, Reuther had worked with his brother in Nizhni-Novgorod's State Automobile Factory (GAZ) from roughly 1933 to 1935. See N. Lichtenstein, *Most Dangerous Man*. On GAZ, see Siegelbaum, *Cars for Comrades*, 36–79.
4. The U.S. government was informed of the Soviet press's coverage and afforded translations of some articles. See note 8 below. On the role of

the Soviet press in exposing wrongdoing and mobilizing workers, see Stalin, "Pechat' kak kollektivnyi organizator," in *Sochineniia*, 5:281–85; and Lenoe, *Closer to the Masses*.

5. On the persistence of ethnic animosity and anti-Semitism, see, for example, S. Davies, *Popular Opinion*, 82–90, 135–37; Hoffmann, *Peasant Metropolis*, 124–25; Kuromiya, *Freedom and Terror*, 147–48, 160, 198, 246; Martin, "Origins of Soviet Ethnic Cleansing"; and Siegelbaum and Sokolov, *Stalinism as a Way of Life*, 42–43, 71–72, 259–67, 364, 369–70.

6. On the propagandistic significance of the Traktorostroi on an international level, see Schultz, "American Factor," 136–48.

7. See "Opyt massovogo primeneniia truda amerikanskikh rabochikh i tekhnikov na Stalingradskom traktornom zavode," RGASPI, f. 495, op. 30, d. 648, ll. 120–26; and note 8 below. For the population total, see "Zasedanie sekretariata TsK VSRM ot 17 avgusta 1930 g.," Gosudarstvennyi arkhiv Rossiiskoi Federatsii (GARF), f. 5469, op. 14, d. 382, l. 4; and Records of the Department of State Relating to Internal Affairs of the Soviet Union, 1930–1939, 861.5017—Living Conditions, National Archives and Records Administration (NARA).

8. "Obvinitel'noe zakliuchenie po delu izbieniia rabochego negra na Stalingradskom traktornom zavode," GARF, f. 5469, op. 14, d. 382, ll. 15–18. Robert Robinson's version of the assault, which he recorded fifty years later, does not deviate much from the unpublished trial record. Given that he composed his memoir to expose Soviet racism, it is unlikely that he would have deliberately misrepresented the altercation. See *Black on Red*, 65–73. *Pravda* provided the description of the fight that corresponded most closely to that found in the trial record. See "19 avgusta—sud nad amerikanskimi rabochimi, izbivshimi negra," *Pravda*, August 17, 1930, 5. The U.S. legation received its information from the Soviet press and Frank Fetter, a Princeton University professor, who supposedly contacted William Chamberlin. See E. L. Packer to J. Edgar Hoover, August 19, 1930, State Department Decimal Files (SDDF), RG 59, 800.00B Robinson, Robert N./1, NARA; Riga Legation to Washington, September 4, 1930, SDDF, RG 59, 361.11/4045, NARA; and Enclosure No. 1 to Despatch no. 7250, Confidential, Riga Legation to Washington, September 11, 1930, SDDF, RG 59, 361.11/4046, NARA. Thanks to Barbara Keys for sharing these files with the author.

9. "Zasedanie sekretariata TsK VSRM ot 17 avgusta 1930 g.," GARF, f. 5469, op. 14, d. 382, ll. 1–3; "Utverzhdeno prezidumom N.V. kraikoma VSRM

ot avgusta 3og.," GARF, f. 5469, op. 14, d. 35, l. 89; "Saratov, prokuroru nizhnevolzhskogo kraia," GARF, f. 5469, op. 14, d. 382, l. 10; "TsK metallistov srochno vyzval v Moskvu predsedatelia zavkoma stalingradskogo zavoda," *Rabochaia gazeta*, August 11, 1930, 4; "Srochno rassledovat' i privlech' k ugolovnoi otvetstvennosti," *Rabochaia gazeta*, August 13, 1930, 6; "Zavkom Traktornogo vtorichno vyzvan TsK metallistov," *Trud*, August 13, 1930, 1; "Stalingradskaia prokuratura zamalchivaet delo amerikantsa Luisa," *Rabochaia gazeta*, August 17, 1930, 6; "TsK soiuza metallistov ob izbienii rabochego-negra v Stalingrade," *Pravda*, August 18, 1930, 2; "Zavkom Traktornogo budet dosrochno pereizbran," *Rabochaia gazeta*, August 18, 1930, 6.

10. Zhuravlev, *"Malen'kie liudi,"* 47, 143–45.

11. "Pozornyi fakt na Traktornom vskryl slabost' internatsional'noi raboty profsoiuzov Stalingrada," *Trud*, August 10, 1930, 1; "'Ia ostaius' na Traktornom,'" *Trud*, August 12, 1930, 1; "My vsetselo na storone tov. Robinsona," *Trud*, August 14, 1930, 1.

12. "Pis'mo rabochikh Elektrozavoda gazete 'Trud,'" *Trud*, August 14, 1930, 1; "'Trud' prinial predlozhenie Elektrozavoda," *Trud*, August 14, 1930, 1.

13. The trial was originally scheduled to begin on August 19; "Stalingrad, Moskva," GARF, f. 5469, op. 14, d. 382, l. 11.

14. "Conscious" meant Americans sympathetic to Communism; GARF, f. 5469, op. 14, d. 382, ll. 3–4. For brigade members, see "Inostrannye rabochie Leningrada posylaiut obshchestvennogo obvinitelia na stalingradskii protsess," *Trud*, August 17, 1930, 2; "Kak byl izbit tovarishch Robinson," *Trud*, August 18, 1930, 4; "Internatsional'naia rabochaia brigada 'Truda' vchera vyekhala na stalingradskii protsess," *Trud*, August 19, 1930, 1; "Inostrannye rabochie Khar'kova i Rostova poslali obshchestvennykh obvinitelei na stalingradskii protsess," *Trud*, August 20, 1930, 1; and "Luis i Braun pytalis' perenesti na sovetskuiu pochvu fashistskie nravy," *Trud*, August 28, 1930, 1.

15. *Trud*, August 19, 1930, 1. A similar photograph appeared in *Mezhdunarodnoe rabochee dvizhenie* the following month. On women in the press, see Brooks, *Thank You, Comrade Stalin*, 89–93 (quotation 90).

16. The prominence afforded Knut and Rodzinskaia on *Trud's* front page is consistent with the valorization of ordinary workers and the future society they were helping to build in Soviet literature and visual propaganda of the First Five-Year Plan. See Bonnell, "Iconography of the Worker"; and Clark, "'Little Heroes and Big Deeds.'"

17. Zhuravlev, *"Malen'kie liudi,"* 236–40, 272–74.
18. On the use of a woman's figure to represent the weaker partner of an alliance, see Bonnell, *Iconography of Power*, 64–135.
19. "Zaiavlenie Nuisa korrespondentu 'Truda,'" *Trud*, August 21, 1930, 1; "Protsess ob izbienii negra tov. Robinsona otlozhen do 22 avgusta," *Pravda*, August 21, 1930, 5; "'Nikogda bol'she ne budu storonnikom natsional'noi rozni,'" *Izvestiia*, August 22, 1930, 2; "'Nikogda bol'she ne budu storonnikom rozni ras i natsii,'" *Rabochaia gazeta*, August 22, 1930, 6; "Apologizes to Russians," *New York Times*, August 22, 1930, 4; "American Worker Who Attacked Negro Now Regrets His Act," *Daily Worker*, August 25, 1930, 2. The *Daily Worker* reprinted the apology on September 8 without noting that Lewis had long retracted it.
20. Some men may have told Lewis that Soviet officials planned to force him to room with Robinson. See Chamberlin, *Russia's Iron Age*, 364; and Enclosure No. 1 to Despatch no. 7250, Confidential, Riga Legation to Washington, September 11, 1930, SDDF, RG 59, 361.11/4046, NARA. On the American committee, see GARF, f. 5469, op. 14, d. 382, l. 4; and Ferdinand Knut, "Prigovor proletariata," *Trud*, August 31, 1930, 1.
21. GARF, f. 5469, op. 14, d. 382, l. 17; "Prigovor eshche ne vynesen," *Trud*, August 30, 1930, 1.
22. Prior to the trial, Lewis was arrested for sexually assaulting a cleaning woman at the factory. Since sexual assault, like physical assault, lacked political significance and carried a less severe penalty, it was not raised during the trial. See GARF, f. 5469, op. 14, d. 382, l. 6. The *Amsterdam News* reported inaccurately that Lewis was a "member of the Communist Youth League"; "Americans to Be Tried in Russia; Evicted Worker," *Amsterdam News*, August 20, 1930, 1.
23. "V SSSR net mesta rasovoi vrazhdebnosti," *Rabochaia gazeta*, August 11, 1930, 4; Ferdinand Knut, "Rasovaia nenavist'," *Trud*, August 19, 1930, 1; "Segodnia v Stalingrade nachinaetsia protsess ob izbienii negra tov. Robinsona," *Trud*, August 20, 1930, 1.
24. *Rabochaia gazeta*, August 22, 1930, 1. For another Stalingrad trial cartoon, see *Put' MOPR'a* 23–24 (August 1930): 13.
25. *Pravda* and *Komsomol'skaia pravda* set the number in attendance at one thousand, while *Rabochaia gazeta* claimed it to be near two thousand; "Nachalsia sud nad L'iuisom i Braunom," *Rabochaia gazeta*, August 24, 1930, 4; "Delo ob izbienii," 3. Chamberlin and his wife heard the proceedings over a loudspeaker as they approached the factory. See *Russia's Iron Age*, 362–63.

26. "Vyslat' amerikanskikh fashistov iz predelov SSSR," *Rabochaia gazeta*, August 27, 1930, 6; Ferdinand Knut, "Pered sudom vsia sistema kapitalizma," *Trud*, August 29, 1930, 1; "Prikhvostniam fashizma ne mesto v sovetskoi strane!" *Trud*, August 29, 1930, 1; "V Ameriku, k organizatoram sudov lincha!" *Trud*, August 30, 1930, 1.

27. "Lemuel H. Lewis," who was listed in the Detroit city directory from 1929 to 1930 as an "autoworker," appeared in neither the 1920 or 1930 U.S. census records for Detroit. This suggests that Lewis had not yet migrated there from the South for the 1920 census and had departed for Stalingrad before the 1930 census. On the witnesses' testimony and Lewis's residence, see GARF, f. 5469, op. 14, d. 382, ll. 16–19; *Polk's City Directory*, 1316; "Posledovateli lincha na Traktornom zavode," *Komsomol'skaia pravda*, August 26, 1930, 4; and "Amerikanets Nuis ne tol'ko khuligan, no i fashist," *Trud*, August 25, 1930, 1.

28. "Sud nad L'iuisom i Braunom," *Rabochaia gazeta*, August 25, 1930, 6; "Nachalsia sud," 4. On *Rabochaia gazeta*, see Lenoe, *Closer to the Masses*, 40–45.

29. See Padmore, "Socialist Attitude," 196.

30. On "proletarianness" and the "New Soviet Person," see Peris, *Storming the Heavens*, 78–83; Petrone, *Life Has Become More Joyous*, 1–5, 11–13, 66–69, 125; Hoffmann, *Stalinist Values*, 45–56; and Siegelbaum, "Shaping of Soviet Workers' Leisure."

31. "My ne dopustim v SSSR nravov burzhuaznoi Ameriki," *Trud*, August 9, 1930, 1; "My obrashchaemsia k amerikanskim rabochim," *Trud*, August 10, 1930, 1; "'Okruzhim negra Robinsona samym druzhestvennym vnimaniem,'" *Rabochaia gazeta*, August 15, 1930, 6; "Pozor khuliganam s Traktorostroia, izbivshim negra Robinsona," *Rabochaia gazeta*, August 14, 1930, 6; "'Protestuem protiv zverinogo natsionalizma,'" *Trud*, August 11, 1930, 1; "Amerikanskie rabochie osuzhdaiut izdevatel'stvo nad rabochim-negrom na Traktorostroe," *Izvestiia*, August 18, 1930, 3; "Rabochie amerikantsy osuzhdaiut izdevatel'stvo nad rabochim-negrom," *Trud*, August 18, 1930, 4; "Stalingradskaia prokuratura zamalchivaet," 6; "Inostrannye rabochie Khar'kova," 1.

32. "Nuzhen vsesoiuznyi smotr internatsional'nogo vospitaniia," *Trud*, August 28, 1930, 1; "Pionery Ameriki, Anglii, Bel'gii, Ukrainy o stalingradskom dele," *Trud*, August 20, 1930, 1; "Delo ob izbienii rabochego-negra," *Izvestiia*, August 18, 1930, 2; "Usilit' internatsional'nuiu rabotu," *Put' MOPR'a* 23–24 (August 1930): 1; "Obshchestvennyi sud nad

grazhdaninom Tsiprusom," *Komsomol'skaia pravda*, August 18, 1930, 4; note 54 below.

33. "Amerikanskie rabochie dolzhny osudit' postupok Nuisa," *Trud*, August 20, 1930, 2.

34. "Rabochie fabriki Moskvoshvei no. 5 vozmushcheny vystupleniem gr. Tsiprusa," *Rabochaia gazeta*, August 13, 1930, 6.

35. "Grazhdanin Tsiprus iskliuchen iz soiuza," *Trud*, August 18, 1930, 1.

36. "V otvet na antiproletarskuiu vykhodku Tsiprusa dopolnitel'no podpishemsia na zaem," *Rabochaia gazeta*, August 17, 1930, 6; "Prigovor rabochikh mass," *Rabochaia gazeta*, August 18, 1930, 6. The Tsiprus trial bore striking similarities to the comrades-disciplinary courts and agitational-trials of the early Soviet era. See Siegelbaum, "Defining and Ignoring Labor Discipline"; and Mally, "Rise and Fall of the Soviet Youth Theater."

37. See, for example, "Takie ne mogut nazyvat'sia rabochimi," *Rabochaia gazeta*, August 11, 1930, 4; "O chem govorit sluchai na Traktornom zavode," *Trud*, August 12, 1930, 1; "Amovtsy trebuiut vysylki vinovnikov iz predelov SSSR," *Trud*, August 13, 1930, 1; "Na Traktornom pobezhdaet solidarnost' proletariata," *Trud*, August 14, 1930, 1; "Postavit' izbivshikh negra pod ugrozu boikota," *Rabochaia gazeta*, August 15, 1930, 6; "Protest amerikanskikh rabochikh avtozavoda," *Trud*, August 19, 1930, 1; and "Voina shovinizmu," *Rabochaia gazeta*, August 20, 1930, 4.

38. "Prikhvostniam fashizma ne mesto," 1; Knut, "Pered sudom," 1; "Prigovor proletariata," 1; "Vyslat' amerikanskikh fashistov," 6.

39. "Rabochie fabriki 'Moskvoshvei' no. 5 reshitel'no osuzhdaiut amerikanskikh khuliganov," *Rabochaia gazeta*, August 11, 1930, 4; "Moskva, 31 avgusta," *Trud*, August 31, 1930, 1.

40. "Izbienie negra Robinsona—kontr-revoliutsionnyi vypad," *Rabochaia gazeta*, August 15, 1930, 6; "Vylazka kontrrevoliutsionerov," *Trud*, August 29, 1930, 1; *Metallist* 29 (September 20, 1930); "Luis i Braun pytalis' perenesti," 1; "V Ameriku, k organizatoram sudov," 1; "Amerikanets Nuis ne tol'ko," 1.

41. *Pittsburgh Courier*, September 6, 1930, 1. On the integral role of African American newspapers in forging Soviet antiracism, see chapter 4 of this study.

42. "Fashist Luis vysylaetsia iz SSSR," *Trud*, August 31, 1930, 1; "Posledovateli lincha v Stalingrade Liuis i Braun dolzhny byt' osuzhdeny,"

Komsomol'skaia pravda, August 30, 1930, 1; "Prigovor po delu ob izbienii negra Robinsona," *Rabochaia gazeta*, August 31, 1930, 2; "Liuis i Braun vysylaiutsia iz SSSR," *Pravda*, August 31, 1930, 7.

43. Lewis did not endure his deportation quietly. He accused Soviet officials of subjecting the Americans in Stalingrad to life-threatening conditions, a charge that an American worker in Stalingrad vehemently denied in a *Moscow News* editorial. See Donald Day, "450 Americans Reported Held Captive By Reds," *Chicago Tribune*, September 21, 1930, A7; Frank Honey, "Are the Americans Held Slaves by the Soviet Government," *Moscow News*, November 16, 1930, 7; and "Detroit Chauvinist Worker Charge Denied by Soviet," *Liberator*, October 11, 1930, 2. Brown may have remained in the country until his work contract expired in 1931. See "Posledovateli lincha osuzhdeny," *Komsomol'skaia pravda*, August 31, 1930, 1. If this was the case, then Soviet officials clearly were not interested in publicizing it. Robinson, however, maintained in his 1988 autobiography that both men were deported.

44. Argenbright, "Marking NEP's Slippery Path"; Getty, "*Samokritika* Rituals."

45. See "O rabote sredi inostrannykh rabochikh priekhavshikh v SSSR," RGASPI, f. 495, op. 30, d. 648, l. 21; "VTsSPS ot 28/8–30 g.: O rabote sredi inostrannykh rabochikh," RGASPI, f. 495, op. 30, d. 648, l. 101; and note 47 below.

46. "Zadachi profsoiuzov v rekonstruktivnyi period," *Rabochaia gazeta*, July 19, 1930, 3–4; "Za internatsional'noe vospitanie mass," *Rabochaia gazeta*, August 20, 1930, 1; "Sudebnoe sledstvie nachato," *Trud*, August 13, 1930, 1. On international education, see "Soveshchanie ob internatsional'noi rabote," GARF, f. 5469, op. 14, d. 381, ll. 3–45; "Mezhdunarodnaia rabota sovetskikh profsoiuzov," *Rabochaia gazeta*, August 29, 1930, 2; and "Opyt inostrannykh spetsialistov ne ispol'zuetsia," *Rabochaia gazeta*, August 15, 1930, 6.

47. See "Vypiska iz protokola no. 33 zasedaniia sekretariata TsK VSRM ot 25/IX-1930 g.," GARF, f. 5469, op. 14, d. 383, ll. 14–16; "Obzor raboty soiuznykh organizatsii metallistov," GARF, f. 5469, op. 14, d. 383, ll. 34–40; and note 8 above. The press depicted workers as condemning local officials. See, for example, "Usilit' politicheskoe vospitanie amerikanskikh rabochikh v SSSR," *Rabochaia gazeta*, August 15, 1930, 6.

48. A Stalingrad worker claimed that he and other "decent" Americans had complained to officials about these troublemakers, but they did

not address the situation until Robinson was assaulted. See "Doklad o rabote sredi amerikanskikh rabochikh na Stalingradskom traktornom zavode," GARF, f. 5469, op. 14, d. 383, ll. 66–72; "To the Secretariat, CPUSA, 19.11.30," RGASPI, f. 515, op. 1, d. 1870, ll. 136–39; RGASPI, f. 495, op. 30, d. 648, ll. 120–25; GARF, f. 5469, op. 14, d. 383, ll. 39–40; GARF, f. 5469, op. 14, d. 381, ll. 17–18; Nemchik, "Amerikantsy v Stalingrade," *Trud*, October 6, 1930, 4; Bill Dunne, "Detroit Racketeers on the Volga," *New Masses* (September 1931): 10–12; and Strong, *I Change Worlds*, 317–19.

49. For the equation of blackness with the absence of morality, see, for example, D. Davis, *Problem of Slavery*, 447–49, 452–64; McClintock, *Imperial Leather*, 5–7, 56–60; and Lawrence, "Just Plain Common Sense."

50. Mikhail Danilov, "Nuis i Robinson," *Rabochaia gazeta*, August 11, 1930, 4. For a similar sentiment, see *Put' MOPR'a* 23–24 (August 1930): 13. The factory committee's chairman at the Stalingrad Traktorostroi claimed that Robinson told the Americans they had no right to tell him to leave the factory; GARF, f. 5469, op. 14, d. 382, l. 1.

51. "O chem govorit sluchai," 1; "'Ia ostaius' na traktornom,'" 1; "Pozornyi fakt na traktornom," 1.

52. Soviet editors could have bolstered Robinson's image as the ideal international black laborer by elaborating on his work experience in Cuba, Jamaica, and Brazil, hotbeds of Marxist labor activity during this era. See James, *Holding Aloft the Banner*. On Robinson's insistence that his Christian beliefs placed him at odds with Marxism, see R. Robinson, *Black on Red*, 95–111.

53. "Amerikantsy ne byvali na rabochikh sobraniiakh," *Trud*, August 13, 1930, 1; "My ne dopustim v SSSR," 1. See also "Obshchestvennyi sud," 4; "O chem govorit sluchai," 1; and "Pionery Ameriki," 1.

54. Danilov, "Nuis i Robinson," 4; "V SSSR net mesta rasovoi vrazhdebnosti," 4.

55. "V redaktsiiu zhurnala 'Metallist,'" GARF, f. 5469, op. 14, d. 381, ll. 84–85; N. N., "Vozmutitel'nyi sluchai na stalingradskom traktornom zavode, v strane sovetov net mesta natsional'noi vrazhde," *Metallist* 26 (August 20, 1930): 12–14; "My vsetselo na storone tov. Robinsona," 1.

56. U.S. papers and the *Times* of London likewise continued to report erroneously that Lewis had expelled Robinson from the cafeteria. See, for example, Walter Duranty, "Americans Essay Color Bar in Soviet," *New York Times*, August 10, 1930, 9; "More Americans Face Accusations in

Soviet," *New York Times*, August 30, 1930, 5; "Soviet and Colour Prejudice," *Times*, August 13, 1930, 9; and "Americans to Be Tried in Russia; Evicted Worker," *Amsterdam News*, August 20, 1930, 1.

57. "Prikhvostniam fashizma ne mesto," 1.

58. Nineteenth-century white American abolitionists had of course made a similar mistake. See, for example, Fredrickson, *Black Image*, chapter 4.

59. "Pokazatel'nyi sud nad 'tsivilizovannymi' amerikantsami," *Izvestiia*, August 18, 1930, 3 (quotation).

60. "Rasskazy pro fashistov i pro pionerov," *Murzilka* 9 (1933): 7–11, esp. 11.

61. "Shorthand record of the conversation of Comrade Manuilskii with students of the 9th sector of KUTV," RGASPI, f. 532, op. 1, d. 441, l. 11.

62. Ida Murphy, "Most Impressive Country is Russia," *Afro-American*, November 14, 1936, 18.

63. RGASPI, f. 534, op. 3, d. 755, ll. 5, 27. During this period, Robinson was primarily signing a series of one-year labor contracts. See *Black on Red*, 79–82.

64. The *Moscow News* was first published on October 5, 1930. The *Workers News* appeared in February 1931 and quickly became more popular among English-speaking workers in the USSR. See RGASPI, f. 495, op. 30, d. 648, ll. 21, 101; "Predsedateliam ino biuro oblast' i krai sovprofov i instruktoram po rabote sredi inostrannykh rabochikh i inospetsialistov," GARF, f. 5451, op. 39, d. 10, ll. 1–2; "III-i s'ezd MOPRa 19/II-1931 g.," GARF, f. 8265, op. 1, d. 27, ll. 147–85; "Brigada TsK metallistov vyezzhaet na Traktorostroi," *Rabochaia gazeta*, August 13, 1930, 6; "Angliiskaia gazeta dlia inostrannykh rabochikh v SSSR," *Rabochaia gazeta*, August 14, 1930, 6; "New Moscow Paper Fights Chauvinism," *Liberator*, October 11, 1930, 1; Strong, *I Change Worlds*, 300–315, 333–52; and "Why 'Moscow Daily News' Has Begun," *Moscow Daily News*, May 1, 1932, 1.

65. "Organize Worker Correspondents," *Workers News*, August 25, 1931, 5.

66. "American Negro Praises Soviets," *Liberator*, September 19, 1931, 3.

67. "Save the Scottsboro Negro Boys: Appeal of Stalingrad Negro Specialist," *Workers News*, March 12, 1932, 3; R. Robinson, "Wonderful Achievements at Stalingrad," *Workers News*, March 26, 1932, 3. A small photograph of Robinson appeared with the statement of protest.

68. "Honor American Negro in Moscow as Hero of Labor," *Liberator*, November 19, 1932, 2.

69. "Will Report at Ball-Bearing Plant Meet on BRIZ Check-up," *Moscow Daily News*, June 9, 1933, 1; "Shows How Foreign Workers Can Get Rational-

izations Effected," *Moscow Daily News*, June 16, 1933, 4; "Ball-Bearing Plant Foreign Engineers Discuss Troubles," *Moscow Daily News*, March 6, 1933.

70. Zhuravlev, *"Malen'kie liudi,"* 256–60 (quotation 256). During his interview with the U.S. embassy after the 1934 election, Robinson played up his image as a diligent laborer to distance himself from association with the Communist Party. See "Report on Robert Nathaniel Robinson," Moscow to Washington, March 14, 1935, SDDF, RG 59, 800.00B/ Robinson, Robert Nathaniel/2, 3–6, NARA; and Robinson, *Black on Red*, 95–111.

71. See especially Lake and Reynolds, *Drawing the Global Colour Line*. Daniel Peris argues that the objective of most propaganda campaigns during this era was to glorify the enlightened nature of the Soviet state. See *Storming the Heavens*, esp. 99–117.

72. *Trud*, January 14, 1935, 2; "Soviet Union Elects Deputies," *Chicago Defender*, January 26, 1935, 11; "U.S. Youth Is Soviet Leader," *Chicago Defender*, December 15, 1934, 1. See also "Races Mingle in Russian Palace," *Afro-American*, June 6, 1936, 8; "Negro Elected to Soviets," *Negro Worker* 5 (January 1935): 31; *Negro Worker* 5 (February–March 1935): 9; and *Moscow Daily News*, March 10, 1935, 3.

73. Brooks, *Thank You, Comrade Stalin*, 85–86.

74. "Robinson Tells Impressions of Moscow Province Congress of Soviets," *Moscow Daily News*, January 17, 1935, 3.

75. "Mandat deputata Robinsona," *Vecherniaia Moskva*, December 14, 1934, 2. Robinson was also featured in *Ogonek* (November 30, 1935): 18–19.

76. Agapov, *Tekhnicheskie rasskazy*, 276–91. For an announcement of the book's publication with a photograph of Robinson, see L. Rapoport, "Interest Is Woven into Stories of Construction," *Moscow Daily News*, June 9, 1936, 3.

77. Brooks, *Thank You, Comrade Stalin*, 85–86.

78. Agapov, *Tekhnicheskie rasskazy*, 284.

79. Agapov, *Tekhnicheskie rasskazy*, 285. The high esteem with which German workers were held in Soviet factories in the early 1930s, the fact that they constituted the largest group of foreign laborers in the USSR, and the historically prominent and respected role of German Communists in the international revolutionary movement may have encouraged Agapov to highlight the foreman's Germanness (if Robinson had claimed he was German during their interview) or ascribe him this

identity. See Zhuravlev, *"Malenkie liudi,"* 236–40, 272–74. In his autobiography, Robinson does not mention that the man who gave him the opportunity was German. See *Black on Red*, 24–25.

80. Agapov, *Tekhnicheskie rasskazy*, 291. In his memoir about life in the USSR, which he composed after becoming disillusioned with the Soviet system, Homer Smith claimed that Russian women were always willing to dance with him and had no problems sharing the sleeping compartment with him on trains. See *Black Man in Red Russia*, 56–60.

81. See, for example, Dray, *At the Hands of Persons Unknown*; Campt, *Other Germans*, 31–62; and Bland, "White Women and Men of Colour."

82. Agapov, *Tekhnicheskie rasskazy*, 287–89.

83. Agapov may have sought to foster a sense of familiarity and friendliness by referring to Robinson as "Bob." But in doing so, he disclosed his ignorance regarding white Americans' long history of referring to adult blacks by familial, racist terms and by diminutives that signified black inferiority or conveyed the erroneous presumption of friendship. On this history, see for example, Litwack, *Trouble in Mind*, 34–36, 184–97.

84. Although Caribbean migrants to the United States were often startled by the racism they encountered, to portray Robinson as clueless is problematic. See James, *Holding Aloft the Banner*, 1–6, 50–51, 69–89.

85. See especially Blakely, *Russia and the Negro*, 81–104 (quotation 81).

86. Agapov, *Tekhnicheskie rasskazy*, 284, 287.

87. On the contradictory images of Africa and Africans in the Soviet Union, see Quist-Adade, *In the Shadows of the Kremlin*.

88. On his religious faith, see Robinson, *Black on Red*, 78–79.

89. Brooks, *Thank You, Comrade Stalin*, 85–97. The acknowledgment of wives alone reflected the reenshrinement of marriage, family, and childbearing as major sources of the country's stability. See Reid, "All Stalin's Women."

90. This reflects the general Soviet aversion in the 1930s to issues of sexuality. See Petrone, *Life Has Become More Joyous*, 33–34; and Healey, "Sexual and Gender Dissent." Karen Petrone claims that the terms "motherland" and "fatherland" were frequently used to refer to the USSR in the 1930s but that the "fatherland" was never symbolically depicted the way that the "motherland" was (53n30).

91. See, for example, A. Davis, "Rape, Racism, and the Myth of the Black Rapist."

92. See "Obzor raboty soiuznykh organizatsii metallistov," GARF, f. 5469, op. 14, d. 383, ll. 3–38 (l. 36).

93. See, for example, Tillet, *Great Friendship*; Slezkine, "USSR as a Communal Apartment"; and Brooks, *Thank You, Comrade Stalin*, 93–97.

94. Brooks, *Thank You, Comrade Stalin*, 85–86; Siegelbaum, "'Dear Comrade'"; Reid, "All Stalin's Women," 133, 158.

95. Though prerevolutionary Russian intellectuals often spoke of the Russian peasantry as "dark" and "primitive," non-Russians were consistently conceived to be more backward, and in some cases, Russian peasants were used to civilize them. See, for example, Brower and Lazzerini, *Russia's Orient*, esp. 80–114; and Sunderland, *Taming the Wild*.

96. See H. Smith, *Black Man in Red Russia*, 25; and Hughes, *I Wonder as I Wander*, 98.

97. To be sure, it was advantageous to "look non-Russian" during the 1930s. See Slezkine, "USSR as a Communal Apartment," 430–52.

98. On the "display" of non-Russian nationalities in Moscow, see, for example, Brooks, *Thank You, Comrade Stalin*, 93–97; and Zhuravlev, "*Malen'kie liudi*," 255–58. On the shift from "brotherhood" to "friendship" of peoples, see Martin, *Affirmative Action Empire*, 441, 452–56, 460.

99. For a discussion of socialism as "the antidote to capitalism," see Kotkin, *Magnetic Mountain*, esp. 149–55.

100. Hirsch, "Race without the Practice of Racial Politics"; Weiner, "Nothing but Certainty."

101. On the connection between the Stalingrad and Yokinen trials, see "V Congress-19th Session," RGASPI, f. 534, op. 1, d. 145, ll. 115–16; *Race Hatred on Trial*; I. Amter, "Significance of the Yokinen Trial," *Daily Worker*, March 9, 1930, 4; Cyril Briggs, "Workers' Mass Trial in Harlem March 1," *Liberator*, February 21, 1931, 1; and Roman, "Another Kind of 'Freedom,'" 113–21.

102. See, for example, Fitzpatrick, *Everyday Stalinism*, 67–75, 132–38; Hellbeck, "Speaking Out"; Alexopoulos, "Victim Talk"; Siegelbaum and Sokolov, *Stalinism as a Way of Life*, 315–16, 408–12.

103. On Acropolis's connections to the CIA, see Keys, "African-American Worker," 34.

104. Robinson, *Black on Red*, 65–73 (quotation 72).

105. Straus, *Factory and Community*, 136–37, 175, 187, 200–205, 244–46, 276.

2. "This Is Not Bourgeois America"

1. Becker, *Soviet and Russian Press Coverage*, 1.
2. Lenoe, *Closer to the Masses*, 42–45, 72–73.
3. For U.S. racism as the "ultimate evil" with the advent of the Third Period, see Wald, "Black Nationalist Identity," 12–13.
4. On the Soviet press's role in the 1920s in conveying the superiority of Soviet society in relation to capitalist countries, see Brooks, "Official Xenophobia," 1438.
5. On the Soviet state's cooptation of writers, journalists, and others involved in cultural production into concealing violence in Soviet society and glorifying Stalin's regime, see, for example, Zubok, *Zhivago's Children*. On violence, see also Davies and Wheatcroft, *Years of Hunger*; and Iakovlev, *Century of Violence*.
6. On MOPR's organizational objectives, see chapter 3 of this study.
7. On this unique community of anticolonial activists, see Mukherji, "Erasure of American Anticolonialism."
8. Il'f and Petrov arrived in the United States in October 1935 and returned to Europe in late January 1936. The remaining portions of *Odnoetazhnaia Amerika* appeared in *Roman-gazete* and *Khudozhestvennaia literatura* in 1937. See Il'f and Petrov, *Odnoetazhnaia Amerika*, 499.
9. On the conflation of nationality with class in U.S. proletarian literature, see Foley, *Radical Representations*, 175–77, 182.
10. "Dat' zhestochaishii otpor," *Rabochaia gazeta*, August 13, 1930, 6; "Kogo linchuiut v SASSh?" *Trud*, September 5, 1930, 2; "V 'tsivilizovannoi' filadel'fii," *Mezhdunarodnoe rabochee dvizhenie* 23–24 (August 1930): 32–33. This information on black workers is well documented in scholarship on black migration. See, for example, Thomas, *Life for Us*.
11. Louis Enghdal, "Negry v Amerike," *Prozhektor* 48 (November 25, 1928): 12. See also George Padmore, "Kak zhivut chernokozhie krest'iane v soediennykh shtatakh," *Put' MOPR'a* 26–27 (September 1930): 2, 9.
12. "Torgovlia negrami v SASSh," *Pravda*, November 12, 1932, 4.
13. On the origins and meanings of the term in the United States, see Waldrep, *Many Faces of Judge Lynch*. On *samosud*, see, for example, Frierson, "Crime and Punishment."
14. "The Red Trade Unions and IRA," RGASPI, f. 534, op. 1, d. 197, ll. 64–70 (quotation l. 69).
15. *Prozhektor* 48 (November 25, 1928): 12.
16. McKenna, *All the Views*, 16, 40 (quotation).

17. *Rabochaia gazeta*, August 17, 1931, 1.

18. On the practice of portraying information in *Pravda* as "factually correct," see McKenna, *All the Views*, 16. For reports on the escalation of lynching, see, for example, "Zavoiuem storonnikov sredi amerikanskikh rabochikh," *Mezhdunarodnoe rabochee dvizhenie* 23–24 (August 1930): 32; "Vylazka kontrrevoliutsionerov," *Trud*, August 29, 1930, 1; Ferdinand Knut, "Pered sudom vsia sistema kapitalizma," *Trud*, August 29, 1930, 1; "SASSh: Sud Lincha," *Put' MOPR'a* 20 (July 1930): 9; "Prisoediniaius' k protestu rabochikh SSSR," *Put' MOPR'a* 23–24 (August 1930): 13; "SASSh: Sud Lincha," *Put' MOPR'a* 22 (August 1930): 9; and "SASSh: 'Zakona' Lincha," *Put' MOPR'a* 29 (October 1930): 9. Vladimir Maiakovskii connected revolutionary activity and lynching. See *Maiakovskii ob Amerike*, 120–21. The most intense period of lynching occurred between 1890 and 1910, but the number of recorded incidents increased between the 1920s and early 1930s. See Wood, *Lynching and Spectacle*, 1–10.

19. U.S. authorities were disturbed by the sale of lynching postcards. See RG 84, MLR Number 435, USSR Embassy, 1935, vol. 28, Entry 60, 840.1, NARA.

20. *Trud*, August 28, 1930, 1; *Komsomol'skaia pravda*, August 28, 1930, 1. See also *Ogonek* 17 (June 20, 1931): 13; and *Workers News*, May 17, 1931, 2. On the Marion lynching, see especially Madison, *Lynching in the Heartland*; and Allen, Als, Lewis, and Litwack, *Without Sanctuary*.

21. On lynchings as "galas," see Wood, *Lynching and Spectacle*, 19–44; and Marriott, *On Black Men*, 1–22 (esp. 5).

22. *Rabochaia gazeta*, August 11, 1930, 4. On the victim, George Hughes, see Dray, *At the Hands of Persons Unknown*, 328–30.

23. David Marriott quotes Richard Wright as saying that "the law is white." See *On Black Men*, 5.

24. As Jacqueline Goldsby argues, U.S. photographers used these images to "remind the photograph's viewers that black achievement was a transgression punishable by death as much as any other crime." Antilynching activists like Ida B. Wells used these photographs to incite national and international outrage. See Goldsby, *Spectacular Secret*, 231; Waldrep, *African Americans Confront Lynching*; and Hill, *Men, Mobs, and Law*.

25. *Komsomol'skaia pravda*, August 30, 1930, 1.

26. *Komsomol'skaia pravda*, August 26, 1930, 4. As editors indicated, the cartoon was from the *Daily Worker* (August 12, 1930, 2). On Soviet car-

toons' depiction of "the American businessman" and "the U.S. government" as responsible for racial injustice, see McKenna, *All the Views*, 42. On the capitalist's standard image, see chapter 3 of this study.

27. "Neistovstva n'iu-iorkskoi politsii," *Komsomol'skaia pravda*, July 1, 1930, 6; "Novye ubiistva rabochikh v SASSh," *Trud*, July 3, 1930, 4; "Ubiistva revoliutsionnykh rabochikh v Amerike," *Rabochaia gazeta*, July 3, 1930, 8; "Pochetnyi karaul u groba ubitogo v SASSh ozverelymi politseiskimi negra tov. Levi, delegata organizatsii bezrabotnykh," *Pravda*, July 25, 1930, 2.

28. On the novel's availability in the USSR, see Hughes, "Negroes in Moscow." On the work's significance, see A. Lichtenstein, "Chain Gangs, Communism, and the 'Negro Question.'"

29. *Komsomol'skaia pravda*, October 27, 1932, 1; *Komsomol'skaia pravda*, December 23, 1932, 1; John Spivak, "Negr iz Georgii," *Internatsional'nyi maiak* 1 (January 1933): 10–11; 2 (January 1933): 12–13; 4 (February 1933): 14–15; 5–6 (March 1933): 14–15; 7–8 (April 1933): 15; 10 (May 1933): 15.

30. "Eshche shesterym grozit elektricheskii stul," *Trud*, November 15, 1930, 2.

31. "Amerikanskaia burzhuaziia ne doveriaet negram oruzhiia," *Pravda*, August 2, 1932, 4.

32. *Trud*, December 21, 1930, 2.

33. On the greater attention to the international movement in children's magazines and newspapers in the late 1920s and early 1930s, see Kelly, *Children's World*, 76–81 (esp. 77).

34. *Murzilka* was the most popular magazine for Octobrists (ages ten and younger). See O'Dell, *Socialisation through Children's Literature*, 122.

35. V. Gavrikov, "Dzhim Krou," *Murzilka* 4–5 (April–May 1931): 18–21.

36. Anna Greenberg, "Rasskazy pro fashistov i pro pionerov: Negritianskie pionery," *Murzilka* 9 (1933): 7–11 (esp. 11).

37. See Kelly, *Children's World*, 101–2 (quotation), 104–8. On the "instinctive bonds" that Soviet children were depicted possessing with children of foreign countries, who were often shown deprived of education, see O'Dell, *Socialisation through Children's Literature*, 84–85, 141.

38. For the de-emphasis on motherhood, see Goldman, *Women, the State and Revolution*. The Soviet state's promotion of motherhood by 1936 reflects a general trend in modern Western societies of this era. See Hoffmann, "Mothers in the Motherland."

39. The interracial proletarian movement in the United States was also articulated in an entirely "masculinist discourse." See Kelley, *Race Rebels*, 112–13.

40. For the conceptualization of some ideas expressed here, see Cambridge and Feuchtwang, *Where You Belong*, esp. 110–19.

41. Steiner, *Stories for Little Comrades*, 104–5.

42. On the siege mentality characteristic of this era, see Peris, *Storming the Heavens*, 102–17; and Rittersporn, "Omnipresent Conspiracy," 101–20.

43. See, for example, M. Smith, "Film for the 'Soviet East.'"

44. Westad, *Global Cold War*, 57.

45. Matusevich, "Exotic Subversive," 67.

46. At the Fourth Profintern Congress in 1928, James Ford was one of three delegates of African descent. See "Problems of Organization of the Negro Liberation Movement," GARF, f. 5667, op. 5, d. 7, ll. 44–45; and Moore Papers, Box 6, Folder 6, 29–30, Schomburg Center. In July 1930 the Comintern denied CPUSA leaders' request that Harry Haywood return to the United States since so many black Communists would be in Moscow. See "To the Political Commission (2.7.30)," RGASPI, f. 515, op. 1, d. 1869, l. 45.

47. The ITUCNW was established in name only in 1928. On the organization and conference, see "Instructions on Leading the International Conference of Negroes," RGASPI, f. 495, op. 155, d. 86, ll. 7–8; "Ob organizatsii i funktsiiakh mezhdunarodnogo profkomiteta negrov v Gamburge," RGASPI, f. 495, op. 155, d. 85, ll. 25–26; "Minutes of Meeting of Trade Union Committee of Negro Workers of RILU," RGASPI, f. 495, op. 155, d. 83, ll. 96–97; "Resolution on the Organization and Functions of the ITUCNW," RGASPI, f. 495, op. 155, d. 96, ll. 2–4; "V RILU Congress, 17.8.30," RGASPI, f. 534, op. 1, d. 137, ll. 171, 174–76, 179–90. See also Solomon, *Cry Was Unity*, 59–61.

48. See *Rabochaia gazeta*, August 11, 1930, 4; *Rabochaia gazeta*, August 13, 1930, 6; *Rabochaia gazeta*, August 18, 1930, 6; *Trud*, August 11, 1930, 1; *Rabochaia gazeta*, August 20, 1930, 6.

49. For the verification of McClain's identity, see RGASPI, f. 534, op. 1, d. 170, l. 42; and Haywood, *Black Bolshevik*, 328–29. The last article on the first International Conference of Female Workers that *Trud* published had appeared three days earlier on August 6.

50. *Komsomol'skaia pravda*, August 21, 1930, 1; *Trud*, August 15, 1930, 2; *Pravda*, August 27, 1930, 2; *Mezhdunarodnoe rabochee dvizhenie* 23–24

(August 1930): 32; and *Internatsional'nyi maiak* 6 (February 1932): 6. Although her name is absent from the list of U.S. delegates, there is a chance that another African American woman, Williana Burroughs, attended the Congress. Fred Beal, a white American delegate to the Fifth Congress, portrayed McClain in a racist manner in his 1971 memoir. See *Proletarian Journey*, 247–49.

51. Burroughs moved to the Soviet Union in 1937 and became an announcer for Radio Moscow. She returned to America in 1945 with her son Neal and died shortly thereafter as a result of poor health. She had requested to return to the United States in 1940 and 1942 but was denied. See Klehr, Haynes, and Firsov, *Secret World*, 199–201; and Carew, *Blacks, Reds, and Russians*, 85–86, 177–78.

52. *Trud*, August 11, 1928, 1.

53. *Trud*, August 16, 1928, 1. The image accompanied speeches denouncing the Second International's support of imperialism and advocating Indonesia's independence from Holland.

54. *Internatsional'nyi maiak* 16 (June 1932): 15. Charles and Neal retained their U.S. citizenship and completed their secondary education in the Soviet Union. The former had the distinction of serving in the Soviet and U.S. military during the Second World War. See Klehr, Haynes, and Firsov, *Secret World*, 199–200; and Carew, *Blacks, Reds, and Russians*, 178–79.

55. See, for example, *Pravda*, August 28, 1930, 2; *Izvestiia*, August 22, 1930, 2; and *Mezhdunarodnoe rabochee dvizhenie* 25–26 (September 1930): 8.

56. *Pravda*, August 16, 1930, 2; *Izvestiia*, August 22, 1930, 2; *Trud*, August 23, 1930, 1; *Komsomol'skaia pravda*, August 23, 1930, 1; *Mezhdunarodnoe rabochee dvizhenie* 25–26 (September 1930): 10. For the verification of Hawkins as "Jack Bell," see RGASPI, f. 534, op. 1, d. 170, l. 42.

57. Other images of Ford, for example, were printed in *Trud* (on four separate occasions), *Izvestiia*, and *Mezhdunarodnoe rabochee dvizhenie*.

58. "Pozornyi fakt na Traktornom vskryl slabost' internatsional'noi raboty profsoiuzov Stalingrada," *Trud*, August 10, 1930, 1.

59. "Piatyi kongress Profinterna," *Pravda*, August 22, 1930, 2; "Opyt millionov-na organizatsiiu revoliutsionnykh boev," *Rabochaia gazeta*, August 21, 1930, 1; "Negritianskie rabochie i Profintern," *Trud*, August 16, 1930, 2; "Negritianskii proletariat vystupaet na revoliutsionnuiu arenu," *Trud*, August 20, 1930, 3; "Revoliutsionnoe dvizhenie sredi negrov," *Izvestiia*, August 19, 1930, 2. See also "Usilim rabotu sredi

negritianskikh mass," *Metallist* 27 (September 1930): 7–9; "Zavoiuem storonnikov sredi amerikanskikh rabochikh," *Mezhdunarodnoe rabochee dvizhenie* 23–24 (August 1930): 32–33. Only *Mezhdunarodnoe rabochee dvizhenie* published what was supposedly an interview with Reid.

60. G. P., "Workers Defend the International Trade Union Committee"; and George Washington, "Negroes in the Struggle for Bread," *Workers News*, January 12, 1932, 4. For the identity of "George Washington," see chapter 5 of this study. On Fort-Whiteman, see Gilmore, *Defying Dixie*, 31–66.

61. This photograph of "Comrade Bruce" also appeared in *Trud* with the same caption on March 8, 1930.

62. On Soviet images of the body in the second half of the 1930s, see Brooks, *Thank You, Comrade Stalin*, 91; and Hoffmann, "Bodies of Knowledge," 271–72.

63. *Izvestiia*, July 8, 1936, 2. Robert Ross (Gary Johnson), a worker and boxer from Minneapolis, arrived in the USSR in 1930 as a student. Ross was expelled from KUTV in 1932 on charges of inappropriate conduct but remained in the Soviet Union, where he thrived as a propagandist. See McClellan, "Black Hajj to 'Red Mecca,'" 71–76; and Carew, *Blacks, Reds, and Russians*, 40–41, 160, 163–65, 184.

64. On *Uncle Tom's Cabin*, see Blakely, *Russia and the Negro*, 31–32, 94. The Afro-Cuban male protagonist in Vladimir Maiakovskii's famous poem "Syphilis" is also named Tom. See *Polnoe sobranie sochinenii v trinadtsati tomakh*, 7:24–30.

65. Foreign children finding refuge from persecution in the USSR was a common theme since it encouraged Soviet children to recognize that they were the luckiest in the world. See O'Dell, *Socialisation through Children's Literature*, 141; and Kelly, *Children's World*, 101–8.

66. Lina Neiman, "Tom Dzhons," *Murzilka* 9–10 (September–October 1932): 12–15.

67. The illustrator was identified as V. Shcheglova. On similar portrayals of blacks in 1960s Soviet textbooks, see Quist-Adade, "African Russians," esp. 166.

68. Fort-Whiteman articulated his concerns in a letter to Anatolii Lunacharskii, the Commissar of Enlightenment. See, for example, RGASPI, f. 495, op. 155, d. 27, l. 71; McClellan, "Black Hajj to 'Red Mecca,'" 62–65; and Baldwin, *Beyond the Color Line*, 65–66. Baldwin's discussion of Fort-Whiteman's letter was helpful in articulating these ideas. See also Quist-Adade, *In the Shadows of the Kremlin*, esp. 43–60.

69. Steiner, *Stories for Little Comrades*, 99–107.

70. D. Kunin, "Neponiatnoe slovo," *Krokodil* (September 1931): 7. A 1928 children's story titled *Tale of a Negro Boy* did not contain stereotypical illustrations of the black American protagonist named "John." See Steiner, *Stories for Little Comrades*, 104–5.

71. "Tom," *Internatsional'nyi maiak* 17–18 (June 1931): 2.

72. Brown and Brown, *Guide to Soviet Russian Translations*, 13–15, 76–77, 151, 208, 210 (quotation 15). See also Gilenson, "Afro-American Literature in the Soviet Union."

73. Gilenson, "Afro-American Literature in the Soviet Union," 25, 28; Foley, *Radical Representations*, 69; Brown and Brown, *Guide to Soviet Russian Translations*, 52, 84–85, 98–101.

74. Page lived in the Soviet Union in the early 1930s as a *Daily Worker* correspondent. The book was first published in the USSR in 1932 and appeared in English in the United States in 1933. On the novel, see Foley, *Radical Representations*, esp. 69, 198–99, 235–39, 369–70, 375–78. *Internatsional'nyi maiak* published excerpts from the novel that concerned violence against black workers. See "Buria nadvigaetsia," *Internatsional'nyi maiak* 25 (September 1932): 10–11; and 26–27 (September 1932): 10–11.

75. Rogger, "How the Soviets See Us," 125. See also Wolf, *Ilf and Petrov's American Road Trip*, x; and Pomorska, "Vision of America," 396–97.

76. On Soviet interest in America, see Brooks, "Official Xenophobia," esp. 1447; Starr, *Red and Hot*; Rogger, "*Amerikanizm* and the Economic Development"; and Stites, *Russian Popular Culture*, esp. 62, 74.

77. See Il'ia Il'f and Evgenii Petrov, "Amerikanskie fotografii," *Ogonek* 11–17 and 19–23 (1936).

78. For the translation of this particular exchange, see Wolf, *Ilf and Petrov's American Road Trip*, 115.

79. Il'ia Il'f and Evgenii Petrov, "Negry," *Ogonek* 22 (August 10, 1936): 14–17; Il'f and Petrov, *Odnoetazhnaia Amerika*, 392–94.

80. Il'f and Petrov, *Odnoetazhnaia Amerika*, 379.

81. "Mr. Adams" was Solmon Trone, a retired engineer from Latvia who spent some time in the Soviet Union as a representative for General Electric. His wife, Florence, was American-born yet spoke Russian fluently. She did most of the driving. See Wolf, *Ilf and Petrov's American Road Trip*, ix–xv; and Etkind, *Tolkovanie puteshestvii*, esp. 163–64.

82. Il'f and Petrov, *Odnoetazhnaia Amerika*, 412.

83. Il'f and Petrov, *Odnoetazhnaia Amerika*, 228–29.

84. Il'f and Petrov, "Negry," 14–15.

85. Il'f and Petrov, "Negry," 17; Wolf, *Ilf and Petrov's American Road Trip*, 122, 125.

86. Il'f and Petrov, "Negry," 16.

87. Il'f and Petrov, "Negry," 14–15; Wolf, *Ilf and Petrov's American Road Trip*, 121; Il'f and Petrov, *Odnoetazhnaia Amerika*, 394–95.

88. Il'f and Petrov, *Odnoetazhnaia Amerika*, 390. On notions of the Russian and African American "soul," see Peterson, *Up from Bondage*.

89. See Matusevich, "Exotic Subversive," 64. Il'f and Petrov's praise of American industry, roads, efficiency, and work ethic as a model of development, and vehement rejection of American values and mores, was consistent with the Bolsheviks' stance and Russian attitudes toward the West throughout history. See, for example, Ball, *Imagining America*, 139.

90. Il'f and Petrov, *Odnoetazhnaia Amerika*, 500–501, 508–9.

91. See Il'f and Petrov, *Odnoetazhnaia Amerika*, 487–89 (quotation 489).

92. The fact that they had also used U.S. racism in a 1935 play titled *Under the Big Top* also suggests some interest in it. This play served as the basis for Grigorii Aleksandrov's 1936 musical comedy, *Circus*. See the epilogue of this study. By the time Il'f returned to the Soviet Union he had become completely disillusioned with the notion of social progress in which he had had so much faith at the beginning of the decade. See Nakhimovsky, "Death and Disillusion."

93. The articulation of this idea was influenced by Steiner's analysis of the illustrations in Soviet children's book; Steiner, *Stories for Little Comrades*, 199n42.

94. On the black belt thesis, see the introduction to this study.

95. The focus on black oppression in American proletarian literature of this era often contradicted the theme of interracial solidarity. See Foley, *Radical Representations*, 57.

96. "Soviet exceptionalism" is defined here as a synthesis of Marxist-Leninist ideology and Russian exceptionalism. See Westad, *Global Cold War*, 72, for a discussion of how these two influences shaped Soviet leaders' understanding of the role of the USSR in the world.

97. See, for example, V. Liadova, "Fashizm—rasovaia nenavist,' sotsializm—bratstvo narodov," *Trud*, July 14, 1936, 2 (quotation); and Iur., "V strane rasovogo izuverstva," *Izvestiia*, June 17, 1936, 2. For the overwhelm-

ing focus on Germany in *Pravda* by the mid-1930s, see McKenna, *All the Views*, esp. 10.

98. On Soviet leaders' belated acknowledgment of fascism as a distinct, serious threat, see Petro and Rubenstein, *Russian Foreign Policy*, 28–29. On the targeting of Soviet territory in the Nazi Party's propaganda, see especially Mazower, *Hitler's Empire*.

99. See especially Baldwin, *Behind the Color Line*, 149–251.

100. Matusevich, "Journeys of Hope"; Hessler, "Death of an African Student."

101. On the concept of two competing models of modernity, see Westad, *Global Cold War*, esp. 8–72.

3. The Scottsboro Campaign

1. Yelena Khanga (b. 1962), the granddaughter of African American Oliver Golden, was born and raised in the Soviet Union. She claims in her 1992 autobiography that the Scottsboro case was still well known in the country. See *Soul to Soul*, 90.

2. The German Communist Klara Zetkin served as MOPR's head from 1924 until her death in 1933. At that time, Elena Stasova, the deputy head of MOPR and the leader of its Soviet branch since 1927, replaced her. See Stasova, *Vospominaniia*, 185–92. See also Avrus, *MOPR v bor'be protiv terrora i fashizma*; and Ryle, "International Red Aid," 36–37, 82.

3. For the foundational texts on the Scottsboro case, see Carter, *Scottsboro*; and Goodman, *Stories of Scottsboro*. For the U.S. Communist Party's response to the Scottsboro case and the ILD's prosecution of it, see Solomon, *Cry Was Unity*, esp. 191–206, 240–49.

4. Miller, Pennybacker, and Rosenhaft, "Mother Ada Wright."

5. For phraseology, see "Vyrvat' uznikov skottsboro iz ruk palachei," *Internatsional'nyi maiak* 8–9 (March 1932): 6. See also "Tretii plenum TsK MOPR 7.4.32 g.," GARF, f. 8265, op. 1, d. 45, ll. 236, 245; "Za edinyi internatsional'nyi front zashchity vos'mi rabochikh-negrov ot smertnoi kazni," *Pravda*, March 8, 1932, 4; "Osvobodim uznikov skottsboro," *Sputnik moprovtsa* 7 (April 1932): 1–2; "Osvobodite uznikov skottsboro," *Sputnik moprovtsa* 8 (April 1932): 13; and "Vyrvem iz ruk iustitsii dollara deviat' molodykh rabochikh negrov," *Sputnik moprovtsa* 17 (September 1932): 25–27.

6. This was the objective of most propaganda campaigns of this era. See Peris, *Storming the Heavens*.

7. On Soviet leaders' increasing concern over the security of the border regions during the early 1930s, see Martin, "Origins of Soviet Ethnic Cleansing."

8. On the efforts to portray the solidarity campaign with the Spanish Republic as popular, see Kowalsky, *Stalin and the Spanish Civil War*, esp. chapter 4 (55–65, 70–75).

9. "Vsem TsK natsrespublik, kraikomam, i obkomam MOPR," GARF, f. 8265, op. 1, d. 41, l. 79.

10. See "Vchera priekhal v Moskvu Maksim Gor'kii: Da zdravstvuet velikii pisatel' proletariata!" *Literaturnaia gazeta*, May 15, 1931, 1; and "Velikii pisatel' proletariata," *Ogonek* 15 (May 30, 1931): 3. For the attacks on Gor'kii, see Fitzpatrick, *Cultural Front*.

11. On Lunacharskii's role as Commissar of Enlightenment, see Fitzpatrick, *Commissariat of Enlightenment*. For his removal on the grounds of having an alleged "soft-line" on culture, see Fitzpatrick, "'Soft' Line on Culture." *Rabochaia gazeta*'s editor, Tsekher, was also prosecutor in the 1930 Tsiprus trial discussed in chapter 1. For the remaining members, see "V zashchitu 8 negritianskikh rabochikh, prigovorennykh k kazni na elektricheskom stule," *Rabochaia gazeta*, June 23, 1931, 4; and note 14 below.

12. "Vtoroi plenum TsK MOPR SSSR," GARF, f. 8265, op. 1, d. 31, l. 25.

13. "Predvaritel'naia informatsionnaia svodka provedeniia kampanii po spaseniiu deviati negritianskikh iunoshei v skottsboro SASSh," GARF, f. 8265, op. 1, d. 39, ll. 222–25 (esp. l. 222).

14. "Preliminary Informational Summary of the Campaign in Defense of the 9 Negro Youths in Scottsboro, USA, Measures Taken on the Part of the C.C. of the MOPR/IRA Section in the USSR," RGASPI, f. 539, op. 5, d. 127, ll. 105–8 (esp. l. 105).

15. "V zashchitu uznikov skottsboro," *Izvestiia*, June 29, 1931, 3; "Obrashchenie komiteta sodeistviia MOPR," *Trud*, June 29, 1931, 1; "Mezhdunarodnaia solidarnost' rabochego klassa dolzhna spasti rabochikh negrov," *Rabochaia gazeta*, June 29, 1931, 4; "Vyrvem uznikov skottsboro iz ruk palachei," *Komsomol'skaia pravda*, June 29, 1931, 4; "Vyrvem uznikov skottsboro na svobodu!" *Internatsional'nyi maiak* 19 (July 1931): 3–4; "In Defense of the Negro Workers Condemned to Death," *Workers News*, July 1, 1931, 4.

16. "Pozor amerikanskomu fashizmu!" *Literaturnaia gazeta*, July 5, 1931, 1.

17. In their appeals to children, MOPR referred to the defendants as "young

proletarians," reaffirming that the main source of their innocence was their class status rather than their "boyishness." See "Ko vsem shkol'nikam i detiam trudiashchikhsia SSSR," GARF, f. 8265, op. 1, d. 42, l. 33.

18. The Loyalists' fate in the Spanish Civil War was similarly connected with the national security of the USSR. See Kowalsky, *Stalin and the Spanish Civil War*, conclusion (1–10). On the "siege mentality" characteristic of this period of Soviet history, see Peris, *Storming the Heavens*, 102–17.

19. "'K trudiashchimsia vsego mira,'" GARF, f. 8265, op. 1, d. 41, l. 80. See also B. Shleifer, "Zverskie kazni i linchevanie rabochikh v sev. amerike," *Leningradskaia pravda*, June 3, 1931, 2.

20. "Ne dadim kaznit' uznikov skottsboro!" *Prozhektor* 7 (April 15, 1932): 31.

21. In a 1926 account of his U.S. trip, N. Osinskii compared the myth of the black rapist to the tsarist-era "ritual legend" about Jews' use of Christian children's blood. See *Po tu storonu okeana*, esp. 41–44.

22. On the use of festivals and meetings to showcase the Soviet regime's popular support, and as sites of alternative discourse, see, for example, Petrone, *Life Has Become More Joyous*; and von Geldern, *Bolshevik Festivals*.

23. "V zashchitu uznikov skottsboro: Internatsional'nyi miting leningradskikh uchenykh i pisatelei," *Izvestiia*, July 6, 1931, 2; notes 43 and 46 below. For a photograph of the meeting, see *Leningradskaia pravda*, July 5, 1931, 4.

24. For Scottsboro meetings in movie houses and theaters, see "Dek. 32 g. TsK MOPR SSSR," GARF, f. 8265, op. 1, d. 57, ll. 80–83; "O khode kampanii protesta protiv kazni 9 negritianskikh iunoshei skottsboro v 1932 g.," GARF, f. 8265, op. 1, d. 57, l. 68–79 (esp. l. 69); and "Operativnyi plan kampanii skottsboro," GARF, f. 8265, op. 1, d. 57, ll. 84–85.

25. For articles and photographs concerning the meeting, see "V zashchitu 8 negritianskikh rabochikh," *Rabochaia gazeta*, July 4, 1931, 3; "V zashchitu uznikov skotsboro [*sic*]," *Rabochaia gazeta*, July 7, 1931, 3; "Scottsboro Demonstration at Moscow Show," *Liberator*, August 8, 1931, 2; and "O'Neill and Scottsboro at the Kamerny," in Dana Collection of Russian Theatrical Scripts and Papers, Box 38, Folder 10, Houghton Library.

26. For the Soviet actors in blackface, see "'Negr' O'Neilia—Kamernyi Teatr," *Sovremennyi teatr* 10 (March 5, 1929): 156–57; and the photographs in the Dana Collection of Russian Theatrical Scripts and Papers, Box 38, Folder 10, Houghton Library. The play reinforces stereotypical

images of black men even though Eugene O'Neill's intention was to indict U.S. racial norms. See Robeson, *Undiscovered Paul Robeson*, 77–81; and Carby, *Race Men*, 74–77.

27. "Monolog," *Literaturnaia gazeta*, July 5, 1931, 1.

28. *Komsomol'skaia pravda*, January 27, 1932, 4.

29. A. Lunacharskii, "Palacham ne uiti ot suda istorii," *Komsomol'skaia pravda*, July 10, 1931, 2.

30. Nikolai Aseev, "Pesenka ob alabame," *Literaturnaia gazeta*, July 30, 1931, 2. For other poems, see, for example, *Rabochaia gazeta*, July 11, 1931, 1; and *Internatsional'nyi maiak* 35 (December 1931): 3.

31. For phraseology, see S. White, *Bolshevik Poster*, 43.

32. Bonnell, *Iconography of Power*, 187–224. See also Hobsbawm, "Man and Woman in Socialist Iconography."

33. For other Scottsboro cartoons featuring the standard image of the capitalist, see *Komsomol'skaia pravda*, May 30, 1931, 1; *Komsomol'skaia pravda*, June 29, 1931, 4; *Komsomol'skaia pravda*, April 21, 1932, 1; and *Workers News*, July 6, 1931, 1.

34. "Palachi vkliuchaiut elektricheskii tok," *Komsomol'skaia pravda*, March 3, 1932, 1.

35. V. Federovskii, *Pravda*, March 10, 1932, 1. For phraseology, see *Prozhektor* 7 (April 15, 1932): 31. See also "Vyrvat' uznikov skottsboro iz ruk palachei!" *Internatsional'nyi maiak* 8–9 (March 1932): 6–7.

36. Bonnell, *Iconography of Power*, 216–17. The other Scottsboro cartoons in the central press that featured a swastika also appeared in 1932. See *Komsomol'skaia pravda*, March 29, 1932, 1; and *Workers News*, March 30, 1932, 1.

37. As Richard Taylor notes, capitalism and fascism were used interchangeably in Soviet propaganda of this era. See "Illusion of Happiness," 604. See also note 36 above.

38. The representation of a Christian official colluding with the bourgeois capitalist was a common feature of Soviet political posters since the civil war, including a few Moor designed. See, for example, White, *Bolshevik Poster*, 48; Baburina, *Rossiia—20 vek*, 48; and Rickards, *Posters of Protest*, no. 101.

39. See "Terror kapitalistov protiv negritianskikh rabochikh v Amerike," RGASPI, f. 539, op. 5, d. 76, ll. 252–53. For distribution numbers, see GARF, f. 8265, op. 1, d. 57, l. 69. Gor'kii's essay was printed in *Internatsional'nyi maiak* 25 (September 1931): 3–4; *Negro Worker* 1 (January 1932): 13–15; and *Workers News*, September 1, 1931, 2.

40. For other Scottsboro pamphlets, see, for example, RGASPI, f. 539, op. 5, d. 127, l. 105.
41. "Vsem TsK natsrespublik, kraevym i oblastnym komitetam MOPR," GARF, f. 8265, op. 1, d. 42, l. 45; "'Demokratiia' politseiskikh banditov Ameriki," *Rabochaia gazeta*, July 20, 1931, 1; "Kak pogib negr Grei," *Trud*, July 20, 1931, 4; "Politseiskaia okhota na negrov v Amerike," *Komsomol'skaia pravda*, July 20, 1931; "Na zashchitu smertnikov iz skottsboro," *Leningradskaia pravda*, July 20, 1931, 2; "Police Terror Against Negro Workers in USA," *Workers News*, July 21, 1931, 1; "Ubiistvo v dedville," *Internatsional'nyi maiak* 33 (November 1931): 7. On the Camp Hill violence, see Kelley, *Hammer and Hoe*, 41–43.
42. During the Cultural Revolution Tolstoi was criticized as a "petty bourgeois 'fellow traveler.'" See Platt, "Rehabilitation and Afterimage."
43. Aleksei Tolstoi, "Osvobodite nashikh chernykh tovarishchei!" *Izvestiia*, July 8, 1931, 3; "History Has a Long Memory," *Workers News*, July 16, 1931, 4.
44. Secretariat of the Executive Committee, "Resolution of the IRA," 188–93.
45. For the phraseology, see Mukherji, "Erasure of American Anticolonialism," 14. See also Baldwin, *Beyond the Color Line*, 80–84; and note 47 below.
46. "Pisateli i akademiki Leningrada protestuiut protiv kazni 8 rabochikh negrov," *Rabochaia gazeta*, July 3, 1931, 4; "Rabochie, akademiki, pisateli sovetskogo soiuza protestuiut protiv gotoviashcheisia v SASSh kazni negritianskikh rabochikh," *Izvestiia*, July 3, 1931, 2. On the Academy of Sciences, see Fitzpatrick, "Cultural Revolution as Class War"; and Suny, *Soviet Experiment*, 209–13.
47. On Russians' contested whiteness and its impact on their policies toward non-European peoples, see Brower and Lazzerini, *Russia's Orient*; and Wolff, *Inventing Eastern Europe*.
48. Kate Baldwin contends that Russians' "illegitimate" whiteness necessarily informed Soviet perceptions of African Americans and vice versa. See *Beyond the Color Line*, 80–84. On Russian exceptionalism, see note 105 below.
49. "Na ikh storone sochuvstvie proletariata vsego mira," *Rabochaia gazeta*, June 27, 1931, 2.
50. "Svobodu uznikam skottsboro!" RGASPI, f. 539, op. 5, d. 126, ll. 68–71. For "Freedom for the Scottsboro Prisoners!" as an official MOPR slogan,

see "Lozungi TsK MOPR SSSR k 10-letiiu MOPR i vsemirnomu kongressu," GARF, f. 8265, op. 1, d. 49, l. 943.

51. See, for example, "Volnoi gnevnogo protesta udarim po rukam pala-chei!" *Komsomol'skaia pravda*, May 27, 1931, 2; "Ostanovit ruku pala-cha!" *Komsomol'skaia pravda*, May 30, 1931, 1; "Trebuem otmeny krovavogo prigovora!" *Komsomol'skaia pravda*, May 31, 1931, 1; "Ala-bamskoe ubiistvo dolzhno byt' predotvrashcheno," *Komsomol'skaia pravda*, June 8, 1931, 1; "Smertniki Alabamy vse eshche pod ugrozoi," *Komsomol'skaia pravda*, June 9, 1931, 1; "Palachi v sudeiskikh-manti-iakh glukhi k golosu millionnykh mass," *Komsomol'skaia pravda*, June 26, 1931, 1; "Cherez sem' dnei palachi gotoviatsia vkliuchit' tok," *Komsomol'skaia pravda*, July 4, 1931, 1; and "Alabamskie ubiitsy vkliu-chaiut tok," *Komsomol'skaia pravda*, March 27, 1932, 1.

52. For an account of resolutions supposedly received from over five thou-sand MOPR sections, see "Massovye kampanii," GARF, f. 8265, op. 1, d. 48, ll. 200–201. By A. I. Avrus's account, MOPR reportedly received over three thousand resolutions in 1931 alone. See *Proletarskii internatsional-izm v deistvii*, 65. See also note 53 below.

53. The editors of *Leningradskaia pravda* pursued a similar strategy. See "Na segodnia naznachena kazn'," *Leningradskaia pravda*, July 10, 1931, 1; and "Kazni ne dopustim," *Leningradskaia pravda*, July 2, 1931, 2. See also "V ozhidanii elektricheskogo stula," *Internatsional'nyi maiak* 16 (June 1931): 4; "Stroim internatsional'nyi detskii dom," *Internatsional'nyi maiak* 19 (July 1931): 16; "Ne dopustim kazni nashikh chernykh tova-rishchei," *Internatsional'nyi maiak* 20–21 (July 1931): 7; and "Svobodu uznikam skottsboro! po zavodam, fabrikam, uchrezhdeniiam," *Sputnik moprovtsa* 5–6 (March 1932): 6.

54. RGASPI, f. 539, op. 5, d. 126, ll. 68–71.

55. "Doloi krovavyi fashistskii terror," *Trud*, July 7, 1931, 1. For other artic-ulations of indignation, see, for example, *Komsomol'skaia pravda*, June 26, 1931, 1; and "Rabochie Leningrada vozmushcheny krovavym terro-rom amerikanskoi burzhuazii," *Trud*, June 7, 1931, 1.

56. For a summary of these pledges, see "Biuro pechati TsK MOPR o kam-panii skottsboro," RGASPI, f. 515, op. 1, d. 3012, ll. 59–63 (l. 60); RGASPI, f. 539, op. 5, d. 127, l. 105; and "Vyrvat' uznikov skottsboro iz ruk pala-chei," *Internatsional'nyi maiak* 7 (March 1932): 2.

57. By this time, two defendants were sentenced to life imprisonment. For the photograph, see *Internatsional'nyi maiak* 29–30 (October 1932): 5.

58. See "Svobodu uznikam skottsboro po zavodam, fabrikam, uchrezh-deniiam," *Sputnik moprovtsa* 7 (April 1932): 6; "Vyrvem 7 negrov iz ruk fashistov po zavodam, kolkhozam, shkolam," *Sputnik moprovtsa* 11 (June 1932): 4; and "Po zavodam, kolkhozam i uchrezhdeniiam," *Sputnik moprovtsa* 9–10 (May 1932): 5.

59. "Brigady imeni 8 molodykh negrov," *Komsomol'skaia pravda*, July 4, 1931, 1.

60. RGASPI, f. 539, op. 5, d. 127, ll. 106–8 (quotation l. 108). For further examples of pledges to engage in a series of tasks, see note 51 above; "32,000 Putilov Workers Condemn Death Sentence," *Workers News*, July 6, 1931, 1; and "Resolution against Scottsboro Sentence," *Workers News*, March 16, 1932, 3. On traditional images of women of the Caucasus as particularly "backward," see Layton, *Russian Literature and Empire*; and Hokanson, "Literary Imperialism."

61. "Vsem TsK natsrespublik, kraikomam i obkomam MOPR," GARF, f. 8265, op. 1, d. 41, l. 79.

62. "TsK MOPR SSSR no. 6050," GARF, f. 8265, op. 1, d. 42, l. 48. The reverse side of this directive lists the twenty-five derelict regions, many of which appeared successful in organizing the campaign by 1932.

63. Peris, *Storming the Heavens*, 99–106 (quotation 102).

64. For Soviet rallies, see, for example, "Spasti uznikov skottsboro!" *Pravda*, April 12, 1932, 4; "Protest inostrannykh rabochikh," *Pravda*, April 11, 1932, 4; *Trud*, July 7, 1931, 1; *Leningradskaia pravda*, July 5, 1931, 4; and *Internatsional'nyi maiak* 19 (July 1931): 3, 5. For protests abroad, see *Trud*, June 9, 1931, 2; *Leningradskaia pravda*, July 2, 1931, 2; *Leningradskaia pravda*, July 3, 1931, 4; *Trud*, June 5, 1931, 1; *Komsomol'skaia pravda*, July 10, 1931, 2; *Rabochaia gazeta*, July 10, 1931, 4; *Izvestiia*, July 10, 1931, 2; *Rabochaia gazeta*, July 12, 1931, 4; *Komsomol'skaia pravda*, August 22, 1932, 4; *Pravda*, May 7, 1932, 4; *Internatsional'nyi maiak* 11–12 (April 1932): 2; and *Internatsional'nyi maiak* 13 (May 1932): 2.

65. See, for example, "Vsem TsK natsrespublik, kraikomam i obkomam MOPR i RK, vydelennym pod nabliudenie TsK," GARF, f. 8265, op. 1, d. 41, ll. 7–8a.

66. The Defense Committee emphasized that Soviet citizens had raised the strongest protest; "Vyrvat' uznikov skottsboro iz ruk palachei!" *Internatsional'nyi maiak* 8–9 (March 1932): 6. See also note 5 above.

67. GARF, f. 8265, op. 1, d. 57, ll. 68–78. For similar reports from individual cells, see, for example, "Tezisy doklada raikoma MOPR o realizatsii

postanovleniia prezidiuma TsK MOPR o rabote na krupnykh predpri-iatiiakh," GARF, f. 8265, op. 1, d. 39, ll. 256–58; and "Rabota MOPR na luganstroe," GARF, f. 8265, op. 1, d. 47, l. 137.

68. GARF, f. 8265, op. 1, d. 57, l. 74.

69. See Stasova, *Vospominaniia*, 195 (quotation). On this unrest, see, for example, Grant, "Average Azeri Village (1930)"; Altstadt, "Nagorno-Karabakh"; Croissant, *Armenia-Azerbaijan Conflict*; and Suny, *Revenge of the Past*.

70. Among a survey of newspapers, Azerbaijan, Khar'kov, the Central Black Earth Oblast', and the North Caucasus (also a site of intense collectivization) were commended for dedicating substantial coverage to Scottsboro. See RGASPI, f. 539, op. 5, d. 127, ll. 106–8; GARF, f. 8265, op. 1, d. 57, ll. 72–73, 75.

71. Fitzpatrick, *Stalin's Peasants*, 49–79; Lewin, *Making of the Soviet System*, 142–77.

72. "Women" as a separate category of participants appeared inconsistently in this data and in MOPR directives and appeals. This inconsistency reflects the general ambivalence among central and local officials during this era regarding whether women should be mobilized as "women" or appealed to as "workers" and "collective farmers." On this ambivalence, see, for example, Reid, "All Stalin's Women"; and Gorsuch, *Youth in Revolutionary Russia*.

73. GARF, f. 8265, op. 1, d. 57, l. 73.

74. The "exact" totals for shock brigades: Ukraine (550), Urals (313), Leningrad (199), Armenia (50), Western oblast' (43), Eastern Siberia (39), Lower Volga (25), Vitebsk (12), and Far East (11). Hectares sown: Ukraine (100), Lower Volga (25), Eastern Siberia (24), Far East (5), and Western oblast' (1). Ruble donations: Ukraine (10,935), Eastern Siberia (4260), Belorussia (3,650), Western oblast' (1,035), and Far East (742). See "Massovye kampanii," GARF, f. 8265, op. 1, d. 48, ll. 200–204 (esp. l. 203); "O sostoianii raboty udarnykh MOPRovskikh brigad," GARF, f. 8265, op. 1, d. 49, l. 832; GARF, f. 8265, d. 57, ll. 71, 73–77. For statements of donations from individual industrial and agricultural enterprises, see RGASPI, f. 539, op. 5, d. 127, l. 108; d. 126, ll. 73–74; "Materialy: sostoianiia raboty MOPR na luganskom parovozo-stroitel'nom zavode," GARF, f. 8265, op. 1, d. 47, ll. 130–37; and "Material o sostoianii raboty sredi inostrannykh rabochikh," GARF, f. 8265, op. 1, d. 47, ll. 63–68.

75. On the "Ukrainian Crisis," see Martin, *Affirmative Action Empire*, 325–28.

76. See, for example, "Ocherednye zadachi massovoi vospitatel'noi raboty MOPR'a," GARF, f. 8265, op. 1, d. 22, ll. 44–45; "Postanovlenie prezidiuma po dokladu TsK MOPR ukrainy," GARF, f. 8265, op. 1, d. 23, ll. 48–68; and "Doklad o rabote," GARF, f. 8265, op. 1, d. 26, ll. 180–83.

77. "Postanovlenie prezidimuma TsK MOPR SSSR," GARF, f. 8265, op. 1, d. 47, ll. 275–76; "Plan raboty TsK MOPR SSSR na 1932 g.," GARF, f. 8265, op. 1, d. 47, l. 319; "Bor'ba s shovinizmom i mestnym natsionalizmom," GARF, f. 8265, op. 1, d. 48, l. 168; "Tretii plenum TsK MOPR 7.4.32 g.," GARF, f. 8265, op. 1, d. 45, ll. 236–44 (quotation l. 244); "Za upornuiu rabotu po sotsialisticheskomu vospitaniiu mass," *Pravda*, April 13, 1932, 1.

78. For the emphasis on the New Soviet Person thinking in new ways, see especially Hoffmann, *Stalinist Values*, 45–56, 63–67; and Peris, *Storming the Heavens*, 78–81.

79. "Linchevanie i presledovanie negritianskikh trudiashchikhsia v SASSh," RGASPI, f. 539, op. 5, d. 126, ll. 43–54.

80. "Osnovnye fakty o protsesse protiv 9 negritianskikh iunoshei v skottsboro," GARF, f. 8265, op. 1, d. 41, ll. 37–56. See also George Padmore, "Samosud nad negram," *Put' MOPR'a* 32 (November 1930): 6–7; "Kak zhivut chernokozhie krest'iane v soediennykh shtatakh," *Put' MOPR'a* 26–27 (September 1930): 2, 19; and Otto Huiswood, "Ne dadim linchevat' negritianskikh iunoshei," *Mezhdunarodnoe rabochee dvizhenie* 9 (March 1932): 7–9.

81. Khanga, *Soul to Soul*, 90; "ILD (24 April 1932)," RGASPI, f. 515, op. 1, d. 3017, ll. 99–100; RGASPI, f. 539, op. 5, d. 127, ll. 105–6, 108; GARF, f. 8265, op. 1, d. 48, l. 203; d. 57, ll. 69, 73–74, 82, 84. Ross may have been working as a postal worker when he was recruited. See GARF, f. 5667, op. 16, d. 281, ll. 166–68. On the recruitment of lecturers, see also *Internatsional'nyi maiak* 20–21 (July 1931): 15; and *Internatsional'nyi maiak* 35 (December 1931): 7.

82. See *Rabochaia gazeta*, June 27, 1931, 2; *Trud*, April 18, 1932, 4; *Komsomol'skaia pravda*, May 16, 1931, 1; *Komsomol'skaia pravda*, July 10, 1931, 2; *Pravda*, April 9, 1932, 4; *Pravda*, April 11, 1932, 4; *Ogonek* 11 (April 20, 1932): 2; *Workers News*, June 1, 1931, 3; *Workers News*, January 14, 1932, 4; *Workers News*, March 16, 1932, 4; and *Workers News*, January 22, 1932, 1.

83. "Negro Workers to Contrast USA with Soviet Union," *Liberator*, October 17, 1931, 4; "The Soviet Union—A Land without Jim Crowism," *Liberator*, July 1, 1932, 8.

84. See, for example, Carew, *Blacks, Reds, and Russians*; and Blakely, *Russia and the Negro*.

85. *Komsomol'skaia pravda*, July 4, 1931, 1; *Komsomol'skaia pravda*, April 21, 1932, 1; *Komsomol'skaia pravda*, January 27, 1932, 1; *Trud*, June 26, 1931, 1; *Internatsional'nyi maiak* 16 (June 1931): 1.

86. "Ostanovite palachei!" *Pravda*, April 11, 1932, 4.

87. "Za edinyi internatsional'nyi front zashchity vos'mi rabochikh-negrov ot smertnoi kazni," *Pravda*, March 8, 1932, 4.

88. "Zhertvy skottsboro zhdut nashei pomoshchi," *Komsomol'skaia pravda*, April 10, 1932, 1.

89. For signs, see, for example, "Svobodu uznikam skottsboro!" GARF, f. 8265, op. 3, d. 31, ll. 6–7; "Resolution Against Scottsboro Sentence," *Workers News*, March 16, 1932, 3; and "Stop the Hand of the Executioner!" *Workers News*, March 30, 1932, 2.

90. See, for example, "Postanovlenie prezidiuma TsK ot 23/VIII," GARF, f. 8265, op. 1, d. 39, l. 226; "Predvaritel'naia informatsionnaia svodka provedeniia kampanii po spaseniiu deviate negritianskikh iunoshei v skottsboro," GARF, f. 8265, op. 1, d. 39, ll. 222–25; "Vsem TsK natsrespublik, kraikomam, obkomam MOPR," GARF, f. 8265, op. 1, d. 42, l. 156; and GARF, f. 8265, op. 1, d. 31, l. 25.

91. The non-Russian nationalities were likewise portrayed as struggling against tsarist oppression with the guidance of their elder Russian brother. See Tillett, *Great Friendship*. See also Slezkine, "USSR as a Communal Apartment"; and M. Smith, "Film for the 'Soviet East.'"

92. N. Sidorenko, "Inoi bereg," *Internatsional'nyi maiak* 16 (June 1932): 2.

93. GARF, f. 8265, op. 1, d. 57, l. 69.

94. On the film, see chapter 4 of this study.

95. Hughes claimed that the Soviet government had stripped Harris of a lucrative business as head of a brothel. See Hughes, *I Wonder as I Wander*, 83, 87. Glenda Gilmore makes no mention of this business or Harris's political leanings. Relying on Homer Smith's account, Gilmore states without qualification that after Harris was stranded in Moscow by the Louisiana Amazons (a vaudeville group) she married a Russian man and performed as the Black Nightingale. Joy Carew's rendition of Harris differs since she relies primarily on Hughes's memoir. See Gilmore, *Defying Dixie*, 137–38; and Carew, *Blacks, Reds, and Russians*, 135–37.

96. "Cast of 'Black and White' Comments on USSR and Films," *Moscow Daily News*, July 6, 1932, 4. See also Lewis, *When Harlem Was in Vogue*, 290.

West also mentioned her favorable impressions of Soviet citizens in letters to her mother. See chapter 4 of this study.

97. It was predominantly in MOPR publications, not central newspapers, where Ada Wright was presented in print or photograph. See *Internatsional'nyi maiak* 8–9 (March 1932): 6; *Internatsional'nyi maiak* 16 (June 1932): 3; and *Internatsional'nyi maiak* 29–30 (October 1932): 4.

98. On official representations of female revolutionaries bringing enlightenment to others, see Hemenway, "Mothers of Communists," 79, 81, 84.

99. See Records of the Department of the State Relating to Internal Affairs of the Soviet Union, 1930–1939, 861.5017–Living Conditions/419 and 861.5017–Living Conditions/623, NARA.

100. Duberman, *Paul Robeson*, 206.

101. Daniel Kowalsky makes a similar argument with regard to the domestic solidarity campaign organized on behalf of the Spanish Republic. See *Stalin and the Spanish Civil War*, conclusion.

102. The terminology is Zubok's in *Zhivago's Children*. See also Hellbeck, "Speaking Out"; and Straus, *Factory and Community*.

103. Matusevich, "Probing the Limits of Internationalism."

104. See, for example, Rogger, "America in the Russian Mind," esp. 30.

105. Carol Avins argues that America was included in Russians' conception of the West after the October Revolution. See Avins, *Border Crossings*, esp. 3–4. As Odd Arne Westad argues, Marxist-Leninist ideology as well as Russian exceptionalism shaped Soviet leaders' understanding of the role of the USSR in the world. See Westad, *Global Cold War*, esp. 72.

106. Four defendants were cleared of all charges and released from prison on July 24, 1937. The remaining five men would have to wait until the 1940s; the last defendant was released in 1950.

107. During the first few months of 1933, MOPR records and *Internatsional'nyi maiak* contained a few directives admonishing citizens and officials against forgetting about the Scottsboro prisoners. But as Christopher Waldrep claims, even the International Labor Defense, the U.S. affiliate of MOPR, had difficulty maintaining interest and participation in the campaign beyond 1932. See *Many Faces of Judge Lynch*, 164.

108. Saul, *Friends or Foes*, 269–301 (quotation 269).

109. Phillips, "Rapprochement and Estrangement."
110. See, for example, Al. Vasil'ev, "Amerikanskii i iaponskii imperialism gotoviatsia k bor'be za novyi peredel mira," *Pravda*, April 3, 1932,
3; "SASSh snabzhaiut Iaponiiu oruzhiem," *Pravda*, May 31, 1932, 1;
"Nepisannoe amerikano-iaponskoe soglashenie o podgotovke inter-
ventsii," *Pravda*, May 30, 1932, 1.
111. On the defense of the Soviet Union assuming precedence over
international revolution after the adoption of socialism in one country, see Eley, *Forging Democracy*, 249–50; and Petro and Rubenstein,
Russian Foreign Policy, 28.
112. A discussion that Dmitri Manuilskii had in January 1933 with students of KUTV bears out this point. See "Shorthand Record of the Conversation of Comrade Manuilskii with students of the Ninth Sector of
KUTV," RGASPI, f. 532, op. 1, d. 441, ll. 1–12.

4. African American Architects

1. Its African American readership was never large. On efforts to
increase the journal's circulation in the colonies, see RGASPI, f. 534,
op. 2, d. 754, ll. 3–4.
2. Financial constraints, political developments, and internal disputes
(surrounding the role of race in the revolutionary struggle) disrupted
the publication of the *Liberator* and *Negro Worker*. The last issues of
these periodicals appeared in 1935 and 1937. See Solomon, *Cry Was
Unity*, 259, 262–64; B. Edwards, *Practice of Diaspora*, 245–61; and note 9
below.
3. "To Aid Soviet Negro Film," *New York Times*, June 14, 1932, 26.
4. Among the reasons the Comintern cited to justify George Padmore's
expulsion was that he wrote articles for the *Pittsburgh Courier*, the
Amsterdam News, *Chicago Defender*, and *The Crisis*. See B. Edwards, *Practice of Diaspora*, 286; and Helen Davis, "The Rise and Fall of George Padmore as a Revolutionary Fighter," *Negro Worker* 4 (August 1934): 17
5. *Negro Worker* 2 (June 1932): 20–23; *Negro Worker* 2 (September–October
1932): 2; *Negro Worker* 3 (June–July 1933): 20; *Negro Worker* 5 (February–
March 1935): 29; *Liberator*, November 4, 1932, 5.
6. See *Liberator*, November 4, 1932, 5; *Liberator*, October 17, 1931, 2, 4;
Liberator, November 19, 1932, 2; *Liberator*, July 1, 1932, 6; and *Negro
Worker* (April–May 1933): 23. See also "Bob Turner Greets Young Workers Convention in Name of Soviet Youth," *Liberator*, June 20, 1931, 6;

"3 Negro Workers on Delegation to the Soviet Union," *Liberator*, October 10, 1931, 4; "Negro Workers to Contrast USA with Soviet Russia," *Liberator*, October 17, 1931, 4. On the scientists, see Blakely, "African Imprints," 47–48; and Carew, *Blacks, Reds, and Russians*, 90–112.

7. "Liberator Offers Free Trip to Soviet Union," *Liberator*, May 10, 1930, 1, 4; "Best Liberator Agent Goes to Soviet Russia in Drive for 10,000 New Readers," *Liberator*, March 28, 1931, 2; "Do You Want to Go to the Soviet Union for May Day?" *Liberator*, October 24 and 31, 1931, 1.

8. "Job for Negro Mechanics Aplenty in Soviet Russia," *Liberator*, June 20, 1931, 2.

9. Wilson, *Russia and Black Africa*, 215.

10. "'Down with Racial and National Chauvinism,'" *Negro Worker* 2 (February 1931): 15–18. For other artifacts of and references to the Stalingrad trial, see "How to Organize for Mass Action," *Negro Worker* 2 (February 1931): 21–22; and Margaret Clyde, "Race Prejudice in England," *Negro Worker* 6 (June 1931): 12–14.

11. *Liberator*, November 4, 1932, 5.

12. "I Am Among My Own People in My Own Country," *Negro Worker* 5 (July–August 1935): 32–34. Glascow's essay was published as "Negro Mother, Now a Shock Worker," in Rosenblit and Schüller, 60 *Letters*, 10–14. Glascow was the mother of Lloyd Patterson, a *Black and White* cast member, and grandmother of James Patterson, who played "Jimmy" in the 1936 musical comedy *Circus*. For James Patterson's recollections of his grandmother, see Kossie-Chernyshev, "Reclaiming 'D. Patterson.'"

13. See, for example, "Soviet Youth Hail Struggles Negro Masses—Call for United Fight of Working Youth," *Liberator*, May 16, 1931, 4; "Letter from USSR Workers Reveals Keen Interest in Negro Masses Struggle," *Liberator*, July 11, 1931, 6; "Soviet Youth Hails the Young Liberators and Pledge Support," *Liberator*, June 13, 1931, 7, "Soviet Youth Calls for Fight to Save 9 Negroes," *Liberator*, June 13, 1931, 2; "Soviet Workers Protest United States Frame-Up," *Liberator*, June 27, 1931, 5; "Soviet Children Pledge Support for Scottsboro 9," *Liberator*, October 31, 1931, 3; "Russian Pioneers Fight for American Lynch-Law Victims," *Liberator*, November 21, 1931, 2; and "Soviet Union in Mass Protest!" *Liberator*, August 1, 1931, 3. See also "Russian Workers Indignant over Lynching," *Negro Worker* 10–11 (October–November 1931): 37.

14. See also "Negro Lawyer, in Moscow, Sees Communism as the Way," *Liberator*, October 17, 1931, 4.

15. Interruptions to its circulation, as the result of government interference and incompetence on the part of distributors, caused George Padmore considerable consternation. See RGASPI, f. 534, op. 3, d. 756, ll. 2, 11–13, 14–15, 18, 20–29; d. 755, ll. 4, 75, 78; d. 754, ll. 7, 135, 156, 170.

16. Wilson, *Russia and Black Africa*, 219; B. Edwards, *Practice of Diaspora*, 257–59.

17. The phraseology is Wilson's regarding the *Negro Worker*. See *Russia and Black Africa*, 214. On the instructions of the Eastern Secretariat of the Comintern regarding the journal's general content and "simple" writing style, see RGASPI, f. 495, op. 155, d. 96, l. 4.

18. Kelley, *Race Rebels*, 103–21.

19. B. Edwards, *Practice of Diaspora*, 248.

20. Von Eschen, *Race against Empire*, 12 (quotation).

21. B. Edwards, *Practice of Diaspora*, 248, 261–64; Wilson, *Russia and Black Africa*, 212–15.

22. B. Edwards, *Practice of Diaspora*, 264.

23. RGASPI, f. 534, op. 3, d. 755, ll. 5, 27. An article by Robinson did not appear in the *Negro Worker*. Robinson possibly did not receive Padmore's letters because it was during this period that he was transferred to the First State Ball Bearing Plant in Moscow.

24. Solomon, *Cry Was Unity*, 179–80; Wilson, *Russia and Black Africa*, 259–60.

25. See, for example, Solomon, *Cry Was Unity*, 178. For Padmore's criticisms, see "An Open Letter to Earl Browder Secretary of the American Communist Party," RGASPI, f. 495, op. 155, d. 102, ll. 123–25. On criticism of the Comintern, see also Naison, *Communists in Harlem*, 131–32.

26. Solomon, *Cry was Unity*, 177–83. See also Hooker, *Black Revolutionary*.

27. Padmore, "The Socialist Attitude to the Invasion of the USSR," 196 (quotation).

28. Padmore, *Pan-Africanism or Communism*, 291–93. On Pushkin in the African American press, see note 97 below.

29. Marable, *African and Caribbean Politics*, 110.

30. Marable, *African and Caribbean Politics*, 45, 110–12. Marable argues that Padmore underestimated the power of British, French, and U.S. leaders to co-opt the newly independent nations of Africa. He also acknowledges Padmore's continued admiration for the USSR's domestic policies "'in the sphere of inter-racial relations.'"

31. On Padmore's willingness to cooperate with individuals across the political spectrum even though he was a staunch anti-Communist, see Von Eschen, *Race against Empire*, 14–15.

32. See Carew, *Blacks, Reds, and Russians*, 120–23.

33. On the prompt repayment of money and salaries, see Hughes, *I Wonder as I Wander*, 73–77, 95–98.

34. On cooperation between Cooper's firm and Soviet leaders, see Ball, *Imagining America*, 122–23.

35. Cooper became an outspoken supporter of Soviet recognition in 1928. At the New York banquet celebrating rapprochement in November 1933, Cooper served as its master of ceremonies. See Saul, *Friends or Foes*, 216; and S. J. Taylor, *Stalin's Apologist*, 191.

36. Davies and Khlevniuk, *Stalin-Kaganovich Correspondence*, 113–14.

37. See Saul, *Friends or Foes*, esp. 254–77; and Bose, *American Soviet Relations*, 187.

38. As noted elsewhere, in 1933 D. Manuilskii confirmed circuitously that the film was cancelled to avoid jeopardizing recognition. See "Shorthand record of the conversation of Comrade Manuilskii with students of the Ninth Sector of KUTV," RGASPI, f. 532, op. 1, d. 441, ll. 1–13.

39. The company had originated in Germany in 1921 as a relief organization intended to help victims of famine in the Soviet Union. Its funds were then used to rebuild the Soviet film industry, and it later merged with the Russian film company Rus' to form Mezhrabpom-Rus, only to completely take over the company and become Mezhrabpom Film. See Kepley, "Workers' International Relief," 12–14, 18–19; and Kepley, "First Perestroika," 36–37; Kenez, *Cinema and Soviet Society*, 38–39; and R. Taylor, *Film Propaganda*, 36–37, 140.

40. "22 Negroes and Meschrabpom," RGASPI, f. 495, op. 72, d. 201, ll. 264–65. Junghans was also directly responsible for this inactivity. See "Dear Comrade," RGASPI, f. 495, op. 72, d. 201, l. 198; and "'Black and White' New Film, Illustrates the Class Struggle in USA: Appeal for Aid from Americans," *Moscow Daily News*, June 28, 1932, 4.

41. "Langston Hughes, August 23, 1932," RGASPI, f. 495, op. 72, d. 201, ll. 213–15. Grebner cowrote screenplays with Anatolii Lunacharskii in the 1920s. See Youngblood, "Entertainment or Enlightenment," 49.

42. Hughes, *I Wonder as I Wander*, 78. On Fort-Whiteman's short stories, see Gilmore, *Defying Dixie*, 139–41. Gilmore notes one version of the Grebner-Fort-Whiteman script was called "Blacks and Whites," 491n171.

43. Gilmore, *Defying Dixie*, 140–41.

44. RGASPI, f. 495, op. 72, d. 201, l. 214. On dissension among Mezhrabpom officials, see also Schoots, *Living Dangerously*, 74, 78.

45. For Junghans's profile, see Hughes, *I Wonder as I Wander*, 79–80. On Junghans's other film, see Jack El-Hai, "Black and White and Red," 87. See also Carew, *Blacks, Reds, and Russians*, 124–25.

46. "Directors Meschrabpom Film, August 25, 1932," RGASPI, f. 495, op. 72, d. 201, l. 208.

47. Hagener, *Moving Forward*, 159–201.

48. Though most accounts indicate that Alan McKenzie was the group's only Communist Party member, Comintern records suggest that Lewis was also a Party member at the time. See "Anglo-American Secretariat, CI, Moscow, August 23, 1932," RGASPI, f. 495, op. 72, d. 201, l. 207; and "June 17th," RGASPI, f. 495, op. 72, d. 201, ll. 196–97.

49. Interestingly, four days later Alberga was one of sixteen cast members who signed a statement claiming that "we in no wise agree with the minority statement presented by them to Commintern [sic]." See "WE, the undersigned . . . ," RGASPI, f. 495, op. 72, d. 201, l. 242. Also curious, Henry Lee Moon eventually published an article claiming that the Soviet Union had achieved gender equality. See "Woman under the Soviets," *The Crisis* (April 1934): 108.

50. "Say Race Bias Here Halted Film," *New York Times*, October 5, 1932, 26.

51. Fort-Whiteman, a close associate of the discontents, arguably had a role in crafting the first statement, which contained more Communist jargon. See Gilmore, *Defying Dixie*, 144–45.

52. "Moscow, USSR 8/22/32," RGASPI, f. 495, op. 72, d. 201, l. 205. For the basis of this argument, see Hellbeck, "Speaking Out." Mark Solomon argues that the dissenters "ironically mimicked the polemical jargon of the Communists." See *Cry Was Unity*, 176.

53. Comintern officials removed the racialized language found in the group's draft and infused the final statement with a class analysis. See "For Immediate Release," RGASPI, f. 495, op. 72, d. 201, ll. 199–200; and "Majority Statement by Members of the Negro Cast for 'Black and White,'" RGASPI, f. 495, op. 72, d. 201, l. 251. See also "Negro Film-Group in Russia Denounces Lying Rumors," *Liberator*, October 15, 1932, 2. The signatories included Louise Thompson, Matt N. Crawford, Mildred Jones, Dorothy West, Constance W. White, Sylvia Garner, Lloyd Patterson, Langston Hughes, Juanita Lewis, Loren Miller, Alan McKenzie, Homer Smith, Wayland Rudd, Mollie V. Lewis, and F. Curle Monte.

54. "Negro Actors in USSR Well Provided For," *Liberator*, October 1, 1932, 2.

55. James W. Ford, "In the Soviet Union, There Is No Compromise with Race Hatred!" *Liberator*, October 20, 1932, 8.

56. Carew, *Blacks, Reds, and Russians*, 129. See also Gilmore, *Defying Dixie*, 128, 147.

57. "My dear Miss Thompson," RGASPI, f. 495, op. 72, d. 201, ll. 256–57. On his position, see Baldwin, *Beyond the Color Line*, 96.

58. Quoted in Gilmore, *Defying Dixie*, 147. See also note 56 above.

59. Naison, *Communists in Harlem*, 73. This implies, however, that the four dissenters had traveled to Moscow for the purpose of artistic expression and were incensed by their inability to act on it.

60. Gilmore, *Defying Dixie*, 145–46.

61. Dorothy West's personal correspondence also indicates that she did not expect the film would be made in the summer of 1933. See "March 5th Mummy dearest darling," Dorothy West Collection (85-M139), Carton 1, Folder 1, Schlesinger Library, Radcliffe Institute.

62. "Reasons for Abandonment," RGASPI, f. 495, op. 72, d. 201, ll. 266–67 (esp. l. 267). See also note 63 below.

63. "Statement of Group, August 23, 1932," RGASPI, f. 495, op. 72, d. 201, ll. 209–12; "Political Results," RGASPI, f. 495, op. 72, d. 201, ll. 273–75. They also accused Otto Katz of deceit. See "Mescrabpom Ineficiencies [sic]," RGASPI, f. 495, op. 72, d. 201, ll. 270–72.

64. RGASPI, f. 495, op. 72, d. 201, ll. 264–65; "The group would like to . . . ," RGASPI, 495, op. 72, d. 201, l. 269; RGASPI, f. 495, op. 72, d. 201, ll. 213–15. Comintern leaders, who sought to win the group to Communism, likewise expressed distress that Mezhrabpom did not organize excursions since they feared that their idleness was corrupting them. See "Odessa, August 9, 1932, Dear Comrade Randolph," RGASPI, f. 495, op. 72, d. 201, ll. 202–3; and "S. S. Abhazia [sic], August 13, 1932, Dear Comrade Randolph," RGASPI, f. 495, op. 72, d. 201, l. 204.

65. "Following are two . . . ," RGASPI, f. 495, op. 72, d. 201, l. 268.

66. RGASPI, f. 495, op. 72, d. 201, ll. 214–15.

67. Davies and Khlevniuk emphasize that this incident underscores that Soviet leaders were feeling extremely vulnerable at this time. See *Stalin-Kaganovich Correspondence*, 114–15.

68. RGASPI, f. 495, op. 72, d. 201, l. 256.

69. See "March 5th Mummy dearest darling" and "Nov 4th Darling mums," Dorothy West Collection, Carton 1, Folder 1.

70. Records of the Department of the State Relating to Internal Affairs of the Soviet Union, 1930–1939, 861.5017–Living Conditions/791, NARA.

71. "Dearest mummy June 29," Dorothy West Collection, Carton 1, Folder 1.

72. Records of the Department of the State Relating to Internal Affairs of the Soviet Union, 1930–1939, 861.5017—Living Conditions/791, NARA.

73. Comintern authorities were more concerned that the African American press published the majority group's statement. See "Uvazhaemyi t. Miziano," RGASPI, f. 495, op. 72, d. 201, l. 253.

74. Louise Thompson, "The Soviet Film," *The Crisis* (February 1933): 37, 46. Upon returning from the USSR in 1926, W. E. B. Du Bois, *The Crisis*'s founder and editor until 1934, advised blacks to approach the Soviet experiment with an "open mind and listening ears." See Lewis, *W. E. B. Du Bois*, 196.

75. RGASPI, f. 495, op. 72, d. 201, l. 257.

76. On the absence of negative stories about the Soviet Union in *The Crisis* from 1936 to 1939, see Plummer, *Rising Wind*, 57–59, 48–56.

77. For a similar argument, see Rosenberg, *How Far the Promised Land*, 85–88; and Gilmore, *Defying Dixie*, 43–47.

78. Hughes published a short book about his travels in central Asia. See Hughes, *A Negro Looks at Central Asia*. See also Hughes, *I Wonder as I Wander*, 210–11. For a contemporary review of Hughes's short book, see Walt Carmon, "Hughes Discovers Central Asia," *Moscow Daily News*, December 10, 1933, 2. For a literary analysis of Hughes's writings on Central Asia, see Baldwin, *Beyond the Color Line*, 86–148.

79. Langston Hughes, "Going South in Russia," *The Crisis* (June 1934): 162–63. For the testimony of Wayland Rudd, who was one of the group's few professional actors and one of three who chose to live permanently in the Soviet Union, see Wayland Rudd, "Russian and American Theatre," *The Crisis* (September 1934): 267, 278. Rudd constituted the subject of a 1994 piece in the *Washington Post*. See Fred Hiatt, "The Ambivalent American," *Washington Post*, July 10, 1994, F1.

80. Curiously, in his autobiography, Smith gives no indication that he was a member of the *Black and White* cast and had enrolled at KUTV. See Homer Smith, *Black Man in Red Russia*. Joy Carew conjectures that Smith sought to lend greater objectivity to his position as a journalist. See *Blacks, Reds, and Russians*, 79–85.

81. The Party's efforts in Depression-era Baltimore impressed Carl Murphy, the paper's editor, and William N. Jones, the managing editor who visited the USSR in 1935 and dined at the home of the commissar of foreign affairs. See *Afro-American*, September 21, 1935, 1–2. Concern with jeopardizing the support of advertisers by treating Communism too

favorably was never a concern with the *Afro-American*. See Farrar, *Baltimore Afro-American*, 149–53.

82. See Chatwood Hall, "A Column from Moscow," *Chicago Defender*, December 15, 1934, 10; December 22, 1934, 11; and December 29, 1934, 8.

83. Hall, "Column from Moscow," *Chicago Defender*, December 22, 1934, 11.

84. Petrone, *Life Has Become More Joyous*, 129–31.

85. Farrar, *Baltimore Afro-American*, 153; Lewis, *Fight for Equality*, 299.

86. See especially Chatwood Hall, "Full Equality of Races and Nations," *The Crisis* (September 1936): 268; "White American Students in Russia Tell What They Think about U.S. Race Problem," *Chicago Defender*, October 6, 1934, 11; Chatwood Hall, "Race Superiority Called Bunk," *Afro-American*, August 22, 1936, 9; Chatwood Hall, "Parity of Races Held Impossible in U.S. by Tutor," *Afro-American*, August 22, 1936, 9.

87. For a similar argument with regard to *The Crisis* and *Messenger* in the 1920s, see Rosenberg, *How Far the Promised Land*, esp. 75–88, 100, 121–27.

88. "Soviet Union Elects Deputies," *Chicago Defender*, January 26, 1935, 11; "U.S. Youth Is Soviet Leader," *Chicago Defender*, December 15, 1934, 1; Thyra J. Edwards, "Another American Youth Making Good in Moscow," *Chicago Defender*, December 29, 1934, 9; "Races Mingle in Russian Palace," *Afro-American*, June 6, 1936, 8.

89. "College Grads Rave about Soviet Jobs," *Amsterdam News*, September 4, 1937, 23.

90. Chatwood Hall, "A Black Woman in Red Russia," *The Crisis* (July 1937): 203–4. On Coretta Arle-Titz's career, see Carew, *Blacks, Reds, and Russians*, 135–38.

91. I. D. W. Talmadge, "Mother Emma," *Opportunity* (August 1933): 245–47. West claimed that Harris was going to appear in *Black and White*. See "Sunday Darling Dearest Mums," Dorothy West Collection, Carton 1, Folder 1.

92. For a similar argument regarding the *Amsterdam News*'s calculated refusal to adopt a categorically hostile position on Communism, see Naison, *Communists in Harlem*, 74.

93. "Writer Contrasts Soviet Balloting with U.S. Style," *Chicago Defender*, December 15, 1934, 10.

94. "Jones Home from Russia," *Afro-American*, September 28, 1935, 6.

95. This commitment had played a role in W. E. B. Du Bois's 1934 departure from the NAACP and resignation as *The Crisis*'s editor. See Lewis, *Fight for Equality*, esp. 342–46; and Rosenberg, *How Far the Promised Land*, 124.

96. T. Edwards, "Another American Youth," 9 (quotation). This discussion is informed by Rosenberg's arguments regarding the depiction of the Soviet Union in the publications of reform leaders in the 1920s. See *How Far the Promised Land*, 88.

97. Quotation in Anna Heifetz, "Pushkin in Self-Portrayal," *The Crisis* (May 1937): 144, 157. See also William N. Jones, "Pushkin's Books Best Sellers in Russia," *Afro-American*, September 21, 1935, 5; Chatwood Hall, "Was Pushkin's Duel A Frame-Up?" *The Crisis* (December 1936): 365, 370; "Russia's Greatest Poet," *The Crisis* (February 1937): 58; and Guichard Parris, "Pushkin's Negro Blood," *The Crisis* (June 1937): 175. The press ignored Soviet leaders' refusal to highlight Pushkin's African roots in the centennial commemorating his death in 1937. See Petrone, *Life Has Become More Joyous*, 126–29. For a similar argument about African Americans' use of Pushkin, see Lounsbery, "Soul Man." On Pushkin's African great-grandfather, see Barnes, *Stolen Prince*. On Pushkin's attitudes about his African heritage, see Nepomnyashchy, Svobodny, and Trigos, *Under the Sky*.

98. "In Russia They Can Rear Children without Prejudice," *Afro-American*, June 6, 1936, 7; "Russian Wife Like All Others, Says Robeson's Brother-in-Law," *Afro-American*, September 21, 1935, 10; "Va. Girl, Now Teaching in Russia, Pays U.S. a Visit," *Afro-American*, June 13, 1936, 12.

99. See "'Reds' Are Bitter, Resent Action," *Pittsburgh Courier*, August 16, 1930, 1, 4; "Reds to Deport Whites Who Attacked Workers: Detroit and Toledo Race-Haters Must Return to America," *Pittsburgh Courier*, September 6, 1930, 1; "Moscow Stirred by Attack on Negro," *Pittsburgh Courier*, August 23, 1930, 1; "Soviet Union Frowns on Race Prejudice," *Amsterdam News*, August 13, 1930, 1; "Americans to Be Tried in Russia; Evicted Worker," *Amsterdam News*, August 20, 1930, 1; "Prejudiced Americans in Russia to Be Deported," *Amsterdam News*, September 3, 1930, 3; "Russia Acts to Halt Racial Prejudice," *Afro-American*, August 23, 1930, 1; "Russ Workers Won't Stand U.S. Prejudice," *Afro-American*, 4; and "Russians to Deport Prejudiced American," *Chicago Defender*, August 23, 1930, 3.

100. Carew, *Blacks, Reds, and Russians*, 79–85. On this widespread hope among Soviet citizens, see Zubkova, *Russia after the War*.

101. Smith, *Black Man in Red Russia*, esp. 56–66.

102. Solomon, *Cry Was Unity*, 179–80; Wilson, *Russia and Black Africa*, 259–60.

103. See Kepley, "Workers' International Relief," 19–20.

104. Records of the Department of State Relating to Internal Affairs of the Soviet Union, 1930–1939, 861.5017–Living Conditions/519, NARA.

5. The Promises of Soviet Antiracism

1. See especially Weigand, *Red Feminism*, 15–24, 97–113 (quotation 15); and Storch, *Red Chicago*. See also Naison, *Communists in Harlem*; and Kelley, *Hammer and Hoe*.

2. O. Patterson, *Ordeal of Integration*, esp. 51–65.

3. After the Commissariat of Nationality Affairs was abolished in 1923, the Comintern assumed jurisdiction over KUTV and began admitting African Americans and Africans. See Klehr, Haynes, and Anderson, *Soviet World*, 201–2; and McClellan, "Africans and Black Americans in the Comintern Schools." The Fifth Comintern Congress established the Lenin School in 1926 to "bolshevize" the Communist parties of capitalist countries, which encompassed eliminating any social democratic tendencies. For the school mission statement, see "Otchetnyi doklad ispolkomu kominterna ob itogakh dvukhletnei raboty mezhdunarodnoi leninskoi shkoly," RGASPI, f. 531, op. 1, d. 15, ll. 36–51; and "Tsirkular po voprosu o novom nabore studentov M.L.Sh.," RGASPI, f. 531, op. 1, d. 18, l. 9. In 1930 Chinese and Germans were the two largest groups at the Lenin School, comprising 14.19 percent and 14.14 percent, respectively, of the student population. See "Studencheskii sostav M.L.Sh.," RGASPI, f. 531, op. 2, d. 16, ll. 45–46.

4. Preference was given to unmarried manual laborers from large industries with at least three years' Party experience and one year of "practical political work." See "Re Conditions for Admission to the International Lenin Courses," RGASPI, f. 531, op. 1, d. 10, ll. 28–31; "Instructions, Conditions of Acceptance into the International Lenin School," RGASPI, f. 531, op. 1, d. 27, ll. 26–28; and "Selection of Students to the ILS for the New Academic Year," RGASPI, f. 531, op. 1, d. 27, ll. 22–25.

5. "Minutes of the Meeting of the Negro Section of the Eastern Secretariat," RGASPI, f. 495, op. 155, d. 83, ll. 19–21; "Secretariat and Polbureau, CPUSA," RGASPI, f. 515, op. 1, d. 1870, ll. 2–6.

6. On the advisement of the Eastern Secretariat's Negro Section, which also included sending a few white students to KUTV, see "Proposals Adopted at Meeting of Negro Section of the Eastern Secretariat,"

RGASPI, f. 495, op. 155, d. 84, ll. 1–3; and "To the Secretariat, CPUSA, 19.11.30," RGASPI, f. 515, op. 1, d. 1870, ll. 136–39. On the amenities available to Lenin School students, see Wicks, *Keeping My Head*, 83–91. In a letter to Weinstone, Otto Huiswood of the CPUSA's Negro Department emphasized that it was imperative that the Party send more blacks to the Lenin School, given the dearth of qualified black leaders in the United States. See "10 Feb. 1930, to W. W. Randolph in USSR from Otto Huiswood (Negro Dept.)," RGASPI, f. 515, op. 1, d. 1872, ll. 28–29.

7. Exploiting official discourse to frame appeals was not without precedent in Soviet history. For its use among non-Russian nationalities, see especially Hirsch, "Toward an Empire of Nations"; and Martin, *Affirmative Action Empire*, esp. 128–32.

8. For the concept of drawing on and challenging a master narrative to make appeals, see Siegelbaum, "Narratives of Appeal."

9. On KUTV, see McClellan, "Black Hajj to 'Red Mecca'"; McClellan, "Africans and Black Americans"; Klehr, Haynes, and Anderson, *Soviet World*, 201–8, 319–24; and Carew, *Blacks, Reds, and Russians*, 27–48. Regarding African Americans' experiences at the Lenin School, Mark Solomon and McClellan alone briefly mention that a group brought charges of racism to the Comintern's attention in 1932. See Solomon, *Cry Was Unity*, 90; and McClellan, "Africans and Black Americans," 377. On the relationship between the Lenin School and CPUSA, see Klehr, Haynes, and Firsov, *Secret World*, 119–22; Klehr, Haynes, and Anderson, *Soviet World*, 201–2; and Klehr, *Communist Cadre*, 96–97. Klehr demonstrates that Lenin School alumni were less likely to leave the U.S. Communist Party.

10. See Cohen and Morgan, "Stalin's Sausage Machine"; Campbell, Halstead, McIlroy, and McLoughlin, "Forging the Faithful"; and Pantov and Spichak, "New Light from the Russian Archives."

11. For school directives on this issue, see "Confidential Points to the Instructions on Conditions for Admittance," RGASPI, f. 531, op. 1, d. 34, l. 32. See also "Abstract of Testimony of Manning Johnson before Subversive Activities Control Board (McCarran Hearings) Washington, Sept. 17, 18, 19, 1951," Robert Kaufman Research Files, Box 4, Folder 4, Tamiment Library and Robert F. Wagner Labor Archives.

12. Harry Haywood is the only African American alumnus of the Lenin School to pen an autobiography, which Woodford McClellan deems

unreliable ("Black Hajj," 83n82). See Haywood, *Black Bolshevik*. As Erik McDuffie notes, few blacks who joined the Party in the interwar era wrote memoirs, none of whom were women. See "'[She] Devoted Twenty Minutes.'" Besides Soviet records (which are often fragmentary), the greatest source of information we have on the experiences of blacks in the Lenin School comes from the House Un-American Activities Committee.

13. Haywood, *Black Bolshevik*, 395–96.
14. On the politics of self-preservation and survival in the Jim Crow South, see, for example, Litwack, *Trouble in Mind*.
15. See Records of the Department of State Relating to Internal Affairs of the Soviet Union, 1930–1939, Colonel Hugh L. Cooper, 861.5017—Living Conditions/519; John M. Pelikan, 861.77—Living Conditions/4233; John Stafford Cromelin, 861.5017—Living Conditions/371; Samuel George Bloomfield, 861.5017—Living Conditions/575, NARA.
16. See Records of the Department of State Relating to Internal Affairs of the Soviet Union, 1930–1939, Eugene Szepesi, 861.5017—Living Conditions/255, NARA. William C. White, in *Scribner's Magazine*, also emphasized that when most white American men first arrived in the capital, whether Communists or non-Communists, they had a difficult time adjusting to the reality that many black men had "Russian lady friends." See "Americans in Soviet Russia," *Scribner's Magazine* (January 1932): 171–82.
17. See Solomon, *Cry Was Unity*, esp. 129–46; and Wald, "Black Nationalist Identity."
18. Roy Mahoney (Jim Farmer), a member of the Party since 1922, and Robert/Gilbert Brady, a member since only 1926 but described as "well-tested," were also admitted in 1927 but several months after Haywood. Mahoney stayed for two years, Brady for only one. See "Protokol No. 34," RGASPI, f. 531, op. 1, d. 11, ll. 14–15; and "Spisok studentov s 1926-31 god," RGASPI, f. 531, op. 1, d. 31, ll. 1–34 (Amerika ll. 2–4).
19. Haywood, *Black Bolshevik*, 310–15.
20. Hutchins and Hewitt arrived at the Lenin School in September 1930 with Gilbert (George) Lewis, a skilled Party organizer from Birmingham AL. However, Lewis died of tuberculosis nine months later. See "To the Secretariat of the CPUSA (30 April 1931)"; and "WOPAT NEW YORK (2 June 1931)," RGASPI, f. 515, op. 1, d. 2225, ll. 37, 46. The *Liberator* published an article announcing Lewis's death on June 13, 1931. Ferguson

enrolled in the Lenin School in October 1930. Ferguson requested to return to the United States in the summer of 1932 because, as she put it, "I will be the only politically trained Negro Woman in the Party at the present time." See "Lichnoe delo-Fergiuson Romi," RGASPI, f. 495, op. 261, d. 4600, l. 7 (quotation). She returned to Chicago, where she continued her work as a Party organizer. See Storch, *Red Chicago*, 46, 67. On Hutchins, see "Lichnoe delo-Men Robert," RGASPI, f. 495, op. 261, d. 4781. Regarding the transfer of Hutchins and Hewitt to the CPSU, see "5 Sept. 1930, This is to certify," RGASPI, f. 515, op. 1, d. 1869, l. 59a. The identities of Lewis, Hewitt, and Ferguson are further verified in "Students Left in 1930," RGASPI, f. 515, op. 1, d. 1869, l. 59v. The transfer document is reproduced in Klehr, Haynes, and Firsov, *Secret World*, 121–23.

21. See "Lichnoe delo-Patterson Leonard," RGASPI, f. 495, op. 261, d. 4797, ll. 1–10; "Lichnoe delo-Kuper Uil'iam," RGASPI, f. 495, op. 261, d. 3343, ll. 1–9; "Lichnoe delo-Iangblad Dzhon," RGASPI, f. 495, op. 261, d. 2227, ll. 1–6, 8–12, and "Communist Party, District #5 Pittsburgh," RGASPI, f. 515, op. 1, d. 2274, l. 41; "Lichnoe delo-Shumaker Erl," RGASPI, f. 495, op. 261, d. 4940, ll. 1–10; "Lichnoe delo-Iakobi Karl," RGASPI, f. 495, op. 261, d. 4881; "Lichnoe delo-Uil'iams Eduard," RGASPI, f. 495, op. 261, d. 1404, ll. 1–6, 14–15; "Lichnoe delo-Koud Mek," RGASPI, f. 495, op. 261, d. 2549; and "Lichnoe delo-Edvards Dzheims," RGASPI, f. 495, op. 261, d. 4904, ll. 2–12. For further verification of most of these men and of Henry Shelton, see "Amerika," RGASPI, f. 531, op. 1, d. 40, ll. 2–3; and "V TsK VKP(b) komissiiu po perevodu v VKP(b)," RGASPI, f. 531, op. 2, d. 20, l. 20.

22. "To the Secretariat—CPUSA," RGASPI, f. 515, op. 1, d. 2225, ll. 27–29 (esp. l. 28). Huiswood was sent to Moscow after being removed as leader of the Negro Department for his initial opposition to black self-determination and support of the defeated Lovestone faction of the Party. Because he arrived after the start of the semester, Comintern officials decided he would enroll when the next session began in the fall of 1931. See "To the Secretariat, CPUSA, 19.11.30," RGASPI, f. 515, op. 1, d. 1870, ll. 136–39; and "Letter 6 December 1930," RGASPI, f. 515, op. 1, d. 1870, ll. 171–73.

23. On Nzula, who died of pneumonia in 1934, see Davidson, Filatova, Gorodnov, and Johns, *South Africa and the Communist International*, 1:6–8. After 1933 only Americans and Canadians comprised "Sector D," while British, Australian, New Zealand, and South African Communists com-

prised "Sector E." See Campbell, Halstead, McIlroy, and McLoughlin, "Forging the Faithful," 100. The Lenin School landergroups were based on the landersecretariats (regional secretariats) within the Comintern. Their purpose was to strengthen communication between the ECCI and Communist parties of a specific region. See Adibekov, Shakhnazarova, and Shirinia, *Organizatsionnaia struktura Kominterna*, esp. 109–12, 152–55.

24. "Rezoliutsiia politsekretariata po dokladu t. Kirsanovoi o rabote MLSh," RGASPI, f. 531, op. 1, d. 27, ll. 47–49.

25. Nelson explained that almost half the students he traveled with to Moscow were black, and that many had little experience with organizing and formal education. See Nelson, Barrett, and Ruck, *Steve Nelson*, 125–27.

26. "Protokol: sobranie amerikanskoi lendergruppy ot 19/IX-31 g.," RGASPI, f. 531, op. 2, d. 56, ll. 1–34; "Meeting of Special Commission to Investigate the Situation in the American Landergroup, held 14 November 1931," RGASPI, f. 531, op. 2, d. 56, ll. 38–46, 56–74, 96–165. These problems pertain to the first of two groups to cross the Atlantic that summer en route to the Lenin School.

27. RGASPI, f. 531, op. 2, d. 56, ll. 3–4, 65, 131–32, 147, 158, 161. For Riley, see "V TsK VKP(b) komissiiu po perevodu v VKP(b)," RGASPI, f. 531, op. 2, d. 20, l. 17. Incidents involving white Communists barring or removing blacks from dance floors in U.S. workers' clubs were common in the 1930s and became part of the Party's campaign against white chauvinism. See, for example, Solomon, *Cry Was Unity*, 129–46.

28. "Rezoliutsiia," RGASPI, f. 531, op. 2, d. 56v, ll. 4–11. On Dalton's identity and defense of her actions, see "Statement by Mary Dorn 4/9–32 g.," RGASPI, f. 495, op. 261, d. 2947, l. 2; and "V TsK VKP(b) v komissiiu po perevodu v VKP(b)," RGASPI, f. 531, op. 2, d. 20, l. 67.

29. RGASPI, f. 531, op. 2, d. 56, ll. 116–19.

30. RGASPI, f. 531, op. 2, d. 56, ll. 3–4, 56–57, 65, 115, 132, 140, 147, 161. For the identities of these female students, see RGASPI, f. 531, op. 2, d. 20, l. 67; and "Amerika," RGASPI, f. 531, op. 1, d. 40, ll. 2–3. Demery had joined the Party in 1924.

31. RGASPI, f. 531, op. 2, d. 56, ll. 115–16, 122–24, 162–63. Black female Communists, like black women in general, were also presumed promiscuous. See Kelley, *Hammer and Hoe*, 79–80, 85. On Hall, whose alias was "Malone," see "Gus Hall—Moscow-Trained Boss of the CPUSA," in Swearingen, *Leaders of the Communist World*, 580–95.

32. RGASPI, f. 531, op. 2, d. 56, ll. 155–56.

33. For the contradictory coexistent racial stereotypes of blacks as sentimental and insubordinate, see especially Fredrickson, *Black Image*, 53–58, 102–9, 168–71.

34. RGASPI, f. 531, op. 2, d. 56, ll. 57–59, 116–17, 119, 132, 162–65.

35. "Meeting of the American Delegation with the Lenin School," RGASPI, f. 515, op. 1, d. 2226, ll. 1–2.

36. "Rezoliutsiia," RGASPI, f. 531, op. 2, d. 60, l. 2; "Resolution of the Nucleus Bureau of the ILS on the Directives of the District Committee about the Insufficient Tempo in the Realization of the Decision of the District Committee and of the General Party Meeting and about the Tendencies to Disorientate the Party Collective (25/12/31)," RGASPI, f. 531, op. 2, d. 60, l. 8. The former Menshevik A. G. Slutskii was at the center of Stalin's letter. See McIlroy, "Establishment of Intellectual Orthodoxy," 210–11.

37. In early 1932, after Stalin accepted Iaroslavskii's public recantations, Kirsanova resumed her post in the Lenin School. In 1937 she was arrested as a Trotskyite oppositionist. See Pantov and Spichak, "New Light from the Russian Archives," 32–33.

38. Mackinnon, "Writing History for Stalin," 15–16. Mints recovered quickly from this incident. By May 1932 he had become the leading figure in the production of a multivolume history of the civil war owing largely to his close relationship with Maksim Gor'kii. See Enteen, "Marxist Historians during the Cultural Revolution," 160–66; and Tucker, *Stalin in Power*, 152–59. Haywood fondly recalled taking classes with Mints. See *Black Bolshevik*, 209–12.

39. "Communist Party of the Soviet Union," RGASPI, f. 531, op. 2, d. 59, ll. 22–30.

40. RGASPI, f. 531, op. 2, d. 59, ll. 24, 30. Nowell accused white Communists of feeling threatened by his equivalent if not superior education. See RGASPI, f. 531, op. 2, d. 56, ll. 57–59, 116–19, 132, 162–65.

41. See, for example, Clark, "Engineers of Human Souls."

42. On the routine functioning of this device to discredit and delegitimize the testimony of members of an oppressed group, see McBride, *Why I Hate Abercrombie and Fitch*, esp. 3–4.

43. "Rezoliutsiia o polozhenii v amerikanskoi gruppe M.L.Sh.," RGASPI, f. 515, op. 1, d. 2602, ll. 37–43; "Draft Resolution on the Situation which Developed in the American Landergroup of the ILS," RGASPI, f. 531, op.

2, d. 60, ll. 10–17 (esp. ll. 14–15). The draft resolution can also be found in RGASPI, f. 515, op. 1, d. 2602, ll. 76–83.

44. On Clarence Hathaway, a Lenin School alumnus, see Klehr, Haynes, and Anderson, *Soviet World*, esp. 40–48.

45. "Resolution on the Situation in the American Lander Group of the ILS," RGASPI, f. 531, op. 2, d. 60, ll. 75–77 (esp. l. 76); RGASPI, f. 531, op. 2, d. 60, ll. 16–17.

46. "American Landergroup. 12.24.31," RGASPI, f. 531, op. 2, d. 56a, ll. 1–178 (esp. ll. 19, 26, 33–36, 76, 100–102, 110, 118, 135, 143–45).

47. RGASPI, f. 531, op. 2, d. 60, ll. 16–17, 76.

48. "Resolution," RGASPI, f. 531, op. 2, d. 60, ll. 50–52 (esp. l. 50); ll. 10–12, 75, 77. On Lenin's formula for internationalism, which required members of the oppressing nation to make concessions and even place themselves in a disadvantaged position in relation to members of an oppressed nation to eradicate the distrust that resulted from centuries of enslavement, see "Theses on the National and Colonial Question Adopted by the Second Comintern Congress," July 28, 1920, in Degras, *Communist International*, 1:138–44 (esp. 144).

49. RGASPI, f. 531, op. 2, d. 60, ll. 11–12, 75–76.

50. "Anglo-American Lander Group Meeting ILS (22.4.32)," RGASPI, f. 531, op. 2, d. 56b, l. 25; "Draft Notes for the Conclusions of the Commission of the AA Secretariat Regarding the Carrying out of the CI Resolution of 27 February 1932 (9 April 1932)," RGASPI, f. 531, op. 2, d. 60, ll. 18–20; "Proekt rezoliutsii o khode realizatsii resheniia politkomissii IKKI o polozhenii v amerikanskoi lendergruppe," RGASPI, f. 531, op. 2, d. 60, ll. 5–7 (esp. ll. 5–6).

51. See "Postanovlenie komissii IKKI po voprosu o polozhenii v anglo-amer. sektore MLSh," RGASPI, f. 531, op. 2, d. 60, l. 1; ll. 5, 19–20; and "Statement on My Position in the Carrying through of the ECCI Resolution in the American Landergroup," RGASPI, f. 531, op. 2, d. 56v, l. 29; d. 56b, l. 71.

52. On Nessin's career in New York, see Klehr, *Heyday of American Communism*, 52–53, 236, 433.

53. RGASPI, f. 531, op. 2, 56b, ll. 6, 35–37, 66; d. 56a, ll. 52, 165–66.

54. This discussion is informed by Roediger's introduction to *Black on White*, 1–26; bell hooks, "Representations of Whiteness in the Black Imagination"; and bell hooks, "Refusing to Be a Victim."

55. "Confidential: Resolution of the Anglo-American Sector on the Case of

Comrade Mills," RGASPI, f. 531, op. 1, d. 168, l. 85; "International Control Commission," RGASPI, f. 531, op. 1, d. 168, l. 87.

56. See "Resolution of the Commission of IKKI on the Question about the Position in Anglo-American Sector of ILS," RGASPI, f. 531, op. 1, d. 168, l. 81; "About the Anti-Party Grouping in the Anglo-American Sector," RGASPI, f. 531, op. 2, d. 60, ll. 44–45; "Rezoliutsiia," RGASPI, f. 531, op. 2, d. 60, l. 55; and "Otchet o rabote biuro iacheiki MLSh za vremia s 1-go aprelia 1932 g. po 15-e dekabria 1932 g.," RGASPI, f. 531, op. 2, d. 20, ll. 83–89 (esp. l. 84).

57. Nelson, Barrett, and Ruck, *Steve Nelson*, 125–27.

58. On the involvement of Mary Dalton in antilynching protests, see Solomon, *Cry Was Unity*, 126.

59. Charles White had made a similar suggestion. See RGASPI, f. 531, op. 2, d. 56, ll. 45–46.

60. On the history of the term "Uncle Tom," see Fredrickson, *Black Image*, esp. 110–29; and Bogle, *Toms, Coons, Mulattoes*, 1–10, 47–53.

61. Stalin is of course the most famous example. See, for example, Rieber, "Stalin: Man of the Borderlands."

62. On the first accusations of Uncle Tomism leveled in the fall of 1931, see RGASPI, f. 531, op. 2, d. 56, ll. 1l–13, 96, 99, 113–14, 136–39, 147–49, 157–58, 160; d. 56a, l. 120.

63. For the Judas charges leveled in the spring of 1932, see RGASPI, f. 531, op. 2, d. 56b, ll. 9, 43, 71–73, 77–79, 98, 109; d. 60, ll. 19–20.

64. RGASPI, f. 531, op. 2, d. 56, ll. 96, 99; d. 56a, ll. 102, 110, 154; d. 59, l. 28.

65. Kelley mentions that this occurred in some rare cases in Alabama. See *Hammer and Hoe*, 113.

66. On the "triple burden" African American women in the CPUSA faced, see McDuffie, *Sojourning for Freedom*; Davies, *Left of Karl Marx*; Maxwell, *New Negro, Old Left*, 125–30; Weigand, *Red Feminism*, 99–113; Naison, *Communists in Harlem during the Depression*, 136–37, 259–60; and Kelley, *Hammer and Hoe*, 21–22, 33, 79–80, 206–7. Women comprised 15 percent of the U.S. student body, which was slightly higher than the percentage of women in the entire Lenin School; RGASPI, f. 531, op. 2, d. 16, ll. 45–46. On the Party's negligence in organizing women until the Popular Front era, when female membership increased, see Weigand, 19–24.

67. On the central role of the emasculation of black men in American

racial politics, see, for example, Orlando Patterson, *Rituals of Blood*. On stereotypical images of black women, see Wallace, *Black Macho and the Myth of the Superwoman*; Morton, *Disfigured Images*, esp. 1–16; Wallace-Sanders, *Mammy*; and McElya, *Clinging to Mammy*.

68. Haywood, *Black Bolshevik*, 312–13. In the 1930s some African American female Communists protested the proliferation of relationships between black men and white women in the Party. See Naison, *Communists in Harlem*, 137–38; and Weigand, *Red Feminism*, 99–100.

69. On black female Communists reshaping notions of respectability, see Harris, "Running with the Reds," 23 (quotation), 32–37. For the foundational study on the politics of respectability, see Higginbotham, *Righteous Discontent*. See also Wolcott, *Remaking Respectability*.

70. On this notion of a new form of black masculinity that challenged traditional notions of respectability, see Summers, *Manliness and Its Discontents*, 149–69, 287–90.

71. "Section Meeting (Anglo-American Nucleus Bureau Report)," RGASPI, f. 531, op. 2, d. 60, ll. 64–68.

72. "Report of the Resolution Commission, October 15–16," RGASPI, f. 531, op. 2, d. 60, ll. 56–63.

73. RGASPI, f. 531, op. 2, d. 56v, ll. 6–7. Accusations of anti-Semitism and Jewish chauvinism were also leveled among American students in the Lenin School. See RGASPI, f. 531, op. 2, d. 60, ll. 50–51; "15 June 1932," RGASPI, f. 531, op. 2, d. 56v, ll. 15–22; RGASPI, f. 531, op. 2, d. 20, l. 83.

74. RGASPI, f. 531, op. 2, d. 60, l. 60.

75. See RGASPI, f. 531, op. 2, d. 56a, ll. 130–32; d. 60, ll. 56–60.

76. RGASPI, f. 531, op. 2, d. 56, ll. 63, 132; d. 56a, l. 87; d. 60, ll. 56–57, 60. Authorities also rebuked other students for waiting too long to report white chauvinism. See, for example, "Draft Resolution on the Allegations Concerning Comrade Smith," RGASPI, f. 531, op. 2, d. 60, ll. 70–71; ll. 16–17.

77. For a similar argument, see Kotkin, "Coercion and Identity," 301–6. See also Hirsch, *Empire of Nations*; and note 7 above.

78. In 1928 William Patterson wrote the students' appeal regarding living conditions at KUTV. See "Dokladnaia zapiska," RGASPI, f. 495, op. 155, d. 65, ll. 2–3; "To the American Political Bureau," ll. 8–9; and "William Wilson, Dictation, 21.8.28," ll. 10–12.

79. For a synopsis of the plot of *Geisha* (1896) and its popularity, see Richards, *Imperialism and Music*, 264–66.

80. For verification of Kenyatta as "Jochen," see "Lichnoe delo-Ken'iata Dzhonson (Dzhoken)," RGASPI, f. 495, op. 198, d. 1211.

81. "Shorthand record of the conversation of Comrade Manuilskii with students of the Ninth Sector of KUTV," RGASPI, f. 532, op. 1, d. 441, ll. 1, 3, 7. For further discussion of this meeting, see McClellan, "Africans and Black Americans," 381–88.

82. For Vallade, see "Lichnoe delo-Villade Monro," RGASPI, f. 495, op. 261, d. 5565. The play was based on a children's book of the same title. See Rozanov and Sats, *Negritenok i obez'iana*. For photographs and letters regarding the play, see *The Moscow Theatre for Children*, esp. 30–34, 37. On the racist association between peoples of African descent and apes, see D. Davis, *Problem of Slavery*, 452–59; and Jordan, *White Over Black*, 29–32, 235–39, 490–97.

83. RGASPI, f. 532, op. 1, d. 441, ll. 2, 8. The 1995 unabridged Oxford Russian-English dictionary defines "black child" as "pickaninny." On the history of the term "pickaninny," see *Toms, Coons, Mulattoes*, 7–8. On the pervasive use of these and similar derogatory terms in U.S. newspapers and leading literary magazines, see Logan, *Betrayal of the Negro*, 215–74.

84. RGASPI, f. 532, op. 1, d. 441, l. 3. For Lister as "Johnson" and his origins in Cleveland, see RGASPI, f. 532, op. 1, d. 439, l. 6; and "Eastern University," RGASPI, f. 515, op. 1, d. 1869, l. 59v.

85. On Mofutsanyana, see Davidson, Filatova, Gorodnov, and Johns, *South Africa and the Communist International*, 1:6–8.

86. RGASPI, f. 532, op. 1, d. 441, l. 3.

87. RGASPI, f. 532, op. 1, d. 441, ll. 8–9.

88. McClellan, "Africans and Black Americans," 385.

89. RGASPI, f. 532, op. 1, d. 441, l. 5. For verification of "Wells" as Walter Lewis, see "Spisok studentov sektora 'A' sektsii No 9 (Negry)," RGASPI, f. 532, op. 1, d. 439, l. 6; and "Lichnoe delo-L'iuis U.," RGASPI, f. 495, op. 261, d. 1658. Lewis attended the International Conference of Negro Workers and Fifth Profintern Congress, and enrolled in KUTV in the fall of 1930, having just joined the CPUSA that February. On Lewis's activities prior to Moscow, see Kelley, *Hammer and Hoe*, 14–15, 17.

90. For verification of "Dewing" as John Hyde Rhoden, see RGASPI, f. 532, op. 1, d. 439, l. 6. Rhoden joined the CPUSA in early 1930 and arrived at KUTV on October 27, 1930. He received a stronger evaluation than Lewis. See "Duing," RGASPI, f. 532, op. 1, d. 440, l. 4.

91. RGASPI, f. 532, op. 1, d. 441, ll. 6–8. Sobia, who joined the CPSA in 1932,

attended KUTV from 1932 to 1934. See Davidson, Filatova, Gorodnov, and Johns, *South Africa and the Communist International,* 1:xxxviii.

92. RGASPI, f. 532, op. 1, d. 441, l. 10. His personal file, which is one page long, claims that Lister had joined the CPUSA in 1929. See "Lichnoe delo-Lester R.S.," RGASPI, f. 495, op. 261, d. 1937.

93. For the basis of this argument, see Hellbeck, "Speaking Out."

94. RGASPI, f. 532, op. 1, d. 441, ll. 10–11.

95. RGASPI, f. 532, op. 1, d. 441, ll. 10–12. On the history of European visitors' disdain for Russian "crudeness," see especially Wolff, *Inventing Eastern Europe.*

96. RGASPI, f. 532, op. 1, d. 441, ll. 12–13.

97. See Hellbeck, *Revolution on My Mind;* and note 93 above.

98. RGASPI, f. 532, op. 1, d. 440, ll. 3–4; "Vel's," RGASPI, f. 532, op. 1, d. 440, ll. 3–4.

99. *Two Universities; Patrice Lumumba Friendship University in Moscow;* Rosen, *Development of Peoples' Friendship University.* On African students' experiences, see Hessler, "Death of an African Student"; and Matusevich, "Journeys of Hope."

100. RGASPI, f. 532, op. 1, d. 440, l. 4; McClellan, "Africans and Black Americans," 386. To this point, Walter Lewis and other African Americans had discussed the plight of African American workers with Manuilskii in September 1930. See "Interview with American Negro Comrades and Comrade Manuilskii," RGASPI, f. 495, op. 155, d. 89, ll. 28–50.

101. On the precarious existence of African students in Moscow since the fall of Communism, see, for example, J. Allina-Pisano and E. Allina-Pisano, "'Friendship of Peoples' after the Fall."

102. Winston James argues that the preponderance of Caribbean-born blacks in U.S. radical movements in the early twentieth century is due partly to the fact that they came from societies where "blacks" (as defined in the binary U.S. sense) comprised the majority of the population and were hence more intolerant of white Americans' racist conduct. See *Holding Aloft the Banner.*

103. Wallace Daniels, "The Negro Feels at Home in the USSR," *Moscow Daily News,* February 11, 1933, 2.

104. "To the Comintern," RGASPI, f. 532, op. 1, d. 441, ll. 15–16, 18; "Resolutions in Connection with the Derogatory Portrayal of Negroes in the Cultural Institutes of the Soviet Union," RGASPI, f. 532, op. 1, d. 441, ll. 26–27. McClellan reproduces the latter document as an appendix to his essay "Africans and Black Americans," 389–90.

105. As Maxim Matusevich argues, racist caricatures of Africa and Africans marked various forms of Soviet cultural expression throughout the country's history and in spite of anticolonial rhetoric. See "Exotic Subversive"; and Matusevich's introduction in his edited collection *Africa in Russia.*

106. The *Negro Child and the Monkey* was also staged, with the help of its director Natal'ia Sats, in children's theaters in various European countries. See Sats, *Sketches from My Life.* On Baker and Europeans' obsession with "primitivism," see, for example, Sweeney, *From Fetish to Subject*; Macmaster, *Racism in Europe*; Berliner, *Ambivalent Desire*; and Stovall, *Paris Noir.*

107. This discussion is informed by hooks, *Killing Rage*, 51–61.

108. See Kotkin, "Coercion and Identity," 294–96, 307. See also Straus, *Factory and Community.*

109. hooks, "Refusing to Be a Victim."

110. McDuffie, "'[She] Devoted Twenty Minutes,'" 235–37; and Kelley, *Hammer and Hoe*, 92–137.

111. See especially Hall, "'Mind that Burns.'"

112. See Hellbeck, "Speaking Out," esp. 74–75, 80–81, 84–85.

113. See "Browder—1004," RGASPI, f. 531, op. 2, d. 56a, ll. 175–76; and "Declaration by Comrade Cooper," RGASPI, f. 531, op. 2, d. 56v, l. 36. One year after testifying before the 1948 Canwell Committee, in which he aided the Washington state legislature's crusade against several intellectual and cultural figures, Hewitt was hospitalized for psychotic episodes. Patterson left the Party in 1937 and Hewitt in 1944. On the history of HUAC and its various incarnations ("little HUACs"), see Woods, *Black Struggle*, esp. 26–38, 85–111.

114. Marable, *Race, Reform, and Rebellion*, 29–30. Harry Haywood denounced Nowell at the Eighth Party Convention in Cleveland in April 1934 for leveling indiscriminate accusations of "Uncle Tomism." He claimed Nowell was a government agent while a member of the CPUSA. See *Black Bolshevik*, 431, 667; and Klehr, *Heyday of American Communism*, 340, 471.

115. Kelley, *Hammer and Hoe*, 132.

Epilogue

1. On Soviet citizens' familiarity with *Circus*, see Ratchford, "*Circus* of 1936," esp. 91–92.

2. On the film's popularity and its Georgian director, Ivan Perestiani, see Youngblood, *Movies for the Masses*, 33, 77–78, 164; Stites, *Russian Popular Culture*, 161; and Leyda, *Kino*, 168.

3. On Tom Jackson and excerpts from the script, see von Geldern and Stites, *Mass Culture in Soviet Russia*, 36–52 (esp. 36, 42, 45).

4. As Peter Kenez notes, Jackson's character is not the film's only departure from reality. See *Cinema and Soviet Society*, 45, 92, 111.

5. Macheret and Glagoleva, *Sovetskie khudozhestvennye fil'my*, 1:450.

6. The film is known alternatively as *Love and Hatred* (*Liubov' i nenavist'*) and *One Enemy* (*Vrag odin*). Murray was probably played by a white actor in blackface. See Macheret and Glagoleva, *Sovetskie khudozhestvennye fil'my*, 1:463.

7. The name of the black protagonist was perhaps inspired by Mark Twain's character "Jim" from *Tom Sawyer* and *Huckleberry Finn*. Scholars argue that the film stretched the boundaries of reality when it left the shtetl for Magnitigorsk. See Hoberman, "Face to the *Shtetl*"; Kenez, "Jewish Themes in Stalinist Cinema"; and Leyda, *Kino*, 288.

8. The same year, Mezhrabpom released a short animated film titled *Black and White*, which was set on a sugar plantation in Cuba and was based on a Vladimir Maiakovskii poem of the same title. See Macheret and Glagoleva, *Sovetskie khudozhestvennye fil'my*, 2:24. This short film has recently been rereleased.

9. Stites, *Russian Popular Culture*, 89; Hoberman, "Face to the *Shtetl*," 140.

10. It was released in fourteen Moscow movie theaters on May 25, 1936. For contemporary glowing reviews of the film, see A. Timofeev, "'Tsirk,'" *Vecherniaia Moskva*, May 21, 1936, 3; "Successful New Film Comedy," *Moscow Daily News*, May 24, 1936, 3; N. D., "Zhizneradostnyi fil'm," *Literaturnaia gazeta*, May 30, 1936, 5; and "'Tsirk,'" *Izvestiia*, May 23, 1936, 4. For the U.S. embassy's assessment of the film, see Enclosure No. 1 to Dispatch No. 1622 of May 27, 1936, from the American Embassy, Moscow USSR, to Secretary of State, RG 84, MLR Number 363, USSR Embassy, 1936, vol. 35, 840.6, NARA.

11. On its premiere, see "Rasskazy i fel'etony (1932–1937)," in Il'f and Petrov, *Sobranie sochinenii v piati tomakh*, 3:539–40. For the play, see "Pod kupolom tsirka," 3:438–70.

12. See Stites, *Russian Popular Culture*, 89. For an extended discussion of the differences between the film and Il'f and Petrov's play, see Holmgren, "*Blue Angel* and Blackface." See also R. Taylor, "Illusion of Happiness."

13. Aleksandrov's wife, Liubov' Orlova, played Dixon. In the play the woman's name is not Marion Dixon but "Alina." For different theories regarding why Aleksandrov changed the character's name, see Holmgren, "*Blue Angel* and Blackface," 12–13; and R. Taylor, "Illusion of Happiness," 611–12.

14. On Kneishits's character, see Stites, *Russian Popular Culture*, 89.

15. Holmgren, "*Blue Angel* and Blackface," 12–17.

16. On his Aryan-like features, see Ratchford, "*Circus* of 1936," 91.

17. R. Taylor, "Illusion of Happiness," 612.

18. On Dixon's coming to consciousness, see R. Taylor, "Illusion of Happiness," 613.

19. Allison Blakely identifies the man in the film as Ross. See Blakely, "African Imprints," 50.

20. Holmgren, "*Blue Angel* and Blackface," 20.

21. On Dixon's revirginalization, see Holmgren, "*Blue Angel* and Blackface," 16–17.

22. "Soviet Hollywood Shows Wonders of Film Technique," *Moscow Daily News*, May 18, 1935, 3.

23. Ratchford, "*Circus* of 1936," 91.

24. *Under the Big Top* claims that Marion's character had been married to a black man. See Il'f and Petrov, "Pod kupolom tsirka," 469.

25. See especially Holmgren, "*Blue Angel* and Blackface," 17–18.

26. Aleksandrov expressed relief that his assistants were able to find a black child to play Dixon's black son. See Aleksandrov, *Epokha i kino*, 202.

27. On this trope, see Kayiatos, "Sooner Speaking than Silent."

28. The Soviet press compared article 123 in the draft constitution guaranteeing racial equality with the policies of the Nazi German state and the bourgeois democracies of the United States, France, and England. See note 42 below. The draft of the new constitution was released for nationwide "discussion" in June 1936, shortly after the film's release. See, for example, Siegelbaum and Sokolov, *Stalinism as a Way of Life*, 158–206; and Wimberg, "Socialism, Democratism, and Criticism."

29. See Scott, *Domination and the Arts of Resistance*, 174–79, 187.

30. For the official promotion of motherhood and family by 1936, see, for example, Goldman, *Women, the State and Revolution*.

31. This song was released prior to *Circus*'s premiere, and according to R. Taylor it was effective in inculcating the film's main message. See "Illusion of Happiness," 607.

32. Petrone, *Life Has Become More Joyous*, 54–55.

33. Reflecting her status as the film's heroine, Dixon was featured in the majority of promotional advertisements for *Circus*, but Jimmy was not. See, for example, the advertisements on page 4 in *Vecherniaia Moskva* on May 8, 11, 16, 17, 20, 21, 22, and 23, 1936.

34. Allison Blakely identifies the woman as Vivian Jones. See "African Imprints," 50. She might be the same woman who the *Afro-American* featured in a 1936 article and identified as "Vivienne France." See "Va. Girl, Now Teaching in Russia, Pays U.S. a Visit," *Afro-American*, June 13, 1936, 12.

35. On the history of African American female domestic workers, see Jones, *Labor of Love*, esp. 22–27, 127–34, 154–67, 256–60.

36. On the coexistence of the contradictory Mammy and Jezebel images of black women, see D. White, *Ar'n't I a Woman?*, esp. 27–61. See also Thurber, "Development of the Mammy Image."

37. See especially Campt, *Other Germans*, 31–62.

38. On Lloyd Patterson, see Carew, *Blacks, Reds, and Russians*, 167–68, 213. After pursuing a naval career, James Patterson began writing poetry, graduated from the Literary Institute, and had his work published in several Soviet journals, some of which can be found in *Rossiia. Afrika. Stikhi i poema*. In a 2004 interview Patterson emphasized that Orlova was like a second mother. See Kossie-Chernyshev, "Reclaiming 'D. Patterson.'"

39. On Khanga's experiences, see *Soul to Soul*, esp. 18–22. On Golden and Bialek, see also Blakely, "African Imprints," 47; Garb, *They Came to Stay*, 36–40; and Carew, *Blacks, Reds, and Russians*, 99–112, 160–66. On Khanga's celebrity status in post-Communist Russia, see Baldwin, *Beyond the Color Line*, 253–62.

40. "In Russia They Can Rear Children without Prejudice," *Afro-American*, June 6, 1936, 7. See also "Racial Angle Sends Wife to Psychopathic Ward," *Chicago Defender*, December 22, 1934, 1, 2. Mark Solomon mentions the couple. See *Cry Was Unity*, 175–76.

41. Aleksandrov, *Epokha i kino*, 190. See also Holmgrem, "*Blue Angel* and Blackface."

42. See, for example, Iur., "V strane rasovogo izuverstva," *Izvestiia*, June 17, 1936, 2; Iu. Shaksel', "Rasovoe uchenie, nauka i proletarskii internatsionalizm," *Izvestiia*, June 18, 1936, 2; and V. Liadova, "Fashizm-rasovaia nenavist', sotsializm-bratstvo narodov," *Trud*, July 14, 1936, 2.

43. On the lynching of African American women, see Dray, *At the Hands of Persons Unknown*, esp. 245–47.

44. Holmgren, "*Blue Angel* and Blackface," 19.

45. R. Taylor, "Illusion of Happiness," 610.

46. See, for example, "Protesty v ssha protiv linchevaniia negrov," *Izvestiia*, August 1, 1946, 4; "Progressivnaia obshchestvennost' ssha vozmushchena terrorom protiv negrov," *Trud*, August 2, 1946, 4; "Demokraticheskie organizatsiia ssha trebuiut zapreshcheniia ku-kluks-klana," *Pravda*, August 3, 1946, 4; "Obshchestvennost' ssha trebuet provedeniia zakona protiv linchevaniia," *Trud*, August 7, 1946, 4. The reports that Il'ia Ehrenburg wrote about America for *Izvestiia* in July and early August 1946 likewise reflect this change. See also Johnson, *Urban Ghetto Riots*.

BIBLIOGRAPHY

Archival Sources

Beinecke Rare Book and Manuscript Library, Yale University, New Haven, Connecticut
Langston Hughes Papers, 1862–1980
Gosudarstvennyi arkhiv Rossiiskoi Federatsii (GARF) (State Archive of the Russian Federation)
f. 5283 Vsesoiuznoe obshchestvo kul'turnoi sviazi s zagranitsei
f. 5451 Vsesoiuznyi tsentral'nyi sovet professional'nykh soiuzov
f. 5458 Tsentral'nyi komitet professional'nykh soiuzov rabochikh shchveinoi promyshlennosti
f. 5469 Tsentral'nyi komitet vsesoiuznogo professional'nogo soiuza rabochikh-metallistov (TsK metallistov)
f. 5667 Mezhdunarodnye komitety propagandy i deistviia
f. 8265 Tsentral'nyi komitet mezhdunarodnoi organizatsii pomoshchi bortsam revoliutsii SSSR
Houghton Library, Harvard College Library, Cambridge, Massachusetts
Henry Wadsworth Longfellow Dana Collection of Russian Theatrical Scripts and Papers
National Archives and Records Administration (NARA), College Park, Maryland
Records of Foreign Service Posts, Diplomatic Posts, Record Group 84
Records of the Department of State Relating to the Internal Affairs of the Soviet Union, 1930–1939
State Department Decimal Files, Record Group 59
Radcliffe Institute for Advanced Study, Arthur and Elizabeth Schlesinger Library, Cambridge, Massachusetts
Dorothy West Collection

Rossiiskii gosudarstvennyi arkhiv sotsial'noi i politicheskoi istorii (RGASPI) (Russian State Archive of Social and Political History)

f. 495 Ispolnitel'nyi komitet Kominterna (IKKI)

op. 30 Otdel propagandy IKKI

op. 72 Anglo-amerikanskii lendersekretariat IKKI

op. 155 Negritianskoe biuro (sektsiia) Vostochnogo sekretariata IKKI

op. 261 Lichnye dela (SShA)

f. 515 Kommunisticheskaia partiia SShA

f. 531 Mezhdunarodnaia leninskaia shkola (MLSh)

f. 532 Kommunisticheskii universitet trudiashchikhsia Vostoka (KUTV)

f. 534 Krasnyi internatsional profsoiuzov (Profintern)

f. 538 Mezhdunarodnaia organizatsiia rabochei pomoshchi

f. 539 Mezhdunarodnaia organizatsiia pomoshchi bortsam revoliutsii (MOPR)

Schomburg Center for Research in Black Culture, New York City

Richard B. Moore Papers, 1902–1978

Tamiment Library and Robert F. Wagner Labor Archives, New York University

James W. Ford Papers, 1928–1957

Mark Solomon and Robert Kaufman Research Files on African Americans and Communism

Published Sources

Adibekov, G. M., E. N. Shakhnazarova, and K. K. Shirinia. *Organizatsionnaia struktura Kominterna, 1919–1943*. Moscow: Rosspen, 1997.

Agapov, Boris. *Tekhnicheskie rasskazy*. Moscow: Khudozhestvennaia literatura, 1936.

Aleksandrov, G. V. *Epokha i kino*. Moscow: Izd-vo polit. lit-ry, 1976.

Alexopoulos, Golfo. "Victim Talk: Defense Testimony and Denunciation under Stalin." In *Russian Modernity: Politics, Knowledge, Practices*, edited by David L. Hoffmann and Yanni Kotsonis, 204–20. New York: St. Martin's Press, 2000.

Allen, James, Hilton Als, John Lewis, and Leon F. Litwack. *Without Sanctuary: Lynching Photography in America*. Santa Fe NM: Twin Palms, 2000.

Allina-Pisano, Jessica, and Eric Allina-Pisano. "'Friendship of Peoples' after the Fall: Violence and Pan-African Community in Post-Soviet Moscow." In Matusevich, *Africa in Russia, Russia in Africa*, 175–98.

Altstadt, Audrey L. "Nagorno-Karabakh: 'Apple of Discord' in the Azerbaijan SSR." *Central Asian Survey* 7, no. 4 (1988): 63–78.

Anderson, Benedict. *Imagined Communities: Reflections on the Origins and Spread of Nationalism*. London: Verso, 1983.

Anderson, Carol. *Eyes Off the Prize: The United Nations and the African American Struggle for Human Rights, 1944–1955*. Cambridge: Cambridge University Press, 2003.

Argenbright, Robert. "Marking NEP's Slippery Path: The Krasnoshchekov Show Trial." *Russian Review* 61 (April 2002): 249–75.

Avins, Carol. *Border Crossings: The West and Russian Identity in Soviet Literature, 1917–1934*. Berkeley: University of California Press, 1983.

Avrus, A. I. MOPR *v bor'be protiv terrora i fashizma, 1922–1939*. Saratov: Izdatel'stvo Saratovskogo universiteta, 1976.

——. *Proletarskii internatsionalizm v deistvii: Iz istorii Mezhdunarodnoi organizatsii pomoshchi bortsam revoliutsii*. Saratov: Izdatel'stvo Saratovskogo universiteta, 1971.

Baburina, Nina. *Rossiia—20 vek: Istoriia strany v plakate*. Moscow: Panorama, 1993.

Baldwin, Kate A. *Beyond the Color Line and the Iron Curtain: Reading Encounters between Black and Red, 1922–1963*. Durham NC: Duke University Press, 2002.

Balibar, Etienne. "Racism and Nationalism." In *Race, Nation, Class: Ambiguous Identities*, edited by Etienne Balibar and Immanuel Wallerstein, 37–68. London: Verso, 1988.

Ball, Alan M. *Imagining America: Influence and Images in Twentieth-Century Russia*. Lanham MD: Rowman and Littlefield, 2003.

Barnes, Hugh. *The Stolen Prince: Gannibal Adopted Son of Peter the Great, Great-Grandfather of Alexander Pushkin, and Europe's First Black Intellectual*. New York: ECCO, 2006.

Beal, Fred E. *Proletarian Journey: New England, Gastonia, Moscow*. New York: Da Capo Press, 1971.

Becker, Jonathan A. *Soviet and Russian Press Coverage of the United States: Press, Politics, and Identity in Transition*. New York: Palgrave, 2002.

Berliner, Brett A. *Ambivalent Desire: The Exotic Other in Jazz Age France*. Amherst: University of Massachusetts Press, 2002.

Blackmon, Douglas A. *Slavery by Another Name: The Re-enslavement of Black People in America from the Civil War to World War II*. New York: Doubleday, 2008.

Blakely, Allison. "African Imprints on Russia: An Historical Overview." In Matusevich, *Africa in Russia, Russia in Africa*, 37–59.

——. *Russia and the Negro: Blacks in Russian History and Thought*. Washington DC: Howard University Press, 1986.

Bland, Lucy. "White Women and Men of Colour: Miscegenation Fears in Britain after the Great War." *Gender and History* 17, no. 1 (April 2005): 29–61.

Bogle, Donald. *Toms, Coons, Mulattoes, Mammies, and Bucks: An Interpretive History of Blacks in American Films*. New York: Continuum Publishing, 1989.

Bonnell, Victoria E. *Iconography of Power: Soviet Political Posters under Lenin and Stalin*. Berkeley: University of California Press, 1997.

——. "The Iconography of the Worker in Soviet Political Art." In *Making Workers Soviet: Power, Class, and Identity*, edited by Lewis H. Siegelbaum and Ronald G. Suny, 341–75. Ithaca NY: Cornell University Press, 1994.

Borstelmann, Thomas. *The Cold War and the Color Line: American Race Relations in the Global Arena*. Cambridge MA: Harvard University Press, 2002.

Bose, Tarun Chandra. *American Soviet Relations*. Calcutta: Firma K. L. Mukhopadhyay, 1967.

Brooks, Jeffrey. "Official Xenophobia and Cosmopolitanism in Early Soviet Russia." *American Historical Review* 97, no. 5 (December 1992): 1431–48.

——. "The Press and Its Message: Images of America in the 1920s and 1930s." In *Russia in the Era of NEP: Explorations in Soviet Society and Culture*, edited by Sheila Fitzpatrick, Alexander Rabinowitch, and Richard Stites, 231–52. Bloomington: Indiana University Press, 1991.

——. *Thank You, Comrade Stalin! Soviet Public Culture from Revolution to Cold War*. Princeton NJ: Princeton University Press, 2000.

Brophy, Alfred L. *Reconstructing the Dreamland: The Tulsa Riot of 1921 Race, Reparations, and Reconciliation*. New York: Oxford University Press, 2002.

Brower, Daniel R., and Edward J. Lazzerini, eds. *Russia's Orient: Imperial Borderlands and Peoples, 1750–1917*. Bloomington: Indiana University Press, 1997.

Brown, Glenora W., and Deming B. Brown. *A Guide to Soviet Russian Translations of American Literature*. New York: King's Crown Press, 1954.

Brubaker, Rogers. *Citizenship and Nationhood in France and Germany*. Cambridge MA: Harvard University Press, 1992.

Burleigh, Michael, and Wolfgang Wippermann. *The Racial State: Germany, 1933–1945*. Cambridge: Cambridge University Press, 1991.

Cambridge, Alrick, and Stephan Feuchtwang. *Where You Belong: Government and Black Culture*. London: Avebury, 1992.

Campbell, Alan, John Halstead, John McIlroy, and Barry McLoughlin. "Forging the Faithful: The British at the International Lenin School." *Labour History Review* 68, no. 1 (April 2003): 99–128.

Campt, Tina. *Other Germans: Black Germans and the Politics of Race, Gender, and Memory in the Third Reich*. Ann Arbor: University of Michigan, 2003.

Carby, Hazel V. *Race Men*. Cambridge MA: Harvard University Press, 1998.

Carew, Joy Gleason. *Blacks, Reds, and Russians: Sojourners in Search of the Soviet Promise*. New Brunswick NJ: Rutgers University Press, 2008.

Carter, Dan. *Scottsboro: A Tragedy of the American South*. 1969. Reprint, Baton Rouge: Louisiana State University, 1979.

Chamberlin, William Henry. *The Russian Revolution*. 1935. Reprint, New York: Macmillan, 1965.

———. *Russia's Iron Age*. Boston: Little, Brown, and Company, 1934.

Chase, William J. *Enemy within the Gates: The Comintern and the Stalinist Repression, 1934–1939*. New Haven CT: Yale University Press, 2001.

Clark, Katerina. "Engineers of Human Souls in an Age of Industrialization: Changing Cultural Models, 1929–1941." In *Social Dimensions of Soviet Industrialization*, edited by William G. Rosenberg and Lewis H. Siegelbaum, 248–64. Bloomington: Indiana University Press, 1993.

———. "'Little Heroes and Big Deeds': Literature Responds to the First Five-Year Plan." In Fitzpatrick, *Cultural Revolution in Russia, 1928–1931*, 189–206.

Cohen, Gidon, and Kevin Morgan. "Stalin's Sausage Machine: British Students at the Lenin School, 1926–1937." *Twentieth-Century British History* 13, no. 4 (2002): 327–55.

Conklin, Alice. "Colonialism and Human Rights, a Contradiction in Terms? The Case of France and West Africa, 1895–1914." *American Historical Review* 103, no. 2 (April 1998): 419–42.

Cooper, Frederick, and Ann Laura Stoler. "Between Metropole and Colony: Rethinking a Research Agenda." In *Tensions of Empire: Colonial Cultures in a Bourgeois World*, edited by Frederick Cooper and Ann Laura Stoler, 1–56. Berkeley: University of California Press, 1997.

Cooper, Wayne. *Claude McKay: Rebel Sojourner in the Harlem Renaissance: A Biography*. Baton Rouge: Louisiana State University Press, 1987.

Croissant, Michael P. *The Armenia-Azerbaijan Conflict: Causes and Implications*. London: Praeger, 1998.

Davidson, Appollon B., Irina Filatova, Valentin Gorodnov, and Sheridan Johns, eds. *South Africa and the Communist International: A Documentary History*. Vol. 1, *Socialist Pilgrims to Bolshevik Footsoldiers, 1919–1930*. New York: Routledge, 2002.

Davies, Carole Boyce. *Left of Karl Marx: The Political Life of Black Communist Claudia Jones*. Durham NC: Duke University Press, 2008.

Davies, R. W., and Oleg V. Khlevniuk, eds. *The Stalin-Kaganovich Correspondence, 1931–1936*. New Haven CT: Yale University Press, 2003.

Davies, R. W., and Stephen G. Wheatcroft. *The Years of Hunger: Soviet Agriculture, 1931–1933*. New York: Palgrave, 2004.

Davies, Sarah. *Popular Opinion in Stalin's Russia: Terror, Propaganda, and Dissent, 1934–1941*. Cambridge: Cambridge University Press, 1997.

Davis, Angela Y. "Rape, Racism, and the Myth of the Black Rapist." In *Women, Race, and Class*, by Angela Y. Davis, 172–201. New York: Random House, 1981.

Davis, David Brion. *The Problem of Slavery in Western Culture*. Ithaca NY: Cornell University Press, 1966.

Degras, Jane, ed. *The Communist International, 1919–1943 Documents*. Vol. 1. London: Oxford University Press, 1965.

Draper, Theodore. *American Communism and Soviet Russia: The Formative Period*. New York: The Viking Press, 1960.

Dray, Philip. *At the Hands of Persons Unknown: The Lynching of Black America*. New York: Modern Library, 2002.

Duara, Prasenjit. *Rescuing History from the Nation: Questioning Narratives of Modern China*. Chicago: University of Chicago Press, 1995.

Duberman, Martin Bauml. *Paul Robeson*. New York: Alfred A. Knopf, 1988.

Dudziak, Mary L. *Cold War Civil Rights: Race and the Image of American Democracy*. Princeton NJ: Princeton University Press, 2000.

Edwards, Brent Hayes. *The Practice of Diaspora: Literature, Translation, and the Rise of Black Internationalism*. Cambridge MA: Harvard University Press, 2003.

Eley, Geoff. *Forging Democracy: The History of the Left in Europe, 1850–2000*. New York: Oxford University Press, 2002.

El-Hai, Jack. "Black and White and Red." *American Heritage Magazine* 42, no. 3 (May–June 1991): 83–92.

Enteen, George M. "Marxist Historians during the Cultural Revolution: A Case Study of Professional In-Fighting." In Fitzpatrick, *Cultural Revolution in Russia, 1928–1938*, 154–79.

Etkind, Aleksandr. *Tolkovanie puteshestvii: Rossiia i Amerika v travelogakh i intertekstakh*. Moscow: Novoe literaturnoe obozrenie, 2001.

Farrar, Hayward. *The Baltimore Afro-American, 1892–1950*. Westport CT: Greenwood Press, 1998.

Ferrer, Ada. *Insurgent Cuba: Race, Nation, and Revolution, 1868–1898*. Chapel Hill: University of North Carolina Press, 1999.

Fitzpatrick, Sheila. *Commissariat of Enlightenment: Soviet Organization of Education and the Arts under Lunacharsky October 1917–1921*. 1970. Reprint, Cambridge: Cambridge University Press, 2002.

——. *The Cultural Front: Power and Culture in Revolutionary Russia*. Ithaca NY: Cornell University Press, 1992.

——. "Cultural Revolution as Class War." In Fitzpatrick, *Cultural Revolution in Russia, 1928–1931*, 17–22.

——, ed. *Cultural Revolution in Russia, 1928–1931*. 1978. Reprint, Bloomington: Indiana University Press, 1984.

——. *Everyday Stalinism: Ordinary Life in Extraordinary Times: Soviet Russia in the 1930s*. Oxford: Oxford University Press, 1999.

——. "The 'Soft' Line on Culture and Its Enemies: Soviet Cultural Policy, 1922–1927." *Slavic Review* 33, no. 2 (June 1974): 267–87.

——. *Stalin's Peasants: Resistance and Accommodation after Collectivization*. Oxford: Oxford University Press, 1994.

Fletcher, Yael Simpson. "City, Nation, and Empire in Marseilles, 1919–1939." PhD diss., Emory University, 1999.

Foley, Barbara. *Radical Representations: Politics and Form in U.S. Proletarian Fiction, 1929–1941*. Durham NC: Duke University Press, 1993.

Foner, Philip S., and James S. Allen, eds. *American Communism and Black Americans: A Documentary History, 1919–1929*. Philadelphia: Temple University Press, 1987.

Fredrickson, George M. *The Black Image in the White Mind: The Debate on Afro-American Character and Destiny, 1817–1914*. New York: Harper and Row, 1971.

Frierson, Cathy. "Crime and Punishment in the Russian Village: Rural Concepts of Criminality at the End of the Nineteenth Century." *Slavic Review* 46, no. 1 (Spring 1987): 55–69.

Garb, Paula. *They Came to Stay: North Americans in the USSR*. Moscow: Progress Publishers, 1987.

Getty, J. Arch. "*Samokritika* Rituals in the Stalinist Central Committee, 1933–38." *Russian Review* 58 (January 1999): 49–70.

Getty, J. Arch, Oleg V. Naumov, and Benjamin Sher. *The Road to Terror: Stalin and the Self-Destruction of the Bolsheviks, 1932–1939*. New Haven CT: Yale University Press, 2010.

Gilenson, Boris. "Afro-American Literature in the Soviet Union." *Negro American Literature Forum* 9, no. 1 (Spring 1975): 25–29.

Gilmore, Glenda Elizabeth. *Defying Dixie: The Radical Roots of Civil Rights, 1919–1950*. New York: W. W. Norton, 2008.

Gilroy, Paul. "One Nation under a Groove: The Cultural Politics of 'Race' and Racism Britain." In *Becoming National: A Reader*, edited by Geoff Eley and Ronald G. Suny, 352–70. New York: Oxford University Press, 1996.

——. *"There Ain't No Black in the Union Jack": The Cultural Politics of Race and Nation*. Chicago: University of Chicago Press, 1987.

Goldman, Wendy Z. *Women, the State and Revolution: Soviet Family Policy and Social Life, 1917–1936*. Cambridge: Cambridge University Press, 1993.

Goldsby, Jacqueline. *Spectacular Secret: Lynching in American Life and Literature*. Chicago: University of Chicago Press, 2006.

Goodman, James. *Stories of Scottsboro*. New York: Vintage Books, 1994.

Gorsuch, Anne E. *Youth in Revolutionary Russia: Enthusiasts, Bohemians, Delinquents*. Bloomington: Indiana University Press, 2000.

Gottlieb, Peter. *Making Their Own Way: Southern Blacks' Migration to Pittsburgh, 1916–1930*. Urbana: University of Illinois Press, 1997.

Grant, Bruce. "An Average Azeri Village (1930): Remembering Rebellion in the Caucasus Mountains." *Slavic Review* 63, no. 4 (Winter 2004): 705–31.

Grossman, James R. *Land of Hope: Chicago, Black Southerners, and the Great Migration*. Chicago: University of Chicago Press, 1989.

Hagener, Malte. *Moving Forward, Looking Back: The European Avant-Garde and the Invention of Film Culture, 1919–1939*. Amsterdam: Amsterdam University Press, 2007.

Hall, Jacquelyn Dowd. "'The Mind that Burns in Each Body': Women, Rape, and Racial Violence." In *Powers of Desire: The Politics of Sexuality*, edited by Ann Snitow, Christine Stansell, and Sharon Thompson, 328–49. New York: Monthly Review Press, 1983.

Hanebrink, Paul A. *In Defense of Christian Hungary: Religion, Nationalism, and Antisemitism, 1890–1944*. Ithaca NY: Cornell University Press, 2006.

Harris, Lashawn. "Running with the Reds: African American Women and the Communist Party during the Great Depression." *Journal of African-American History* 94, no. 1 (Winter 2009): 21–43.

Haywood, Harry. *Black Bolshevik: Autobiography of an Afro-American Communist*. Chicago: Liberator Press, 1978.

Healey, Dan. "Sexual and Gender Dissent: Homosexuality as Resistance in Stalin's Russia." In *Contending with Stalinism: Soviet Power and Popular Resistance in the 1930s*, edited by Lynne Viola, 139–69. Ithaca NY: Cornell University Press, 2002.

Hellbeck, Jochen. *Revolution on My Mind: Writing a Diary under Stalin.* Cambridge MA: Harvard University Press, 2006.

———. "Speaking Out: Languages of Affirmation and Dissent in Stalinist Russia." *Kritika: Explorations in Russian and Eurasian History* 1, no. 1 (Winter 2000): 71–96.

Hemenway, Elizabeth Jones. "Mothers of Communists: Women Revolutionaries and the Construction of a Soviet Identity." In *Gender and National Identity in Twentieth-Century Russian Culture,* edited by Helena Goscilo and Andrea Lanoux, 75–92. DeKalb: Northern Illinois University Press, 2006.

Hessler, Julie. "Death of an African Student in Moscow: Race, Politics, and the Cold War." *Cahiers du Monde russe* 47, nos. 1–2 (January–June 2006): 33–64.

Higginbotham, Evelyn Brooks. *Righteous Discontent: The Women's Movement in the Black Baptist Church, 1880–1920.* Cambridge MA: Harvard University Press, 1994.

Hill, Rebecca N. *Men, Mobs, and Law: Anti-Lynching Defense and Labor Defense in U.S. Radical History.* Durham NC: Duke University Press, 2008.

Hine, Darlene Clark. "Rape and the Inner Lives of Black Women in the Middle West: Preliminary Thoughts on the Culture of Dissemblance." In *Unequal Sisters: A Multicultural Reader in U.S. Women's History,* edited by Ellen Carol DuBois and Vicki L. Ruiz, 292–97. New York: Routledge, 1990.

Hirsch, Francine. *Empire of Nations: Ethnographic Knowledge and the Making of the Soviet Union.* Ithaca NY: Cornell University Press, 2005.

———. "Race without the Practice of Racial Politics." *Slavic Review* 61, no. 1 (Spring 2002): 30–43.

———. "The Soviet Union as a Work-in-Progress: Ethnographers and the Category *Nationality* in the 1926, 1937, and 1939 Censuses." *Slavic Review* 56, no. 2 (Summer 1997): 251–78.

———. "Toward an Empire of Nations: Border-Making and the Formation of Soviet National Identities." *Russian Review* 59 (April 2000): 201–26.

Hoberman, J. "A Face to the *Shtetl*: Soviet Yiddish Cinema, 1924–1936." In *Inside the Film Factory: New Approaches to Russian and Soviet Cinema,* edited by Richard Taylor and Ian Christie, 124–50. London: Routledge, 1991.

Hobsbawm, Eric J. *The Age of Extremes: A History of the World, 1914–1991.* New York: Vintage, 1994.

———. "Man and Woman in Socialist Iconography." *History Workshop* 6 (Autumn 1978): 121–38.

Hoffmann, David L. "Bodies of Knowledge: Physical Culture and the New Soviet Man." In *Language and Revolutions: Making Modern Political Identities*, edited by Igal Halfin, 269–86. London: Routledge, 2002.

——. "Mothers in the Motherland: Soviet Pronatalism in its Pan-European Context." *Journal of Social History* 34, no. 1 (Autumn 2000): 35–54.

——. *Peasant Metropolis: Social Identities in Moscow, 1929–1941*. Ithaca NY: Cornell University Press, 1994.

——. *Stalinist Values: The Cultural Norms of Soviet Modernity, 1917–1941*. Ithaca NY: Cornell University Press, 2003.

Hokanson, Katya. "Literary Imperialism, *Narodnost'* and Pushkin's Invention of the Caucasus." *Russian Review* 53 (July 1994): 336–52.

Holmgren, Beth. "*The Blue Angel* and Blackface: Redeeming Entertainment in Aleksandrov's *Circus*." *Russian Review* 66 (January 2007): 5–22.

Holquist, Peter. "'Conduct Merciless Mass Terror': Decossackization on the Don, 1919." *Cahiers du monde russe* 39 (1998): 197–208.

Holt, Thomas C. *The Problem of Freedom: Race, Labor, and Politics in Jamaica and Britain, 1832–1938*. Baltimore: Johns Hopkins University Press, 1992.

Hooker, James R. *Black Revolutionary: George Padmore's Path from Communism to Pan-Africanism*. New York: Frederick A. Praeger, 1967.

hooks, bell. "Refusing to Be a Victim: Accountability and Responsibility." In *Killing Rage: Ending Racism*, by bell hooks, 51–61. New York: Henry Holt, 1995.

——. "Representations of Whiteness in the Black Imagination." In *Black Looks: Race and Representation*, by bell hooks, 165–78. Boston: South End Press, 1992.

Horne, Gerald. *Black and Red: W. E. B. Du Bois and the Afro-American Response to the Cold War, 1994–1993*. Albany: State University of New York, 1986.

Howe, Glenford D. *Race, War, and Nationalism: A Social History of West Indians in the First World War*. Kingston, Jamaica: Ian Randle, 2002.

Hughes, Langston. *I Wonder as I Wander: An Autobiographical Journey*. New York: Hill and Wang, 1956.

——. "Negroes in Moscow: In a Land Where There Is No Jim Crow." *International Literature* 4 (1933): 78–81.

——. *A Negro Looks at Central Asia*. Moscow: Society of Foreign Workers in the USSR, 1933.

Iakovlev, A. N. *A Century of Violence in Soviet Russia*. New Haven CT: Yale University Press, 2002.

Il'f, Il'ia, and Evgenii Petrov. *Odnoetazhnaia Amerika: Pis'ma iz Ameriki*. Moscow: "Tekst," 2003.

——. "Pod kupolom tsirka." *Sobranie sochinenii.* Vol. 3. Moscow: "Khudozh. lit-ra," 1994.

——. *Sobranie sochinenii v piati tomakh.* Vol. 3. Moscow: Gosudarstvennoe izdatel'stvo khudozhestvennoi literatury, 1961.

James, Winston. *Holding Aloft the Banner of Ethiopia: Caribbean Radicalism in Early Twentieth-Century America.* London: Verso, 1998.

Jenkinson, Jacqueline. *Black 1919: Riots, Racism, and Resistance in Imperial Britain.* Liverpool: Liverpool University Press, 2009.

Johnson, Ann K. *Urban Ghetto Riots, 1965–1968: A Comparison of Soviet and American Press Coverage.* New York: Columbia University Press, 1996.

Jones, Jacqueline. *Labor of Love, Labor of Sorrow: Black Women, Work, and the Family from Slavery to the Present.* New York: Basic Books, 1985.

Jordan, Winthrop D. *White Over Black: American Attitudes toward the Negro, 1550–1812.* Baltimore: Penguin, 1971.

Kayiatos, Anastasia. "Sooner Speaking than Silent, Sooner Silent than Mute: Soviet Deaf Theatre and Pantomime after Stalin." *Theatre Survey* 51 (2010): 5–31.

Kelley, Robin D. G. *Hammer and Hoe: Alabama Communists during the Great Depression.* Chapel Hill: University of North Carolina Press, 1990.

——. *Race Rebels: Culture, Politics, and the Black Working Class.* New York: Free Press, 1994.

——. *Scottsboro, Alabama: A Story in Linoleum.* New York: New York University Press, 2002.

Kelly, Catriona. *Children's World: Growing Up in Russia, 1890–1991.* New Haven CT: Yale University Press, 2007.

——. *The Little Citizens of a Big Country: Childhood and International Relations in the Soviet Union.* Trondheim, Norway: Program on East European Cultures and Societies, 2002.

Kenez, Peter. *Cinema and Soviet Society, 1917–1953.* Cambridge: Cambridge University Press, 1992.

——. "Jewish Themes in Stalinist Cinema." *Journal of Popular Culture* 31, no. 4 (Spring 1998): 159–69.

Kepley, Vance, Jr. "The First Perestroika: Soviet Cinema under the First Five-Year Plan." *Cinema Journal* 35, no. 4 (Summer 1996): 31–53.

——. "The Workers' International Relief and the Cinema of the Left, 1921–1935." *Cinema Journal* 23, no. 1 (Fall 1983): 7–23.

Kershaw, Ian. *The Nazi Dictatorship: Problems and Perspectives of Interpretation.* London: Arnold, 1993.

Keys, Barbara. "An African-American Worker in Stalin's Soviet Union: Race and the Soviet Experiment in International Perspective." *The Historian* 71 (Spring 2009): 31–54.

Khanga, Yelena. *Soul to Soul: A Black Russian Jewish Woman's Search for Her Roots*. New York: W. W. Norton, 1994.

Khlevniuk, Oleg. *1937-i: Stalin, NKVD i sovetskoe obshchestvo*. Moscow: Izd-vo "Respublika," 1992.

Klehr, Harvey. *Communist Cadre: The Social Background of the American Communist Party Elite*. Stanford: Hoover Institution Press, 1978.

——. *The Heyday of American Communism: The Depression Decade*. New York: Basic Books, 1984.

Klehr, Harvey, John Earl Haynes, and Kyrill M. Anderson. *The Soviet World of American Communism*. New Haven CT: Yale University Press, 1998.

Klehr, Harvey, John Earl Haynes, and Fridrikh Igorevich Firsov. *The Secret World of American Communism*. New Haven CT: Yale University Press, 1995.

Kossie-Chernyshev, Karen. "Reclaiming 'D. Patterson' (J. Patterson), Child Star in Grigori Alexandrov's *Circus*: A Reconstructive History." *Sound Historian* 8, no. 2 (2004): 61–72.

Kotkin, Stephen. "Coercion and Identity: Workers' Lives in Stalin's Showcase City." In *Making Workers Soviet: Power, Class, and Identity*, edited by Lewis H. Siegelbaum and Ronald Grigor Suny, 274–310. Ithaca NY: Cornell University Press, 1994.

——. *Magnetic Mountain: Stalinism as a Civilization*. Berkeley: University of California Press, 1995.

Kowalsky, Daniel. *Stalin and the Spanish Civil War*. New York: Columbia University Press, 2004. Gutenberg-e.

Kuromiya, Hirokai. *Freedom and Terror in the Donbass: A Ukrainian-Russian Borderland, 1870s–1990s*. Cambridge: Cambridge University Press, 1992.

Lake, Marilyn, and Henry Reynolds. *Drawing the Global Colour Line: White Men's Countries and the International Challenge of Racial Equality*. Cambridge: Cambridge University Press, 2008.

Lapidus, Gail Warshofsky. "Women in Soviet Society: Equality, Development, and Social Change." In *Stalinism: The Essential Readings*, edited by David Hoffmann, 213–36. New York: Wiley-Blackwell, 2002.

Lawrence, Errol. "Just Plain Common Sense: The 'Roots' of Racism." In *The Empire Strikes Back: Race and Racism in '70s Britain*, 47–94. London: Hutchinson, 1982.

Layton, Susan. *Russian Literature and Empire: Conquest of the Caucasus from Pushkin to Tolstoy.* Cambridge: Cambridge University Press, 1994.

Lenoe, Matthew. *Closer to the Masses: Stalinist Culture, Social Revolution, and Soviet Newspapers.* Cambridge MA: Harvard University Press, 2004.

Lewin, Moshe. *The Making of the Soviet System: Essays in the Social History of Interwar Russia.* 1985. Reprint, New York: New Press, 1994.

Lewis, David Levering. *W. E. B. Du Bois: The Fight for Equality and the American Century, 1919–1963.* New York: Henry Holt and Company, 2000.

——. *When Harlem Was in Vogue.* 1969. Reprint, New York: Oxford University Press, 1989.

Leyda, Jay. *Kino: A History of the Russian and Soviet Film.* 1960. Reprint, New York: Collier Books, 1973.

Lichtenstein, Alex. "Chain Gangs, Communism, and the 'Negro Question': John L. Spivak's *Georgia Nigger.*" *Georgia Historical Quarterly* 79 (Fall 1995): 633–58.

Lichtenstein, Nelson. *The Most Dangerous Man in Detroit: Walter Reuther and the Fate of American Labor.* New York: Basic Books, 1995.

Litwack, Leon F. *Trouble in Mind: Black Southerners in the Age of Jim Crow.* New York: Knopf, 1998.

Livezeanu, Irina. *Cultural Politics in Great Romania: Regionalism, Nation Building, and Ethnic Struggle.* Ithaca NY: Cornell University Press, 1995.

Logan, Rayford W. *The Betrayal of the Negro: From Rutherford B. Hayes to Woodrow Wilson.* 1954. Reprint, New York: Da Capo Press, 1997.

Lounsbery, Anne. "Soul Man: Alexander Pushkin, the Black Russian." *Transition* 84 (2000): 42–61.

Lucassen, Leo. "'Harmful Tramps': Police Professionalization and Gypsies in Germany, 1700–1945." *Crime, History, and Societies* 1, no. 1 (1997): 29–50.

Lusane, Clarence. *Hitler's Black Victims: The Historical Experiences of Afro-Germans, European Blacks, Africans, and African Americans in the Nazi Era.* New York: Routledge, 2002.

Macheret, Aleksandr Veniaminovich, and N. A. Glagoleva. *Sovetskie khudozhestvennye fil'my: Annotirovannyi catalog.* Vol. 1, 1918–1935, and Vol. 2, 1930–1957. Moscow: Gosudarstvennoe izdatel'stvo "iskusstvo," 1961.

Mackinnon, Elaine. "Writing History for Stalin: Isaak Izrailevich Mints and the *Istoriia grazhdanskoi voiny.*" *Kritika: Explorations in Russian and Eurasian History* 6, no. 1 (Winter 2005): 5–54.

Macmaster, Neil. *Racism in Europe, 1870–2000.* New York: Palgrave, 2001.

Madison, James H. *A Lynching in the Heartland: Race and Memory in America.*
New York: Palgrave, 2001.
Maiakovskii, Vladimir. *Maiakovskii ob Amerike: Stikhi, ocherki gazetnye interv'iu.* Moscow: Sovetskii pisatel', 1949.
———. *Polnoe sobranie sochinenii v trinadtsati tomakh.* Vol. 7. Moscow: Gos. izd-vo khudozhestvennoi literatury, 1958.
Mally, Lynn. "The Rise and Fall of the Youth Theater TRAM." *Slavic Review,* 51, no. 3 (Autumn 1992): 411–30.
Marable, Manning. *African and Caribbean Politics: From Kwame Nkrumah to the Grenada Revolution.* London: Verso, 1987.
———. *Race, Reform, and Rebellion: The Second Reconstruction in Black America, 1945–1990.* Jackson: University of Mississippi Press, 1990.
Marriott, David. *On Black Men.* New York: Columbia University Press, 2000.
Martin, Terry. *Affirmative Action Empire: Nations and Nationalism in the Soviet Union, 1923–1939.* Ithaca NY: Cornell University Press, 2001.
———. "The Origins of Soviet Ethnic Cleansing." *Journal of Modern History* 70 (1998): 813–61.
Matusevich, Maxim, ed. *Africa in Russia, Russia in Africa: Three Centuries of Encounters.* Trenton NJ: Africa World Press, 2007.
———. "An Exotic Subversive: Africa, Africans and the Soviet Everyday." *Race and Class* 49, no. 4 (April 2008): 57–81.
———. "Journeys of Hope: African Diaspora and the Soviet Society." *African Diaspora* 1 (2008): 53–85.
———. "Probing the Limits of Internationalism: African Students Confront Soviet Ritual." *Anthropology of East Europe Review* 27, no. 2 (Fall 2009): 19–39.
Maxwell, William J. *New Negro, Old Left: African-American Writing and Communism Between the Wars.* New York: Columbia University Press, 1999.
Mazower, Mark. *The Dark Continent: Europe's Twentieth Century.* 1998. Reprint, New York: Vintage, 2000.
———. *Hitler's Empire: How the Nazis Ruled Europe.* New York: Penguin Press, 2008.
McBride, Dwight A. *Why I Hate Abercrombie and Fitch: Essays on Race and Sexuality.* New York: New York University Press, 2005.
McClellan, Woodford. "Africans and Black Americans in the Comintern Schools, 1925–1934." *International Journal of African Historical Studies* 26, no. 2 (1993): 371–90.
———. "Black Hajj to 'Red Mecca': Africans and Afro-Americans at KUTV, 1925–1928." In Matusevich, *Africa in Russia, Russia in Africa,* 61–83.

McClintock, Anne. *Imperial Leather: Race, Gender and Sexuality in the Colonial Conquest*. New York: Routledge, 1995.

McDuffie, Erik S. "'[She] Devoted Twenty Minutes Condemning All Other Forms of Government but the Soviet': Black Women Radicals in the Garvey Movement and in the Left during the 1920s." In *Diasporic Africa: A Reader*, edited by Michael A. Gomez, 219–50. New York: New York University Press, 2006.

———. *Sojourning for Freedom: Black Womaen, American Communism, and the Making of Black Left Feminism*. Durham NC: Duke University Press, 2011.

McElya, Micki. *Clinging to Mammy: The Faithful Slave in Twentieth-Century America*. Cambridge MA: Harvard University Press, 2007.

McIlroy, John. "The Establishment of Intellectual Orthodoxy and the Stalinization of British Communism, 1928–1933." *Past and Present* 192 (August 2006): 187–230.

McKay, Claude. *A Long Way from Home*. New York: Lee Furman, 1937.

———. *Negroes in America*. Translated by Robert J. Winter. Port Washington NY: Kennikat, 1979.

———. *Trial by Lynching: Stories about Negro Life in North America*. Translated by Robert Winter. Mysore, India: The Centre for Commonwealth Literature and Research, 1977.

McKenna, Kevin J. *All the Views Fit to Print: Changing Images of the U.S. in Pravda Political Cartoons, 1917–1991*. New York: Peter Lang, 2001.

Miller, James A., Susan D. Pennybacker, and Eve Rosenhaft. "Mother Ada Wright and the International Campaign to Free the Scottsboro Boys, 1931–1934." *American Historical Review* 106 (April 2001): 387–430.

Mills, Charles W. *The Racial Contract*. Ithaca NY: Cornell University Press, 1997.

Moch, Leslie Page. "Foreign Workers in Western Europe: The 'Cheaper Hands' in Historical Perspective." In *European Integration in Social and Historical Perspective, 1850 to the Present*, edited by Jytte Klausen and Louise A. Tilly, 103–16. New York: Rowman and Littlefield, 1998.

Morton, Patricia. *Disfigured Images: The Historical Assault on Afro-American Women*. New York: Praeger, 1991.

The Moscow Theatre for Children. Moscow: Co-operative Publishing Society of Foreign Workers in the USSR, 1934.

Mukherji, Ani. "The Erasure of American Anticolonialism in Moscow: Race and the Redefinition of Political Space." Paper presented at the Center for the United States and the Cold War, New York University, May 4, 2007.

Naiman, Eric. *Sex in Public: The Incarnation of Early Soviet Ideology*. Princeton NJ: Princeton University Press, 1997.

Naison, Mark. *Communists in Harlem during the Depression*. New York: Grove Press, 1983.

Nakhimovsky, Alice. "Death and Disillusion: Il'ia Il'f in the 1930s." In *Enemies of the People: The Destruction of Soviet Literary, Theater, and Film Arts in the 1930s*, edited by Katherine Bliss Eaton, 205–88. Evanston IL: Northwestern University Press, 2002.

Nelson, Steve, James R. Barrett, and Rob Ruck. *Steve Nelson: American Radical*. Pittsburgh: University of Pittsburgh Press, 1981.

Nepomnyashchy, Catharine Theimer, Nicole Svobodny, and Ludmilla A. Trigos, eds. *Under the Sky of My Africa: Alexander Pushkin and Blackness*. Evanston IL: Northwestern University Press, 2006.

O'Dell, Felicity Ann. *Socialisation through Children's Literature: The Soviet Example*. Cambridge: Cambridge University Press, 1978.

Osinskii, N. *Po tu storonu okeana: Iz amerikanskikh vpechatlenii i nabliudenii*. Moscow: Gosudarstvennoe izdatel'stvo, 1926.

Padmore, George. *Pan-Africanism or Communism*. 1955. Reprint, Garden City NY: Doubleday, 1971.

——. "The Socialist Attitude to the Invasion of the USSR." *Left* 60 (September 1941): 193–99.

Pantov, Alexander V., and Daria A. Spichak. "New Light from the Russian Archives: Chinese Stalinists and Trotskyists at the International Lenin School in Moscow, 1926–1938." *Twentieth-Century China* 33, no. 2 (April 2008): 29–50.

The Patrice Lumumba Friendship University in Moscow. Moscow: Novosti Press, 1973.

Patterson, James L. *Rossiia. Afrika. Stikhi i poema*. Moscow: Molodaia gvardiia, 1963.

Patterson, Orlando. *The Ordeal of Integration: Progress and Resentment in America's "Racial" Crisis*. Washington DC: Civitas, 1997.

——. *Rituals of Blood: Consequences of Slavery in Two American Centuries*. Washington DC: Civitas Counterpoint, 1998.

Peabody, Sue. *"There Are No Slaves in France": The Political Culture of Race and Slavery in the Ancien Regime*. New York: Oxford University Press, 1996.

Peabody, Sue, and Tyler Stovall, eds. *The Color of Liberty: Histories of Race in France*. Durham NC: Duke University Press, 2003.

Pennybacker, Susan. *From Scottsboro to Munich: Race and Political Culture in 1930s Britain*. Princeton NJ: Princeton University Press, 2009.

Peris, Daniel. *Storming the Heavens: The Soviet League of the Militant Godless.* Ithaca NY: Cornell University Press, 1998.

Peterson, Dale. *Up From Bondage: The Literatures of Russian and African American Soul.* Durham NC: Duke University Press, 2000.

Petro, Nicolai, and Alvin Z. Rubenstein. *Russian Foreign Policy: From Empire to Nation-State.* New York: Longman, 1997.

Petrone, Karen. *Life Has Become More Joyous, Comrades: Celebrations in the Time of Stalin.* Bloomington: Indiana University Press, 2000.

Phillips, Hugh D. "Rapprochement and Estrangement: The United States in Soviet Foreign Policy in the 1930s." In *Soviet-U.S. Relations, 1933–1942,* edited by Kim Pilarski, 9–17. Moscow: Progress Publishers, 1989.

Pipes, Richard. *The Formation of the Soviet Union: Communism and Nationalism, 1917–1923.* 1954. Reprint, Cambridge MA: Harvard University Press, 1997.

Plach, Eva. *The Clash of Moral Nations: Cultural Politics in Pilsudski's Poland, 1926–1935.* Athens: Ohio University Press, 2006.

Platt, Kevin M. F. "Rehabilitation and Afterimage: Aleksei Tolstoi's Many Returns to Peter the Great." In *Epic Revisionism: Russian History and Literature as Stalinist Propaganda,* edited by Kevin M. F. Platt and David Brandenberger, 54–57. Madison: University of Wisconsin Press, 2006.

Plummer, Brenda Gayle. *Rising Wind: Black Americans and U.S. Foreign Affairs, 1935–1960.* Chapel Hill: University of North Carolina Press, 1996.

Polk's City Directory, 1929–1930; People's Wayne Country Bank Serving Detroit, Highland Park, Hamtramck, Dearborn, River Rouge, Ecorse. Detroit: A. L. Polk and Co. Publishers, n.d.

Pomorska, Krystyna. "A Vision of America in Early Soviet Literature." *Slavic and East European Journal* 11, no. 4 (Winter 1967): 389–97.

Pratt, Mary Louise. *Imperial Eyes: Travel Writing and Transculturation.* London: Routledge, 1992.

Quist-Adade, Charles. "The African Russians: Children of the Cold War." In Matusevich, *Africa in Russia, Russia in Africa,* 153–73.

———. *In the Shadows of the Kremlin and the White House: Africa's Media Image from Communism to Post-Communism.* Lanham MD: University Press of America, 2001.

Race Hatred on Trial. New York: Workers Library Publishers, 1931.

Ratchford, Moira. "*Circus* of 1936: Ideology and Entertainment under the Big Top." In *Inside Soviet Film Satire: Laughter with a Lash,* edited by Andrew Horton, 83–93. Cambridge: Cambridge University Press, 1993.

Reid, Susan E. "All Stalin's Women: Gender and Power in Soviet Art of the 1930s." *Slavic Review* 57, no. 1 (Spring 1998): 133–74.

Richards, Jeffrey. *Imperialism and Music: Britain, 1876–1953*. Manchester: Manchester University Press, 2002.

Rickards, Maurice. *Posters of Protest and Revolution*. New York: Walker, 1970.

Rieber, Alfred J. "Stalin: Man of the Borderlands." *American Historical Review* 106, no. 5 (December 2001): 1651–91.

Rittersporn, Gabor Tamas. "The Omnipresent Conspiracy: On Soviet Imagery of Politics and Social Relations in the 1930s." In *Stalinism: Its Nature and Aftermath*, edited by Gabor Tamas Rittersporn and Nick Lampert, 101–20. Armonk NY: M. E. Sharpe, 1992.

Robeson, Paul, Jr. *The Undiscovered Paul Robeson: An Artist's Journey, 1898–1939*. New York: John Wiley and Sons, 2001.

Robinson, Cedric J. *Black Marxism: The Making of the Black Radical Tradition*. 1983; Reprint, Chapel Hill: University of North Carolina Press, 2000.

Robinson, Robert. *Black on Red: My 44 Years Inside the Soviet Union*. Washington DC: Acropolis Books, 1988.

Roediger, David R. *Black On White: Black Writers on What It Means to Be White*. New York: Schoken Books, 1998.

Rogger, Hans. "America in the Russian Mind: Or Russian Discoveries of America." *Pacific Historical Review* 47, no. 1 (February 1978): 27–51.

———. "*Amerikanizm* and the Economic Development of Russia." *Comparative Studies in Society and History* 23, no. 3 (July 1981): 382–420.

———. "How the Soviets See Us." In *Shared Destiny: Fifty Years of Soviet-American Relations*, edited by Mark Garrison and Abbott Gleason, 107–46. Boston: Beacon Press, 1985.

Roman, Meredith L. "Another Kind of 'Freedom': The Soviet Experiment with Antiracism and Its Image as a 'Raceless' Society, 1928–1936." PhD diss., Michigan State University, 2005.

———. "Making Caucasians Black: Moscow since the Fall of Communism and the Racialization of Non-Russians." *Journal of Communist Studies and Transition Politics* 18 (June 2002): 1–27.

Rosen, Seymour M. *The Development of Peoples' Friendship University in Moscow*. Washington DC: U.S. Department of Health, Education, and Welfare, 1973.

Rosenberg, Jonathan. *How Far the Promised Land: World Affairs and the African American Civil Rights Movement from the First World War to Vietnam*. Princeton NJ: Princeton University Press, 2006.

Rosenblit, N. S., and R Schüller, eds. 60 Letters: Foreign Workers Write of Their Life and Work in the USSR. Moscow: Co-operative Publishing Society of Foreign Workers in the USSR, 1936.

Rowe, Michael. Policing, Race, and Racism. Portland: Willan, 2004.

Rozanov, Sergei, and Natal'ia Sats. Negritenok i obez'iana. Moscow: Gosizdat, 1930.

Ryle, James Martin. "International Red Aid: A Case Study of a Communist Front Organization." MA thesis, Emory University, 1962.

Sats, Natal'ia. Sketches from My Life. Moscow: Raduga Publishers, 1934.

Saul, Norman E. Friends or Foes? The United States and Soviet Russia, 1921–1941. Lawrence: University Press of Kansas, 2006.

Schoots, Hans. Living Dangerously: A Biography of Joris Ivens. Amsterdam: Amsterdam University Press, 2000.

Schultz, Kurt. "The American Factor in Soviet Industrialization: Fordism and the First Five-Year Plan, 1928–1932." PhD diss., Ohio State University, 1992.

Scott, James C. Domination and the Arts of Resistance: Hidden Transcripts. New Haven CT: Yale University Press, 1990.

Scott, John. Behind the Urals: An American Worker in Russia's City of Steel. 1942. Reprint, Bloomington: Indiana University Press, 1989.

Secretariat of the Executive Committee. "Resolution of the IRA on Work among the Negroes; October 16, 1930." In Ten Years of International Red Aid, 188–93. Moscow: Executive Committee of the IRA, 1933.

Siegelbaum, Lewis H. Cars for Comrades: The Life of the Soviet Automobile. Ithaca NY: Cornell University Press, 2008.

——. "'Dear Comrade, You Ask What We Need': Socialist Paternalism and Soviet Rural 'Notables' in the Mid-1930s." Slavic Review 57, no. 1 (Spring 1998): 107–32.

——. "Defining and Ignoring Labor Discipline in the Early Soviet Period: The Comrades-Disciplinary Courts, 1918–1922." Slavic Review 51, no. 3 (Winter 1992): 705–30.

——. "Narratives of Appeal and the Appeal of Narratives: Labor Discipline and Its Contestation in the Early Soviet Period." Russian History/Histoire Russe 24, nos. 1–2 (Spring–Summer 1997): 65–87.

——. "The Shaping of Soviet Workers' Leisure: Workers' Clubs and Palaces of Culture in the 1930s." International Labor and Working-Class History 56 (Fall 1999): 78–92.

Siegelbaum, Lewis, and Andrei Sokolov. Stalinism as a Way of Life. New Haven CT: Yale University Press, 2000.

Slezkine, Yuri. "USSR as a Communal Apartment, or How a Socialist State Promoted Ethnic Particularism." *Slavic Review* 53, no. 2 (Summer 1994): 414–52.

Smart, Christopher. *The Imagery of Soviet Foreign Policy and the Collapse of the Russian Empire.* Westport CT: Praeger, 1995.

Smith, Homer. *Black Man in Red Russia.* Chicago: Johnson Publishing, 1964.

Smith, Michael G. "Film for the 'Soviet East': National Fact and Revolutionary Fiction in Early Azerbaijani Film." *Slavic Review* 56, no. 4 (Winter 1997): 654–78.

Solomon, Mark. *The Cry Was Unity: Communists and African Americans, 1917–1936.* Jackson: University Press of Mississippi, 1998.

Stalin, Joseph V. *Sochineniia.* Vol. 5. Moscow: Gos. izd-vo polit. lit-ry, 1950.

Starr, S. Frederick. *Red and Hot: The Fate of Jazz in the Soviet Union, 1917–1980.* New York: Oxford University Press, 1983.

Stasova, E. D. *Vospominaniia.* Moscow: Izdatel'stvo "Mysl," 1969.

Steiner, Evgenii. *Stories for Little Comrades: Revolutionary Artists and the Making of Early Soviet Children's Books.* Translated by Jane Anne Miller. Seattle: University of Washington Press, 1999.

Stites, Richard. *Russian Popular Culture: Entertainment and Society since 1900.* Cambridge: Cambridge University Press, 1992.

Stoler, Ann Laura. *Race and the Education of Desire: Foucault's History of Sexuality and the Colonial Order of Things.* Durham NC: Duke University Press, 1995.

Storch, Randi. *Red Chicago: American Communism at Its Grassroots, 1928–1935.* Urbana: University of Illinois Press, 2007.

Stovall, Tyler. "The Color Line behind the Lines: Racial Violence in France during the Great War." *American Historical Review* 103, no. 3 (June 1998): 737–69.

———. "Colour-blind France? Colonial Workers During the First World War." *Race and Class* 35, no. 2 (1993): 35–55.

———. *Paris Noir: African Americans in the City of Light.* Boston: Houghton Mifflin Company, 1996.

Straus, Kenneth M. *Factory and Community in Stalin's Russia: The Making of an Industrial Working Class.* Pittsburgh: University of Pittsburgh Press, 1997.

Strong, Anna Louise. *I Change Worlds.* New York: Henry Holt and Company, 1936.

Summers, Martin Anthony. *Manliness and Its Discontents: The Black Middle Class and the Transformation of Masculinity, 1900–1930.* Chapel Hill: University of North Carolina Press, 2004.

Sunderland, Willard. *Taming the Wild: Colonization and Empire on the Russian Steppe*. Ithaca NY: Cornell University Press, 2004.

Suny, Ronald Grigor. *Revenge of the Past: Nationalism, Revolution, and the Collapse of the Soviet Union*. Stanford CA: Stanford University Press, 1993.

——. *The Soviet Experiment: Russia, the USSR and the Successor States*. New York: Oxford University Press, 1998.

Suny, Ronald Grigor, and Terry Martin, eds. *A State of Nations: Empire and Nation-Making in the Age of Lenin and Stalin*. Oxford: Oxford University Press, 2001.

Swearingen, Roger, ed. *Leaders of the Communist World*. New York: Free Press, 1971.

Sweeney, Carole. *From Fetish to Subject: Race, Modernism, and Primitivism, 1919–1935*. Westport CT: Praeger, 2004.

Szobar, Patricia. "Telling Sexual Stories in the Nazi Courts of Law: Race Defilement in Germany, 1933–1945." *Journal of the History of Sexuality* 11, nos. 1–2 (January–April 2002): 131–63.

Tabili, Laura. "Women 'of a Very Low Type': Crossing Racial Boundaries in Imperial Britain." In *Gender and Class in Modern Europe*, edited by Laura L. Frader and Sonya O. Rose, 165–90. Ithaca NY: Cornell University Press, 1996.

Taubman, William. *Khrushchev: The Man and His Era*. New York: W. W. Norton, 2003.

Taylor, Richard. *Film Propaganda: Soviet Russia and Nazi Germany*. 1979. Reprint, London: I. B. Tauris, 1998.

——. "The Illusion of Happiness and the Happiness of Illusion: Grigorii Aleksandrov's *The Circus*." *Slavonic and East European Review* 74, no. 4 (October 1996): 601–20.

Taylor, S. J. *Stalin's Apologist: Walter Duranty, the New York Times's Man in Moscow*. New York: Oxford University Press, 1990.

Thomas, Richard. *Life for Us Is What We Make It: Building Black Community in Detroit, 1915–1945*. Bloomington: Indiana University Press, 1992.

Thurber, Cheryl. "The Development of the Mammy Image and Mythology." In *Southern Women: Histories and Identities*, edited by Virginia Bernhard, Betty Brandon, Elizabeth Fox-Genovese, and Theda Perdue, 87–108. Columbia: University of Missouri Press, 1995.

Tillery, Tyrone. *Claude McKay: A Black Poet's Struggle for Identity*. Amherst: University of Massachusetts Press, 1992.

Tillett, Lowell. *The Great Friendship: Soviet Historians on the Non-Russian Nation-alities.* Chapel Hill: University of North Carolina Press, 1969.

Trotter, Joe William, Jr., ed. *The Great Migration in Historical Perspective.* Bloomington: Indiana University Press, 1991.

Trouillot, Michel-Rolph. *Silencing the Past: Power and the Production of History.* Boston: Beacon Press, 1995.

Tucker, Robert C. *Stalin in Power: The Revolution from Above, 1928–1941.* New York: W. W. Norton, 1992.

Tuttle, William M., Jr. *Race Riot: Chicago in the Red Summer of 1919.* 1970. Reprint, Urbana: University of Illinois Press, 1996.

Two Universities: An Account of the Life and Work of Lumumba Friendship University and Moscow State University. Moscow: Novosti, 1963.

Tzouliadis, Tim. *The Forsaken: An American Tragedy in Stalin's Russia.* New York: Penguin, 2008.

Verdery, Katherine. *What Was Socialism and What Comes Next?* Princeton NJ: Princeton University Press, 1996.

Von Eschen, Penny. *Race against Empire: Black Americans and Anticolonialism, 1937–1957.* Ithaca NY: Cornell University Press, 1997.

von Geldern, James. *Bolshevik Festivals, 1917–1920.* Berkeley: University of California Press, 1993.

von Geldern, James, and Richard Stites, eds. *Mass Culture in Soviet Russia: Tales, Poems, Songs, Movies, Plays, and Folklore, 1917–1953.* Bloomington: Indiana University Press, 1995.

Wald, Alan. "Black Nationalist Identity and International Class Unity: The Political and Cultural Legacy of Marxism." In *Radical Relevance: Toward a Scholarship of the Whole Left,* edited by Steven Rosendale and Laura Gray Rosendale, 3–30. Albany: State University of New York Press, 2005.

Waldrep, Christopher. *African Americans Confront Lynching: Strategies of Resistance from the Civil War to the Civil Rights Era.* Lanham MD: Rowman and Littlefield, 2009.

——. *The Many Faces of Judge Lynch: Extralegal Violence and Punishment in America.* New York: Palgrave, 2002.

Wallace, Michele. *Black Macho and the Myth of the Superwoman.* New York: Warner Books, 1980.

Wallace-Sanders, Kimberly. *Mammy: A Century of Race, Gender, and Southern Memory.* Ann Arbor: University of Michigan Press, 2008.

Weigand, Kate. *Red Feminism: American Communism and the Making of Women's Liberation.* Baltimore: Johns Hopkins University Press, 2001.

Weiner, Amir. *Making Sense of War: The Second World War and the Fate of the Bolshevik Revolution*. Princeton NJ: Princeton University Press, 2002.

———. "Nothing but Certainty." *Slavic Review* 61, no. 1 (Spring 2002): 44–53.

Weitz, Eric D. "Racial Politics without the Concept of Race: Reevaluating Soviet Ethnic and National Purges." *Slavic Review* 61, no. 1 (Spring 2002): 1–29.

Westad, Odd Arne. *The Global Cold War: Third World Interventions and the Making of Our Times*. Cambridge: Cambridge University Press, 2007.

White, Deborah Gray. *Ar'n't I a Woman? Female Slaves in the Plantation South*. New York: W. W. Norton, 1985.

White, Stephen. *The Bolshevik Poster*. New Haven CT: Yale University Press, 1988.

Wicks, Harry. *Keeping My Head: The Memoirs of a British Bolshevik*. London: Socialist Platform, 1992.

Williams, Chad L. *Torchbearers of Democracy: African American Soldiers in the World War I Era*. Chapel Hill: University of North Carolina Press, 2010.

Wilson, Edward T. *Russia and Black Africa before World War II*. New York: Holmes and Meier, 1974.

Wimberg, Ellen. "Socialism, Democratism, and Criticism: The Soviet Press and the National Discussion of the 1936 Draft Constitution." *Soviet Studies* 44, no. 2 (1992): 313–32.

Wolcott, Victoria W. *Remaking Respectability: African American Women in Interwar Detroit*. Chapel Hill: University of North Carolina Press, 2001.

Wolf, Erika, trans. *Ilf and Petrov's American Road Trip: The 1935 Travelogue of Two Soviet Writers*. Princeton NJ: Princeton Architectural Press, 2006.

Wolff, Larry. *Inventing Eastern Europe: The Map of Civilization on the Mind of the Enlightenment*. Stanford CA: Stanford University Press, 1994.

Wood, Amy L. *Lynching and Spectacle: Witnessing Racial Violence in America, 1890–1940*. Chapel Hill: University of North Carolina Press, 2009.

Woods, Jeff. *Black Struggle, Red Scare: Segregation and Anti-Communism in the South, 1948–1968*. Baton Rouge: Louisiana State University Press, 2004.

Youngblood, Denise. "Entertainment or Enlightenment: Popular Cinema in Soviet Society, 1921–1931." In *New Directions in Soviet History*, edited by Stephen White, 41–61. New York: Cambridge University Press, 1992.

———. *Movies for the Masses: Popular Cinema and Soviet Society in the 1920s*. Cambridge: Cambridge University Press, 1992.

Zhuravlev, Sergei. *"Malen'kie liudi" i "bol'shaia istoriia": Inostrantsy moskovsk-*

ogo Elektrozavoda v sovetskom obshchestve 1920-kh–1930-kh gg. Moscow: Rosspen, 2000.

Zubkova, Elena. *Russia after the War: Hopes, Illusions, and Disappointments, 1945–1957*. Armonk NY: M. E. Sharpe, 1998.

Zubok, Vladislav. *Zhivago's Children: The Last Russian Intelligentsia*. Cambridge MA: Harvard University Press, 2009.

INDEX

Page numbers in italics refer to illustrations.

white Americans in, 159–79, 190, 198

Communist University of the Toilers of the East (KUTV), 8, 19, 49, 127, 156–57, 176, 179–90

Conklin, Alice, 11

Cooper, Hugh L., 137, 140, 143, 145, 247n35

The Crisis, 127, 146–48, 150

Cultural Revolution, 93–94, 103

Daily Worker, 146

Dalton, Mary, 162

Daniels, Wallace, 180–81, 187–88

Demery, Pearl, 163–66, 169, 175

Derzhavin, N. S., 104

Domingo, W. A., 142, 145–46

Du Bois, W. E. B., 6, 89, 205, 208n25, 250n74, 251n95

Dunaevskii, Isaak, 198

Edwards, Brent Hayes, 130

Eisenstein, Sergei, 151

Elektrozavod, 25, 27–29, 34, 38–39, 53, 75, 128, 151

Emery, Jane, 202

Father Divine, 85–86

Federovskii, V., 97, *98*, 113, *114*, 115

Ferguson, Romania, 160, 166, 175–76, 255n20

First Five-Year Plan, 7, 8, 26, 30, 46, 61

First State Ball Bearing Plant, 43, 45–46

Ford, James, 13, 21–22, 28, 71, 74–75, 128, 136, 141, 151, 212n72

Ford Motor Company, 27, 40, 194

Fort-Whiteman, Lovett, 9, 75–76, 78–79, 94, 112, 138, 142, 180, 188

Foster, William, 13

France, 108; African Americans in, 12–13; imperial policy of, 11–12, 14, 130, 181, 201

Freeman, Samuel, 182

Garvey, Marcus, 14

Geisha, 180, 182

Gilmore, Glenda, 3, 75–76, 138, 242n95

Glascow, Margaret, 129, 201, 245n12

Golden, Oliver, 9, 112, 127, 202

Gor'kii, Maksim, 94, 102, 120, 258n38

Gray, Nathan Varne, 182

Grebner, Georgii, 138, 247n41

Grey, Ralph, 102

Hall, Gus, 163

Hall, Otto, 13

Harris, Emma, 117–18, 150, 242n95

Harris, Joel Chandler, 82

Hathaway, Clarence, 168

Hawkins, Isaiah, 35, 71, 74, 159

Haywood, Harry, 13, 21–22, 158–59, 162, 176, 228n46, 254n12, 264n114

Hellbeck, Jochen, 185

Hewitt, George, 159, 160, 167, 191, 255n20, 264n113

Hill, Leonard, 141

Hirsch, Francine, 10, 14, 54

Holmgren, Beth, 197

Holt, Thomas, 11

House Un-American Activities Committee (HUAC), 191, 255n12

Houston, Marie, 176

Howard, Joseph, 158

Hudson, Hosea, 158

Hughes, Langston, 5, 82, 117, 137, 138–39, 144, 147, 242n95

Huiswood, Otto, 4–5, 44, 52, 144, 153, 175, 254n6, 255n22

Humphrey, Hubert H., 1, 58, 204–5

Hutchins, H. R., 159–60, 255n20

Iaroslavskii, Emel'ian, 165, 258n37

Il'f, Il'ia, 18, 59, 82–88, 196, 232n92;

Il'f, Il'ia (*cont.*)
    One-Story America, 59, 82–88,
        231n81; *Under the Big Top*, 196–97,
        203, 232n92
International Labor Defense (ILD), 92,
    243n107
International Lenin School (ILS), 8, 19,
    155–79, 190–92, 253nn3–4, 257n23
International Organization for Assis-
    tance to Revolutionary Fighters
    (MOPR), 29, 54, 58–59, 60, 91–94, 96,
    102, 115, 122–23; Central Commit-
    tee of, 95, 105, 108–11; Executive
    Committee of, 93, 105, 107, 112,
    119–20
International Trade Union Commit-
    tee of Negro Workers (ITUCNW), 20,
    70–71, 125–26, 131–32, 153
Internatsional'nyi maiak, 58, 66, 72, 97,
    102, 105
Izvestiia, 74, 75, 77, 94, 197

James, C. L. R., 131, 133
James, Winston, 20
Japan, 122–23, 137
Jenkins, Katherine, 141
Jones, Mildred, 201
Jones, Vivian, 201
Jones, William N., 149, 250n81
Junghans, Carl, 138–39, 144

Kaganovich, Lazar, 137, 145, 165
Kalmek, Pierre, 181–85, 187, 191
Kamernyi Theater, 96–97, 180
Kataev, Valentin, 196
Katayama, Sen, 208n12
Katz, Otto, 139, 144
Kelley, Robin D. G., 3, 16, 130
Kenyatta, Jomo, 180–81, 186–87
Khanga, Yelena, 202, 233n1
Khar'kov, 29, 34

Khrushchev, Nikita, 1, 58, 204, 207n3
Kirsanova, Klavdiia Kirsanova, 165,
    258n37
Knut, Ferdinand, 29, 35
Kolomoitsev, Pavel, 194–95
Komsomol'skaia pravda, 59; and black
    prisoners, 66; and lynching car-
    toons, 64, 65, 66; and lynching pho-
    tographs, 63–64; and the Scottsboro
    campaign, 94, 97, 98–99, *98, 100,*
    101–2, 105, 107
Krokodil, 79–80
Kuusinen, Otto, 14, 15

Langford, Sam, 113
League of Struggle for Negro Rights
    (LSNR), 43, 125
League of the Militant Godless, 108
Leningrad, 28–29, 35, 96, 150, 240n74
Leningradskaia pravda, 102, 105
Levy, Alfred, 66
Lewis, Abraham, 113
Lewis, Lemuel, 16–17, 25–28, 30–39,
    41–42, 53, 60, 63, 71, 185, 217n27,
    219n43
Lewis, Thurston McNairy, 139, 141–42,
    146, 248n48
Lewis, Walter, 182–83, 185–87, 262n89,
    263n100
Liberator, 43, 125–30, 151, 244n2
Lister, Roddy, 181, 183, 187
Literaturnaia gazeta, 95, 97
Little Red Devils, 77, 193–94
Lovestone, Jay, 13
Lunacharskii, Anatolii, 94, 98–99, 180
lynching, 2, 121, 151–52, 185, 203,
    226n24; lecture guide about, 111–
    12; and myth of the black rap-
    ist, 95–96, 112, 119, 190, 198; and
    Scottsboro verdict, 95–99, 102;
    Soviet postcards of, 63; and the

Ross, Robert, 9, 77, 112, 197, 199, 230n63
Rostov-on-Don, 29, 35
Rudd, Wayland, 9

Samoilovich, A. N., 103
Sample, George, 141
Saul, Norman, 122
Scottsboro campaign, 18, 54, 92, 126, 129, 183, 186, 188, 190, 243n107; and cartoons, 97, 98–99, *98, 100,* 101, 113, *114,* 115; and collective farmers, 93, 95, 105–6, 108–10, 240n74; and the Defense Committee, 93–97, 105, 107, 112, 115, 120; in Europe, 92, 95, 108; and expressions of indignation, 106–7; and fascism, 101–2, 106, 236n37; and image of Soviet racelessness, 104, 115–20; and intellectuals, 93–104, 107, 122; and paternalism, 115–16, 119; and photographs, 113; and protest resolutions, 95, 105–7; and rallies, 96–97, 102, 109, 111–13, 117–18, 180; and representations of defendants, 94–99, 101–2, 113–16; and soldiers, 105–6, 108; and the trial, 91, 122, 148, 243n106; in the United States, 92, 95, 108; and women, 107, 118–20; and workers, 92–95, 105–10, 118, 240n74
Second Five-Year Plan, 7, 8, 46
Shaw, George Bernard, 131
Shelton, Henry, 160
Shipp, Thomas, 63
Slezkine, Yuri, 14–15
Smith, Abraham, 63
Smith, Homer, 9, 148–49, 152–53, 223n80, 250n80
Sobia, Nikin, 183, 187
Solomon, Mark, 3, 21

Soviet antiracism, 1–4, 7–8, 24, 54; and cartoons, 31, 61, 62, 64, 65, 66, 97, 98–99, *98, 100,* 101, 113, *114,* 115; and children's stories, 67–69; and film, 126, 136–46, 193–204; as hard-line policy, 16–17, 57, 59–60, 70, 82, 126, 130–31, 198–99; and image of Soviet racelessness, 70–71, 74–81, 85, 125–36, 145–53, 181, 184, 187–91; and literature, 6, 81–88; and lynching, 60–66, 75, 95–96, 98–99, 102, 106–7, 116, 121, 151, 184, 203; as masculine discourse, 22–23, 118–20, 149–50; paternalism of, 40, 50–52, 69–70, 79, 104, 115–16, 119–20; and photographs, 61–67, 71–77, 88–89, 127–28; and poems, 81, 99, 116–17; post–World War II, 89, 121–22, 186, 204–6; and the press, 4, 6, 57–81, 88–89, 122, 146–52; as soft-line policy, 18, 19, 59, 76–77, 83, 193–94, 198–99, 203–4; and whiteness, 103–4, 128–29, 148, 167–68, 171–72, 186–87, 237n48
Soviet Union: Americans (white) in, 27, 29, 31–32, 35, 121, 145, 153, 158–59, 186, 255n16; and anti-Semitism, 26, 178, 185, 261n73; and caricatures of blacks, 78–82, 135, 179–83, 188–89, 264n105; and childhood, 68; English-language newspapers in, 42–43; foreign workers in, 25, 28–30, 33, 36, 39, 43–44, 53–54, 213n3; and graphic artists, 61, 99–101; and the "Great Terror," 9; and heroes, 47, 50–51; and international education, 37, 43, 110–11, 118; nationality policy of, 14–15, 23, 30, 51–52, 69, 104, 170, 259n48; national security of, 8, 10, 58–59, 66–67, 83, 92–96, 99, 120, 205, 209n31,

West, Dorothy, 118, 121, 145, 249n61
White, Charles, 160, 162
White, Maude, 23
whiteness, 103–4, 128–29, 148, 167–68, 171–72, 186–87, 237n48
white supremacy, 186–90. *See also* racism
Wikman, Morris, 113
Williams, Edward, 160
Wilson, Edward, 128, 130, 134
women: and African Americans, 6, 23, 71–72, 80, 84–86, 117–20, 160, 175–77, 201, 203, 257n31, 261n68; and

Soviet citizens, 30, 68, 107, 119–20, 200–201, 203, 216n22, 223n90, 240n72; and white Americans, 119–20, 162–64, 190, 198–204
Workers News, 43, 75, 76, 94–95, 102, 132, 221n64
Wright, Ada, 119, 243n97

Yokinen, August, 54
Youngblood, John, 160–62, 164, 172

Zhuravlev, Sergei, 28, 30, 44
Znamia, 59

CPSIA information can be obtained
at www.ICGtesting.com
Printed in the USA
LVHW041830141119
637379LV00001B/55